A LASTING LEGACY

A Practical Guide to Secure
your *FUTURE*, your *FAMILY*, your *FINANCES*
and your *FAITH*

in **uncertain times**

Doug Hagedorn

www.xulonpress.com

LIVES CHANGED AND ADVANCE PRAISE FOR *A LASTING LEGACY*, THE AUTHOR AND MORE!

"Doug Hagedorn is a man with a passion to help others and a wealth of knowledge to accomplish it. He gracefully guides, directs and coaches those who desire a life that matters. How much better to learn how to have *A Lasting Legacy* than from a man who is actually doing it!"

Chuck Bentley, author of *The Root of Riches*
Chief Executive Officer, Crown Financial Ministries

"Doug Hagedorn has created a veritable banquet of inspiration, instruction, and eternally impactful resource that will recharge, redirect, and refocus families on the how-tos of leaving a legacy worth everything. Throughout Hagedorn's text, *A Lasting Legacy*, readers will be delighted (and informed) by the author's lively storytelling and his countless interactive exercises (which are both interesting and insightful) that all lead to developing a worldview and lifestyle that honors God and changes lives (ours and those we impact) today and into all our tomorrows."

Michele Howe, author of
*Burdens Do a Body Good: Meeting Life's Challenges
with Strength and Soul*
www.michelehowe.wordpress.com

"This book covers it all! With great passion and clarity Doug gently encourages us to make our lives count. As a fellow traveler, he then equips us with the tools and eternal wisdom to change our own personal economy now and leave a Godly legacy for the future."

Steve Moore, Host, Moneywise, www.compass1.org
Co-host, 23 years with Larry Burkett and Howard Dayton, Christian Financial Concepts, Crown Ministries

"Raising a family in the 21st Century isn't easy. In fact, the negative influences in the culture can leave you feeling trapped, submerged, isolated, and hopeless. Against those kinds of odds, it may seem as though the goal of effective parenting is merely surviving. But I'm convinced that God has more in store for us than just holding on. I believe it is possible to not only survive in this life but to actually thrive in the process of living life, raising a family, and leaving a legacy. Doug Hagedorn has poured his heart and soul into providing a practical roadmap to help you accomplish this task. *A Lasting Legacy* is one of the most useful resources I have ever read, and I know you will benefit from these principles which will help you lead your family with certainty in uncertain times."

Roger Marsh, author of *Internet-Protect Your Kids*
Executive Producer, "HomeWord with Jim Burns"

Comments from others who have read *A Lasting Legacy*:

"With humility, passion, and wisdom, you provide us a practical manual for our future, family, finances and faith. With your engaging style of writing, your book becomes easy and delightful to read. I personally thank you for taking the time to pen *A Lasting Legacy*, which is now your precious legacy to us."

"To sit down and read a book that is encouraging me in pursuit of leaving a legacy- a godly legacy, and to enjoy and apply what is written into my everyday life is something I think is rare. The way Doug writes to different types of readers and grabs the attention of them is amazing."

"It is a book to be read over and over, as the Lord points out different areas and grows us in different ways through the many seasons of life. I truly believe *A Lasting Legacy* is a life changing book"

"Passing this book on to friends and family will be a priority for me, as I know so many people who are looking to make their lives count for more than just the here and now."

"The strength of this book is the writer's personal testimony on what he has learned, where he is and his plans. I enjoyed the personal stories and testimony."

"I liked most that you not only write about these issues, but that you live them. You not only teach us how to experience and make changes that will lead to fulfillment and fruitfulness, but you have given practical and doable steps to achieve these goals. You backed it up with real life experience and stories."

"The question of "so what?" is answered with practical application to my life. You are very gifted—you are an emotional, yet factual writer. There is hope!"

"Love the quotes throughout the book. Great mirror moments. Fun quizzes. Perfect balance of great principles to guide your family and Biblical teachings of how and why to do it."

"It is full of good advice and sound wisdom. Powerful stuff—eye opening! Your personal testimony is wonderful!"

"Very well written—practical, personal and funny!! Very hopeful and helpful. Practical ideas."

"I love all the practical tools and suggestions along with explanations and ideas. Wonderful combination to put ideas into action."

"Life and eternal changing information for your audience!"

"My favorite part of *A Lasting Legacy* is the theme of God's grace and redemption. You continually show how to do things, but if you have stumbled or missed an opportunity, here is how you can start anew today. What a beautiful reflection of God's love for us in all we do, whether it is family, financial or our relationship with Him.

"I really enjoyed *A Lasting Legacy* and believe it will benefit the readers tremendously. This effort to rebuild the foundations of our society is much needed. I really appreciate the way you wove the Bible throughout."

"I was truly drawn to the unique ideas of including "mirror moments", "Selah stops", and "tune ties"—just what this book needed to be personal and life changing."

"I liked the questions, discussions, details and challenges presented. There are a lot of good topics and checklists. The approach is progressive."

"Thorough and I liked the idea of *A Lasting Legacy* not being a quick fix, but more for the marathon which we are running."

"I liked the read and reflect stops. It is so easy to read a book and think I will come back to that later or dig deeper later, but the stops and questions cause you to do that."

"Great resources and great topics. I loved the appendixes at the end. I liked your honesty, hitting the hard things in life."

"Loved the format, that you can stop and spend a greater amount of time in one area or use it as a resource that you can continuously flip back to as needed."

Comments from church leaders and churches from multiple denominations

"Doug Hagedorn was a fine guest on our nationwide talk show! His enthusiasm, passion and knowledge made for excellent radio and assisted thousands of listeners—evidenced by the response from the shows. He has a genuine, natural ability to touch people's minds and hearts. . . .Though I am impressed by Doug's writing, teaching, interviewing and communicating skills, what impresses me the most is his humbleness, Christ-likeness and priority to ensure that God receives the glory for all that has been accomplished through this vital ministry.

—Marlin Maddoux
Founder/Host, Point of View radio talk show
National Religious Broadcasters Hall of Fame

"Doug led and taught us, and all were blessed because of his teachings. Doug's heart and compassion were impactful. We cannot thank Doug enough for his ministry and teaching."

"We all sensed in you a spirit-filled man who has God's call in hand. You were a great help to my family and my church."

"Your presence and work among us bears fruit of Christ's work in your life, and we are so grateful for what He has done through you. Thank you for coming to help others experience the victories that you yourselves have experienced."

"Doug reflected our heartbeat in his teachings. He is very practical, down to earth, encouraging and challenging. The response of our group was excellent. He addressed some tough topics in a relevant and biblical manner. His book, and his testimony, gives you an idea of his passion to see people be unhindered in living for God's purposes."

Comments about his writing style and approach (from *Ease the Squeeze*)

"A truly first rate instructional manual. . . very strongly recommended as being a truly first-rate instructional manual appropriate for all readers of all economic and educational backgrounds"
---Midwest Book Review, 5 stars

"Mr. Hagedorn, I've just finished reading your book. This book probably had more of a SPIRITUAL impact on me than any other book that I've read, except the Bible. Thank you for your book. It really did move me spiritually more than any other book I've read."

"He writes straight from the heart and backs up his writing with biblical truth. This book is encouraging, motivational, and I commend him for having the conviction and strength to write it."
— Amazon, 5 star review

"It is a book from the heart and a powerful testimony adds significant weight to the teaching it provides."
---Amazon, 5 star review

"This book is honest, insightful, and hopeful. By changing one heart and one family at a time through Biblical common sense principles, our families, churches, and communities will be better places to live and work."
---Amazon, 5 star review

"Doug truly has a heart for people.
He has been a real blessing in our lives."

DEDICATION

To:
Emily—always my sweety
Jacob—always my buddy
Justin—always my little man

I love you!
You are my *inspiration* and *motivation* for this book.

May you one day be blessed to have the genetics and talent to sing like an angel to your very own children and grandchildren. Ensure that your legacy explodes by passing this critical baton with such classic gentle wake-up calls as "Wake up, wake up you sleepy head" and "Arise and shine."

Remember always to lean on the Lord and not your own understanding. He will direct your paths. The name of the Lord is a strong tower; the righteous run to it and are safe.[1]

Remember that being a leader often means making decisions that will result in loneliness and separation. Don't be afraid to lead. Be faithful in the little things. Whatever you do, work at it with all your heart, as working for the Lord, not men. [2]

Counterfeits in life will be plentiful. Be real. Give yourself away. Be a true Christian. Be a hero when no one is looking.

"To be a true hero you must be a true Christian. To sum up, then, heroism is largely based upon two qualities—truthfulness and unselfishness, a readiness to put one's own pleasure aside for that of others, to be courteous to all, kind to those younger than yourself, helpful to your parents, even if that helpfulness demands some slight sacrifice of your own pleasure. You must remember that these two qualities—truthfulness and unselfishness— are true signs of Christian heroism. If one is to be a true Christian, one must be a Christian hero."

—G.A. Henty (1832–1902)

To the future spouses of my children and their parents

****

To Dad, Mom and Dana—thanks for your legacies and impact. I stand on your shoulders and shoulder to shoulder with you.

****

To Larry Burkett, Marlin Maddoux, and Chuck Colson. Thanks for your Lasting Legacies!

****

To those who are laboring and sacrificing to share the good news with every nation and every people group. Thank you for your work to ensure that God's love is made real and that each person alive and those not yet born will have the same opportunity that we each have had—an opportunity to gain a spiritual inheritance. You are making Jesus Christ famous and leaving a lasting legacy in all nations for generations to come!

One hundred percent of the net proceeds
from sales of this book will be given to
World Missions.

Psalms 78:1–8

LEGACY BUFFET MENU

Table of Contents

PART I: YOUR FUTURE, YOUR LIFE

PART 2: YOUR FAMILY

PART 3: YOUR FINANCES

PART 4: YOUR FAITH

APPENDICES

Foreword

*Y*ou hold in your hands a book that can literally change your life and the legacy you leave for your loved ones. Doug Hagedorn does an excellent job of helping you assess your life and helps you plan your future. Many people climb the ladder of success only to find that it is leaning against the wrong wall. Then they begin to think about meaning and significance in their lives. What legacy are you leaving? This book helps you answer that question.

What about your family? Do you have a plan for your family? Once again this book helps you think through many important issues related to your family. Not only are you parenting the next generation, but you are raising the future. You will gain practical insight on raising children and building a strong family.

This book also addresses your finances. Someone once said that if you want to know a people's priorities, look at their Daytimer and their check book. We might update that today to say, look at their smartphone and their online banking account. How you spend your time and money says everything about your priorities. Do you know what to do with your finances in these uncertain economic times? Once again this book helps you think through the important issues of your finances.

Throughout the book you are given opportunities not only to read wise counsel but to apply it in a practical way. You will find "Mirror Moments" that give you time to reflect on what you are learning. There are "Selah Stops" that call for you to put the book aside and take action. And there are "Legacy Lessons" that summarize the main theme of the chapter so that once again you can consider what you must do to be faithful.

I highly recommend this book. Buy it. Read it. Apply it. There is great wisdom, and it will change your life and help you leave a lasting legacy.

Kerby Anderson
President of Probe Ministries
Host of Point of View radio talk show

Introduction

We are ALL leaving a legacy—the question is "what kind of legacy"?

I have had a heavy burden for years that families and individuals would be able to develop a generational mindset and action plan and not be so overwhelmed with the flames of today's fires—their problems and challenges. Some have inherited a negative legacy. Others have been gifted a great legacy. If you truly want to live a purposeful, successful life in all seasons and at every age of this journey called life, and want to pass the baton effectively to your children and grandchildren successfully, then this book is for you.

We are living in epic times with uncertainty and turmoil not seen in generations, especially for those approaching "halftime" or those who are already living out the "Second Half" of life. World unrest. Regimes toppling. Wars. Devastating worldwide disasters. The rise of radical terrorism. Economic turbulence. Crushing debt. Decaying morals. Closer to your home address is an urgency that is growing by the day: there is a shortage of future. That is true whether it is your age, due to your children or grandchildren getting older, or the feelings that crisis events seem to be at every turn.

You might be seeking financial freedom that enables a secure future or a stronger, more authentic and rewarding spiritual life. You might want more successful family relationships or a more real, authentic relationship with others or with God. You might want to better understand why previous generations left you a great legacy and help others do the same. However, *desire* and *reality* often seem to be separated by a Grand Canyon of fear, doubt, worry, or just a plain lack of knowing what to do and how to do it.

Most people I know struggle with developing a practical plan for a successful, influential future. They might not have had the best examples in their past or present to help with the "how-to's" for living a connected, joyful, influential, and vibrant life. As our world and our families career towards a crisis at the crossroads, what can you do? In these turbulent times, NOW is the time for you to lead your family, develop a generational mindset, and secure your future. *A Lasting Legacy* will assist you in this endeavor.

As I hold up my life mirror, I realize that I am not getting any younger. Yes, I experience those depressing morning mirror moments when the wrinkle count or hair tally is just not as favorable as it once was. But those moments are not what led me to conclude that this book needed to be written. I was spurred by others who had influenced me. I was spurred by my own failures and life lessons learned.

My approach provides practical and applicable solutions and plans. Anyone can slap words onto a paper, brag about a few successes, or come up with a few great ideas. But my sole purpose for writing this book is *YOU*! I want to partner with you to make your life count and to help revive and renew your heart, mind, and soul. I pray that a sense of excitement and expectation will begin to stir inside of you as you launch into a more passionate pursuit for living life to the fullest. A mundane life with no influence is not rewarding. You have a God-given purpose, and you must not only start strong but also finish strong. It is time to dream again and to run your race called life with purpose. It matters not whether you are running with a tailwind or you are running up a steep hill and into a headwind. You might have a crowd cheering you on, or you might feel that you are running this race alone with tears streaming down your face and with no one to see or care. Whether you are on top of the mountain, standing on an ant pile of problems, or sinking in the quicksand of worry or fear, God knows your every need. He knows the blind spots in your life. He loves you more than you can ever realize. You are of great worth. Let Him love you and help you.

A Lasting Legacy not only articulates the problems and challenges but also provides a "why to," "how to," and "what to" practical, proven toolkit that will help transform your **future**, your **family**, your **finances**, and your **faith** for generations to come. I have not taken this material lightly. It has percolated for decades and been soaked, saturated, and marinated in prayer, fasting, and years of research. I don't believe it is accident or happenstance that you are reading this now. God personally cares about your future. As you read this book, my prayer is that my written words and ideas will be accompanied by the power of the Holy Spirit.[3] If that prayer is answered as you read the book—and I believe it will be—then I simply ask that you have an open mind and heart, that you obey any direction, act upon any conviction, and listen as He speaks to you personally.

This book is about you, but it is about so much more than you. Sometimes that makes it challenging. Permission is granted to feel anger or regret, to laugh or cry, and to change. I give you license to "emote." Please grant yourself permission. Learning to pass the baton of life effectively to your children and grandchildren takes a lifetime. The format and approach of the book is to offer an "idea buffet" from which you can sample—a solution smorgasbord. It is a menu of appetizer ideas, meat-and-potato action plans, and a dessert table loaded with rewards. It may not all taste good. **DO NOT** be overwhelmed or discouraged as you read the book. Take it in bite size chunks and skip that which does not apply.

Take your Medicine

The healthy do not need a doctor. The sick do.[4] Sometimes we know that we are sick. The symptoms are obvious. At other times, we don't know we are sick until we have a physical. Participate in the reflection moments and activity opportunities that are presented throughout the book. Let them be your "physical." They will help with the diagnosis. You might know that you are healthy in certain sections of the book. Take a pass on those treatments or medicine.

1. Admit the areas where you are sick.
2. Be willing to explore those unshared private areas where you might be sick.
3. Get some help; get to a doctor.
4. Take the medicine. Take action!

You will be brought to the front of a mirror to come to face to face with some of the things that matter the most in your life. We often see ourselves as family- or faith-focused, but we often don't stop long enough to look more closely. The focus of this book is PERSONAL APPLICATION.

Although the challenge at hand might require an introspective season in your life, it might also be that you *already* know what you have to do. Now it is time to do it! It is time to develop purposeful and specific plans to leave a strong heritage and a lasting legacy. Understanding our generations, ourselves, and our differences will help in those plans.

Many "self-help" books are "self-destruction" books and promote a quick fix—"Five steps to six ways to eighteen reasons"—or make you more efficient in going the wrong direction. They may lead you to believe that a sprint to success will take only sixty days. Those approaches are more hype and cotton candy for the soul than anything. My hope and prayer is that as a result of investing your time and money in this book you will be able to think and act for the "marathon" you are running. If it helps you or blesses you, tell others of the book, share it with a small group, or pass it on to someone else. You might know that a chapter or section will help a relative or a friend. One section might be more applicable to your current season of life than another. Another chapter might be more appropriate down the road. Although the book can be read straight through, it might make a manual for some people. You might need to soak in some sections longer than others.

As painful as it is for me in some areas, this book was not born out of theory but of practice. It is also born out of data. This book is loaded with data, facts, and research to ensure that the dictum "trust, but verify" has been followed. Facts and data can be stubborn things, but when coupled with life experience, they are a powerful combination.

How to Get the Most from the Book

Building a strong family, creating a secure future, and living a real faith so you can make a generational impact is not light work. Are you willing to do some heavy lifting? Some sections of the book will challenge you greatly. You may be able to skim through others. I heard recently of a major league baseball pitcher who was struggling. He was one of the best pitchers in the league, yet some of his arm motion mechanics needed to be tweaked. He revealed that every year he had to go back and read a book called *The Art of Pitching* by Tom Seaver. In fact, he confessed that often he would pick the book back up four or five times a year to challenge himself in areas where he was weak. My goal is that for sections that are not "light reading" for you, or that challenge you, you read them often. Highlight, dog-ear as necessary, develop a plan, and refer back to those sections. Every tool and checklist may not be for you. To help you determine your priorities and action plan, and to hold yourself accountable, I have included an Appendix called "Idea Buffet Checklist".

To maximize personal application, you will find a number of activities, questionnaires, exercises, and ponder-pause opportunities along the way. These are called Selah Stops, Mirror Moments, Tune Ties, and Legacy Lessons. Take advantage of those activities. Discuss them with a spouse, a family member, or a friend. Teach or share ideas and actions with your friends, loved ones, etc. When you teach something to others you really learn it and apply it best to your own life.

	Mirror Moment = Look a little deeper. Self-reflect and introspect. Maybe have someone else hold up the mirror. Take time to pray.
	Selah Stop = This is a time to do more than reflect; it is a time to set the book down and take action.
	Tune Tie = This indicates a song that is relevant to the topic at hand and that might connect with your soul. If you are reading the e-book, you can link to Itunes or other digital music services. If you are reading the hard copy, I encourage you to stop and listen to the song.
	Generational Hall of Fame = A story of an individual that made a generational impact.
	Legacy Lesson = A Legacy Link that summarizes the chapters main intent in Leaving a Lasting Legacy

Read and Reflect

I was joking with my kids that although I was writing a book on leaving a strong heritage, I wish that I could leave a more robust "hairitage" for my boys. As usual, what would have gotten a roaring laugh when the kids were in elementary school was instead greeted with a weak, half-hearted chuckle and "Good one, Dad." I told them that a few of the book readers might appreciate my attempt at humor more than they did. Fortunately, I can't see the eyerolls from your end. Although my hairline is suffering from its own mid-age crisis, I know that our family legacy or heritage is not about our looks, my hairline, our financial success, or what rung I am clinging to on that career ladder. Rather, it is about much deeper things.

As you read and reflect, think about not only your callings, your dreams, and your passions but also what you can do to discover and cultivate those gifts, dreams, and passions in your family, community or circle of influence. It is critical to understand the seasons you and your family are in, and to prepare for the next season. If you can begin to have a generational mindset, it will shift your focus from just treading water today. You will no longer focus on shallow temporal success but live a transformational life of purposeful significance.

Hope

Though the world around us is literally quaking, in these epic times of uncertainty and turmoil not seen in generations, you CAN experience peace. Although regimes are toppling and war, terrorism and devastation seem to be commonplace, you CAN have hope. Regardless of the lack of leaders who govern with action and with an uncompromising moral rudder, you CAN design your future. You CAN live a significant, purposeful life, despite the ever-increasing tremors of economic turbulence and the headwinds of crushing debt, and a flood of personal and national financial pressures. Have you lived a "half-full" or a "half-empty" life? Despite your past failures, feelings of worry, or spiritual drought, you CAN overcome fear and regret. You may not feel it or believe it, but I believe without a shadow of doubt that you CAN leave a *Lasting Legacy*! You CAN transform *your future, your family, your finances,* and *your faith.*

My true belief is that *A Lasting Legacy* will help you live a rich, exciting, rewarding, secure life so that you can know beyond a shadow of doubt that your heritage and your life will not only radically influence your *present world* but also change our *future world* one home and one family at a time. This book is about the past, the present, and the future. It will help you preserve your past. It will help you live life loud in the present. And it will help you make a generational impact beyond your life. Your future is now!

Your family needs you to thrive. Future generations need you to lead. This country needs strong families. May you sense the urgency to change your world one home at a time.

Legacy Smorgasboard

A Lasting Legacy is segmented into four buffet areas:

Part 1 addresses your **future**. There is no legacy if you are not addressing your own future, your own life. It will help you determine what you want to do with the rest of your life and help you create a plan to achieve it.

Part 2 addresses your **family**. This will help you build a strong family and pass the baton successfully. It will focus on parenting, marriage, and practical tips to improve both.

Part 3 addresses your **finances**. It will lay out a case for your economic future; how you can invest effectively; and how you can get ready for retirement, pay for college, budget effectively, and get out of debt.

Part 4 addresses your **faith**. It will help you ask some introspective questions and develop a plan that will lead to peace, hope, and a joyful life.

A Lasting Legacy is a practical toolkit to help transform your **future**, your **family**, your **finances** and your **faith** for generations to come. It is an essential, comprehensive guide manual for LIFE! It will give you hope, rekindle your dreams, and help you live a significant, purposeful, secure, healthy, and peaceful life. It will help you conquer past regret and failure and attack fear and worry head on. You will be able to build a thriving family, prepare for college and retirement, deal with debt and investment questions, and help secure your family in these uncertain times. It will diagnose and treat. It will refresh and revive. It will encourage, challenge and help you LIVE AND LEAVE a rich, memory-filled, generational, "no-regrets" legacy.

Time Marches On.
Make your Life Count.
Slow the Hourglass.
Pass the Baton.
Diffuse the Time bomb.

Leave a Lasting Legacy!

PART 1

YOUR FUTURE, YOUR LIFE

"Twenty years from now you will be more disappointed by the things you didn't do than by the ones you did. So throw off the bowlines, sail away from the safe harbor, catch the trade winds in your sails. Explore. Dream. Discover."
—Mark Twain

CHAPTER 1

THE FUTURE IS NOW! MOTIVATION AND INSPIRATION

"I will not just live my life. I will not just spend my life.
I will invest my life."
-Helen Keller

What do you want your life to be like five years from now? Ten years? Twenty years? How about your children or grandchildren? This book is about envisioning the future and then taking practical actions to move successfully toward it. The clock is ticking, and the years tend to slip away quickly. We must deal with the future, but we must also deal with the *now* in parallel. It is hard enough to have a "one-year mindset," let alone a multi-generational multiplication mindset. Our problem is that we are overcome with the urgencies of the day. We are running faster but are more exhausted and less fulfilled. It is time to see the bigger picture of your future and deal with the vitally important things of *now*.

This is your life. Are you who you want to be?

People tend to fear the future and failure. We will look briefly at our past and how it affects our future, but most of this book will focus on the future. I truly believe that we are on the cusp of dynamic things in this country. It could involve a spiritual revival, a financial calamity, or another terrorist attack on our country. It could be all of those things. I don't know or pretend to know, but almost everyone I talk to feels the same way. We all can sense the ticking and the tremors around us. All we can do is prepare our families for the future. We must plan now to protect, preserve, influence, lead, and deflect what is coming. We are really preparing for battle—spiritual battles, moral battles, and financial battles. Your future begins now.

Delay of Game

Why is it that we put off until tomorrow what we probably could have done today? Neil Fiore, author of *The Now Habit*,[5] says that "procrastination is a mechanism for coping with the anxiety associated with starting or completing any task or decision." In other words, procrastinating tendencies are often triggered by fears that are not articulated. It could be a fear of failure, a fear of the results, nervousness or stress associated with making a change, or just some rationale as to why we don't have the time or expertise to make a change.

I would guess that in addition to fear and stress, plain old laziness also plays a part in our inaction. It is much easier to sit in front of the television, computer, or a good book than to take action with our health, family, or finances. So what exactly needs action or change? A quick assessment of your "Legacy" thermometer might provide some insight. However, as you score yourself, don't beat yourself up too much! The following example will help you create a framework for your future!

 Score yourself from 1 to 5, with 1 being a failing grade and 5 being an A.

Future

I feel like I am living a purposeful life	1	2	3	4	5
I have a documented plan for my future	1	2	3	4	5
If I lost my job or retired, I have a Plan B	1	2	3	4	5
I effectively balance work and family time	1	2	3	4	5
I have discussed dreams/future with my spouse	1	2	3	4	5
I am prepared for retirement	1	2	3	4	5
I have my dreams written down	1	2	3	4	5

Family

I feel like I am a good spouse	1	2	3	4	5
I feel like I am a good parent	1	2	3	4	5
I give my family enough quality time	1	2	3	4	5
I am teaching my children life principles	1	2	3	4	5
I am training my children spiritually	1	2	3	4	5
I am purposeful about memory making	1	2	3	4	5
I connect well with my kids	1	2	3	4	5

Finances

I am spending less than I make	1	2	3	4	5
I know where my money goes	1	2	3	4	5
I am saving for the future	1	2	3	4	5
I am reducing my debt	1	2	3	4	5
I have a written plan for retirement	1	2	3	4	5
I live on a budget	1	2	3	4	5
I am on track for college/retirement	1	2	3	4	5

Faith

I feel a peace in my soul	1	2	3	4	5
I daily talk to God and read the Bible	1	2	3	4	5
I am a positive spiritual influence	1	2	3	4	5
I am passing the baton effectively	1	2	3	4	5
I have positive, faith-filled relationships	1	2	3	4	5
I feel secure about my future	1	2	3	4	5
I have a multigenerational mindset	1	2	3	4	5

If you enjoy a measure of pain or torture, add up your scores for each section. If you scored > 30 in any one section, congratulations, you are a rare bird and on the Legacy Dean's List. If you scored > 20 in any one section, you have started the Legacy journey in that area. If you scored < 20 in any one section, you are a candidate for a Legacy tune-up or improvement. (We will address all of these areas in *A Lasting Legacy*.)

Take an all-important Mirror Moment and reflect on this little quiz. While I was writing this book, the song that seemed to scream at me and yet encourage me was the following. (If you are reading the E-book, link to Itunes or other digital music service; if you are reading the hard copy, I encourage you to pause and listen).

"This is Your Life"—Switchfoot

Seldom do we spend as much time contemplating the consequences of *not* taking action as we do the excuses or rationale for staying stuck. Consider a few ideas from Fiore:

- Replace "I have to" with "I choose to" or "I will."
- Replace "I must finish" with "When can I start?"
- Replace "This project is so big and important" with "I can take one small step."
- Replace "I don't have time" with "I must take time."
- Replace "I wish I had done that" with "What small step can I take now."

 What are some "I will" or "I must" life shifts that you know *must* be addressed immediately? (Use the Legacy Thermometer scores above to help you.)

Act-Now Pledge[6]

As I read *The Greatest Salesman in the World*, these words jumped off the page at me. I turned it into a pledge or commitment. If you are serious about making some changes, read these words aloud and then sign your name at the bottom of the pledge.

"My dreams are worthless, my plans are dust, my goals are impossible. All are of no value unless they are followed by action.
I WILL ACT NOW."

"Action is the food and drink that nourish my success.
I WILL ACT NOW."

"My procrastination which has held me back was born of fear. Now I know that action reduces the lion of terror to an ant of calmness.
I WILL ACT NOW."

"I will not avoid the tasks of today and delay until tomorrow, for I know that tomorrow never comes.
I WILL ACT NOW."

"It is better to act and fail than not to act and flounder.
I WILL ACT NOW."

I will act now!
I will act now!
I will act now!

I believe a powerful tool is to spend thirty days documenting how you spend your time. Usually within two weeks people realize that taking a small chunk of time from television, work, or housework and reallocating that to family, exercise, finances, or spiritual growth will free up the time needed to take some necessary actions in life.

STOP Spend at least the next week documenting how you spend your time. Take thirty seconds to say aloud an honest prayer from your heart: *"Lord, help show me where I need change, and help me follow through to act now. Stir me and speak to me, please, as I read this book. Amen."*

> "You're more likely to act yourself into feeling
> than feel yourself into action."
> —Jerome Bruner

Stay Strong! Look Long!

Taking action and making changes often requires us to skip or delay an immediate pleasure or desire so as to reach a longer term goal. The challenge is to resist the short-term reward or gratification and exercise self-control to gain a larger reward, whether that be health, long life, financial freedom, or a successful family. Dr. Mark Muraven, a University of Albany professor who studies self-control, states that "self-control is a deliberate, conscious effortful, and resource intensive process of restraining an impulse in order to reach a long-term goal."[7]

Wow! Deliberate. Conscious. Intense. Restraint. Sounds tough! And you know it will be. A "must-do" key to success is for each of us to wrestle with the motivation for our change. If you don't want it bad enough, it will not stick. In a Muraven study, "a plate of cookies was placed in front of participants with the instructions to please not eat them unless absolutely necessary. They were then asked why they did not eat the cookies. People who did not eat the cookies for more self-determined reasons (e.g., because it was important to ME) exhibited better self-control as compared to those who did not eat the cookies for more external reasons (the experimenter would get mad at me)."[8] Thankfully, the moral is not to reject that next batch of chocolate chip cookies. The real moral is that *you gotta want it*! Your children, your life, and your impact should be great motivation for making some consequential changes.

 What is your motivation for living a purposeful second-half life?

Now, I flip the hand-held mirror back around toward your angelic face. Wouldn't the tragedy of all tragedies be for you to come to the end of your road and realize that you missed all that life had to offer, that your legacy was one that you were not proud of? Do not wait until age 65 to assess your legacy and life opportunities. If you are 65 or older, it is not too late. Everyone wants his or her life to count, to make an impact, and to be an influencer. We often struggle with our confidence or ability to do this successfully. With

many people, the first half of life is consumed with pursuits—careers, success, and a chaotic, bustling, mad-dash life where one fails to be contemplative or introspective about the
future. There just doesn't seem to be any time. There are seldom authentic, purposeful
relationships, and many people try to hide "their blemishes" or "keep up with the Joneses."
I believe that you can live an incredible "next half" or "next third" of your life that will blow
away your expectations.

We were recently in Europe and toured the Vatican museums. The beauty and varia-
tion of the artwork, the statues, and the paintings was absolutely amazing. A recollection of
a stroll through the Gallery of Maps and the Hall of Tapestries, reminds me of the parallels
with your life and your God. You were created uniquely. You have wisdom and insight that
others do not have. You have gifts, capabilities, and capacities that others do not have. You
might not view your life as a Michelangelo or DaVinci work. But know that you are just
that. You are not a carbon copy of anyone. God is the Artist or Sculptor. He is molding you,
shaping you, and creating this majestic piece of art that is so valuable and so beautiful that
it does not have a price tag on it. He cherishes you, invests in you, pursues you, and loves
you. He is not rushing this piece of work!

May this book be an opportunity for you to realize that His work in you has only just
started. Let Him do His work. Respond. Participate. Slow down, and do not rush through
the buffet sections that are for you. Force the rose-petal ideas or thoughts to your nos-
trils, ponder them, meditate on them, and be open to becoming more "self-aware," and
then make some mid-course corrections. Take advantage of the mirror moments contained
within, but also ensure that you have some treadmill moments as well! My prayer is that
you are developing a multi-generational, multiplication mindset. One cannot truly understand the future without first understanding the past. "*Remember* the days of old, consider
the years of all generations.[9]"

Remember means to "recall," to "recollect," to "remind." It might be difficult to look
back in the rear view mirror, but even God urged the Israelites to remember their detest-
able years of slavery in Egypt. Some Bible horror stories are there for us to learn from the
past. Nations that forget past times of suffering are doomed to experience more of the same.
Don't just remember but learn from your past. Gain an understanding that will improve
your future.

The next few chapters are about looking back. If you haven't taken the time to share
major life events from your past, make sure you do that somehow, someway—and soon.

"You must never confuse faith that you will prevail in the end. . . .with the discipline to con-
front the most brutal facts of your current reality, whatever they might be."
---Admiral James Stockdale

Legacy Lesson: A multi-generational multiplication mindset is not natural. Leaving a legacy will take some mirror moments focused on living with a new sense of
purpose. We need to be inspired to live for now, but also to live for the future.

CHAPTER 2

GENERATIONS OF CONTRAST— HOW TO THINK AND ACT GENERATIONALLY

That which seems the height of absurdity in one generation often becomes the height of wisdom in another.
—Adlai Stevenson

*I*t is important to connect with history to see a generational snapshot, or you think that your recent generational life experiences are the norm. In studying the generational cycle of America and our world, you can often see through a bigger lens. History ebbs and flows, as do generations. People in different age groups think and behave differently as they progress through the different stages of life—childhood, marriage, midlife, and old age. But a collective generational group has "similar attitudes about family life, sex roles, institutions, politics, religion, lifestyle and the future[10]."

What will they say about your generation in 2040? How about in 2100? What milestones have occurred in our nation during this recent generation? What will we be known and remembered for?

- The terrorist attacks of-9/11?
- Massive government debt and financial collapse?
- Reality TV?
- A secular society?
- The beginning of the end for the United States as the world superpower?

Only time will tell.

The rear view mirror will show us clearly one day. Those few things I listed seem so large that we really don't think that we could have affected them or made a difference personally. So let us shut the door, have a seat on the couch, and bring it a little closer to your home. How will your children and grandchildren remember you? What influence did you or will you have with those few precious years you have remaining?

Time flies. We have such a brief window during which to lay a firm foundation for each of our children—a decade maybe. However, we have a lifetime of seventy to eighty years to make an impact that will last beyond our lifetime. Don't waste your time. Make an impact.

I recall a recent survey of individuals over the age of 65. They were asked a simple question: "If you could live your life over again, what would you do different?" Overwhelmingly, the response was, "I would make sure my time and my money were invested in things that made an impact beyond my generation."

Generations

I am a member of the exclusive "cusper club." I am blessed with an extra strand of generational DNA—I straddle the fence between the Boomers and Gen-X, so I tend to take on traits of both. I guess that means one of two things: either I am hopelessly lost and extremely confused, or I can relate to and understand both generations. I am optimistic that it is the latter, but you will soon be the judge.

Bridging the Generation Gap

Because Boomers and the Silent Generation are living longer than ever, we now have four generations colliding in the workplace, the church, and the home. Each generation has its own set of values, life experiences, beliefs, and attitudes. In *Bridging the Generation Gap*[11] and *When Generations Collide,*[12] the authors discuss generational profiles. Here is a brief summary of their findings.

Nickname	Birth years	Characteristics / Traits
Generation Z Millennials/ (35+ million)	1994–present	Connected, confident, self-expressive, open to change, racial/ ethnic diversity, less religious, educated, multi-taskers
Generation Y (75–80 million)	1977–1994	Racial/ethnic diversity, independent, tech revolution, feel empowered, sense of security, optimistic, overindulgent parents
Generation X (45–50 million)	1965–1976	Self-reliant, mistrust institutions, use technology, the MTV generation, tend to ignore leaders, educated, practical, pragmatic
Boomers (75–80 million)	1946–1964	Impatient, divorce generation, richest generation, hard working, self-reliant, goal-oriented, competitive, resourceful, idealists
Silent Generation (50–60 million)	1925–1945	Hard working, strong work ethic, loyal, respectful of authority, technically challenged, traditional values, adaptive

GI Generation	1901–1924	Resourceful, determination, rationalistic, rigid, self-sacrifice, resilient, family cohesion, teamwork

Generational Quiz: Can You Relate?

You know you're a Silent Generation/Traditionalist if

- you read Dr. Spock
- you cheered on Joe DiMaggio and Joe Louis
- you watched John Wayne, Elizabeth Taylor and Bob Hope
- you listened to 45s / LP's of Duke Ellington and Ella Fitzgerald
- you learned to do without and saved for a rainy day
- you survived a world war and a depression

You know you're a Boomer if

- you watched the *Mickey Mouse Club* and *Leave it to Beaver*
- you liked to hula hoop and wear bell bottoms
- you watched McEnroe and Connors
- you used a typewriter
- you listened to the Beatles, the Monkees, and the Stones on cassette tape
- you remember Woodstock, Watergate, and women's rights

You know you're a Gen-Xer if

- you wore a shirt with an alligator or a horse on the chest
- you played Atari and Asteroids
- you watched Jordan, Rodman, and O.J.
- you know who shot J.R., who ran Microsoft, and who Monica Lewinsky was
- you know what "all skate" means
- you had a record player and listened to Madonna

You know you're a Gen-Yer/Millennial if

- you listened to CDs, then ditched them for digital
- you cooked in the microwave or ate out all the time
- you used e-mail, then switched to texting
- you watched the steroid boys, Mark McGwire and Sammy Sosa, and Lebron
- you watched *Harry Potter*, *Survivor*, and *Lost*
- you can text, talk on the phone, check Facebook, and study at the same time

Each generation goes through events that shape them: the American Revolution, the Civil War, the Great Depression, Pearl Harbor, World War II, Woodstock, the Apollo moon landing, 9/11, etc. "There are two types of social moments where history shapes generations or generations shape history: secular crises and spiritual awakenings"[13]. According to

Strauss and Howe in *Generations*, the spiritual awakenings we have been through are the Reformation Awakening, a Puritan Awakening, the Great Awakening, the Transcendental Awakening, the Missionary Awakening, and the Boom (Jesus Movement) Awakening. I've chosen to list a few of the influential "giants" of each period, but there were many more.

Reformation	1517–1539	Martin Luther, John Calvin, John Knox
Puritan	1621–1640	John Winthrop, John Cotton, Anne Hutchinson
Great	1734–1743	Jonathan Edwards, George Whitefield, the Wesley brothers
Transcendental	early 1800s	Charles Finney, Charles Spurgeon
Missionary	1886–1903	Dwight Moody, Charles Parham, William Seymour
Jesus Movement	1967–1980	Bill Bright, Billy Graham, Keith Green, Martin Luther King Jr.

Each of these movements has connection points. Many of the Puritans had great-great-grandparents who had learned alongside Martin Luther and John Calvin and were burned at the stake as Protestant heretics. Some heard these stories by word of mouth and others read them in the *Book of Martyrs* by John Foxe. Each of these giants had a major impact on the church centuries later: Martin Luther's Ninety-Five Theses on the church door at Wittenberg, Calvin's and Knox's influence on the Protestant Reformation, the preaching, the theology, the ministries, the social impact—this list runs long.

"We shall be as a city upon a hill," 42-year-old John Winthrop told the passengers aboard their flagship *Arabella* as it sailed for Massachusetts in 1630. Winthrop's message was a generational clarion call. The Puritans were influenced by the Reformation. Cotton and Hutchinson, born in England, were Puritans and played prominent roles in colonial America.

The youth propelled Great Awakening that began as a series of isolated spiritual revivals in the Connecticut Valley, spread quickly and brought a passion to the church. Jonathan Edwards called some members of the older generations "moral neuters," and clergyman Samuel Dexter confessed in admiration of the younger George Whitefield "ten thousand worlds would I give. . .to feel and experience what I believe that man does." The Wesley brothers' influence was felt in their preaching, hymns, and in the founding of the Methodist movement. A generational revival was on America's doorstep. The Great Awakening, led by many people in only their mid-twenties was credited with the founding of 250 new churches and 200,000 conversions.

Charles Finney was the "father of revivals," and Charles Spurgeon was called the "prince of preachers." Both men had a great influence in the early and mid-1800s. D.L. Moody's influence on missions, education, and publishing is still felt today. Parham and Seymour were instrumental in the Azusa Street Revival and the explosion of the Charismatic Movement.

The Boom Awakening, started in the late 1960s, during times of inner-city riots and the sexual revolution. The rise of the "Jesus movement" led to resurgent evangelism, massive crusades with Billy Graham, many blossoming ministries such as Campus Crusade for Christ, and the growth of the contemporary Christian music scene. Martin Luther King's influence both spiritually and socially also changed the world. This was the most active era of church formation of the twentieth century. Church attendance rose by nearly 30 percent. The face of American religion was changing drastically. During the 1980s, the Boomers migrated out of established mainline churches and surged into New Age and evangelical sects. America's fastest growing church was the Assemblies of God, the number of "Charismatic or "Pentecostal" Catholics quintupled, and America now had more Muslims than Episcopalians.

Futurist

According to the article *"The Generation of Contrast"* in *Relevant Magazine,*[14] twenty- and thirty-somethings are part of a generation that is "reshaping the world we live in, while experiencing seismic cultural shifts that are defining our times." This generation

- is ready to change the world, but a little numb
- will alter how faith is practiced and perceived
- is increasingly alienated from institutions and traditions that once epitomized the American way of life
- is skeptical of all kinds of authority
- is engaging politically with increasing intensity
- is using technology and social media regularly, and obsessed with mobility and connectivity
- is doing family in a different cultural context and experiencing "family" in all shapes and sizes
    - In 1960, 5 percent of babies were born to unwed moms; today that is 41 percent.
    - In 1970, 17 percent of those in their late 20s were single; today that is 56 percent.
    - Determined not to repeat their parents mistakes, the divorce rate among 18- to 34-year-old Christians is actually dropping.

This generation is wrestling with its spirituality as well:

- They wonder how to be "in but not of" this world, but to connect faith with the world they live in.
- They want to know where the boundaries are.
- Only one-third of them believe that spiritual maturity is best measured by the rules of the Bible.
- They are not comfortable being labeled "Christian left" or "Christian right."
- More than half of the 18-to-29-year-olds with a Christian background are less active in church than they were at age 15.
- A mere 26% of them say that they grew up learning to view their gifts/passions as part of God's calling.

31

Being the richest man in the cemetery doesn't matter to me. . . .
Going to bed at night saying we've done something wonderful—that's what matters to me.
—Steve Jobs, founder Apple, CNNMoney/Fortune, May 25, 1993

Old Boomer Bloomer

I discovered this past month that I was officially old. It wasn't the hairline or the blinding glare emanating from the bathroom mirror. It wasn't even my lagging hundreds of yards behind my kids as we biked eight miles to Baskin-Robbins. It was that now-familiar request from someone at work to share my career experiences with a group of Gen-Yers and Millennials. They assured me it was "my experience" and "my seasoned stories" that would be helpful to those up-and-comers. It wasn't even this one request that made me feel old, though; it was that this request has become a regular request.

Telling a group of Millennials my career path story was a challenge. A bunch of young up and comers sat with notepads and pens at the ready, contemplating their future. I recall my dad's telling me to "bloom where you are planted." The advice was sound and I heeded it *after* I uprooted from Michigan and headed to Texas. I tended to interpret this quotation as "Do the best you can with what you are given"—the talents, the boss, the economy, etc.

I chose my major in college based on the 100 percent placement rate and the Motown automobile industry's need for purchasing majors. I interviewed for an internship at Texas Instruments (TI) in Dallas, Texas, and they loved my paper route, pay-my-way-through-college story so much that I landed a six-month internship during my senior year. I worked hard and received an offer to come to Texas for a full-time position. I never thought I would actually leave Michigan, but this was a great opportunity.

My first purchased car in Texas had no air conditioning. We didn't even bother to look. No wonder we got a good deal! We never had air conditioning in Michigan. I can recall that all my friends were on the "five-year plan" at TI. To them, TI meant Tiny Income or Training Institute. We all planned to strike out on our own or head different directions after five years. I kept blooming where I was planted while my friends flew the coop. My first few assignments helped build my subject matter expertise, confidence, and leadership skills. I was "modeling" or watching my managers to harvest their good leadership skills. No assignment was wasted, I told these up and comers. You might learn writing skills from one person, oral communication skills from another, and the negative lesson of the lack of people skills from another.

I earned my MBA in twenty months at University of Dallas, taking three classes at a time, year round. It was a blur, but I was learning social skills, public speaking, and leadership skills without having actual authority. I was always candid with my bosses about my desires, and it was an open, two-street of communication. I was favored with promotions and raises and soon thereafter met my wife Dana.

My final pieces of advice to the passionate group of youngsters were these: (1) Take some measured risks, and try different things early in your career. You will learn what you are good at and what you have a passion for. (2) Get wisdom in the counsel of many. Don't rely on one person to look out for you or steer you. (3) Be quick to listen and learn. Ask questions. Do what you say you are going to do. Follow through. (4) Respect and reward the people and communicate well. (5) Stick to your core beliefs, and do not waiver.

I closed by telling them not to be afraid to fail. Some of the greatest leaders failed at multiple turns. The key is to avoid making the same mistake over and over and to turn those mistakes into stepping stones for success. Your perception and failures will grow you and build you so much more broadly and quickly than just having success all of the time. Dealing with obstacles and adversity will make you a strong leader.

I am blessed with employment. I have learned to connect with 4 different generations. We can all learn from each other.

How are you influencing other generations? How are they influencing you? What common ground can you work towards? Are you thinking and acting to make a generational impact? Get into other generations world.

"Those individuals who do not look upon themselves as a line connecting the past with the future do not perform their duty to the world."
—Daniel Webster

Legacy Lesson: You come from a unique generation. How can you be a more influential connection point to bridge the gap with your kids, grandkids and co-workers? What will your generation be remembered for? More importantly, what will YOU be remembered for?

CHAPTER 3

MILESTONE MARKERS: PASSING THE BATON

> *"Each **generation** goes further than the **generation** preceding it because it stands on the shoulders of that **generation**. You will have opportunities beyond anything we've ever known."*
>
> —Ronald Reagan, fortieth president of the United States

A screaming, slimy baby, age two minutes, enters the world, March 18, 1965, in Royal Oak, Michigan. It is a milestone for Mom and Dad.

At age twenty-two, with a full head of hair and a college diploma in hand, I was ready to conquer the world, seek my fame and fortune, and live life loud. I was graduating from the dismal gray skies, the snow-capped Plymouths, and the hapless Detroit Lions. I was leaving the good life of delivering newspapers in four-foot snow drifts and from slinging fast-food chicken wings, family size fries, and ocean perch (or was it lake perch?). Ahh, I was entering the new life of seventy-degree winters, rustless vehicles, the Bible belt, and the land of the Alamo, Larry Hagman, oil tycoons, and past presidents (Bush, W. Bush, Eisenhower, and LBJ). It was the state preferred by Autry, Crockett, Dell, Nolan, Trevino, Criswell, Hagee, and even Mary Kay, Steve Martin, and "the Rookie." There was one sore spot, however: I would also now be subjected to the media blitz and fervor of "America's team." I would be a fish out of water to say the least, but I was ready for adventure. Having been a fearful yet fiercely independent teenager brought me to this moment. Or was it more than that? Nevertheless, it was my first milestone.

At age forty-something, I had a full head of scalp, wore a jacket and a tie, was conducting yet another team-building workshop while drifting in and out of reality when the facilitator asked a question that awakened me from la-la land. "Whose shoulders do you stand on?" My brain was suddenly shocked to attention, and the next hour led me on a saunter down Hag History lane and my own personal life milestone markers.

On whose shoulders did I stand and why should I care? It was a great question that forced me to spend much more time on this topic over the next several days than the two minutes I was allotted in class. The obvious answer was my parents. Spending a quarter of a century under the same roof certainly had a major impact. I thought about others who had influenced me and came up with quite a lengthy list of my "Generational Hall of Fame."

These are rear-view reflection moments that will not only create a stirring of gratefulness, but will also no doubt percolate some not-so-pleasant emotions. The fact is that both our ancestors and genetics play a role in who we are. The fact is also that your parents' training or lack of training influenced the shaping of who you are.

My own *past* decisions and choices have not only made me who I am but also have had great influence on my children. More importantly, my *future* decisions and actions will have a monumental influence on my children and grandchildren.

Give some thought to the question: Whose shoulders do you stand on? Who made you what you are today? Who (or what) influenced you the most as a child, as a teenager, as a young adult, and as an aging middle ager? Was it genetics, others, or your own plans and efforts? Or was it plain luck, destiny, or God's plan that made you who you are today?

Hall of Fame or Hall of Shame?

What comes to mind when you read the following names?

- Henry Ford	- Adolf Hitler	- Your mom/dad	- Abraham Lincoln
- Jesus Christ	- Charles Darwin	- Martin Luther	- Babe Ruth
- Michelangelo	- Karl Marx	- Noah	- Beethoven
- Tim Berners Lee	- Benjamin Franklin	- Martin Luther King Jr.	- Christopher Columbus
- Albert Einstein	- Mohammed	- Joseph Smith	- Winston Churchill
- Your grandparents	- George Washington	- Osama bin Laden	- Pope John Paul

These are people who might be in your Generational Hall of Fame—or in your Generational Hall of Shame. Regardless of your feelings about each of them, they had a monumental influence on generations after them. They were hated by some, loved by others, followed by many, and, in many cases, disowned by the people closest to them. Some of them created, invented, and discovered. Others terrified and tortured. Some are worshipped and adored. They were all leaders, examples, and had influence far beyond their years. They failed. They overcame. They all left their mark. They had an impact. Their influence will continue for generations to come.

Generational Giant

You will find some interesting "Generational Giants" at the end of some chapters; people who had an impact on the world, often on our lives directly. I hope that this feature will reinforce the reality that each of us leaves a legacy. Our impact is felt long after our tombstones are marked.

 Take a few minutes to list the people who had a major impact on your life. Those people are members of your "Generational Hall of Fame."

Marking Time—Your Roots

We are still looking in the rear-view mirror and determining how you were shaped and influenced. As you think of the individuals who had a major impact on you, both positively and negatively, you certainly also will recall some major events that were "milestone moments" that were pivotal in helping you determine your future, or that had a major impact on you in some way. Your roots are many and run deep in helping shape who you are.

Many of your milestones are singular particular events or decisions that had a major impact. Certainly seasons of life also had an impact. If you stroll back in time, you will be amazed how these milestones influenced where you are today and where you will be in the future.

Joshua 4:5-9 and 4:21 talks of setting up stones as markers so that your children will ask, "What do these stones mean to you?" Document your milestones and tell the stories behind them. How will you pass on your memories, your stories, your pile of stones? (I will cover how to do this effectively in the Family section.)

I took a few hours and tried to recall all of the "milestone moments" in my own life. Your spouse and kids may help you. Any memories you have collected also will help you recall. Our annual Christmas newsletter, photo albums, and videos helped me recall many such moments.

Milestone Moments:

o The move from Terre Haute, Indiana, to Grand Rapids, Michigan	1974
o The choice of a high school	1980
o The first job—Chicken Coop Restaurant	1982
o The choice of a college/moving from home	1983
o The internship in Texas/moving from Michigan to Texas	1987
o The first job at Texas Instruments	1988
o The first date with Dana	February 3, 1991
o My salvation	February 10, 1991

o The decision to give up specific "material idols" in my life	1991
o Intercession prayer meetings/learning how to pray	1991–1993
o Attending an informational meeting—Fun Farm/Metro Ministries	1991
o Attending a Larry Burkett financial seminar	1992
o My marriage to Dana	March 6, 1993
o The birth of Emily Ann Hagedorn	July 26, 1994
o Teaching at LeTourneau University	1995
o The birth of Jacob Rees Hagedorn	November 14, 1996
o Dad's warning—my decision to make family my major focus	1997
o Lying flat on my back—Bradbury Eggleston Syndrome	1997
o Teaching my first Financial Freedom seminar	1997
o The birth of Justin Douglas Hagedorn	March 7, 2000
o Emily's salvation	2001
o Publication of *Ease the Squeeze*	2001
o Spending a "prayer carpet" night in prayer about starting a school	2002
o Jacob's salvation	2003
o The founding of Cornerstone Christian Academy	2003
o Appearing on the Larry Burkett and Marlin Maddoux radio shows	2004
o Justin's salvation	2007
o The family missions trip	2011
o My heart episode/Surgery—Pacemaker	2011
o Emily's high school graduation	2012
o Publication of *A Lasting Legacy*	2012

As I reflect on these milestones, I realize that many of the roots came from my parents, family influence, or where I grew up, and those influences laid the groundwork for not only my own family tree but also the family branches that would come years later.

- The type of church I chose and the doctrine I believed were influenced by the church I attended and my likes and dislikes of the church at the mere age of nine.
- I developed a lifelong work ethic from the paper routes I owned as a young teenager.
- I made lifelong friendships based on the neighborhood and the school I attended as a teenager.
- The timing of my first job influenced my friends, my future resume, and my eating habits.
- My college choice influenced my social habits, my lack of a spiritual life, my future job, and where my family settled.

- Our decision to attend a financial seminar and develop a plan to get out of debt led to writing *Ease the Squeeze*, conducting seminars, and doing nationwide radio and writing. An offer from a singles-class leader to teach a small Sunday school class one time, though I was *nervous and shaking*, led to a passion for communicating and teaching.
- A two-minute discussion with my dad about my misguided priorities radically changed my life and future generations to come. It eventually led to new family priorities, my books, our starting a school, being involved with ministry, our kids' salvation and success and favor at work, and dozens of other involvements.
- My decision to follow the Lord was fraught with years of arm wrestling and will be covered in a later chapter, but it was the most monumental decision and milestone of my life.
- Our choice of a church and our choice to train our kids led to their salvation, friendships, and many other choices.
- Our decision to start a school has led to the influencing of hundreds of families and of future leaders.
- My decision to destroy my secular music and change how I spent my spare time led to a passion for God and a radical reshaping of how I spend my time and the eventual generational impact that will hopefully take place.
- My decision to move out of state influenced my family relationships, my independence, starting a family, our children's upbringing, our income, my spiritual life, and dozens of other life events.

STOP Take out a clean sheet of paper. What are some of your pivotal Milestone Moments that have shaped your life and will have a generational impact? Read about how memorial stones were used to mark significant events in the Bible. (1 Samuel 7:12; Jeremiah 31:21; and Matthew 26:13).

The decisions and actions we make and take have a profound, monumental impact for our children and grandchildren. Do not take them lightly! Ask for God's help. He will help!

Decisions and Choices

Life is full of milestones. Full of seasons. Full of decisions and choices. Driving for the first time. College. First job. Marriage. Kids. Family. Work. Ministry. Empty nest. Retirement. Grandkids. Loss of family members. Death.

It is amazing the impact that one decision can have on future generations. I was the only Hag kid who left the great state of Michigan for Texas. That one flippant college-kid decision set the wheels in motion for generations to come. It boggled my mind as I began to draw a decision tree and to realize how it had led to major decisions on who my spouse would be, the success of my career, where my children would end up in college, my spiritual life, and ministries that I would be involved with. I created a decision tree with the branches that were created as a result of that one decision:

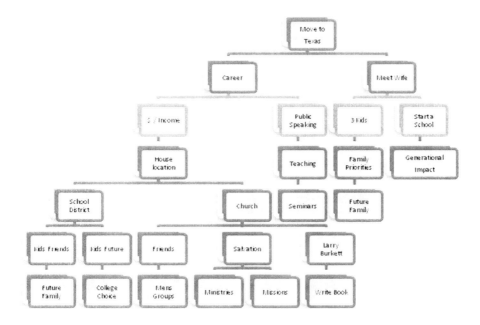

I think you get the point. This exercise makes it crystal clear that your decisions or events can turn out to be either major stepping stones or major hurdles in your life. Some of these "small" or subtle decisions or events have a monumental impact on your family tree, on your children's environment, and many other areas of your life. The multiplication effect is astounding. These milestones are in fact entrance ramps and off ramps for future generations to come. DO NOT TAKE YOUR DECISIONS LIGHTLY!

Reflect on some decisions or events in your life that are affecting your future or your family's future.

Your career decisions influence how much time you have with your family. Your decision to uproot your kids from a school, church, or city at a critical point will have a major impact. Your decision to party or indulge in a secret sin can cut your life short. Your decision to dabble in pornography or flirt with a co-worker can lead to greater sin that can devastate your family. Your decision to make a purchase you can't afford can lead to family conflict.

Your decision to pray with your spouse will have an impact that will surprise you greatly one day. Your decision to read the Bible to your kids or grandkids will help keep them on the straight and narrow path or, at a minimum, start them there and have a narrow path to come back to someday. Your decision to eat healthy and exercise can lengthen your life and lead to a bounce in your step. Our decisions have a generational impact. Some might be big, and others will be little.

I recall deciding to write a book. It wasn't a clear "call from God" or even a matter of obedience or disobedience. Many times we think we should do something or even that we have a leading from God, but we just don't know if we should. It was actually laughable when someone told me I should write a book. I did a short devotional and taught about goalsetting and budgeting in an evening class I was teaching at LeTourneau University. A student said I should write all of this down and then do seminars. The idea was laughable because God was stretching me enough with my time. My pastor asked me, "Why not?"

I was very cautious because God had made it clear about my time management and my need not to waste precious time. He also had made it clear that my family was to be my primary focus and my job was not to be jeopardized, so I was a little apprehensive to embark on a project that would interfere with my primary priorities. I began doing financial seminars and writing *Ease the Squeeze*. I wrote the book over a period of eighteen months while my kids and wife were already in bed, from 10 p.m. until 2 a.m. I would not compromise my family time or job for my own pursuits.

It was a whirlwind and still seems like a dream. It took a lot of hard work, a ton of research, much study, plenty of prayer, and preparation, but God honored the hard work and overcame my inadequacies. I conducted more than 30 radio shows, sold approximately 2,500 books, and gave away 300 others. Now it all seemed to make sense as to why God wanted me to focus on my family and surrender my time early on in our marriage! I thought I had it all figured out! Not. I was now making a small but generational impact!

Sometimes we don't know our gifts until we test the waters. I am forever grateful to my singles pastors. They let me teach a class on getting involved in politics. My friend Andy and I were passionate about seeing people engage in the political process. But that didn't really seem to fit the "normal" Sunday school material. The title of my incredibly spiritual Sunday school inaugural teaching was "Get Involved." The handout included websites, phone numbers, and talk radio show details. I am not sure how well received it was, but it started to burn in me to teach. Marlin Maddoux was my hero at the time, so I taught a lot from a book called *A Christian Agenda* and content from his *Point of View* radio talk show.

Little did I know that ten years later I would be invited by his wife Mary and Warren Kelly to be on his radio program nationwide with Kerby Anderson and that soon after I would appear on Larry Burkett, Howard Dayton, and Steve Moore's *Money Matters* show nationwide. Why? God opened the doors. I had been faithful in a few things. I felt inadequate and unprepared. God said, "This is the one I esteem, he who has a humble and contrite spirit." He used "ordinary, unschooled" men. I fit that description pretty well. Believe that if you make some changes in your little things and are obedient, great things are ahead!

 What little things is God asking you to do? What little things does your family need from you? Be faithful in the little things.

"Enjoy the little things, for one day you may look back and realize they were the big things."
—Robert Brault

Generational Giant

Charles Jennings and Handel: George Frederick Handel[15] faced much adversity. He was on the verge of bankruptcy and in failing health. He recovered from a stroke but was despondent. He decided it was time to retire at age 56. He had decided to give his farewell concert and then gave up. A friend visited Handel later in the year and stirred him to action. Handel decided to try again. Thank you, Charles Jennings! For twenty-four days, Handel worked almost nonstop and produced a 260- page masterpiece called *Messiah*. Although Handel himself had to decide to move forward, a spoken word of encouragement was a major milestone in Handel's life. Do not underestimate how you can influence someone else's decisions and choices.

Whether you turn to the right or to the left, your ears will hear a voice behind you, saying,
"This is the way; walk in it."
- Isaiah 30:21

Legacy Lesson: In looking back we all have milestone markers that greatly shaped us. Our roots run deep. We make decisions that will be our kids and grandkids very own milestone markers. Whose Hall of Fame will you be in? We can learn from the past batons passed (good and bad). Are you allowing God to play a part in the race?

CHAPTER 4

GENERATIONAL GAPS AND GENETICS—UNDERSTAND AND DEAL WITH GENERATIONAL DIFFERENCES

The Leadership Inventory results were in. I scored in the ninetieth percentile on ambition. I was competitive, energetic, and eager to advance, yet I scored very high on prudence, organization, dependability, and thoroughness. I was "off the charts" on being "risk averse/conservative," off the charts on "Type-A traits", way off the charts on "perfectionist/precise/ high standards," and was also "approval dependent/eager to please." I was barely visible on the charts for "impulsive/risk taking," and I was in the ninety-ninth percentile for my traits of "independence, directness." I was in the ninety-fifth percentile for "being practical/down to earth" and in the ninety-ninth percentile for being reserved and quiet, not calling attention to myself, and not minding working alone.

As I reflect on my "first half," I have always known that I enjoy solitude and independence, yet I had to force myself to get out of my comfort zone and speak publicly and work hard at it. I was an introvert being forced out of his box. I was always curious how many of my personality traits and leadership skills were actually attributable to "genetics" and/or "learned from my parents"? Which of those traits were self-learned or learned from others? My gut and the knowledge of my parents led me to believe that many of these traits were also evident in my parents. I interviewed them and asked them to rate themselves the following on a scale of 1 to 10:

	Doug	Dad	Mom
Ambitious/competitive/energetic	9	7	5
Prudent/organized/dependable/thorough	9	7	9
Risk averse/conservative	9	7	10
Perfectionist/precise/high standards	9	7	7

Approval dependent/eager to please	8	6	10
Impulsive/risk taker	3	5	1
Independent/direct	9	7	3
Practical/down to earth	9	7	8
Reserved/not call attention to self/don't mind working alone	9	6	7

It was an interesting dialogue and exercise with my parents. We have inherited traits and learned traits. I was NOT a risk taker in part quite possibly because my parents were not. We might also find some "negative traits" from our parents and determine not to repeat some of those (i.e., alcoholism, smoking, anger issues, gambling, or abuse). Some of the traits might be harder to change and influence than others. It is possible to change some of your genetic traits if you have the will power, the money, or in some cases, the guts. Of course, you might have to move to another state after you get your hair transplant.

 Take your own "Learned Legacy Inventory."

What would my last words be to my dad? To my mom?	
Describe the parenting style of dad. mom.	
Describe how your parent treated his or her spouse.	
Finish the following sentences:	
The most fruitful family times were. . . .	
The most destructive family times were. . . .	
I felt most secure when my dad would. . . .when my mom would. . . .	
My fondest memories of my dad were. . . .of my mom were. . . .	
My fondest family memories were when. . . .	
How did your dad show you love? Your mom?	
What were the best qualities in your dad? Your mom?	
What were the worst qualities in your dad? Your mom?	

Describe your parents approach to discipline.	
Describe how much quality time and quantity time you experienced with your parents.	
What was the spiritual impact of your dad? Your mom?	

Genes or Jeans?

The word *generation* comes from the root word *Gene* and is an English derivative of the Latin word *genus*, meaning "birth, offspring, or creation." A gene is a unit of heredity in a living organism. I will not get into the detail of DNA and RNA, nor will I cover the nonfunctional structure of a gene, a study of chromosomes or dominant and recessive traits, or try to increase your knowledge of molecular inheritance.

Genealogy means "account," "order of birth," "descendants," "biography," or "generations." Generational lineage and history are even addressed in the Bible. "The messianic promise was first made in Genesis 3:15, then again through Isaiah's prophecy in Isaiah 7:14 and then fulfilled in the birth of Jesus Christ in Matthew 1:18–25."[16]

The Bible is God's history book, giving us great insight into learning from past generations. "Genesis 5 records Adam's genealogy, 10 generations from Adam to Noah. Genesis 11 records the 10 generations from Shem to Abraham. There are 10 other genealogies in Genesis. Matthew 1 depicts 42 generations from Abraham to Jesus Christ. Luke 3 lists the genealogy of Jesus in ascending order."[17] (If you really want to go deep into biblical genealogies, I highly recommend *The Genesis Genealogies* by Rev. Abraham Park.)

The question is not *whether* genes contribute to who you are today but rather *how much* they contribute to who you are. Genes do hold the information to build and maintain an organism's cells, and one does pass genetic traits to offspring. Traits such as your eyes, your hair, your blood type, your risk of certain diseases, and some body traits such as limb size and traits, a nose, a hairline or even the size of your caboose (and thus the size of your jeans) are traits that could be passed down. (Sorry kiddos—think on the many *good* things we passed on.)

Even some of your taste bud desires can be passed down. A recent study showed that our need for caffeine is in our DNA! (Now I have an excuse!) "Researchers made this discovery by comparing the genes and caffeine consumption habits of more than 47,000 Americans of European descent."[18]

These and other traits *might* be passed on, but they also can skip a generation or more. We inherit a set of "potentials," some of which might lie dormant for generations. We wish that some of them had lain dormant! I see myself in pictures of my great grandparents. You can have a blue-eyed person somewhere in your family tree that lingered for generations before becoming evident. You can have the potential to grow to 6' 5" but have poor nutrition, be subjected to different environmental conditions, or just get the luck of the draw and be 6' 0". Genes and your environment influence who you are.

You might find it interesting that you have some of the same areas of talent as one of your parents. Genes can contribute differently for different traits. *Forbes* magazine recently cited a study on entrepreneurial talents by Scott Shane[19], a behavioral economist and professor at Case Western Reserve University. Did you inherit any of your parents social or entrepreneurial traits? You bet! Shane even studied, analyzed, and estimated how much:

A person's ability to recognize new opportunities	45 percent inherited
Openness to new challenges	45 to 61 percent inherited
Being extroverted	Up to 66 percent inherited
Entrepreneurship	30 to 40 percent inherited

This made sense as I reviewed the results of my brief survey of my parents cited above. The results were a mix of inheritance and acquiring.

If genetics floats your boat, you might enjoy studying Gregor Mendel, Pythagoras, or Aristotle on your own time, but they are not the purpose of this book. We do pass on some of our genetic material. We learn traits. We can also unlearn traits we are not happy with. Some behavioral change will take much more work than others. The truth is that we are uniquely created by God. We are fully human and fully created by God. We make choices. We can change some things on our own. For other things, we need God's help or deliverance. Some physical things we are just stuck with! The good news is that He knows us better than we know ourselves. He even knows the number of hairs on our head.[20]

> *For you created my inmost being;*
> *You knit me together in my mother's womb.*
> *. . . I am fearfully and wonderfully made;*
> *. . . I was made in the secret place.[21]*

Legacy Lesson: Taking inventory of your past and impacting your future will require "reflection" that turns to "action". We all leave an inheritance to future generations. Some of these traits they will acquire, and some they will learn. Some will be genetic. Influence the traits that you can in your kids and grandkids.

CHAPTER 5

EPIC TIMES REQUIRE EPIC MEASUES: CHANGE

"The world belongs to the energetic."
—Ralph Waldo Emerson

What, Me Change?

"*P*eople do change!" the grizzled, inner-city preacher[22] nearly shouted. Then he paused for effect before finishing the short sentence with a throaty whisper, "*—but not much.*" His gravelly words sliced through the air and felt like a sharp, pungent bee sting to a silent crowd. The splinter seemed to linger for a while as we all took in that simple statement. *"People change, but not much."* I didn't realize the abounding profundity of those simple words at the time. His point was that, although our world has many needs, most people are not willing to man up and make some major personal sacrifices or radical changes so that they can influence their world. They are unwilling to lay down their own desires or needs for someone else. The preacher meant for his message to stir comfortable pew dwellers to action. We all have these splinters of inaction, and sometimes the truth hurts. But my hope is that you are reading this book because you know the hourglass that represents your life is draining quicker than you thought it would and that you do, in fact, want to make some changes. My hope and prayer has been that you will break out of that cocoon of desire and experience such a desperation for a life metamorphosis that you know you *must* act, that you *must* change! Future generations depend upon it.

"The greatest inspiration is often born of desperation."
—Comer Cotrell

As you sat through those monotonous high school and college classes with biology beakers, trigonometry tables, or chemistry chaos, did you wonder how those courses would benefit you outside the walls of the classroom? As you clawed and scratched to earn enough money to pay the bills and get to the next paycheck, how often did you think and plan for ten or twenty years down the road? As you climbed the career ladder or embarked on the pursuit of success, how well were you being prepared for your future and your children's future? How many classes did you take on marriage, staying out of debt, raising a family, or preparing for retirement? If you are typical, very few.

Did your parents sit you down and share the finer points of how to live a purposeful life, how to turn your dreams into reality or how to choose a college? Did they share with you how long it took them to pay off their house or have a good talk with them about some of the parenting mistakes they made so you could avoid the same? Did a professor or Sunday school teacher instruct you how to make great family memories, build a strong family, choose the best college for your kids, or how to live a secure, purposeful life?

If your answer is no to most of those questions, be encouraged—you are normal. Most of us are ill prepared to leave a Lasting Legacy. The starting place must be to change your mindset. Are you ready to change? Why should you change?

Which "-tion"?

I have heard it said that people change because of either *inspiration* or *desperation.*[23] Either way, making changes will take some *perspiration* and *motivation* by you. Inspiration, desperation, perspiration, and motivation! Do you have any motivation to make some changes? Are you ready to roll up your sleeves and perspire? How desperate are you? What do you need to inspire you?

You can expect to experience a handful of divine intersections[24] in life. They might be major decisions or choices, or they might be major events beyond your control. You might be coming upon a new season in your life that could be an intersection. Such an intersection could be a graduation, a child leaving home, a missions trip, a job loss or career change, a broken relationship, a financial setback, a health problem, or the death of a loved one. It will provide perspective to your life but will also lead to choices—a choice to be bitter, a choice to go deeper with God, or a choice to quit. The two worst forms of failure are (1) not trying or (2) giving up too quickly.

Ray Kroc, founder of McDonald's, often used to quote Calvin Coolidge:

"Nothing in the world can take the place of persistence. Talent will not; Genius will not; Education will not; Persistence and determination alone are omnipotent."
—Calvin Coolidge

But there is one more "-tion" to consider, my favorite and a red-letter, haunting challenge: *Multiplication.*

"I tell you the truth, unless a kernel of wheat falls to the ground and dies, it remains only a single seed. But if it dies, it produces many seeds."[25]

This process of planting and thought of death reminds us that we must not have a focus not only on today but also on the future. I am that kernel of wheat for my children and future generations. You, too, are that kernel. What is our willingness to think beyond today's problems and challenges, look beyond our generation, beyond our needs, beyond our desires, and beyond our personal levels of comfort?

Read Psalm 144:4 and James 4:13–15.

What weedy areas of your life do you need to put out of their misery? What areas do you need to water and fertilize? We need a multiplication mindset. We need a multigenerational multiplication mindset. We need not only the mindset but also a plan of action. We are conditioned to live paycheck to paycheck or are consumed by the next child or household problem. We worry about the next financial quarter, the next 401k statement, or the next spousal or employment blowup. We have such a strong focus on the "near term," the today, that we seldom devote a significant amount of time to planning a purposeful future. Quite possibly we do so financially, whether it is retirement or our children's college education, but not so much with our family or our faith.

A multiplication effect is just waiting to be set in motion that will affect your family, your friends, your community, and future generations. The multiplication effect begins with *your* "perspiration"!

No Such Thing as a Small Change

Good habits are the key to success. Bad habits are often the door to failure. We must make good habits and ultimately become slaves to them. You have probably heard it said that it takes twenty-one days to make or break a habit. Has this been true in your life? I know in my own life that depends on what habit or what change I am trying to make and how motivated I am to make that particular change. My health problems, which I will talk about later, radically shook me, and I pursued instantaneous and consequential life-long (hopefully) changes. In other areas, however, I think that I am approaching the 17,000-day mark, and I'm still not there yet.

Recent research published in the European *Journal of Social Psychology* discussed this "how long" question. Dr. Phillippa Lally, an expert in habitual behavior, and colleagues from University College London, recruited ninety-six people who were interested in forming a new habit (such as eating a piece of fruit with lunch or doing a fifteen-minute run each day). Participants were then asked daily how automatic their chosen behaviors felt. Many of the participants showed a curved relationship between practice and automaticity."[26] On average, after sixty-six days the habit was as much a habit as it ever would be.

"However, certain habits, like drinking a glass of water daily became automatic very quickly, but doing fifty sit-ups before breakfast required more dedication. Research showed that missing a single day, did not reduce the chance of forming a habit, however early repetitions gave the greatest boost in automaticity."[27] Unfortunately, it seems that there is no such thing as a small change; the twenty-one-day generalization might, in fact, be an underestimation—unless the only change you make as a result of reading this book is to drink a daily glass of water!

We are living in epic times, so my hope is that your eyes will be opened and your mind will be changed or transformed to that of a generational mindset. Start with some small immediate changes. One improved habit will lead to another, and a brook will turn into a river, and a river will soon become a roaring sea!

"All habits gather by unseen degrees;
As brooks make rivers, rivers run to seas."
—John Dryden

Legacy Lesson: We are living in epic times. These times require a willingness to change. One motivation to make some changes is to enable you to make an impact on your future—your children, your grandchildren, your community, and your nation. A generational mindset is a change in thinking for most of us.

CHAPTER 6

WHAT SHOULD I DO
WITH THE REST OF MY LIFE?

"If you live each day as if it was your last, someday you'll most certainly be right."
It made an impression on me, and since then, for the past 33 years, I have looked in the
mirror every morning and asked myself: 'If today were the last day of my life, would
I want to do what I am about to do today? Whenever the answer has been no for
too many days in a row, I know I need to change something."
"No one wants to die. Even people who want to go to heaven
don't want to die to get there. And yet death is the destination we all share. No one has
ever escaped it. Your time is limited, so don't waste it living someone else's life. . . .Don't let
the noise of others' opinions drown out your own inner voice. And most important,
have the courage to follow your heart and intuition."
—Steve Jobs, 2005 commencement speech, Stanford University

*W*e were joking at a recent family reunion about the receding hairlines, the new gray streaks, and the few extra pounds. One of my wife's cousins said, "My life mission statement is to die of old age!" Yes, we are all getting older, but what are you doing about it? Some people spend too much time looking in the rear-view mirror. Others avoid the reflections and mirror moments and are obsessed with the future. And many others are just plodding along trying to make it through today's challenges.

I love the attempt by "Dr. Lucy" to go deeper with Charlie Brown in the following Peanuts comic.[28]

We might be more like Charlie Brown than we care to admit. We don't want to get trapped spending our second half looking back and yearning for yesterday, but we don't want to dwell fully on the future without appreciating the gift of today. We can't control the past, and we must make the most of the rest of our lives!

> *"Whoever watches the wind will not plant;*
> *Whoever looks at the clouds will not reap."*
> —Ecclesiastes 11:4

Take a Bow

Most curtain calls come after a great performance. The crowd roars and beckons the performer back to the stage for a "bonus show." How about a curtain call for almost all of us? Our average life expectancy continues to rise and has increased by more than 50 percent in the last century. The benefits are obvious. (We will address some of the challenges that should be planned for in the financial section of the book.) What if I really live to be 100? Will I die broke? Am I neither ready to retire nor able to afford it? What will I do with this "curtain call" of extra years?

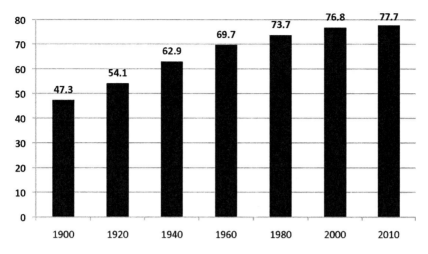

Source: U.S. Life Tables, CDC[29]

Because of our increased life expectancy, we have a new life stage between midlife and death that is a new phenomenon. This new chapter of life between middle and old age can lead to increased financial needs late in life, and it will almost certainly swamp Medicare and Social Security (but more on that later). The exciting thing is that it also creates a great opportunity for a "second half" that can combine meaningful work with the opportunity to stay active longer. Marc Freedman calls these the "encore years."[30]

The Harvard School of Public Health[31] recently published a report called "Reinventing Aging." Here is a pivotal question: "Are you aging?" I guess that the answer for all is yes. Anyone who is getting older is aging. Duh. In fact, "studies have shown that after age 25, the number of newly formed cells in our body is less than the number of cells that die. In plain terms, our body begins to die around our 25th year."[32] That is sobering, but when confronted with the reality of our death, "I am forced to consider whether this quick vapor I call my life will have any impact on the world."

Now that you have looked death in the mirror, you have the opportunity to redefine your meaning and purpose in your later years. Call it "post-25-year-old cell milestone." Call it your "Second Half." Call it a Bridge Career or Encore Career. Call it Retirement. Call it Rehirement. Call it Living a Significant Life. These things can occur *whenever* you want them to. They don't just magically happen for everyone at a set age or life season. Don't wait until retirement. Rick Warren, author of Purpose Driven Life says it rather bluntly: "You know you're going to die, so whatever you're going to do with your life, you'd better get on with it."[33] Warren challenges people to ask three questions:

1) Who am I?
2) Do I matter?
3) What's my purpose in life?

With people living longer, we are in the process of redefining the meaning, purpose, and influence of the older years. The boomer generation is beginning this process now. The average age of retirement has risen. "Although close to one-third of boomers say they expect to participate in community service after retirement, there is a difference between intentions and actions, and boomers may need a push."[34] You will hear the word *active senior*. The question is "Active doing *what?*" You hear "golden years." The questions are "Golden for *whom?*" and "When do you have enough gold?"

Future generations have a great opportunity to define an influential second half. Instead of "retirement," it is really becoming a mix of paid and unpaid activities: "service", "volunteer," "second career," and "entrepreneurial volunteerism." "Retirement, too, was largely a 20th-century creation and after the introduction of Social Security in the mid-1930s, which established 65 as the age of eligibility for public pension benefits, more men began retiring in their mid-60's."[35]

"Between one-third and one-half of people who leave their full-time career jobs move into what have been called "bridge jobs," which presumably bridge the transition from work to retirement."[36] Others leave the work force and later return, and as many as half of current retirees left the work force earlier than they planned, most often due to poor health or adverse economic events."[37] [38] Empty-nesters and early retirees often are working longer because of financial challenges or family health issues. The challenge will be the health and well-being of the Boomers' financial savings and the future health of public programs such as Medicare and Social Security. Many people can begin the "bridge" process in parallel with getting involved with nonprofit organizations, local or state governments, educational institutions, churches, or special interest clubs where gifts/talents can be nurtured and grown.

The tug of war between "reward yourself" and "serve" is hard at work. Only 20 percent of Boomers anticipate retiring and not working at all, and 28 percent of Boomers defined getting older as a "time to help others." Fifty-nine percent of adults said they have volunteered or done community service work in the past year.[39] Fifty-five percent of Boomers felt that it would be a time to "indulge yourself," 68 percent viewed it as a time of leisure, and 74 percent viewed it as a time to pursue your interests or hobbies. Seventy-five percent of Boomers felt that their generation was more self-indulgent than their parents. The question is, what will you do with your second half? A Roper Reports survey found that a family focus was the most important component of leisure time. Sixty-eight percent felt that time with family was a very important part of leisure."[40] Fifty percent of older persons value the time for enhanced spiritual involvement while 47 percent said that "more time to enjoy one's self" was most important.

The buck stops here! What will you do in your 2nd Half?

You often hear of the story of someone who had a passion for making a late career change but just couldn't pull the trigger. Then you hear about a layoff that was a blessing in disguise. Regardless of your situation, age, or season, begin those mirror moments now to plan the rest of your life. Contemplate your purpose and answer Rick Warren's 3 introspective questions: Who Am I? Do I Matter? What's my Purpose?

Legacy Lesson: Contemplating your purpose is the key to living a fulfilling 2nd Half. Live purposefully!

CHAPTER 7

LIVING A SIGNIFICANT AND PURPOSEFUL LIFE! YOUR SECOND HALF

"So many people walk around with a meaningless life. They seem half-asleep, even when they're busy doing things they think are important. This is because they're chasing the wrong things. The way you get meaning into your life is to devote yourself to loving others, devote yourself to your community around you, and devote yourself to creating something that gives you purpose and meaning."
—Morrie Schwartz

I read a short but unique and captivating book during my research for this book. It was a story called *Tuesdays with Morrie* by Mitch Albom. This book kind of snuck up and grabbed my heart and brought perspective to life in the fast lane. I recall reading it on airplane and having to stop reading at one point because I couldn't control my blubbering— and I rarely blubber over a book, especially not in public. The book is about a professor who is teaching his final course and the choices he faced of whether to withdraw from the world or to live life fully. In each of our "second half's," we have to come to grips with a similar crossroads. Will we choose to live with a self-absorbed temporal focus or with a generational mindset?

In the book, Albom discusses the "stone walls built between my present and my past."[41] We run the risk of doing that with some of our negative past experiences instead of fully learning from them and integrating those lessons in our future legacy path. Hence, the Milestones exercise in Chapter 3. We often have made other decisions or choices in our past that have built those walls. It might have been trading our dreams for a bigger paycheck, and not even realize we were doing it. It might have been focused on the temporary instead of the long-lasting relationships.

Everyone lives in his or her own life cocoon. Some people are wrapped up in the cocoon of busyness, others in the cocoon of career or pursuit of money. Most of us are in the "get-me-through-today" cocoon with our many errands, actions, and to-do lists.

We neither have the time nor make the time to reflect on life's purpose. We spend so much time on meaningless things when we could be squeezing out every minute possible with our spouse and kids. We must rediscover the essentials and put our time and energies there. You might need to shove away some things and let God in. We must be strong enough to say no to the mindless cultural magnets that draw us from what is important. We need people in our lives to poke and prod us to focus on the correct priorities. I might be that finger jabbing you in the side right now.

The pursuit of career or success, although temporarily fulfilling, can often end in emptiness. Sometimes the gap that needs to be filled is "cause." Are our contributions in life leading to a cause that is purposeful and meaningful? We all want our lives to count, but often we are barraged with the need to meet the next payroll, the next stack of bills, the next quarterly report, or the next deadline. Gail Sheehy lists ten hallmarks of well-being and the chart topper is "*my life has purpose and meaning.*" Getting involved with causes or things that are greater than ourselves brings true, lasting satisfaction beyond the moment of the paid bill, the successful presentation, or the accomplishment of the moment.

Peter Drucker, management guru and author of *Managing the Non-profit Organization,* asks people *what they want to be remembered for*—"that is the beginning of adulthood"— according to St. Augustine. The answer changes as we mature—as it should. But unless the question is asked, there is a lack of focus and a lack of direction."

 What do you want to be remembered for? Contemplate the following questions about your future legacy:

- Where do I spend my most time? On what do I spend most of my thoughts?
- What is the center of my life?
- Do I have a generational perspective?
- Am I spending enough time with family? Do I have a balanced life?
- Am I coasting or "giving it everything I've got"?
- Am I passionate about what I do?
- Who am I serving in life?
- Am I satisfied with life?
- Are you looking forward more or backward more?

What do I want to be remembered for? You have an incredible opportunity to create and design a legacy of profound importance. Your life experiences, networks, relationships, and gifts give you the capability and have laid the foundation for your renewed or revised Life Mission. The golden years can be relaxing and full of leisure, but they can also be an incredible time to make a generational impact. Until the end of the nineteenth century, retirement planning was pretty simple: You worked until death. In 1950, 72 percent of men were still participating in the labor force at age 65, and 50 percent were participating at the age of 70. In 2002, only 39 percent were working at age 65 and 18 percent at age 70. The trend has now reversed as a result of the economic challenges, and the retirement age is trending back up.

Americans are known as hard workers, and people in the U.S. have been putting in more hours of work, on average, than those elsewhere in the industrialized world. What motivates people either to continue working or to retire varies. Some people work even when they could afford to retire, often because they derive satisfaction from their work, while many work primarily because they cannot afford to do otherwise.

What impact will you have on your family, your community, your nation, and your world? You really do have the potential to change your world! What will you do in your second half? Some movements need visionaries and risk takers. Others need hard "nose-to-the-grindstone" workers, good followers. Still others just need to be nudged or persuaded. What is your vision for the future, and what are you doing to achieve it?

"George Gallup Jr. says that 84% of Americans declare themselves to be Christians."[42] One of my favorite books, *Halftime* by Bob Buford, asks, "What is in your box? What is that 'one thing' that will consume you? What is the still small voice saying to you? (See 1 Kings 19:11–12) Let God whisper to you.

Although I provide a lot of practical helps in getting ready for your future, one of the worst things I could do would be to omit discussing the most important thing about living a purposeful and significant life. It is so dangerous to begin a major pursuit or your "second half" without God and His infinite wisdom. We often don't include Him in our plans because we think that doing so might slow things down. However, He sees around corners we can't see. He knows the future and will guide us when we ask Him for advice. He knows our intent, our weaknesses, and our strengths. He will order your steps. He will help you to live a God-centered life, not a self-centered life.

STOP Read Proverbs 3:5–6; 5:21; and James 1:5.

Legacy Lesson: Significance, Living for a "cause", Purpose, Your Calling, Leaving a Legacy. . . .all weighty topics. How much have you involved God in this contemplative process?

CHAPTER 8

PLANNING YOUR SECOND HALF / RETIREMENT: NEVER TOO LATE, NEVER TOO EARLY

"Everybody says you've got to get ready financially.
No, no, you've got to get ready psychologically."
—Lee Iacocca

One million miles on American Airlines—a milestone of sorts, I guess. I'm not sure how memorable most of those miles have been, but, ah, the glory. Once in a while, I get an upgrade to first class, get a meal, and even find a home for my carry-on bag. But there is *never* a guarantee to whom my row seatmate will be. My mind drifts as I plop down into my window seat and chuckle as I recall the John Candy scene from *Planes, Trains, and Automobiles* in which he chatters away non-stop, shares his musty sock odor with his rowmates, and falls asleep on Steve Martin's shoulder. Little did I know that I was about to embark on my own four-hour nightmare. My in-flight entertainment was a slightly portly gentleman who believed strongly that he has title to the middle armrest and proves it by leaving it there like it is superglued for the entire flight. He actually bleeds over the armrest by a few inches into my personal airspace, similar to the long station wagon rides when I used to taunt my sister by crossing that invisible "in-your-face-space" line. But that isn't the Candy/Martin moment. I am used to the sight of the mini-bags of peanuts or pretzels that are at most four ounces—good for about ten minutes of munching. Not Vern. My new neighbor broke out a *two-pound* bag of "international flavored corn nuts" (code for mighty, potent, scent filled).

The smell nearly made me heave, the pungent odor burning my nose hairs. The scent is difficult to describe, but imagine an odor like a Dorito/cayenne pepper/tabasco/onion mixture from the bad breath of a stranger, who is a mere twenty-four inches from your nostril hairs, and you kind of get the picture. Only the smell of a skunk in your lap, a dead rodent, or a freshly wafting sour kraut delicacy could top that smell. Oh boy, I can't wait. This was to be my prison cell for the next four hours. My eyes were not deceiving me as his empty left hand headed toward his mouth as if on a mission. *Tell me he is not going to lick his finger!* Nope. Not one finger—all five! *Come on! This is not KFC at home on your couch, ok? This is a public airplane cabin! You have got to be kidding me.* The sights, smells, and sounds continued for two full hours! What a milestone.

I cover this compelling bit of air narrative, not to deter you from flying in your "second half," but just to ensure that you know your traveling buddy. I know your spouse surely doesn't have any bad habits that annoy you as bad as my new pal did, and hopefully most of you don't feel trapped in a life next to a Vern, with no exit in sight. However, life is a long flight, and sometimes you are in a marriage or relationship in which you just have to make the best of circumstances. (More on marriage later, and *no more* on barf bag chronicles, I promise.) However, creating a successful, happy, and peaceful future will take more than munching together every now and again. It will take some discussions and it is never too early to start!

You think you know your spouse, but have you really sat down and talked about your second-half dreams and listened to what your spouse wants of life or what his or her future dreams are? You don't have to settle on a concrete plan, but the next few exercises will help you better understand each other's desires and dreams and how to best make an impact. You can have more fruitful discussions and possibly begin to shift your dreams to find some common ground and a center of gravity that can share some common rungs on a combined Life Ladder.

Retirement—The "What" and the "Where"

Retirement is not an endless vacation. In fact you won't see it discussed in the Bible. Talk to anyone who has recently retired, and they will tell you that approach becomes a recipe for boredom and a feeling of uselessness after a number of months. It is never too early, and never too late to have some fruitful thought and dialogue with your spouse about what to expect and what to plan for.

 Discussion questions:

- What do you look forward to in the "second half" or retirement?
- What are you ultimate dreams in the "second half"?
- What do you fear in the "second half" or retirement?
- What are some talents or interests you see that we could use to earn a partial living or put to use in volunteer work?
- How can you make the greatest impact in your "second half"?

STOP Take the following self-assessment on where your interest areas might lie and *what you* might want to do with your "second half." This is a great tool to discuss with your spouse as well and to identify potential intersection points. Rate each of your interests High, Medium or Low.

The What—Your Interests, Talents, and Skills

	You	Spouse
YOUR INTERESTS		
Example: Camping/Hiking	High	Low
Teach/instruct	___	___
Non-profit volunteer or paid position	___	___
Local or national government positions	___	___
Work/volunteer for a faith-based institution	___	___
Work/volunteer for an educational institution	___	___
Relationship building: socializing, community, clubs	___	___
Writing	___	___
Family time–spouse, children, parents, extended family	___	___
Friend time	___	___
Start a ministry	___	___
Recreation/hobby	___	___
Start a small business	___	___
Outdoor activities- Gardening, Hiking, etc.	___	___
Cooking	___	___
Reading	___	___
Travel	___	___
Spiritual involvement	___	___
_____	___	___

YOUR TALENTS / SKILLS		
Writing	___	___
Marketing	___	___
Teaching	___	___
Organizing	___	___
Creativity	___	___
Hospitality	___	___
Problem-solving	___	___
Caring/Giving/Mercy	___	___
Leadership	___	___
Wisdom	___	___
Faith	___	___
Serving	___	___

Work skills_____	____	____

Next, have a very high-level discussion about your *dream* or ideal state on *what and where* you might want to spend retirement. This is where there might be potential for major disagreements. Again, it's better to know your different ideals now so you can come together over the next years and decades and develop common ground.

Self	Spouse

2 weeks Missions trips
2 weeks Vero/Destin Beaches
2 weeks Camp of the Woods/US Open
6 weeks RVing—seminars, baseball, volunteer
40 weeks—near grandkids, volunteer, vocation

The Where

According to Holmes and Rahe, who developed the life stress scale, which ranks key life events and their stress factors, retirement ranked ten on the scale of forty-three items. It was just below getting fired from your job and just higher than the death of a close friend. Isn't retirement supposed to lead to less stress? If you have planned for it or thought through it, then yes it will. It might be stressful to have some of these hard discussions now with your spouse. But trust me, it will be more stressful if you wait to have these all important discussions of "where" to retire too late in your "second half."

Choosing the spot to retire/live scorecard care-abouts (High, Medium, or Low):

	You	Spouse	Notes
- Low crime rate	____	____	
- Good hospitals	____	____	
- Mild climate	____	____	
- Friendly, like-minded neighbors	____	____	
- Scenic beauty, beach, lake	____	____	
- Low cost of living/housing	____	____	
- Recreational facilities	____	____	
- Active social/cultural environment	____	____	
- Nearby airport	____	____	
- Major city nearby	____	____	
- Sales, state, and property taxes	____	____	
- Retirement communities	____	____	
- Distance from friends, relatives	____	____	
- Part-time employment opportunities	____	____	

- Place of worship location			
- Volunteer opportunities			
- Nearby education			

These exercises were eye opening for us. They are not a one-time discussion; rather, they have built a foundation for an on-going dialogue that helps us plan and position ourselves for the future. We did not have the same vision. That is Okay! We don't have all of the same likes, but it now helps us understand our differences and also points to some common areas we can build upon to develop a common vision.

Take a Test Drive

You don't read much in the Bible about retirement. The concept of retirement is the invention of a wealthy, oversized society. Numbers 8:25 is the only reference in the Bible that comes close and that was for priests of the Temple.

With the state of Social Security, Medicare, pensions and our economy, retirement might no longer be the early option it was in past decades. I loved Ebby Halliday's comment on her ninety-ninth birthday when discussing the recipe for living such a long, successful life: "Don't drink. Don't smoke. Don't retire."[43] I believe in "test driving" your retirement or second half. We test drive our cars and our relationships, why not test drive your retirement? Start with that circle of influence and "practice your retirement." Whether that be starting a small business, volunteering, taking get-aways, relocating, or experimenting with hobbies. Before you take those leaps of faith, test drive. Sit down with your spouse and map out your dreams, ideas, and conflicts. You might have much conflict if you don't have buy-in or a common plan. Map out what a typical week would look like. Volunteer: Monday and Friday. Hobbies: Tuesday/Wednesday. Getaway: Once-a-month weekend. Create a hypothetical monthly calendar and see how it might look.

"According to the Kauffman Index of Entrepreneurial Activity, 45 to 54 year olds accounted for a quarter of all start-ups, while 55 to 64 year olds made up another 23%, up from 15%."[44] Entrepreneurship is not just a kids' game. Often, the older crowd has more capital and more experience to pursue the excitement and risk of "hobbypreneurship." Often, a hobby or business venture that is a passion can be successful since you are totally invested—heart and soul—in this venture.

Start the "test drive" in parallel with your current career. Test drive your finances by setting up a budget for these things. Complete a draft budget for your first year of retirement and live on it for a year. Some expenses will go up, and others will go down. This is very personally specific, and much of this will be dependent upon our country's financial situation, so be sure that you understand the latest impact and risks.

Some of the expenses that might go down after retirement include payroll taxes, retirement or 401k contributions, local taxes, transportation costs, work expenses, clothing and general living expenses, home taxes (if you downsize), mortgage payment (if your loan is paid off), and giving totals. Some of the expenses that might go up after retirement include medical, prescriptions, travel, entertainment, hobbies, home repairs, and car repairs.

The experts say that you can live on 60 to 80 percent of your current income. Don't live with generalities and what the experts say. You might need 120 percent, or you might need

50 percent. Retirement expenses are usually more than you think if you are part of the Generation X/Baby Boomer excessive-spending block. We will discuss more about finances in your second half later, but if you are near retirement, try living on that 50 percent or 120 percent budget for the next six months before you retire and see if you are fooling yourself. Yes, your work-related and college expenses go down, but your greens fees, your giving heart, your entertainment, boomerang kids, college debt, or grandkids expenses might push you higher than you thought.

Planning for your second half is much as an "internal" heart-and-mind exercise as it is an "external" getting-your-goals-on-paper exercise. What will be your balance of pleasure, leisure, and serving, giving, and working? The following passages might not be how you see retirement, but see how they might apply to you.

Read Proverbs 28:19; Acts 20:33–35; Colossians 3:23; 1 Thessalonians 4:11–12; and 2 Thessalonians 3:10.

It is a mistake to look too far ahead. Only one link of the chain of destiny can be handled at a time.
—Winston Churchill

Legacy Lesson: Planning your Future is one of the most difficult things you do. How do you view your 2nd Half? Many don't plan to retire at all, but rather to make a great impact and leave a great impact. Weigh these things before determining the "where", "what" and "when" of your 2nd Half. What actions do you need to take to get ready for your 2nd Half? Have you involved your spouse?

CHAPTER 9

YOUR SECOND-HALF POTENTIAL: A BUFFET OF OPTIONS

"Superficiality is the curse of our age."
—Richard J. Foster

*Y*our second-half options are many. The challenge is trying to find your niche or high-impact area. According to Banning Liebscher in *Jesus Culture*,[45] both Bill Bright and Loren Cunningham identified seven "mountains" or "mind molders" in our culture: Family, Religion, Economy, Education, Government, Arts and media, and Science and technology.

These mountains set the agenda for our society and, in turn, influence our children and generations to come. Where can you plug in and make an impact? It might be a different "mountain" for a different "season." You might be able to influence multiple "mountains." We are living in a Western age of narcissism, a preoccupation with self, with me, with mine, with ours. The "mountain" of self and personal pleasure and comfort are ones we need to descend. The mountaintop experience is short-lived, and empty, yet the allure is great.

James Emery White wrote a compelling book, *Serious Times*,[46] on making your life matter. One of the most intriguing discussions that he uncovers follows a season of goal-oriented pursuits. It is a season of soul-searching during mid-life during which he was seeking for his niche in his second half. He asked the typical questions, "What do I do best? Where can I make the most impact?" He felt like God was saying, "These are the wrong questions." He went on a journey of self-discovery to find God's "call." He could not find a single case in Scripture where people went on a hunt for their niche. Instead, he found the following:

- people who were *invited* to do things (the disciples, Jeremiah)
- people who were *selected* to do things (David, Samuel)
- people who were presented with the *opportunity* to do things (Esther, Deborah)

They lived life faithfully, submitted their gifts to the Lord, and responded to what God brought their way. Some of them even accepted a call they did not want or ask for, and they surely didn't seek it out.

White talks of our "calls." The first call is to become a Christ follower. God first called our hearts to respond to Jesus' forgiveness and to repent and follow Him. The second call is the call of vocation. Our natural tendency is to have compartmentalized Christianity, with our spiritual life targeted at particular times and places and our "jobs/career" at other times and locations. In reality, we must see our jobs as an act of worship and a ministry. Our work is often viewed as a means to end—for leisure or for income. But it can be so much more. It can be an expression of our energy and our creativity. It can be an outlet for using our skills, experiences, and gifts. I have discovered over the years a joy in communicating—both verbally and in writing. I enjoy teaching. Over the years, I have found a way to encompass those skills into my everyday job. Look for those opportunities. How can you bring honor to God in the little things at your work?

Bill Wilson has said that "the need is the call." Sometimes we wait and wait and wait for some spiritual guidance and direction when we just need to look for needs and then fill them. Henry Blackaby says to look around for what God is doing and where He is doing it, and then join others in that. I would highly recommend the study, *Experiencing God*. I had kind of thought that my life would fit cleanly into four seasons that I knew as a kid growing up in Michigan. I was discovering that many people wait for the "big call" from God and expect it like a lightning bolt at the most opportune time. Don't ignore the current season. Be used where you are. I have found that we always need to be ready for the opportunity and then walk through those doors or test the waters at least for that next season. God made it clear to me in my early twenties that I had a "call," that He was going to "use me." I thought that each new season was "it." The call. The full-time deal. I also put that calling in a box, thinking that it was a preaching call and that I needed to pursue that calling.

How often do you read about individuals in the Bible pursuing a calling? Usually it seems that God pursued and then His people either obeyed or disobeyed. His disciples followed. Noah followed. Saul/Paul followed. When you see people pushing their own agenda, taking matters into their own hands or trying to open doors for themselves, the ending usually is not a happy one. The Tower of Babel. The years the Israelites spent in the wilderness. Ishmael. When God speaks, then take that step of faith.

I look at a "call" as not only a pursuit of God but also an asking for Him to close and open doors and bring the right opportunities at the right times. It will require my acting upon needs that present themselves. Seeking God. Listening to God. Looking for Him to speak—and then acting when He does speak. Obedience. In parallel continuing to be faithful in what I am doing now, in what He asked me to do last while waiting/looking/praying. (See Matthew 25:23 and 2 Corinthians 2:12.)

"The primary sense of calling is that it is not for self but for God's glory. Vocation is as much about being faithful where we find ourselves as it is finding where we are to be faithful."
—James Emery White

Your Second Half

Will you consider a new job? Volunteering? A transition from full-time to part-time work? Back to work after empty nesting sets in? Going back to school?

65

Start with prayer and then a clean sheet of paper to brainstorm ideas. Do this alone and then do it with your spouse and some trusted friends. Consider a number of things before you take the plunge or prepare the plan for your second half.

- How much income do you need?
- Do the math and income and expense projections.
- Measure the risk versus the reward. Jobs will be harder to find than ever before.
- Have you assessed what are you good at?
- Are you enjoying your work and contributing?
- What are the fastest growing occupational fields?

Help Wanted!

A recent study showed thirty-two million replacement job openings over the next ten years as baby-boomers exit the workforce.[47] The past recessions and economic changes have reshaped the job and education landscapes, so it is important to plan before deciding. Many low-skill jobs in manufacturing, farming, fishing, and forestry are permanently gone because of automation or off-shore procurement of the resource. America's shift from an agrarian economy to an industrial economy is now giving way to a service/technology economy that requires more education and different skills of its workers. Computers and related inventions are radically reshaping our economy's future, and the jobs required for those industries are different than those of earlier generations. "Nearly two-thirds of the available jobs through 2018 will require workers with at least some college education."[48]

Following are some of the top findings from the Georgetown University "Help Wanted" Study.[49]

- Training is important and can increase employee wages by 3 to 11 percent.
- Higher levels of education increase access to jobs and higher earnings.
- Postsecondary education gives large accumulated earnings over a lifetime:
    - o Earnings of high school graduates increased by 13 percent since 1983.
    - o Earnings of people with bachelor's degrees increased by 34 percent since 1983.
    - o Earnings of people with graduate degrees increased by 55 percent since 1983.
- Workers who use computers earn 15 to 27 percent more than those who do not (varies by degree level).
- Access to technology and computers is important to job access and higher earnings.
- Having a bachelor's degree is worth more than $1.5 million more than having only a high-school diploma.
- Workers with college degrees had the lowest unemployment rates during the most recent recession.

To further illustrate how an emphasis on a college degree has increased greatly, about two-thirds (62 percent) of all employment will require some college education or better by 2018.[50]

	1973	2018
High school dropouts	32%	10%
High school graduates	40%	28%
Some college/Associates degree	12%	29%
Bachelor's degree	9%	23%
Master's degree or higher	7%	10%
Total	100%	100%

If you are considering switching jobs or transitioning to a new career in semi-retirement, be sure that you research not only what "you enjoy" but also where the jobs are. According to the "Help Wanted Study," the top occupations for job openings by education level (degree) through 2018 are as follows:

High school or less

1. Farming, fishing, and forestry occupations
2. Building and grounds cleaning and maintenance operations
3. Construction and extraction occupations
4. Transportation and material-moving occupations
5. Production occupations
6. Food preparation and serving occupations
7. Installation, maintenance, and repair occupations
8. Personal care and service operations
9. Healthcare support occupations
10. Office and administrative support occupations
11. Sales and related occupations

Bachelor's Degree

1. Financial specialists
2. Architects and technicians
3. Arts, design, entertainment, sports, and media occupations
4. Computer and mathematical science occupations
5. Business operations specialists
6. Life and physical scientists
7. Community and social services occupations
8. Management occupations
9. Education occupations
10. Healthcare practitioners and technical occupations
11. Social scientists and technicians

Master's Degree and Higher

1. Life and physical scientists
2. Social scientists and technicians
3. Legal occupations
4. Education occupations
5. Community and social services occupations
6. Architects and technicians
7. Healthcare practitioners and technical occupations
8. Computer and mathematical science occupations
9. Management occupations
10. Business operations specialists
11. Financial specialists

Note that many of these jobs cross two different educational degree categories; the healthcare practitioners jobs actually cross three categories. Another part of the study breaks occupations into "clusters." The clusters with the *highest rate of growth* (in order) for those with some college experience projected through 2018 are as follows. Average wages for these occupations are in parenthesis (full-time, full-year workers).

1. Healthcare professional and technical ($77,827)
2. Education ($46,258)
3. Science, technology, engineering, mathematics, and social sciences, the STEM occupations ($74,958)
4. Community services and arts ($49,168)
5. Managerial and professional office ($82,254)
6. Sales and office support ($46,521)
7. Healthcare support ($28,446)
8. Food and personal services ($26,222)
9. Blue collar ($41,347)

Again, high occupational employment is projected in healthcare, technology, and service sectors. The highest pay projections are in the healthcare professional, technical, and managerial fields.

Wage and Job Winners > $100,000![51]

Recent data from *Forbes* magazine showed that some of the big job-and-wage winners for the next decade were:?

	Mean wage	New Jobs
Lawyers	$129,440	98,500
IT managers	$123,280	49,500
Pharmacists	$109,380	45,900

Financial managers	$116,970	41,200
Marketing managers	$122,720	21,900
Dentists	$158,770	18,400
Engineering managers	$125,900	11,300

Education Pays!

If you are considering finishing your degree or getting additional degrees, chances are good that it will pay off in the long run. Consider the statistics from the United States Bureau of Labor Statistics. If you have at least some level of college degree, your chances of being employed increase greatly, not to mention your pay will also be much higher.[52]

Unemployment rate in 2010 (%)	Education attained	Median weekly earnings in 2010 ($)
1.9	Doctoral degree	$1,550
2.4	Professional degree	1,610
4.0	Master's degree	1,272
5.4	Bachelor's degree	1,038
7.0	Associate's degree	767
9.2	Some college, no degree	712
10.3	High-school graduate	626
14.9	Less than high-school diploma	444
8.2	All Workers	782

As you consider your future career/occupation or your child's college educational focus area, ensure that you are emphasizing education, training, and technology. You should also consider the risk sectors if we continue to have a failing economy. (I have written about the worldwide economy in the financial section of this book.)

Legacy Lesson: Your 2nd Half options are many. Money is only part of the equation. What about your passions? Your gifts? Your calling?

CHAPTER 10

THE SEASONS OF LIFE

First we are children to our parents, then parents to our children, then parents to our parents, then children to our children.
—Milton Greenblatt

I fondly remember raking up a pile of leaves from our seventy plus trees on two acres and piling them up so the kids, dogs, and I could jump in them, roll in them, and enjoy the coolness, crispness and color of the fall season. I recall as a young teen counting down the days until spring training when pitchers and catchers reported to their baseball camps in Florida. The problem was that the Michigan winter still raged, often into April. That waiting and anticipating made spring even more special. I recall a few April blizzards in Grand Rapids, Michigan, and how I slogged through the four-foot snow drifts to deliver newspapers. I recall watching my boys play tennis in the summer of 2010 in Dallas, where the constant blistering heat never seemed to stop. We had eighteen consecutive days of 100 degrees or more.[53] What always got us through to the next sauna-like day was the knowledge that fall was just around the corner.

I always have a short but riveting debate with myself when spring rolls around and then fall arrives. The internal arm-wrestling match is focused upon which season is my favorite. I love the cool crispness of the fall after a miserable, boiling, Texas summer, but I also love the finality of the winter season and the transition to 80-degree days and 50-degree evenings. The only problem with both these seasons is that they seem to last but the blink of eye, while summer heat always to seems to have its way stealing the pleasant, but brief spring season and also inevitably delaying the start of the fall season.

The beauty of our natural seasons is that there is a regular ebb and flow to the seasons. We are comfortable with knowing what is coming, the order and regularity of it all. You know summer and winter are about the same length each year. You know that winter will give birth to spring, which will eventually give way to summer, which will lead into fall. There is no fear or worry that we will be trapped in snow drifts 365 days of the year. In our personal lives, we don't have the luxury of forecasting the length of a season or when it might end. I am always struck by the simplicity in the book of Ecclesiastes: Generations come, and generations go. . . .

Read Ecclesiastes 3:1–8.

You might have a laundry list of "seasons" you have experienced, are longing to experience, or are afraid to experience. Here are some of those seasons.

o Seasons of loneliness
o Seasons of flourishing relationships
o Seasons of testing
o Seasons of peace
o Seasons of persecution and trouble
o Seasons of victory
o Seasons of lack
o Seasons of plenty
o Seasons of blessing
o Seasons of spiritual drought
o Seasons of age
o Seasons of children
o Seasons of mourning
o Seasons of resting
o Seasons of doing
o Seasons of joy
o Seasons of war

One of the hardest seasons is the season of waiting. If you are in this season, be patient and trust God. Read Psalm 27:14; 40:1; and 2 Chronicles 16:9a.

The Coaster

The sprawling roller coaster stared at me from the distant heavens. It seemed to be taunting me, jeering at me as I moved slowly forward in the line. My mind was engaged in an all-out tug of war. "Stick it out, you wimp." "What if I pass out?" "Your ten-year-old is doing this, you knucklehead." "What if it gets stuck in that loop at the top?" I was exhausted by the time I arrived at the front of the line. The anticipation was worse than the ride itself (the Titan at Six Flags over Texas). Despite my mental battle, my aging body won the battle. I did it—I rode the Titan! I took on death and won!

Everyone knows he or she is going to die, but few live like it. When you are ready for death, you are fully living. I am not sure I felt like I was fully living when that line inched forward, but all of my senses were wide awake, and I was very focused on the task at hand. Life is similar. Maybe you have taken on death in a more dramatic way than a roller coaster. Most of us are not excited about aging, about traveling "over the hill." Some people try to avoid the thought, others convince themselves that 50 is the new 30. Which is true in many respects. Aging can actually be exciting if embraced. It can be a time of growth, maturity, and fulfillment and a culmination of your life experiences. This is a chance anew to live a fulfilled life. Accept who you are. Embrace it!

71

Age is Irrelevant

In the Old Testament, Uzziah was crowned king of Israel at age 16. Josiah became King at the age of 8. They both lacked experience, credentials, and even resources. Uzziah, at age 16, did not rely on human help. He cried out to God for help! "When you are weak, I am strong," says the Lord. Later in life, Uzziah was strong in his own strength, and pride filled his heart. If he had maintained that child-like faith and innocence and looked to the Lord, he might have finished strong.[54] Age is irrelevant. Whether you are young, old, or middle-aged, don't waste your years!

You might think your retirement will be golfing, cooking, and traveling. There might be seasons of that, but why not make a great impact as well? You might be younger and approaching "halftime"—in your twenties to forties. Thomas Jefferson authored the Declaration of Independence at age 33 in 1776. Patrick Henry uttered, "Give me liberty or give me death!" at age 39 in 1775. Jesus ministered in his early thirties. You might be older and already deep into your "second half." Michelangelo was named chief architect of St. Peters basilica in 1546 at the age of 72![55] Recently, his last sketch was found, presumably the work of his hand in his eighties. Billy Graham was still conducting crusades in his late eighties. Our fortieth president of the United States, Ronald Reagan, took office just sixteen days shy of his seventieth birthday. I love the story about Rose Gilbert, a millionaire, who is still teaching AP English in Los Angeles at age 88. She wants to pass on her love of life. "I want them all to love literature, love poetry and love life."[56] There are no wasted seasons, and seasons do not discriminate.

Some people let age limit their dreams or their "purpose fulfillment plans," or they simply settle for a mundane retirement. I enjoyed the inspiring stories from *What Should I Do With The Rest of My Life?*[57] The book contains a dozen or so true diverse stories of "late achievers" in their fifties and beyond who sorted out a fulfilling, meaningful "second act."

One story featured a man who had been laid off. At age fifty-nine he earned his PhD and then began a new career, volunteered, and became a full time therapist at age 72. His story reminded me that the mind often runs the body. I have been confronted over and over with the fragility of my body and the reality of mortality. It shouldn't take that to drive us to do something with our lives. Don't leave so many parts of your life for "later." Don't leave relationship business unfinished. Don't lead a compromising, lukewarm lifestyle. Life is too short. Know that anything is possible.

I Am too Old[58]

> "...When I am old and gray, do not forsake me Oh God,
> till I declare your power to the next generation."
> —Psalm 71:18

If you say you are too old and your winter season of life is one of wasting away, I beg to differ with you. It is time to get up and take action! Here are some more examples to encourage you.

- At the age of 85, Caleb was given Hebron (Joshua 14:6–15). The secret to his success can be found in Numbers 14:24.

- The Lord appeared to Abraham at age 99, Sarah gave birth at age 90 (Genesis 17).
- Moses led the children of Israel from Egypt at age 80.
- Aaron served as Moses' spokesman from age 83 to age 123.
- Joshua led Israel until age 110.
- Anna fasted and prayed and served at age 84.
- John the disciple was nearly 90 when he was exiled to Patmos, where he wrote Revelation.
- Mother Teresa served until her death at 87.
- Michelangelo painted *The Last Judgment* on the ceiling of the Sistine Chapel at age 59.
- Winston Churchill was the British prime minister at age 81.
- Picasso completed some of his greatest works late in life and painted until age 90.
- Benjamin Franklin was elected to be a delegate to the U.S. Constitutional Convention at age 81.
- Bob Hope entertained troops at age 87.
- Connie Mack coached the Philadelphia Athletics at age 87.
- Strom Thurmond completed his eighth term as a U.S. senator at age 100.
- Billy Graham, Bill Bright, Truett Cathy—the list goes on.

"There is still no cure for the common birthday."
—John Glenn

Only the Lord knows the end of our days and when the finish line is. Our age means nothing to God. We are but a vapor, so let us not waste our days. It is possible to waste a season of life. I think of the Israelites—a whole generation wasted. They turned an eleven-day journey into forty years (Deuteronomy 1:2–6)! Maybe you are taking the long or convenient road to the finish line. It is time to find a new mountain! Despite the Israelites wilderness years, God was kind, and His favor was evident. He will do the same for you and desires to get you to a more fruitful promised land. Arise! Be strong and of good courage.

 Read Deuteronomy 1:2–6; Joshua 1:1–9; 3:7; and Psalm 39:4–5.

"You have stayed long enough at this mountain."
—Deuteronomy 1:6

Refreshing, not Doing

How long do we stay in a season? That is always the question that rarely seems to get answered. Sometimes we can control that, but at other times we cannot. This book seems to fault on the side of "doing." God might be calling you, in fact, to a season of *do now*. You have been fed, focused on yourself, and now it is a season of giving. This section might be for those who need a season of *be now*. Or you might have an imbalance that needs fixing.

In one season of life, I was serving on three boards, my wife was teaching and remodeling, and we both were trying our best to keep up with our kids' activities and our own spiritual priorities. We were enjoying serving together and starting a school. It was a busy but rewarding season of life. My wife and I are creatures of action and doing. Neither of us is a person of rest; we don't enjoy doing nothing. We like to be productive. We were living the classic North American "doing machine." I was, in fact, living and feeding spiritually off others without knowing it during this busy season. I had no time for a rich personal relationship with my Creator. It was soon time for a seasonal chiropractic adjustment. If you are similar to us or a Type-A personality, you know that it is harder to sit, rest, and worship than it is to "do."

For everything there is a season.[59]

STOP It might be hard for you to transition from a season of busyness or ministry to a season of rest. Ask God to lead you in His timetable to the next season. When in doubt, stay on the same path until He opens a door or you sense His Spirit moving you. Take some time to ask God to give you His peace and direction. Just relax and rest in Him. Take a few minutes and rest in this Tune Tie. Close your eyes and get hidden away.

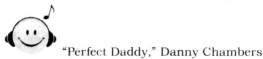

"Perfect Daddy," Danny Chambers

Pruning

We are nearing the finish of winter here in Texas. We had our two days of snow, and it is time to get the yard ready for spring! I am not a perfect gardener, but I can tell when certain trees or plants need a good trimming. If I don't see it, my wife is quick to point them out. It is not fun pruning branches, but it needs to be done. God is our gardener. He knows when we are producing fruit and when we need some dead branches pruned. Sometimes we just know that we are withering away, and we need a break. You might know that you have been dormant too long, and now it is time to bear fruit. Fruit implies seasons. We might not even realize that we need pruning. Winter is not the time to fertilize, and spring is not the time for idleness. If God's Word is showing you some things or God is using people to send you a message, let Him prune. Remain in Him. He is the vine, and we are the branches. He loves you very much. Remain in His love. He chose us and appointed us. Doesn't He really know best?

Your heart might be going through a winter season. Perhaps you lost a job or a loved one, or your child is not following God as you desire. Your spouse might not be meeting your needs. You might be lonely. Be real with God (Psalm 88). Imagine singing that in your church on Sunday. Jesus Christ is fully aware of your suffering (Isaiah 53:3). You will come out of winter. Spring is approaching! Lean on your gardener. Trust in the Lord with all your heart. Don't lean on your own understanding. In all your ways acknowledge Him, and He will direct your path.[60]

"Seasons call for rhythm. Each requires a pace and a motion for moving through it that best matches that season's demands, its limits, its opportunities. Just as kayaking requires a different rhythm from wood chopping, so winter requires a different rhythm from fall and that from spring. The rhythm of winter is waiting. The rhythm of spring, preparing. Summer, enjoying. Fall, gathering. Better yet, as we move in rhythm with each season, we find Christ in the midst of each. Best of all, He finds us. He walks with us. He speaks to us. He loves us. For everything there is a season."[61]

Kids seasons

The first half of our lives is ruined by our parents
and the second half by our children.
—Clarence Darrow

As we move through different seasons of our own lives, the journey often comes with the additional complication and stress of having our children move through different seasons in parallel. It becomes a very intricate balancing and understanding of each of the family member's seasons. A lot is in play here: maturity (or immaturity), emotions, hormones, the grapple for independence, the grapple for loss of control. These seasons can be very frustrating, but they can also be very fruitful.

What teaching moments are there for us, not just for the children? What is God trying to teach me during this process? Sometimes we are so focused on the child, the problem, or the discipline that we forget to engage God during "the process." Can I see it through His lens?

Intimacy with Him is first and foremost. Are we individually being faithful in the little things that He has already spoken? Are we communicating with Him, two-way, including worship and listening instead of "the list." We might need a really candid prayer: "Lord, help me to *love* this child or spouse, when I really don't *like* them right now." You might need a P.S. prayer that asks, "Lord what do you want to prune in me right now?" God wants to work on our hearts, and the heart can be deceitful. One of the most difficult prayers you can pray is, "God, search my heart and examine my mind."[62]

As I sat in the bleachers, I was truly enjoying my son's tennis match. I reflected on this season, just enjoying my child, spending time with him. I had no to-do list. I was not concerned with performance or results. I think father was enjoying this more than son. I wonder how much God truly enjoys those times when we just sit with Him? When we have no agendas, no seeking for answers, no "study"—just soaking in His presence and, seeking to know Him.

This parenting season had been quite a journey for all of us. We had been through the joys and the emotional ups and downs of high-caliber, select baseball and had watched our son hoist a state trophy after closing out the game on the mound with a save. We had watched our daughter gain acceptance in the National Honor Society and photographs win local awards and a best in show! We had watched her art go to state competitions. We had seen good grades, and watched our son win a baseball tournament and move to the next level of tennis prowess. We had also witnessed devastating losses—sitting on the bench, pieces and photos not selected for awards. We had witnessed tears from hurt feelings. We had seen success and failure up close. We had also experienced the humbling feelings of not always being the best in the eyes of man or a victim of favoritism or politics. We have experienced being bypassed by other talented, gifted individuals—and have also done the bypassing. We also failed plenty as parents.

We have told our children that these successes and failures are "great practice for life." Life is a roller coaster. Get ready. We have had many teachable moments, and throughout the times of struggle or failure we tell them, "Hagedorns aren't quitters," and they stick it out. We have said it with boldness and confidence, yet deep down inside we wanted to quit ourselves. Oh, but the joys of watching your children grow. Growing means success and it means failure. It means that perseverance and character are being developed.

This particular match was a loss. Not a failure. A temporary setback. A learning experience. The key as a parent was that it was all about relationship. Sometimes we as parents focus on the end goal, the mission, the results instead of enjoying the journey. You will see dreams die or shift. You will see dreams birthed. One relationship is built, and another broken. You will live through seasons of success and seasons of failure. Seasons of victory and seasons of defeat. Seasons of joy and seasons of loneliness. Time flies. Don't miss their growing up. Time flies. Enjoy the seasons. No regrets.

Decisions and Dreams

One of the hardest yet most rewarding parts of raising a teenager is allowing your kids to participate in key decisions and even to make their own decisions in certain areas. Sometimes they fall flat on their faces. Sometimes they excel. It is an important process during their transition to adulthood. Here are a few changes we have witnessed and participated in recently:

- Emily—Making a school change, choosing a college, starting a relationship
- Jacob—Making a school change, leaving a tennis academy
- Justin—sports choices and school choices
- All—A family/job move, various opportunities

As reality clashes with your children's dreams, or your dreams for your children (they are two very distinct things), such as playing in the World Series or winning a U.S. Open, how are you to handle it as parents? You build them up, encourage them, teach them to dream big, feed and finance the dream—and then the dream evaporates, becomes dormant, or gets replaced with more urgent things, such as the reality of a child growing up, social needs, or spiritual needs. Do you reject the child? Certainly not. The opportunities for bitterness, anger, or guilt trips are plenty. A new season emerges. As parents, we must prepare for how to handle multiple paths, multiple scenarios. God is building adults before our very eyes. Allowing them to learn from their mistakes, gradually giving them responsibility and decision making opportunities is much harder than I thought. It is a balance of teaching, disciplining, guiding, and allowing them to take on more "adult roles" as they mature.

Sometimes we wish that some seasons were longer than others. This is where trust comes into play.

> *Praise be to the name of God for ever and ever: wisdom and power are His.*
> *He changes times and seasons.*
> —Daniel 2:20–21

Generational Giant

I love my grilled Kentucky Fried Chicken. Talk about seasons of life, failures along the way, and blooming late. Colonel Sanders dropped out of school in seventh grade, his dad beat him, he joined the Army at 16, and he couldn't seem to keep a job in his early years. At 40, he cooked chicken dishes at his service station and didn't even own a restaurant during his fifties and sixties. At the age of 65, his store failed, and he used his first Social Security check to start his franchising business. He didn't quit and didn't dream small, despite failures, struggles, a difficult upbringing, and a late start. The business flourished during his late season of life and even long after he was gone. More than 20,000 stores in more than 100 countries are now selling that heavenly grilled KFC. Each of us has a destiny, and we have choices to embrace it, pursue it, or run from it. Enjoy each step of the journey. Walk with a slower pace. Linger a little longer. Smell the roses. Enjoy the current season—but prepare now for the next season.

Legacy Lesson: Don't waste your season. Life is full of different seasons. Regardless of your age or the type of season you are in: doing, being, planning, pruning, waiting, risking——involve God and trust God!

CHAPTER 11

YOUR HEALTH: INVESTING IN YOU!

Everybody thinks of changing humanity
and nobody thinks of changing himself.
—Leo Tolstoy

Wow! This next page could radically alter your entire life. Why else would I start a chapter with *Wow*!

Do you want to decrease your stress, reduce your emotional distress, quit a habit, increase your emotional control, eat healthier, improve with your household chores, meet your commitments, improve your spending habits, improve your self-regulation/self-control, and improve your study habits? This is not an infomercial for anything, I promise. It is, however, proven that just one word answers these questions—exercise.

In a recent study in Sydney, Australia,[63] participants who exercised showed significant improvement in *all* of these areas! Easier said than done, I know. Whether it is getting started with exercise, making some dietary changes, eating or drinking too much, or spending instead of saving, we all fail often. The preliminary evidence showed that exercise over two weeks begins to have influence on other tasks that require self-control. If one study doesn't convince you, there are many others.

The Oaten/Cheng study[64] showed that when people participated in an exercise program over a two-month period, significant improvements in a wide range of self-regulation behavioral areas, including tobacco, caffeine and alcohol consumption, more healthful eating, less stress, less impulse spending, improved moods, more energy, less loss of ones temper, improved study habits, more consistent performance of household chores, and many other areas. Exercising will make you a more productive person, help you exercise more self-control, and potentially influence your life and behavior in all areas.

If you need to assess your overall health progress and your "biological age," you can take a free on-line test at www.realage.com. I was pleased to see that I was five years younger than I really am. My wife would say that I act twenty years younger than I am and that I need to grow up. So, the consensus is that I am not as old as I am.

The benefits[65] of regular exercise are significant:

- improves feelings of self-worth and elevates mood
- reduces bad cholesterol

- decreases body fat and suppresses appetite signals
- decreases the chance of diabetes
- lowers stress levels and relaxes you
- helps alleviate moderate levels of depression
- improves your appearance
- strengthens your heart, improves circulation and lowers blood pressure
- helps fight cold viruses
- increases muscle strength and endurance
- improves joint flexibility
- decreases the chance of getting gallstones
- adds or slows loss of bone mass
- helps prevent factures of the spine
- lowers the risk of some cancers
- allows you to fall asleep more easily and sleep better
- improves the efficiency of the lungs and delivers more oxygen
- decreases the risk of falling by improving balance and coordination
- increases energy
- hones planning, goal-setting, and decision-making skills

Exercise is good for you! It is wise to consult a doctor if you are embarking on an exercise program for the first time, but don't let that prevent you from taking some action. Not taking action can have severe consequences. In the United States it has been reported that obesity will soon overtake smoking as the primary cause of preventable deaths.

A major MOJO life shift is just two weeks away for you!

Mojo/Snowball

As you can readily attest, exercise, dieting, living on a budget, having your daily devotions, or controlling your temper is not easy. Our self-control efforts fail more often than they succeed. However, a great source of motivation should be that IF you are successful at making some *small* changes, it can accelerate other changes in your life, almost like a snowball effect. Dr. Mark Muraven's research suggests that self-control is like a muscle. "People can strengthen their self-control muscle by exercising that self-control. Practicing self-control will increase your stamina."[66] Push yourself in one area to begin with. You will be surprised at the momentum it creates in other areas. The results of this study showed that practicing self-control can increase your self-control power and help overcome more powerful impulses. If you mix in prayer and fasting, they can also be powerful factors.

Have you overcome a temptation or taken a specific action that required self-control and afterward felt energized and strengthened? In a 2009 study, two groups of participants engaged in either (1) a *strong training* program or (2) a *weak training* program. At the end of this training, participants returned to the laboratory and engaged in several different tasks that required self-control. Those who underwent the *strong training* held their hand in ice water significantly longer, performed better on other tasks that required attention and concentration, and reported better health-related behaviors."[67] Be wise, but push yourself as a result of this book (with your doctor's permission)!

A little change will lead to a snowball effect and momentum that can influence generations to come.

Wake-up Call

My wife faithfully gets her annual physicals and age-appropriate testing with no pushing, poking, or prodding. I, on the other hand, waited until my forties to have my first physical since high school—a mere thirty years late. Experiencing an army of doctors, years of testing, and multiple ER and hospital visits in the late 1990s led to one of many miracle stories, which I cover in *Ease the Squeeze,* so I won't belabor that here. I was in no hurry to *voluntarily* agree to visit the doctor just for a "checkup." The thought of getting "a physical" made as much sense to me as bringing my car to the mechanic when it ran perfectly fine and plunking down some hard-earned cash just to make me feel better (or maybe it was my wife).

I sat stunned that January day in 2008 when my physician told me that the EKG showed evidence of a possible silent heart attack. My cardiologist confirmed that I had some abnormalities and an enlarged left side of my heart, and he gently lectured me on my off-the-charts cholesterol levels. I was all ears as he asked me questions that seemed to penetrate my ear drums and my body in its entirety. All of my being leaned forward in the chair with a newly amplified and intensified mission at hand. "How often do you exercise? How are your eating habits?" Each question seemed like a blaring alarm clock going off. I think the cholesterol level readings had given him all of the answers he needed to those questions; the verbalization of the questions was a mere formality. It was like a switch that flipped inside me that ignited a zeal and a purpose for making some changes.

I knew that I needed to make some changes immediately and permanently. I exercised very little. I enjoyed donuts, fast food fries, beef, cookies, sweets, and anything with sugar, all on a regular basis. I immediately made some radical dietary changes and started reading nutritional labels as if they were a New York Times bestseller beckoning me. I scrutinized my cholesterol intake as if each percentage point threatened my very life. I committed immediately to no more fast food, beef only every couple of weeks, and started exercising regularly. I wanted to live, and I put that desire into action. I cut my cholesterol levels in half in less than a year and have been faithful with my new zeal for health and diet for nearly four years.

Cardiovascular disease is the leading cause of death and serious illness in the United States. The Framingham Heart Study[68] researched the leading causes of heart disease and stroke. Five thousand two hundred and nine men and women between the ages of 30 and 62 went through extensive physical examinations and lifestyle interviews to be analyzed for patterns. The researchers have studied participants for three generations, since 1948. The major risk factors should come as no surprise: high blood pressure, high cholesterol, smoking, obesity, physical inactivity, and diabetes.

"I don't like going to exercise; I like having gone to exercise."[69]

Supersize It

The media barrage from the superficial magazine cover screams at you: "Flatbelly Secrets Inside!" "Beautiful buns in 30 days!" "New beauty and aging secrets discovered!" "Sexy hair!" "Toned body!" "Style in a snap!" This was a sample from just 30 seconds of reading in one grocery store! You get the picture! Many magazines, newspapers, and TV programs are now loaded with weight-loss ads and super models with pearly whites, beach-ready bods, and six-pack abs. The message blares for us to do something, to swallow their pill, get on their plan, or simply follow their seven steps to thirty pounds in thirty days. Reality is that a "marathon" approach is needed, not a short-term pill-pop or diet fad that comes tempting you daily. Most of these "sprint solutions" often are unhealthy and require unrealistic behavioral changes.

Throughout most of human history, food was scarce. That might be true today with half the world, including Third World countries, but not so much in the Western world. Weight-related illnesses and disease are overwhelming our health-care system. Obesity doubles the risk of heart failure in women, and a man with 22 extra pounds has a 75 percent greater chance of having a heart attack than one at healthy weight. Gaining just 11 to 18 pounds doubles the risk of developing Type 2 diabetes.[70] Technology has also led to reduced activity levels. This makes for a deadly combination. The following is a stunning comparison in how portion sizes have changed radically in the past generations. We are eating ourselves to death[71]:

	Then	Now
Fast-food hamburger (1957)	1 oz., 210 calories	6 oz, 618 calories
Movie theater popcorn (1957)	3 cups, 170 calories	16 cups, 900 calories
Butterfinger (1990)	2.1 oz, 270 calories	5.0 oz., 680 calories
Coca-Cola (1894)	6.5 oz.	20 oz.

We are also barraged with a discounted "super-size" bargain that beckons us at many restaurants. We are offered ten varieties of nearly everything at our grocery stores and restaurants, and reality-based weight-loss television is the new entertainment of the day. Often weight gain is due to a complex mix of emotional and psychological factors, and food plays a key role in how people deal with these issues. Some of the reality shows might be inspiring, but often the training methods are extreme and unsustainable.[72]

We are in good company. America continues to supersize.[73] More than 61 percent of adults are overweight,[74] and about one-third of all American adults are now obese. Obesity is common, serious, and costly. Approximately 72.5 million U.S. adults are obese. The warnings are obvious that much of the population is at dangerously high risk of diabetes, heart disease, and other chronic and costly illnesses."[75] Poor diet and physical inactivity contribute to weight increase and are major causes of chronic diseases and premature death.

"In the 30 years since the debut of the USDA's Dietary Guidelines, the number of Americans considered obese has skyrocketed from 15 percent to 34 percent."[76] It is so easy to plop down in front of the television, and that one show or one sporting event can turn into hours before we know it. The average American watches four hours of television per day. According to the British Journal of Sports Medicine, "watching six or more hours of TV per day can shorten life expectancy by nearly five years! That means that TV watching is as bad for you as not getting exercise, being obese, and smoking cigarettes."[77]

Sugar Blues

I remember reading a book called *Sugar Blues* as a kid. I'm not sure why, other than that I had heard some of the statistics about how much sugar was in my favorite beverage, Coca-Cola, and it blew my mind. "The average 12-ounce soda contains more than 8 teaspoons of sugar! The average American now consumes 22 teaspoons of sugar a day. Early humans ate about *4 pounds* of sugar per year. In 2008 the average American ate *136 pounds* of sugar per year! Our sweet tooth isn't just making us fat—it's triggering all kinds of inflammation that can lead to diabetes, heart disease, autoimmune disorders, and even increasing our risks of cancer."[78]

Sugar consumption is an addiction. Sugar activates feel-good substances in our brain and gives us a big rush. In a recent study, "94% of laboratory rats chose sugar water over cocaine. Refined sugars were absent in the diet of most people until very recently in human history. Our diets rich in sugar contribute with other factors to drive our current obesity epidemic. The pleasure of the sweet taste of sugar is often compared to drug addiction. [79]

Be careful about replacing sugars with more artificial sweeteners. Some of them can be up to "1300 times sweeter than sugar itself, and disrupt the body's natural insulin-regulating and calorie-counting mechanisms. Numerous studies suggest that artificial sweeteners also negatively affect weight loss."[80]

My Plate

Remember the old food pyramid? The U.S. Department of Agriculture developed it twenty years ago. That old icon has now evolved to the "choosemyplate.gov" icon, which has portional slices of "fruits, grains, vegetables, and protein and dairy". The USDA nutritional recommendations vary by age and gender. "For example, a man between age 19 and 30 needs 60% more grains than a girl between 9 and 13."[81]

The USDA released its long-overdue updated dietary guidelines,[82] and although nothing will jump off the page as a major revelation, maybe you can start with this "idea buffet" and choose to do one or two of the following things immediately and have someone hold you accountable:

Balancing calories:
- Enjoy your food, but eat less.
- Avoid oversized portions.
- Increase physical activity.

Foods to increase:
- Make half of your plate fruits and vegetables.
- Switch to fat-free or low-fat (1 percent) milk.
- Consume at least half of all grains as whole grains.
- Consume foods fortified with vitamin B12 (for individuals age 50 and older).

Foods to reduce:
- Compare sodium in foods like soup, bread, and frozen meals—and choose the foods with lower numbers.
- Drink water instead of sugary drinks.

Stay Consistent/Get Back on the Horse

You are in good company if you have started exercising and then quit. "Research suggests that most adults are inactive or irregularly active and that ~50% of adults joining exercise programs will drop out within 3 to 6 months."[83] Don't let the excuses—lack of time, cost, no energy, risks, etc.—keep you from getting back on the horse again. Exercise that self-control muscle. Get ready for some radical changes.

The more people do things, the more those things become automatic. Be consistent. The benefits of exercise are obvious, but recent research also shows that people who regularly exercise at moderate-to-intense levels might have a 40 percent lower risk of developing brain damage linked to strokes, dementia, and mobility problems. The American Heart Association's guidelines for ideal cardiovascular health includes 150 minutes of moderate activity or 75 minutes of vigorous intensity per week. [84]

Baby Steps

Baby steps. Start with a 20-minute walk. Make the right choices daily. Make long-term lifestyle changes, not kamikaze, 30-day programs. Always consult a physician before making any major changes. Do some soul searching to resolve the issues that might have caused weight gain in the first place. Ali Vincent, the first female winner of *The Biggest Loser*, said that "people expect me to talk about diet and exercise, but that's really only 10 percent of the whole weight-gain equation. It's really about how you process your thoughts, your self-image and what issues you have."[85]

How do you see yourself? What issues do you need to take action upon?

Invest in YOU!

Many people spend time monitoring the stock market or college fund shortfall. They monitor the bills that are due or the checks that are bounced, but they just don't take the time to invest in themselves. The most important investment you can make is in YOU! Your body is God's church, His temple. You wouldn't look at your 401k statement once every ten years or look at your checking account balance every two to three years.

Almost all of the key diseases that are fatal to Americans could largely be prevented by lifestyle changes—exercise and a healthful diet—but people don't know exactly what to do or how to change. As our bodies age, exercise also keeps our brains sharp, and there is nothing like a younger, smarter brain! "Exercise promotes a process where the brain creates new neurons that help keep our brains flexible and limber."[86] Here are some practical steps to help you take some baby steps in investing in YOU.[87]

 Check the areas in which you might need some improvement
or to take some action

🍎 See yourself as God sees you. He loves you right now—unconditionally—just as you are.

🍎 Your body is your most valuable asset; respect it, take care of it, and make it last. Ask God to help you fully realize that your body is God's temple; it is not your own.[88]

🍎 Focus on the inside first, then on the external appearance. Man looks at the outward appearance, but God looks at the heart.[89]

🍎 Change one or two habits every few weeks, and then build on that. Most people cannot sustain multiple changes at once (diet, smoking, drinking, exercise).

🍎 Drink eight glasses of water a day—start with that.

🍎 Find an accountability partner that you trust who will encourage and challenge you but not shame you.

🍎 Find an exercise/fitness activity that you enjoy. The drudgery of doing something you dislike will lead to quitting.

🍎 Don't skip meals. Eat three meals a day plus a snack. You tend to overeat and oversnack if you miss a meal.

🍎 Eat healthful foods. Increase your fruit and vegetable intake, add lean meats, whole grains, and low-fat dairy.

🍎 Build a shopping list before going to the store. Build it around a core of fruits, vegetables, whole grains, low-fat dairy products, and protein sources.

🍎 Minimize sugar, saturated fats, and trans fats.

🍎 Shatter the cookie jar, don't hide it. Don't buy the cookies in the first place. The temptation is too great!

🍎 Wait! Eat something healthful when you have a craving, then wait thirty minutes and the craving might pass.

🍎 Exercise portion control. Choose a small piece of candy or half of your usual portion.

- Cut your habits before eliminating them. Go from four sodas to two sodas for a couple weeks, then eliminate them.

- Reduce dining out or split an entree. Portion sizes are greater than you eat at home, and oil and fat content is usually higher. Research the entries online to understand fat and cholesterol content before going.

- Morning mocha is a mockery. That whipped cream, shot, or sugar packet all add up. Go low-fat or small size.

- Dressing fat and calorie content is stunning. I discovered this while on my cholesterol journey. Go low-fat dressing.

- Eliminate the soda. According to the center for Science in the Public Interest, 21 percent of Americans' calories come from beverages.

- Eat fruit!

- Read the labels. Don't get tricked by the "serving size" lingo.

- Turn off the TV! The ads will get you, but also a sedentary lifestyle will pack on the pounds, not to mention the overall value and productivity of that time that could be used elsewhere!

- Add fiber. This might also help you reduce total caloric intake.

- Join a fitness club. Increase your level of fitness activity.

- Get health screenings done— cholesterol, blood sugar, blood pressure, body mass index, mammogram, etc.— it might just save your life.

- Get colorectal cancer screening (recommended at age 50).

- Get a routine physical exam! It probably saved my life!

- Get recommended immunizations.

- Start or join a weight loss competition—with family, neighbors, or friends, or track your progress on Facebook.

- Make your commitments public. That makes it harder for you to quit.

- Walk the dogs and/or take a walk with the family.

- Make healthier food choices.

🍎 Get nutritional counseling, or come up with your own plan.

🍎 Be tobacco free.

🍎 Limit alcohol intake.

 What are the top three actions from the preceding list that you commit to work on beginning *now*?

1. _____ , 2. _____ , 3. _____

Choices

Can you guess the most commonly given excuse for not exercising? Yep. "No time." According to Gina Demillo Wagner in her article "25 Ways to Make Time for Fitness," "we usually find that it is not a lack of time, but rather a lack of motivation, lack of enjoyment, fear or possibly low self-esteem. It seems we find it easier to make time for television, social networking, or even household tasks." Fear might be the biggest reason of all. It could be that we have a "fear of embarrassment, failure, or of getting hurt." What we really ought to fear are the *results* of not exercising, or the *results* of the cost of inactivity.

Live Life Long

According to the "The Longevity Project,"[90] the best childhood predictor of long life is a quality defined as conscientiousness: "the often complex pattern of persistence, prudence, hard work, close involvement with friends and communities" that produces a well-organized person who is somewhat obsessive and not at all carefree". The authors also suggest that the long-term health effects of broken families were often devastating. Parent divorce during childhood was the single strongest predictor of early death in adult years. Parental breakups were the most traumatic and harmful events for children.

Those who faired best in The Longevity Project had a high level of physical activity, gave back to the community, and had a healthy marriage and family life. (We will address these factors in the "Family" and "Faith" sections of the book.)

Make the time. Take the time. We make time in life for exactly what we want to do. I made a choice to make exercising and a diet change a *top* priority in my life. Take those baby steps. The first month was hard; now it is just part of my lifestyle. Here are some practical ways to move out now.

- Find a friend or advocate to partner with in exercise or weight loss.
- Find someone to hold you accountable.
- Put your goals down on paper.
- Lock it into your calendar. Start a weekly ritual.
- Start small. Start with 30 minutes a few times a week, and then add more time as you make this a habit.
- Make this a top priority. Turn off the TV.

- Make it a family event. Our family joined a fitness club. My daughter challenges me some days; I challenge her on other days.

Do you not know that your body is a temple of the Holy Spirit, who is in you,
whom you have received from God? You are not your own.
—1 Corinthians 6:19

The web is a source of information, yet it is also a source of misinformation. I was a "cyberchondriac" second to none. I know I had my wife's head spinning when I quoted to her my life expectancy and some frightening statistics before I had my disease diagnosed. A recent Harris poll showed that 71 percent of us turn to the web for health information.[91] The problem is that not all websites are accurate. Another problem is that the data gets outdated in a hurry, and a search engine can bring you millions of sights to sort through. I googled "heart disease" and a mere 26,800,000 sites were available for my perusal! How in the world do you know where to start?

"I quit therapy because my analyst was trying
to help me behind my back."
—*Richard Lewis, hypochondriac comedian*

Where to Start/Good advice[92]

1) Narrow your search. Find sites that were posted within the last year. Be specific in your search terms.
2) Consider the source. Is it.gov (government) or.edu (educational)? What is the health background of the writer?
3) Seek seals of approval. HON or URAC certifications are independent organizations.
4) Check the date. When was the article written or the site last updated?
5) Look for hidden agendas—ads or sponsorships or conflicts of interest.
6) Get a second and a third opinion.

Some potentially helpful sites (always consult a physician):

o www.familydoctor.org: a flow chart lists various possible causes of your symptoms
o www.medlineplus.gov: the most recent news releases from major medical organizations
o www.pdrhealth.com: the *Physician's Desk Reference*
o www.or-live.com: watch a surgical procedure
o www.webmd.com: symptom checker

Adapt yourself to the life you have been given;
and truly love the people with whom destiny has surrounded you.
—Marcus Aurelius

Legacy Lesson: Your kids need you. Your spouse and family need you. Your grandkids need you. Your years are so precious. Take care of yourself first and maximize your impact years! Start some new disciplines now!

CHAPTER 12

OVERCOMING FEAR, FAILURE, AND REGRET: LIVE A FUTURE-FOCUSED LIFE

"Failure is good. It's fertilizer. Everything I've learned about coaching I've learned from making mistakes."
—Rick Pitino

"I'm not a failure. I failed at doing something. There's a big difference"
—Erma Bombeck

I love reading about others' successes, but it also encourages me to read about their failures or struggles. Failing is more common than succeeding; people just don't share their failures publicly. We usually find out about them late in life in the subject's autobiography. Here are a few good examples.

- What does a "Type A" entrepreneur idea man do when he's stuck in bed for months with health problems? If he's an opportunist like Truett Cathy, he comes up with a million-dollar idea. The time Truett spent out of commission inspired him to play with a new concept. That experiment became the Chick-fil-A sandwich!
- Emperor Ferdinand told Wolfgang Mozart that his opera *The Marriage of Figaro* was "far too noisy" and contained "far too many notes. Good thing Mozart didn't listen to opposing voices.
- Artist Vincent van Gogh sold only one painting in his lifetime. Sometimes a generational impact doesn't occur until down the road. He used his gifts and talents to the best of his abilities.
- Thomas Edison[93] was considered unteachable as a youngster. Later in life, "the genius inventor was faced by two dejected assistants, who told him, "We've just completed our 700th experiment and we still don't have an answer. We have failed." "No, my friends," said Edison, "you haven't failed. It's just that we know more about this subject than anyone else alive. And we're closer to finding the answer, because now we know 700 things not to do." Edison went on tell his colleagues, *"Don't call it a mistake. Call it an education."*

89

- A Munich schoolmaster told Albert Einstein that he would never amount to much.

Some people are paralyzed by a fear of failure or a fear of the future. Others are paralyzed by indecisiveness or overanalysis. Some are stuck in despair, loneliness, or isolation. Still others wallow in regret focused on "what could have been." We all deal with fear, failure, and regret. A focus on the future is all you can control. I recall the lyrics of a song by Steven Curtis Chapman, "*Saddle up your horses, you have a trail to blaze. . . this is a life like no other. . . . this is the Great Adventure.*"

"Surely I am with you always."
—Matthew 28:20

When we open ourselves up to God and to other people, we learn that we are not alone in our fears, inadequacies, failures, struggles, temptations, and uncertainties. Isolation is dangerous, especially when we are battling fears and failures.

.300 Hitter

You will fail. All of us fail regularly. A Hall of Fame baseball player fails at home plate seven times out of ten. I fail at having dinner together with my family every night. I fail and raise my voice. I fail and skip the discipline when I should have spanked or grounded. I fail and put myself ahead of my spouse or family. I fail to meet our goal of volunteering monthly. I miss a dinner or a Bible reading. I fail in prayer, in fasting, and in Bible study. You might have failed at spending too much time at work or spending too much time on the social and not enough on the spiritual. Admit and confess your failures, and then get over it. Forget what is behind and press on toward what lies ahead.[94] Your family is a prize. A gift from God. Open the gift. Pursue the prize. Pursue Him, and you will be better able to pursue them. Don't dwell on the past moments or failures. Make every future moment count. Begin now. Do not be afraid. God is with you. Ask your spouse for help if you need to.

A man who gives a good account of himself is probably lying, since any life when viewed from the inside is simply a series of defeats.
—George Orwell

"Warren Bennis, a pioneer in the field of leadership studies and adviser to four presidents, says the learning person looks forward to mistakes. Of the ninety leaders he studied, a common theme was that they demonstrated persistence, commitment and risk-taking, but above all, learning."[95] Bennis discussed learning from our mistakes: "The worst problem in leadership is basically early success. There's no opportunity to learn from adversity and problems." "People who are truly great at what they do—athletes, musicians, or chefs—concentrate on what they're doing wrong in order to get better. If we are too eager to ignore our mistakes and failures, we can't learn from them."[96] Failure is inevitable. The choice is ours whether we risk failing again or will make the same mistake again.

"God whispers to us in our pleasures, speaks to us in our conscience,
but shouts in our pains. It is His megaphone to rouse a deaf world."
—CS Lewis

Sometimes your greatest failures are a springboard to future success. If you are too paralyzed or polarized to learn from your failures, you can become overwhelmed with shame, guilt, or even depression. People who end up living great lives failed over and over again. Success can happen when you least expect it, so always be ready to pounce.

"It is not the critic who counts; not the man who points out how the strong man stumbled or where the doer of deeds could have done them better. The credit belongs to the man who is actually in the arena; whose face is marred by dust and sweat and blood; who strives valiantly; who errs, and comes short again and again, because there is not effort without error and shortcoming; who does actually try to do the deed; who knows the great enthusiasm, the great devotion and spends himself in a worthy cause; who at the worst, if he fails, at least he fails greatly. Far better it is to dare mighty things, to win glorious triumphs even though checkered by failure, than to rank with those poor spirits who neither enjoy nor suffer much because they live in the gray twilight that knows neither victory or defeat."
—Theodore Roosevelt, "Citizenship in a Republic,"
Speech at the Sorbonne, Paris, April 23, 1910

You are in a battle. Mom, that daily battle is with the teenager. It might include the fight about homework or the speech you gave your kids about staying on a straight and narrow path. Dad, it is the time you are investing in your kids. It might be that failed business attempt or failure in ministry. No regrets. Move on. Live and learn.

"Ninety percent of all those who fail are not actually defeated.
They simply quit."
—Paul J. Meyer

No Regrets

I recall the "death crawl" scene from the movie *Facing the Giants*. He left everything he had on the field. He gave it his very best. Don't die wondering. *I wonder—I wish I had—If only I had. . . .* The missed activities, the misprioritizing of time, the things you said that you wish you could take back, the neglect of children during seasons, the anger, etc.

Paul could have had regrets when he spent key seasons of his life in prison. I assume that was not on his bucket list or one of his Life Ladder goals in how he would spend big blocks of his life. Yet he wrote much of the New Testament during those seasons and made a generational impact.

I think we would all like to look back over our lives and say that we have no regrets. I think the person who can say that is a rare breed. We all make mistakes. It could be that you "did your best," but you still had regrets. It could be that you have no "major regrets" but that you realize your parenting or marriage could have been improved or your faith could have been more robust. I like my friend Andy Postema's[97] take on how best to avoid "regret":

The person who has the most regret is the person who cheated themselves and their family, co-workers, friends and teammates in little ways along shared paths. Hardly noticeable to others and deemed, "well, that's life" by others, it is a blinding and paralyzing light you are sure others can see exposing you in front of them.

The problem with regret is it screams at you in the confines of your own soul. Relief from regret comes in a paradox: people with whom you have let down. You learn to compartmentalize and judiciously guard every part of your soul until you become the master of many, all wrapped in the enigma inside your spirit.

But sin, in any form, chips away at the masterpiece that is you. You cannot live with "who you are not" and you cannot live with "who you are" when "who you are" is not in line with God's vision. You can avoid regret by surrendering the areas you try to hide from God and others. Give everything you have or give nothing at all. Giving less than your best confuses your own spirit and creates tension in your life. You begin to wonder what man is really you. Am I the cheater of time and effort or am I the man God says I am? What man do you want to be?

Control what you can control and be responsible for it.

In degree, the sustained pain of regret is difficult to manage because it stays with you. Dormant at times, it will spring up in moments which sting the soul. No one may know, but you cannot fool yourself.

Postema goes on to discuss "true joy" and how we often give up too easily. It might be the temptation to relax with the paper or television instead of spending quality time with our family or giving in to our weak flesh.

Having no regret starts with your little decisions, your daily decisions, your daily temptations, and your daily sins. How are you dealing with those decisions? It is time to move into a new mindset, one of pursuing your dreams and making the little decisions and taking the little actions now that will set things in motion.[98]

I thank God that I live in a country where dreams can come true, where failure sometimes is the first step to success and where success is only another form of failure if we forget what our priorities should be.
—Henry Lloyd

Failures

My favorite book on failures is just a little simple book written by K.P. Yohannan called *When We Have Failed, What's Next?*[99] As many versions of the Bible as we have available to read, you would think that someone would have come out with the New Perfect People (NPP) version by now. Thankfully, it has not been published yet. Yohannan walks you through a number of biblical "failures" and is grateful that God doesn't "Photoshop these failures." We can learn greatly from them.

- Moses: A dramatic bulrush rescue, a great leader of people, then he kills a man and spends forty years in the desert
- Elijah: A powerful prophet of God, miracles, brings rain, and then lives with terrible discouragement and says "I want to die" (1 Kings 19:4)
- David: A shepherd boy turned king, wins many great battles, a man after God's own heart, then he breaks five commandments, including murder and adultery
- Jacob: Lied to his father, stole a blessing, and then wasted twenty years of his life
- Adam and Eve: gave up their beautiful, perfect garden home for a piece of forbidden fruit

We all fail and have regrets. God takes messed-up people, broken lives, failures, sick bodies, and those living in sin, in prison, outcasts, and losers and uses them! The recipe after failure and past regret is:

- Let God be the strength of your heart (Psalm 73:26)
- His yoke is easy; His burden is light (Matthew 11:28–30)
- Return to Him (Jeremiah 3:1)
- Let Jesus comfort, heal and rebuild you (Psalm 61:1–4)

Jesus knew that Peter would fail Him and deny Him. His prayer was not that Peter wouldn't fail but that his *faith* wouldn't fail (Luke 22:31–32). Don't let Satan accuse you. Be humble. Let God restore you. Accept God's forgiveness. Admit your failure, and be broken before Him. Be the clay, and let God be the potter.

Dust yourself off. Forget the past. Know that He is God. He is all powerful. He understands and knows you. He will give you power and strength. Watch for patterns and warning signs as you press forward. Pursue spousal unity above all.

 Read the following passages, and meditate upon what they mean to you.

- Isaiah 40:29–31—He will give you strength.
- Philippians 3:12–14—Forget what lies behind and press on toward what lies ahead.

Failure is an inside job. So is success. If you want to achieve, you have to win the war in your thinking first. You can't let failure outside you get inside you. Another great book on failing and regret is John Maxwell's *Failing Forward: Turning Mistakes into Stepping Stones for Success*. I believe each person wants to live a life with greater purpose and with no regrets. So, how can you live a more significant life? Learn from your past and put your failures behind you. Do not dwell on your failures as "your legacy". I love the story of Cy Young. The award for baseball's best pitcher each year is named after him. The ironic thing is that Cy Young had 316 career losses—the most in major league history. Cy Young must have learned from his many losses. He also had 511 career wins—also a major league record!

I was told of an individual who concluded that he had largely failed at leaving a legacy with his children so he spent his 2nd Half rebuilding relationships, focusing on the grand-kids, and helping the local school. He determined to not have any more regrets. Failure will occur. Failure is about taking responsibility, learning from your mistakes, being positive, not quitting, moving forward, and being willing to take new risks. Neither success nor failure is a destination, but rather part of the journey. The average for entrepreneurs is 3.8 failures before they finally make it in business.

"If you're not failing, you're not growing."
—John Maxwell

Generational Giant

When making legal arrangements for her new corporation, Mary Kay's lawyer said, "If you are going to throw away your life savings, why don't you just go directly to the trash can? It will be so much easier than what you are proposing." She sank her $5000 life savings into her new business. A month before the business was to open, her husband died. She did not accept defeat. She launched her business on September 13, 1963. Now the company has more than $1 billion sales and employees 3500 people.

"Failure isn't so bad if it doesn't attack the heart.
Success is all right if it doesn't go to the head.
—Grantland Rice

"Success is moving from one failure to another with no loss of enthusiasm."
—Winston Churchill

Legacy Lesson: All have failed. All have regrets. All have plenty of reasons to fear the future. Choose to press on, look ahead and not dwell in the past. Reflect, learn from your failures and regrets and leave a legacy!

CHAPTER 13

LIFE BY DESIGN: CLIMBING YOUR LIFE LADDER

We forego significance for the sake of success and pursue the superficiality of title and degree, house and car, rank and portfolio over a life lived large.
—James Emery White

Life Ladder

Are you ready to live life large? Have you planned out your Life Ladder? One way to look at your Life Ladder would be as the steps of aging or life's seasons. I prefer to look at my Life Ladder as one I can use for any season of life. A Millennial can use it and a Silent Generation member can use it. You might have developed elements already within the Life Ladder. Certainly you have emphasized one step or rung above another. Maybe it is time to shore up some other steps. Your steps may be a different order or weighted differently. Many may be in parallel. You may have additional steps.

The first place to start is with your Life Mission. That will help you establish some Life Guiding Principles that will help you stabilize the ladder and ensure a firm foundation in aiming to climb toward your Life Mission. These will be principles or objectives that you will always fall back on—through good times and bad times. Most businesses and ministries develop a Mission Statement, but very few families develop a Life Mission.

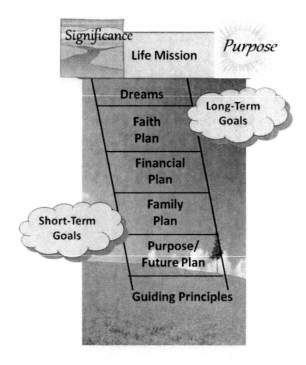

Although you can tailor your Life Ladder as you see fit, I would recommend drafting these ingredients in the following order:

1. Life Mission
2. Dreams, Bucket List, and High-Level Twenty-Year Plan
3. Purpose Plan
4. Life Guiding Principles
5. Family Plan
6. Financial Plan
7. Faith Plan
8. Annual Goals for Each
9. Long Term Goals for Each

The first section of this part of the book will deal with the Life Mission, Purpose Plan, and Guiding Principles. It will also cover Long-term and Short-term goals. Subsequent sections of the book will cover the Family Plan, Financial Plan and Faith Plan.

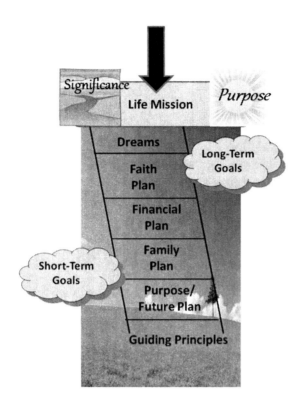

"write the vision and make it plain"
- Habakkuk 2:2

1. Life Mission

I am a Type-A personality. It is easy for me to take on a new ambitious challenge and pour my heart and soul into it. The hard thing for me to do is to say no. I am getting better at it, but it is so critical that we ensure that what we put our time and energy into will be a deposit toward our life mission statement. Is this a project or challenge that will pay dividends for my family? My future? My finances? My faith? Does it align with my Life Mission? With my top life priorities? Is this the right time to pursue this? Does it align with the season of life that I am in? It would have been a disaster for my family if I had written this book while two of them were in diapers. It is critical to consider your life mission and goals regularly. My goals have shifted as the children grew and as our activities shifted. Thus you might also have four "seasonal" ladders in your life:

- High school/college years (teens/20s Ladder)
- Early marriage/young children years (20s–30s Ladder)
- Teenager/children attending college years (40s–50s Ladder)
- Second Half years (40s–90s)

Welcome each seasonal process by looking at your Life Ladder, Life Mission, and Goals. Welcome the aging process by giving back. Someone has said that life is partitioned in three "Acts," although I would argue the third is lifelong:

Act 1: To learn
Act 2: To earn
Act 3: To return

Don't waste any of your acts. The question is whether we are returning enough. Encompass your time, talents, knowledge, and resources in your future plan. Sometimes we let "self" and "safety" limit our life multiplication opportunities. Sometimes we also let busyness of Act 1 and Act 2 limit our dreams or mission fulfillment.

If you have never set a "Life Purpose" or "Life Mission," you should take time to develop this "target." I cover a lengthy section on this in *Ease the Squeeze*. What is your aim? What is your target? What is your life's calling? This is your rudder against which all major decision arrows should be analyzed. I have this pasted everywhere—on all of our computers, in my Bible, and in my Daytimer so that I view it daily. Mine is simple:

Know God. Love one another. Serve others.

"If the ladder is not leaning against the right wall, every step we take just gets us to the wrong place faster."
—Stephen Covey

 Take some time away and draft your Life Mission.

2. Dream Setting/Your Dream Plan—LIVE LARGE!

 "History Maker"- Delirious

"I have learned that if one advances confidently in the direction of his dreams, and endeavors to live the life he has imagined, he will meet with a success unexpected in common hours."
—Henry David Thoreau

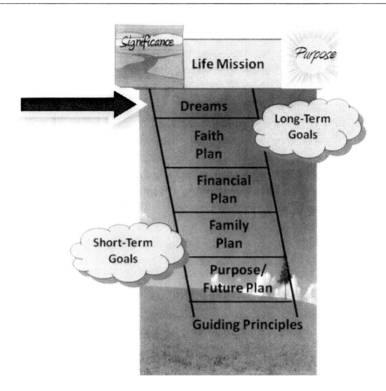

Many people often document their goals, but they don't document their dreams. Often this might be because they don't want to hold themselves to a high standard that they don't expect to achieve. I think that dream documentation is a healthy exercise. You will find your dreams changing from one life season to another. "Getting through the teenage years" is not characterized as a dream, although that and 3 John 1:4 might be the main goals for those years.

My prayer and goal in writing this book is to *stir you up*. Sense the eternal urgency. May God right now begin to stir up your gifts. May His Holy Spirit dust off those talents and light a fire in your gut to do something. It is not too late. That is a lie from the devil. You have kids, grandkids, friends, family, neighbors, and co-workers who need your influence.

More importantly, you have hundreds, even thousands, of people that can be influenced after you are gone enjoying eternity elsewhere (hopefully you are *enjoying*!)

Dream big. Think big. May God infuse you with faith, so that you *will* believe! Your biggest dream killers might be people who are closest to you. Find those people who feed your dream and encourage you. Take action. Start small. You might be thinking, *I thought you said to dream big?* One of my favorite Bible principles is "Be faithful in the little things, and He will put you in charge of many things." It is truth. God has been so faithful with my very scant talent. All He is looking for is obedience. You do your part, and He will do His. Trust Him. Ask Him to help open your spiritual eyes as you read this book.

Leave a legacy. Make a generational impact. The clock is ticking. Will you obey? Take this book in bite-size nuggets, and reflect and act using the Selah Stops. Don't be tempted to skip these sections. Use them to get you jump started, and then He will guide you in how to proceed. Dreams always seem to have a birth, a death, and a resurrection. Usually, the season of "death" or "doubt" or "mid-life reality" is the longest season.

Sometimes dreams and promises take time. Anna, an 84-year-old widow, had been praying and fasting for years. We don't see the years of labor and pain experienced with Anna and Simeon. A season of waiting is the hardest. The nine months that a mother prepares to give birth often seems like years. The big promises in the Bible took big chunks of time. Hannah, Paul in prison, Abraham/Sarah. If you have a big call or a big promise, be prepared to wait! Prayer is often compared to childbirth. All kinds of emotions are present in childbirth—depression, irritation, and restlessness. Don't waste this time of "gestation." Pray.[100]

Here is a summary of my personal dreams for two distinct seasons in my life. Hopefully, it will spur you on. I try to document and update my dreams every few years because they change with the seasons.

My Dreams—"My 30s"

- Being faithful to my spouse until death do us part—have a marriage and family testimony
- That all three children would be saved and stay on the straight-and-narrow path their entire lives, following and fulfilling God's plan and calling for their lives; that we and they would have a generational family testimony; that my children's ministry impact will be multiplied times more than what mine is.
- To spend enough time at home to teach the kids and develop a godly, cohesive family
- To be in "full-time ministry"—teaching, conducting seminars, administrating; itinerant ministry with family in a multidenominational dimension.
- Write a book/books
- Serve and minister to pastors
- Develop a community solace for troubled/inner city kids/families
- Give 50 percent; support missionaries and inner-city ministry
- Communion with the Lord—walking in the Spirit, hearing clearly

My Dreams "Rebooted"—"Mid 40s"

- To know God intimately, to love God passionately, to have an undivided heart, to love one another better than myself
- To be faithful to my spouse until death do us part—have a marriage and family testimony
- To live a successful, holy, uncompromising, bondage-free life to the very end
- Revive/renew Christians to pursue God wholeheartedly
- Ministry that has a generational impact and breaks down denominational barriers
- Publish second book
- Seminars/teachings/conferences to make a generational impact—National
- Launch business ministry that influences generations to come
- Make a direct impact and be directly involved with widows/orphans
- Give 50 percent

Another exercise that ties in to your second-half planning is to document what some people call "a bucket list." This is just a list of "dream activities" for your encore career or second half. For us there is not adequate budget or funds for these activities, but it helps us with our planning and dreaming.

Things to Do in My "Second Half"

- *Live out dreams as God wills and opens doors*
- *Strong involvement in kids' and grandkids' lives*
- *Yearly family vacations with extended family—Camp of the Woods, Vero Beach*
- *Vacation with a purpose*
- *Annual missions trips*
- *Business with ministry—Seminars and teachings—God, life, family, money*
- *Family museum*
- *Youth camp/home*
- *RV travel—all national parks*
- *All professional baseball stadia*
- *Attend all four Grand Slams*
- *Attend U.S. Open for two weeks yearly*
- *Foreign tours—Rick Steves; Australia, Israel, etc.*

Take some time to document your dreams and bucket list with your spouse.

One important thing today is to begin to scratch out a plan in pencil for your second half. You should have much overlap in the specific year windows and you should allow for much flexibility. Have a plan within a plan. Have a Plan A, Plan B, and Plan C. Putting a timeline on a twenty-year plan is hard, but it forces you to give some thought to what lies ahead and will also establish what you need to do with your financial plan (to be discussed later). Remember the following self-examination axioms:

"If you would not be forgotten as soon as you are dead and rotten, either write something worth reading or do something worth writing.
—Benjamin Franklin

"Do what you're good at."—COMPETENCIES, your gifts
"Do what fires you up."—PASSION
"Follow open doors."—God

Twenty-year "Second-Half" Plan (in pencil)
James 4:13–16 ("If the Lord wills")

- Age 45–46—Write as a hobby
- Age 47–50—Work full time, book/teaching as a hobby
- Age 48–50—Research business/ministry, research "2nd half" home base
- Age 45–52—Family focus/kids, determine "second-half" home base
- Age 50–53—Work full time, test family focus business local
- Age 52–55—Launch business ministry, regional, job full time
- Age 55–57—Job part time—27 years of marriage, kids college grad!
- Age 57–60—"Semi-retire," business/ministry, missons, dream list
- Age 57–62—Conduct seminars full time, missions part time
- Age 60–65—Family business, missions, seminars, heritage foster home

3. Purpose Plan- Change Your World

Few will have the greatness to bend history itself;
but each of us can work to change a small portion of events,
and in the total of all those acts will be written the history
*of this **generation**."*
—Robert F. Kennedy

You could just as easily call this a Passion Plan. It is a little more detailed than your Mission Statement. It has a few more specifics and can be summarized in several key sentences. Following is mine.

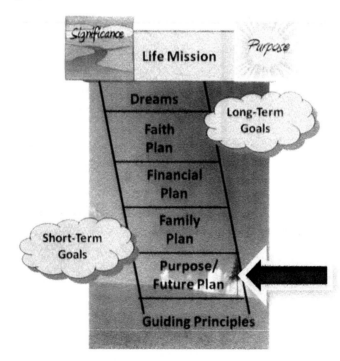

My Purpose Plan

***To renew and revive believers and spur them to a passionate,
uncompromising pursuit of God
To ignite a "think generationally" and "act now" mindset
To build strong, godly, purposeful, families
Secure Future—Strong Family—Real Faith***

Part of your purpose plan is "who" you want to influence. Most professional athletes started small. They developed their skills, then they played on a local team. If they were good enough, they traveled out of city, then out of state, etc. The same thing occurs with a business or possibly a ministry, dependent upon your goals. This is important in defining "how big" you want to get. I did this with my personal life and recent book success and teaching. Start small, and then expand your circle of influence. I will discuss a Family Plan and a Financial Plan in their respective sections.

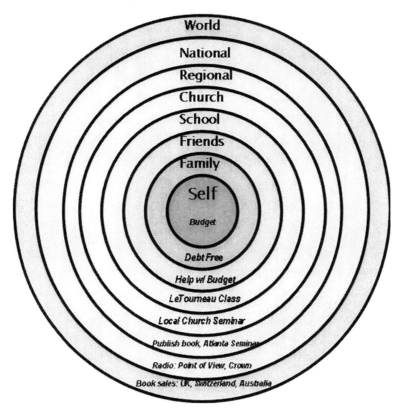

4. Life-Guiding Principles—The Rudder of Life

The next very important thing is to document your Life-Guiding Principles. These can be principles, assumptions, a code of conduct, core values, or doctrinal statements. These are areas you will not compromise and you will always default to. If you see some of these values slipping, it might be a good time for a spiritual, family, or financial "chiropractic adjustment."

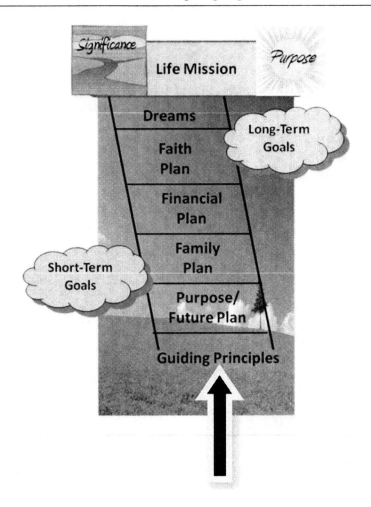

My Life-Guiding Principles are my rudder for life. Here are my principles.

- Put God first; know Him/love Him/pursue Him.
- Love and glorify Jesus Christ in all that I do; surrender all of my desires; abandoned everything to Him.
- Stay in constant two-way communication with Jesus Christ through Bible reading, prayer, and worship.
- Always remaining sensitive to the Holy Spirit's leadings and direction.
- Comply and align with the Bible—my roadmap, GPS, and guidemap for life.
- Be a good steward of all that God has entrusted to us, treating it all as a loan. Pursue debt-free living.
- My family is my highest calling, and time should be given accordingly, no "laters" or "not nows"; be quick to listen, slow to speak, and slow to get angry.
- Marriage is the top priority—follow "5:1" Goals,[101] invest in marriage, Children are a top priority—teach, disciple, and affirm them to move toward godliness; prepare them with a biblical worldview for life and future family.
- Mission-minded—serve communities and the world with my time and money.
- Lay down my life, serve, practice self-denial, sacrificial living, and daily dying to self.

- Seek God—fasting and prayer on major milestones, decisions, and in all seasons.
- Annually update/review the Purpose Plan, Goals, and highlights.
- Preserve family/generational memories through newsletters, documents, and DVD.
- Incur no excessive debt on business/ministry ventures; clear it thru God and Dana.
- Work hard; give it everything I have.
- Don't quit anything until God makes it clear, releases us, and we are in unity.
- Live a lifestyle of generous giving; give at least 10 percent.
- Live a holy, pure life, and run from sin.

Take a first cut at drafting some life-guiding principles. Maybe at the end of each section or chapter you will have some new ideas to consider. Keep that draft as a bookmark, and begin to pencil out some ideas for your Life Mission and Life-Guiding Principles.

Life-guiding Wisdom

Another area that might take many years to document is your Life-Guiding Scriptures. Many of these are included in the Guideposts for Life document I assembled for my children in the appendices. I took an entire two years to put it together. As I read through the Bible in its entirety as research for this book, I highlighted many key scriptures that meant a lot to me. I then went back through those and documented the key ones that were foundational for our family future.

Start a list of your Life-Guiding Principles and Life-Guiding Scriptures that you can add to over the next months and years. This will be a valuable heritage to pass on to your children and grandchildren.

Generational Giant

Martin Luther King Jr. said, "We must keep God in the forefront. Let us be Christian in all of our actions." He had a public role in the civil rights movement. Of his call, King said, "My call was not a miraculous or supernatural something. On the contrary, it was an inner urge calling me to serve humanity." Even after King's house was bombed, he forbade those guarding his home from carrying guns. He was stabbed in the chest while autographing his book *Stride Toward Freedom*. He received death threats and was stoned, arrested, and subjected to solitary confinement. Even such a great man as King was influenced by others. Sometimes we don't realize the power of a spoken word in someone's life. King recalled a phrase spoken by a young woman: "*I have a dream*." Her simple quotation in the hands of a national megaphone had a generational impact. King's influence led to a

U.S. national holiday named after him and quite likely opened the door to America's first African-American president.

Legacy Lesson: Only you and God truly control the design of your future. Many things can change your plans. God will order your steps if you are following Him. Document your plans. What are your dreams? What is your mission? What foundation are you building on? These are all life-changing and generational altering questions.

CHAPTER 14

PURPOSEFUL AND EASY GOAL SETTING: YOUR GPS FOR LIFE

If you don't know where you are going, you'll end up some place else.
—Yogi Berra

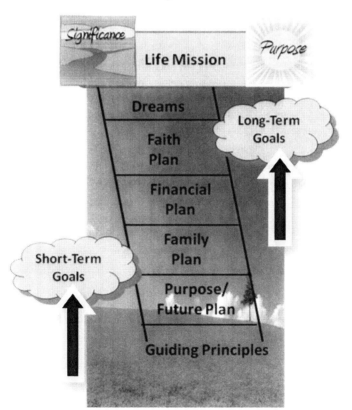

O ne of my favorite movies is *"What About Bob?"* The counselee (Bill Murray) becomes the counselor (Richard Dreyfuss) after a series of family encounters drives Dreyfuss crazy. There was the slurping chicken breast scene, Bob's "I sail" scene, and Bob saving Dreyfuss's life with a memorable Heimlich session. It all came down to baby steps. Bob was trying to develop a life plan that took one step at a time. Now that you have done some dreaming, it is time to clearly document your baby steps, your life plan. The research shows that we are more successful when we "measure" our results.

A direct relationship exists between goal setting and accomplishment. A recent Harvard study of MBA graduates ten years after graduation showed that "3% of these MBA's had accomplished far more than the other 97%. The primary distinguishing characteristic was that the 3% had left Harvard with written goals."[102] For some of you, I know that this section might stretch you. Take baby steps. For example, you know you should exercise five times a week for an hour each session, but reality says that you know that is not at all possible with your schedule. Start with baby steps. For month 1, you set a very specific goal of Monday, Wednesday, and Friday for thirty minutes. Being general—"try to exercise a little more often"—does not cut it. After you create these small blocks of success, you can build upon them. Set up a work-out chart so that you can check off your progress. Things that are measured daily usually show more progress than things that are measured weekly, etc.

I Resolve! Goal Setting

As you plan your future, there are some critical success factors that you must follow-through on. Pilar Gerasimo, Editor in Chief of *Experience Life* magazine and author of *Being Healthy is a Revolutionary Act,* writes of resolutions and the frustration and high failure rates that go along with goal setting. "Set goal. Faltered. Failed. Forgot about it. Repeated 12 months later."[103]

Let's face it—we all fail, and fail often! The challenge in goal setting and making changes is doing a little more analysis about why you are setting the goal and how badly you want to achieve it. That soul searching might help you develop a burning desire to achieve some goals and help you better understand the obstacles and fears that might trip you up in your journey. Gerasimo emphasizes the need to have the right mindset as you enter a goal/resolution-setting mode. Sheer willpower is often not enough, and "self-exploration, self-knowledge, self-mastery, and self-acceptance" are often the key to being successful. Often, the biggest barriers to success come from our own past experiences, failures, or mental battles and coming to grips with that up front can only help you be more successful.

We will cover three steps in the goal-setting process:
1) Specific goals
2) Success Step Summary
3) Long-term Life Goals

Step 1: Set Specific Goals

Don't just say, "I need to lose weight." Doing the self-exploration and answering some questions for yourself before setting a goal will be key to motivating you to succeed. Also writing it down on paper is a must to ensure that all of your thoughts have been translated into a plan. Here are some key success factors in goal setting.

a) **Why:** This might be the most important part of your self-discovery. Why are you pursuing this goal? What are your motives? For weight loss it might be (1) to live longer and fulfill my life calling, (2) to watch my grandchildren grow up, (3) to achieve my bucket list, (4) to feel better about myself, (5) to influence my world, (6) to attract a spouse, (7) to win a "biggest loser" bet with my sister, etc. This will help you stir up the desire and motivate you to succeed.

b) **What/How:** How will the goal be accomplished? Use the S.M.A.R.T. goal philosophy.[104] **S**pecific—Be specific in your goal setting; this is your bull's-eye or your target. **M**easurable—Ensure that you document what makes a successful accomplishment, **A**ttainable—Ensure that it is achievable. **R**ealistic—Ensure that the bar is not too high, or you might quit out of frustration. **T**ime-bound—Ensure that you bind the goal so that it is not open-ended and that you have challenged yourself..

c) **Where:** Defining a specific physical location, if necessary, might also involve understanding your current state and current situation regarding this goal.

d) **When:** When will you start? When does this conclude? When does the goal get reset? You might have a target weight after thirty days and then set another goal after achieving your first milestone.

e) **Who:** Do you need any help or support? Do you need to build your belief?

f) **Barriers/barrier removal:** What are the obstacles or barriers you might see along the way, and how can you overcome them?

g) **Reward:** Identify a reward if that helps motivate you.

Here is an example of the concept in action. (See the appendices for a blank sheet.)

Goal:	Lose Weight	**Priority:**	High	**Rank:**	#1

Why: (1) To live longer and fulfill my life calling, (2) to watch my grandchildren grow up, (3) to achieve my bucket list, (4) to feel better about myself, (5) to influence my world

What/How: <u>Short term</u>: Lose five pounds in the next thirty days. <u>Long term</u>: Lose thirty pounds; decrease cholesterol by 40 percent.

How: (1) Stop eating all fast food and drinking sodas for the next thirty days, (2) jog/speed walk three times a week

Where: The local fitness club; eliminate all unhealthful, tempting food from the pantry and sodas from the fridge

When: Monday/Wednesday/Friday after dinner; target within 30 days

Who: A friend will partner with me and ask me about exercise and sodas

Barriers: Money for fitness club, work schedule, travel

Barrier removal: Find fitness club the cost of which equals my 2 fast-food meals and 6 sodas per week (i.e., $20/week, pick lowest risk work-impact time)

Set one or more goals using the spreadsheet provided in the appendices.

STEP 2: Short-Term Success Step Summary

Nothing will happen if you just set goals. You must measure your success. Your own list might include savings, debts, lifestyle, education, giving, career, etc. In addition, the themes of this book—future, family, finances, and faith—might give you additional ideas. I also cover an exhaustive list of goals in *Ease the Squeeze*.

After reading each section of this book, accumulate your key "Success Steps" to help you climb the Life Ladder quickly. This consolidated summary will be used as your goal scorecard. These are specific goals that you want to monitor daily or weekly. Keep the Success Step Summary near your bed, at your breakfast table, in your Bible, on your refrigerator, or somewhere visible daily.

Short-term goal	1 S	2 M	3 T	4 W	5 T	6 F	7 S	8 S	9 M	10 T	11 W	12 T	13 F	14 S	15 S	16 M	17 T	18 W	19 T	20 F	21 S
Jog 30 minutes	√		√			√					√			√	√		√		√		√
Eat no fast food	√	√		√	√			√	√	√	"	√	√	√	√	√	√	√	√	√	√

We are kept from our goal not by obstacles
but by a clear path to a lesser goal."
—Robert Brault

STOP Once you have documented several goals against which you want to measure your success, then populate this template daily or weekly. A sample blank sheet is provided in the appendices. Also, a summary of "Action Ideas" (Idea Buffet) is provided.

STEP 3: Long-Term Life-Ladder Scorecard

Now that you have started a list of critical short-term goals, in parallel you can create a to-do list of longer-term goals. Create yourself a Life Ladder Planning Scorecard to document your future actions and your targeted dates to accomplish these actions. Grade yourself every three months on each action, and add or subtract items each quarter. Then refresh this list once a year. (A blank scorecard is provided in the appendices.)

Your future action	Target date (self)	Tgt date (spouse)	Tgt date (together)	Quarterly grade
Develop life mission				
Set stress goals				
Set health/fitness goals				
"Second-half" plan				
Document dreams				
My purpose plan				
Life Guiding Principles				
Twenty-year plan bucket list				
Twenty-year timeline				
Set five short-term goals				
Weekly goal table				

The key is not to prioritize what's on your schedule,
but to schedule your priorities.
—Stephen Covey

The CEO of Life Time Fitness, Bahram Akradi, said it well: "All of us have a finite amount of time, and a limited amount of energy. No matter how fully and passionately we embrace or lives, we simply can't do everything. Yes, we may be racking up promotions, possessions and personal bests. We may be achieving goals of fame and fortune, or just having a really good time. But if we're doing those things at the expense of something that matters more to us, then our long-term prospects for enjoying a life well lived are not good."[105]

"Our plans miscarry because they have no aim. When a man does not know what harbor he is making for, no wind is the right wind."
—Seneca, Roman philosopher and statesman (4 BC–65 AD)

"Moving Forward"- Israel Houghton

Legacy Lesson: The benefits of goal setting are obvious to some and simply a root canal to others. Your goals are like gasoline to a car or a map for your journey. Plan your legacy! Hold yourself accountable!

CHAPTER 15

A LEGACY OF HOPE: DEALING WITH STRESS AND OVERLOAD

I am officially a dinosaur. Yes, I have my own Facebook account. Yes, we dumped our landline years ago. I buy almost all of my books online. However, I just can't seem to shake my love for the newspaper and cup of Joe. You, too, officially qualify as a prehistoric middle ager if you do any of the following:

a) walk to the front porch to get your newspaper
b) rent DVDs instead of streaming a movie
c) write letters, lick an envelope, or paste a stamp
d) walk to the phone that still uses a land line
e) visit a local record store or still buy CDs or albums
f) visit a bookstore
g) send an e-mail or pick up the phone instead of texting
h) get your film developed at a local photo finishing store

Just as the industrial revolution went the way of the horse and carriage, many industries are bleeding a slow death as our society begins to trend more to services and continues to outsource labor and manufacturing. According to IBIS World,[106] many of our new technological inventions are introducing a whole new crop of "dying industries."

Technological change, though making our lives easier, is leading to the demise of many profitable industries: wired telecommunications, newspaper publishing, book stores, DVD, game and video rental, record stores, and photo finishing, just to name a few.

The Bureau of Labor Statistics[107] released its list of the thirty fastest growing occupations forecast recently. The high-growth jobs are nearly all in service and professional occupations. That is not bad in itself, it is just that we are no longer competitive with items that are produced outside of the United States. Competition is more fierce, so less is invested in research and development and new product ideas. Manufacturing is dying in America. Mills and apparel manufacturing are on the list of top ten dying industries. Many U.S. manufacturers have shipped production overseas, where wages are low.

Technology & Relationship

The social tapestry is getting more complex and more connected than ever before. We are a wired generation. Technology is now not just a tool or a toy, but a way of life, but rather as necessary for some as breath itself. "A 2010 study by the Kaiser Family Foundation found that students 8 to 18 spend more than 7.5 hours a day engaged with computers, cell phones, TV, music, or video games, and the amount of time all kids spend online daily has tripled in the past 10 years."[108] Forty percent of twenty- and thirty-somethings have viewed Scripture on a cell phone or the internet in the last month."[109]

Children need supervision and guidance. The relationships they are forming are often cemented or grown through digital media. The never-ending media blitz can affect their school performance. "Kids 11 to 14 spend, on average, 73 minutes a day texting; for older teens, it's closer to two hours." Some people might consider this addictive behavior. In fact, Dr. Nora Volkow, director of the National Institute of Drug Abuse, says that "when you get an unexpected text, the dopamine cells in the brain fire up." Dopamine is associated with feelings of pleasure and plays a role in many addictive behaviors, and texting is certainly more pleasurable than studying. "Sixty-seven percent of parents say texting is hurting their kids' school performance." Although the internet and the cell phone certainly might help kids with their schooling, we also must be aware of the risks and monitor their activity.

In a recent article titled "In Defense of Slow,"[110] a good assessment of our dilemma ensued: "In our drive-thru, instant, there's-an-app-for-that culture of fast everything, where our iDevice mobile amusements see to it that no time is dead time, the concept of slowing down seems strange to us. We avoid things that are too slow, because they destroy our rhythm and slow down our pace." The article suggests that we "embrace slow" and pause and turn our eyes and ears to the world around us and truly listen." This takes time, effort, and quietness.

We are living in a surface society in which deep relationships are rarely open, authentic discussions and friendship is a lost art. Our culture even seems to elevate mask wearing and fake fronts. We are enamored of celebrities and gossip about them, the next fad or craze, consumerism, or a polished Facebook profile. Our choices are complicating things. Nothing is simple anymore. Take blue jeans as an example. "In 1980 we could all name the brands. There were half a dozen, dominated by Levi's. Now there are more than 800 blue jean brands sold in the U.S.[111]" This technology and connectivity can lead to stress, worry, and busyness. We are overwhelmed with over choice. Alvin Toffler in *Future Shock* wrote, "The advantages of diversity and individualization are canceled by the complexity of buyers' decision-making process."

Acceleration & Overload

We are numb with busyness. We know it is happening and vow to change it, but before we know it, big chunks of years have passed, and our kids are gone.

The rapid pace of technological, economic, and social change, coupled with our lack of competitiveness, make for a challenging future if we in America want to maintain a leadership position and the strongest economy in the world.

Because this explosion of change seems to be exponential and perpetual, some people have just thrown up their hands with a realization that we just can't keep up anymore. The kids laugh at my ongoing need to purchase CDs and use e-mail. Aren't these relatively new inventions? Not anymore.

At some point, though, we must ask ourselves when enough is enough. I love my GPS, but does it really need to have a conversation with me? How many version updates of the iPod or iPad are really necessary? To what extent is this flood of innovations actually enhancing my life, or is it actually taking from it (time, money, simplicity)? Are the personal conveniences of all of these technological improvements worth the social, psychological, and financial trade-offs? What about quality of life? Have we taken the bait too many times?

The acceleration of technology and connectivity has affected our society and every dimension of how we live. It has radically affected how we work, what products and services we provide, how we educate, how we socialize, how we govern, how we trade, how we communicate, and even how we play. The pace is breathtaking, and the associated stress can be overwhelming.

The scriptures refer to peace, rest and stillness in God. We find it hard to make time for that with the crushing overload. The 7th day should still have "rest elements" associated with. Read Exodus 20:8-10, Ps 37:7, Ps 46:10, Matthew 11:28-29, Phil 4:16-17.

The Genetics of Stress

Taylor Clark references a Kenneth Kendler study that states that "genes account for around 30% of our anxiousness."[112] Although stress or pressure might have a genetic component, "it is mostly the result of what we do to build it up throughout our lives." It will require work to ease the overload, put on the brakes, and slow down to change our habits. It might be doubly hard because some of these traits are learned or even passed down via genetics.

Change Is the Only Constant

Do we really need that version 9.0 cell phone upgrade? Don't you wish you could talk to a human being instead of punching a number eighteen times or repeating an inquiry because the computer could not understand your Texas or North Eastern accent? The never-ending onslaught of gizmos and gadgets will not end anytime soon. The radio, the telephone, the computer, and social media were all game changers that changed the world. Most of them were invented by young people for young people. These will soon be replaced as well. Quite frankly, the onslaught of technology scares the heck out of older generations.[113] Most of the time we try to adapt. If we don't, we are left behind. "At the moment you stop growing, your world will begin to shrink. You'll be able to communicate with fewer people, especially the young. Each new generation seems to build on the technology and innovation of the previous one. The cry will continue to be, "Don't get left behind!"

How to Counter Stress and Overload

- Change what's "In Your Box."
- Develop close relationships.
- Lean on God.
- Learn to Laugh.

115

- Pray.
- Put a Hillsong worship CD in while driving, and worship.
- Rest.
- Exercise.
- Find positive people to hang around with.
- Don't worry.
- Eliminate those things that stress you (unless that is your spouse).
- Slow the rate of change in your life.
- Simplify.
- Bloom where you are planted.
- Stop striving.
- Find stability.
- Value people above pursuit of stuff.

> *"The only trouble with success is that the formula for achieving it*
> *is the same formula for a nervous breakdown."*
> —Chuck Swindoll

Finding Peace

If you are dealing with stress, difficulties or overload or just need God's peace, cry out to God, and He will be your best friend, your comforter, and your rock.

- Let God speak peace into your life (Psa. 85:8–9)
- Do not let your heart be troubled (John 14:27)
- God is your peace (Eph. 2:14)
- Put your hope in God (Psa. 42:11)
- Let God be your anchor of hope (Heb 6:19)
- Find a hope filled church that can encourage you (Heb 10:23-25)
- Consider that these times are temporary and find peace in your eternal destiny (John 14:1-6)
- Know that God's grace is sufficient for you (2 Cor 12:9)

Know that God has "made the heavens and the earth by [His] great power and outstretched arm. Nothing is too hard for [Him]. Cast all your anxiety on Him because He cares for you."[114]

 Find someone who is struggling with worry, stress, or overload, and speak a word of life into their broken world. (See Proverbs 15:23.)

 Exit life's busy interstate and take a country drive or a long walk to do some pondering about how to simplify. Two excellent books on this topic are *Margin* and "*The Overload Syndrome*" by Richard Swenson.

"I Breathe you in God"- Bryan and Katie Torwalt

 "The Desert Song"—Hillsong United

Legacy Lesson: Stress and Overload may feel defeating. You may feel you can no longer dream. Be faithful in the little things. Serve. Sacrifice. Turn to God. Your investment in your kids and grandkids will make a generational impact. Make sure your priorities and time align with your Mission.

CHAPTER 16

LIVING IN THE VALLEY/PEACE FOR YOUR FUTURE: OVERCOMING TRIALS AND WORRY

As I write this section, I have been in the deepest valley of my lifetime. In addition to a rare nervous system disorder (Bradbury Eggleston Syndrome), over the last six months I have had three ER visits for ventricular tachycardia and atrial flutter, more than five thousand incidents of heart arrhythmia or bradycardia over a two-week period, one EP study and pacemaker installation, a five-hour electrophysiological study with a heart ablation, one endoscopy, one gastric emptying test, one abdomen ultrasound, one gall bladder hidascan, one abdomen CT, constant ringing in my ears (tinnitus), nonstop eructation (a fancy name for 24/7 belching), familial tremors throughout my body, two minor thrombosis issues, liver lesions, and trouble with sleeping. It has been my Grand Canyon health valley!

It has been a constant physical and mental battle for hope, peace, and trust in my God. Yet, I daily have had a choice—choose joy and rest in Him or choose worry, negativity, and grumbling. Some days I fail miserably. Other days I pray, "Lord help my unbelief![115]" I must daily choose God's hope and peace and trust him fully. When I do make that choice, I have been able to seek Him wholeheartedly and be totally abandoned to Him rather than to my temporal situation. I am so grateful that when I fail one day, He waits patiently for my approach and welcomes me warmly back with open arms. Overall through this valley, I have had the best and most intimate times with God of my life to date. I have lived in Psalms and read them and prayed them through multiple times. Soaking in them, not just reading them. Meditating on them. Talking to God aloud as I read. Weeping before Him. The honesty has been cleansing for my heart and soul. I was getting to know Him like I never had before and experiencing His love like never before. God is so good.

Here are a few of our valley choices:

- Will I humble myself and ask for prayer and seek encouragement from others or will I live in isolation?
- Will I trust Him and rest in Him, not seeking answers or an exit from the valley. Will I live in His presence?

- Will I accept and know His full love despite the challenges? You are His child and He loves you deeply!
- Will I build myself up through worship, positive relationships, God's word, and honest prayer?
- Will I choose joy and be of good cheer or will I grumble or complain?

I forced myself into writing down specifically why I would choose JOY.

- God has never failed me.
- God is not finished with me.
- I have hope for the future. Where I am is not who I am.
- God's Word encourages me to choose joy.
- In His presence is fullness of joy.
- The joy of the Lord is my strength.
- I have felt/known God's deep love for me.
- The testing of faith has produced patience.
- Many of His promises are yet to be fulfilled.
- He has heard my cries!
- He has heard many prayer warriors' cries!
- Jesus is interceding on my behalf.
- I have had a wonderful time with my best friend, getting to know Him.
- The doctor and incident divine appointments encourage it.
- Insurance!
- Dana, my wonderful wife, has been taking care of me.
- I firmly believe that I will not be defeated.
- My kids are driving me to continue to lead.
- He is my Prince of Peace.

Here are some potential words of encouragement from the fantastic devotional *Jesus Calling*[116]:

"Trust me one day at a time. This keeps you close to Me and responsive to My will. Don't let your need to understand distract you from My Presence. Tomorrow is busy worrying about itself. Stop trying to understand. Seek me. Stay close to Me. Trust Me and don't be afraid. I am your strength. This is a time in your life when you must learn to let go.
Rest in My Presence."

"Trust me with every fiber of your being, instead of trying to figure things out for yourself. Waiting on Me is the way I designed you to live. I have promised blessing to those who wait on Me: renewed strength, living above one's circumstances, resurgence of hope, awareness of My continual
presence. In My Presence is fullness of joy. Be still in My presence.
Nothing is more important than spending time with Me. Do not seek Me
primarily for what I can give you. Stop trying to work things out before their time has come."

Warning: Don't gloss over the scriptures in this chapter if you are in a valley. They are life!

Love in the Valley

Know that He is God. He will bless you for waiting and persevering. Take the time to sense His love and presence. Turn off the noise. You can live above your circumstances. He is the source of strength, hope, and peace. The doctors might let you down. Other people will let you down. Your Heavenly Father, by contrast, will give you a resurgence of hope. You will be aware of His presence. Take some time to know how deep, how wide, how long, and how broad God's love is for you. Read Ephesians 3:14–21, and pray it aloud in your own words. It is a mystery to try to comprehend His love. He is your support, and He truly delights in you. Read Psalm 18:18–19. It is difficult to understand His love, especially with our guilt trips, sin, and performance mentality. But rest with Him, and ask Him to show you that love. He will. Let Him be your peace, your love, and your hope. *Let go!* Rest in His presence.

God is pursuing you. Most people don't allow themselves to experience the full love of God. They don't feel His passion or love. In His presence is fullness of joy. We tend to think more about His judgment than His love. We tend to view God as angry or distant. Yes, He does judge and discipline, but He also loves deeply (Psa. 149:4; 16:11). We guard our hearts and our spirits because humans have failed us. If Jesus is the bridegroom who is soon to return and we are His bride, how much does a bridegroom love His bride? We are His prize, and our success and value are not based on our level of performance or production, our financial success, our talent, or our standing in the community. He desires an intimate relationship with you. The bridegroom desires the bride's time. Instead of trying harder, enjoy God more. That is a lifestyle of being in the Word, praying the Word, and just having candid, honest talks with God. [117]

He is big enough. Be of good courage. Read Jeremiah 29:11–13. His ways are much higher than our ways. He has a future for you. He hears you. Call upon Him. Receive His hope. Seek Him with everything you have. Give Him your time. Give Him your worry. Give Him your mind. Three steps come to mind for living in the Valley.

1) Abide in His Presence (John 15; Psa. 132:1–5).
2) Use the trial to know God and help others (Psa. 119:71; 2 Corinthians 1:3–7; 4:17).
3) Choose joy (James 1:2; John 15:11).

Stop and talk to God. Read and pray these scriptures to God. Have an honest talk with Him.

Embrace the Season

You might be in a season of trial or tribulation. Do not waste the season. There is no wasted time in God's seasons if your heart and mind is set on His will. Trust the season. Seek Him fully during the season. Know Him through His Word. Trust Him. Seek out how you can grow and mature through this process. Get to really know Christ and how this suffering is actually a fellowship of sharing in *His* sufferings. Ask God for help in doing that. No one wants to live in the valley. Be patient. Do not worry. Be of good cheer. Embracing the season is a recipe for hope! You might feel like you are stuck in traffic and cannot move. Find the good things to appreciate during that stuck time. Think generationally, yet live one day at a time.

Blessings in the Valley

I have had unexpected sources of blessing through the valley, simply because I reached out and humbled myself and asked for prayer. If you are dying of thirst in the valley, you seek out those who can bring water. Others will also somehow find you and bring you water in your desert. A boss, co-workers, or a church group might band together to support you. Figure out how you can "deny yourself" and minister to others while you are in your valley instead of that quick prayer. Look and pray for opportunities; there are plenty. Out of the blue, an individual whom I barely knew wrote me a letter of encouragement and sent me a book called *Jesus Calling*. That little devotional book has been a lifeline for me. Little did I know that she was going through the deepest valley of her own life. Yet she found a way where God could use her and comforted someone else in a valley. (See 2 Corinthians 1:3–7.)

I now fully appreciate things that I had taken for granted before: the chirping birds, the warm sunshine, clear hearing, a normal heartbeat, a good night's sleep, and a normal meal digested. Sometimes blessings can come in the form of pain, trouble, or persecution.

Comfort, Peace, and Hope in the Valley

"Peace is my continual gift to you. It flows abundantly from My throne of grace. Just as the Israelites could not store up manna for the future, but had to gather it daily, so it is with My Peace. The day by day collecting of manna kept My people aware of their dependence on me. I am training you to set your mind on me more and more[118]."

The beautiful thing about God's love for us is that it is unconditional. He loves you despite your performance or goodness. He loves you with an everlasting love. Your finite human mind cannot comprehend the depth of His love for you. It is a mystery. He wants to love you fully. Let Him. I recall holding our new baby for hours. As a father, I delighted in the presence of my child. I couldn't articulate the feelings of love and joy because they ran so deep. Sometimes we focus on what we as His children get out of His love. Think about how much *He* enjoys the time we spend with Him. How much more does God love you? Picture His holding you in His arms. Even when a baby is spitting, crying, and pooping, we love them. The same is true of God's love. It is a two-way relationship that He enjoys. Confirm it in the Word.

- *He loves you. He builds you. He draws you (Jer. 31:3).*
- *He rejoices over you with singing (Zeph. 3:17).*
- *Rejoice in Him. Be joyful in Him (Isa. 61:10).*
- *Give thanks to the Lord for His goodness (Psa. 107:8).*
- *Be patient. Count it all joy (James 1:2–4).*

 "Never Once"—Matt Redman

Comfort from God's Word

Wait on the Lord, be of good courage,
and He shall strengthen your heart (Psa. 27:14).
My soul trusts in You; And in the shadow of your wings
I will make my refuge,
until these calamities have passed by (Psa. 57:1).
Rest in the Lord and wait patiently for Him.
The salvation of the righteous is from the Lord.
He is their strength in the time of trouble.
And the Lord shall help them
and deliver them (Psa. 37:7, 39-40).
Let not your heart be troubled, neither let it be afraid (John 14:27).
He Himself is our peace (Eph. 2:14).
In Me you may have peace. In the world you will have tribulation,
but be of good cheer, I have overcome the world (John 16:33).
The peace of God which surpasses all understanding will guard
your hearts and minds through Christ Jesus (Phil. 4:7).
The angel of the Lord encamps around those
who fear Him and delivers them (Psa. 34:7).
Ministering spirits sent forth to minister
for those who will inherit salvation (Heb. 1:14).
Call upon me in the day of trouble
and I will deliver you and you will glorify Me
(Psa. 50:15).
Lord my God I cried out to you and healed me (Psa. 30:2).
Behold, I am with you and will keep you wherever you go. I will not leave you
until I have done what I have spoken to you (Gen. 28:15).

Worry

You may have many justifiable reasons to worry or be discouraged in your life. Many people have found that money, health, lifestyle, relationships and career can bring happiness, but they can also bring worry or extraordinary concern! Even our families and friendships can bring an unhealthy worry to our lives. A recent survey[119] discovered that we worry about a lot of things! Here are the top ones:

- Finances	62%
- Appearance/weight	56%
- Health	55%
- Children	42%

- Lifestyle	40%
- Self-esteem	35%
- Job	34%
- Marriage	31%
- Friendships	27%

Worry not only leads to health problems, relationship turmoil and stress but also provides no solutions, no action plans, and no peace for the future. Pursuit of peace and an action plan for almost all of the items on this list should be one of your key objectives in reading this book.

"My grace is sufficient for you, for my power is made perfect in weakness." Therefore I will boast all the more gladly about my weaknesses, so that Christ's power may rest on me. That is why, for Christ's sake, I delight in weaknesses, in insults, in hardships, in persecutions, in difficulties. For when I am weak, then I am strong.
-2 Corinthians 12:9-10

Read and meditate upon the following scriptures: Matthew 6:25–34 and Philippians 4:4–8, which give you some peace about your worry!

Worry Anecdote

- ❖ Good can come out of bad. I have been through a lot with my health problems over the years. It has driven me to worry often and forced me to trust God. Out of these times have come some monumental generational things. They were not wasted seasons. (See Galatians 4:13–15)
- ❖ Realize that you are growing through these circumstances. Your trials and stress are producing perseverance, character, and hope. (See Romans 5:3–5)
- ❖ Know that sufferings are only for a season. Get hope in knowing that the Spirit is praying for you! (See Romans 8:18, 26, 28, 31, 34)
- ❖ Get God's peace. Let Christ be your peace (John 14:27, Ephesians 2:14)
- ❖ Be of good cheer. It is the best medicine (John 16:33, Proverbs 17:22)
- ❖ Pray instead of worry. (See Philippians 4:6–8)
- ❖ Be still and know that I am God. (See Psalm 46:10)
- ❖ Let God quiet you with His love (Zephaniah 3:17)
- ❖ Let Him give you rest and sleep (Psalm 127:2)
- ❖ Find out who cares (1 Peter 5:6–7)
- ❖ Do not be afraid (Deuteronomy 31:6)
- ❖ Let God help you (Psalm 46:1)
- ❖ God is your rock; let Him deliver you (Psalm 91:2–6)
- ❖ Know that trials are building your character (James 1:1–3)
- ❖ The trials are temporary (2 Corinthians 4:16-17)
- ❖ You are in good company (1 Peter 4:12)

Because of the LORD's great love we are not consumed, for his compassions never fail. They are new every morning; great is your faithfulness. I say to myself, "The LORD is my portion; therefore I will wait for him." The LORD is good to those whose hope is in him, to the one who seeks him; it is good to wait quietly for the salvation of the LORD.
-Lamentations 3:22-26

 Stop and talk to God. Meditate on and memorize His words of love for you!

*"Some say if only my fears and doubts will leave
then I will get to work. But instead you should get to work
and then your fears and doubts will leave."*
- Dwight L. Moody

Legacy Lesson: Turn to God to be your anchor of peace and hope. Trust and lean on Him. Wait on the Lord. He will strengthen you and give you courage!

****

A Generational Mindset

For updated resources and more information you may access
www.futurefoundationbuilders.com.

As we close the "Future" section, I wanted to include a few Life Lesson Batons for a meaningful, successful life.

I polled my Facebook friends[120] and asked them to share their most significant "Life Lesson Batons." Here are a few wisdom nuggets:

1) "Make some decisions ONCE: We decided ONCE that we would go to church every Sunday. It was not a weekly decision. Some things you just WILL do."
2) "Only one life will pass; only what's done for Christ will last. Keep God as the central focus in your life and He will take care of everything else"
3) "Do not rush in to quick decisions. Don't make a decision and then ask God to bless your decision. Talk to Him (prayer and Word) and talk to others and ask God to direct you step by step. Trust His answer and His timing."
4) "God will provide."
5) "Don't compare yourself with others—negative or positive. God makes each of us special and unique. He doesn't make any junk. He will use each individual in His way and in His place."
6) "Start a budget. Use a budget."

7) "Cherish each moment living for kids and marriage, instead of acting invincible to time."

8) "Love who you are even with your flaws."

9) "Pursue God with all that you are and have. Everything else will be taken care of."

10) "Hang around people who make you want to become a better person."

11) "Only consider marriage if you are equally yoked! Your beliefs are so important! Take time together to pray about life decisions."

12) "Have a good savings account set aside before you marry. . .money causes most fights in your marriage!!!!"

13) "Spend time with God daily."

14) "We are never too old or young to learn."

15) "Never, never, go to bed angry with one another."

16) "God made us to be with people. . .trust people and build true raw relationships."

17) "I would have stayed more involved in the positive things in life—exercising, church, nature."

18) "Never duel a Sicilian when death is on the line." (There's always a smart aleck on FB. Thanks, Andy.)

Heavy stuff. I see a generational mindset. I hear themes of authenticity, priorities, love, and relationships—with both God and those around us. When we take action on these life lessons, we not only address our personal yearning for a fulfilling, purposeful life but also our actions influence generations to come. Solomon summarized it in the book of Ecclesiastes. Solomon had tried it all, nothing seemed to satisfy. He tried gratifying himself with wine, he worked hard, he built great houses and had wonderful vineyards. He had servants and greater possessions than anyone then or before him. He was rich beyond dream. He had great wisdom. He had anything he desired, yet all was "grasping for the wind."[121] Our possessions are only temporal. We all have two certainties: birth and death. We will return to dust and take nothing with us. Our years are precious, so my prayer is that you don't waste the ones you have left. Impact your future and future generations now!

> *"One generation passes away and another generation comes."*
> —Ecclesiastes 1:4

> *"Your PAST has been forgiven, your PRESENT has purpose*
> *and your FUTURE is Certain."*
> —John Mark Caton

PART 2

YOUR FAMILY

CHAPTER 17

FAMILY FIRST

The strength of a nation lies in the homes of its people.
—Abraham Lincoln

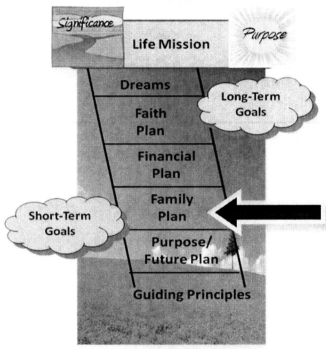

$\mathcal{O}$ur country is at a crossroads. Our churches and communities are at a crossroads. Your family is at a crossroads. As we drive along the highway of life, most of us have passengers aboard. It is not enough just to check the rear-view mirror periodically or simply to keep our eyes on the road and drive the best we can. We must have a destination and then map the route to that destination.

We all have some regret when peering in the rear-view mirror. I believe "Family First" is a true destination goal for most parents. In a recent Radcliffe Public Policy Center study,[122] 82 percent of men ages 20–39 put family time at the top of their list, and 85 percent of women did the same. The survey showed that increasing numbers of young men want to take an active role in raising their children and seek a priority of a family-friendly work schedule. Obviously, gender roles have shifted over the generations, but 68 percent of those polled said they thought one parent should stay home during a child's early years. This is a positive leading indicator that parents want to focus on the family.

The younger Millennials would also agree. In a recent LifeWay Research survey,[123] when asked what's important in life, they say "family comes first, ahead of friends, education, careers, and even religion. Sixty-one percent of Millennials placed family at the top of their priority list." This positive trend could be the response from Boomers' children who saw their parents and an older generation having a great emphasis on work, career, and dual incomes. Thus, they might have experienced a scarcity in family time themselves. This is an encouraging report that the younger generations (Generation X and Generation Y) are refocusing on family.

However, for most of us the decision to make family a priority is merely the first and easiest step toward the destination. Our GPS or map might be old, ragged, or just nowhere to be found. Unfortunately, creating the map is not as simple as pushing a "Family First" button on the GPS. It is even more of a challenge if you had poor parenting or marriage examples in your own lives. It also might be difficult if your children are in their teenage years or have already left the nest. Do not be discouraged. There are plenty of "apps and maps" to help you out! First, let's peer in the rear-view mirror to see the generations that preceded us.

Family in the "Wild West"

Much has changed over the past generations regarding how to "do family" or how to plan for a secure future for your family. Some of that change is helpful and positive; other parts of it might leave us feeling like we are lost on a country road, low on gasoline, with no map in sight. According to Beatrice Gottrieb, author of the *The Family in the Western World*,[124] in past Western civilization history, multiple generations lived together under one roof, and some households contained nonrelatives. At least you had a lot of help raising the family! There was no commonly agreed-upon age for retirement, and employees did not get old-age pensions. Most houses were not very comfortable, and modern notions of comfort, such as spaciousness, privacy, and interior decoration were not normal. A house in the eighteenth and nineteenth centuries meant little more than four walls and a roof, with no division into rooms, and the entire house was the size of many modern living rooms. I guess we have it pretty good!

Even into the twentieth century, only the homes of the very wealthy had separate rooms for varied functions. Sharing a bed with a relative was normal. Most homes were made of wood, weren't very durable, and did not fully keep out the cold and wind. Extra layers of clothing were worn throughout winter. The "hearth" used for warmth and food preparation was a sign of wealth. Stone and brick were materials used by the well-to-do. Water had to be drawn from wells and was not available within the house. Plumbing was only for the very wealthy, and a toilet was a structure outside the house or, for the poor in the country, just a discreet hole in the ground.

Our modern homestead is strikingly different from that of earlier generations. Most people grew their own food, cut wood for fuel, and made their own tools and clothing. They preserved their own food, prepared beverages, and sewed and embroidered for themselves.

The staple food was bread, and meat was only for special occasions, Sundays, and holidays. Home was a place of work, the center of economic activity. The church doubled as an assembly hall and the village gathering place. Prayers, storytelling, and music were household activities. The man read from the Scriptures or recited a prayer in the presence of the assembled household.

After 1900, a stripping-away process began to occur, minimizing the intersections of family members and changing household life and activities greatly. The majority of the population shifted to cities and suburbs, and the household roles also changed. The family "unit" gave way to more individualistic lives, roles, and goals that resulted in a more fragile and splintered family. "Divorce is a very recent phenomenon and has contributed to an emphasis on individual satisfaction in marriage."[125]

Much has changed in family education as well. Regarding the mixture of home and school, "by the end of the 18th century, school was not yet a necessary part of every child's upbringing. Apprenticeship was at one time the model for learning every kind of skill."[126] Family relations were described as "patriarchal." The father filled the role of teacher and father. In our modern society, the man, and sometimes the woman, face a wrenching apart of work and home life. Now, the central activity of fatherhood is outside one's immediate home. Children have slowly moved from economic worker to spoiled consumer. Families must battle for time together as more and more isolation and independence prevails in work, in education, and in worship. A report from Massachusetts during colonial times declared that public funding of elementary schools was not desirable because "the office of instruction belongs to parents. Parents have opportunities to impart instructions, and to gain an influence over their children which the public teacher does not possess."

The Family in the Western World goes on to discuss an "inseparable mixture of literacy and religion. Schools taught religion. They learned reading, writing, arithmetic, and "above all, as the regulations stated, religion, and the fear of God." Family was the DNA of society. These days, social messages about family and family roles are mixed and confusing. Spousal, parental, and spiritual role models are few and far between. Much has changed in the wild, wild, West.

Dysfunctional Days?

The next time you are walking around town, shopping, or even at church, look around and note how rare it is to see a family sitting together, playing together, or walking together. I know there are exceptions: at the local restaurant, the park, Disney World, or other vacation spots. For a number of reasons, our families are splintered or divided. Much of this can certainly be attributed to the change in our societies over the years. Family farming and family businesses are out. Corporate ladders and divided classrooms are in. The one-room household unit is out. The "separate room, separate stuff" culture is in. Large, cohesive families are rare. The soccer mom and the disappearing dad are in. The family dinner and the family activity are out. We have become more inward and self-focused, and the thought of having "too many children" is an inconvenience that will detract from our wants, desires, and priorities for life. This is quite possibly a leading indicator for a decaying society. "As the birth rate fell from 4.0 to 2.0 during the 20th century, the average square footage of homes more than doubled."[127]

A person's value is measured in economic terms rather than in moral and relational terms. Our children are prepared for a life of independent success and salary instead of how their contributions can positively affect their society and even eternity. High schools and colleges are preparing kids for careers more than for life or family. Little emphasis is placed on godly relationships or character, and education and instruction is from strangers, who may or may not claim your values. You might not be able to affect educational institutions, but you can influence your family. The parents must be the ones to set a vision for their future in concrete. The hope is that portions of this vision will be adopted by our children and carried on for generations to come.

The transient world we live in has greatly affected our relationships. Integrated family units are becoming more and more scarce. Dysfunctional families are becoming more the norm. It is incumbent upon father and mother to re-institute a more structured, family-based unit. This is not easy, and those who try it will be swimming upstream against strong currents of the cultural norm. However, a small niche in our society is beginning a radical return to a more integrated family unit.

Family First

As parents, we must be sensitive to people and things that influence our children outside of our own homes. People who influence enter our children's world at a very young age in every area of life, from peers to church leaders to school and extracurricular activities leaders. Some are a good influence, others are not. Who is going to write the script for your child's life?

Influences that shape our kids are all around us. In addition to the genetics discussed earlier, their life experiences, family life, family values, social structure, community, culture, parenting approach, and spiritual influence will mold and shape them into the adults they will soon become (see the following illustration). In addition, as parents, how we handle boundaries, discipline, and conflict resolution will also have a great influence. (Later in this section we will develop a "Family Plan" that will be your GPS.)

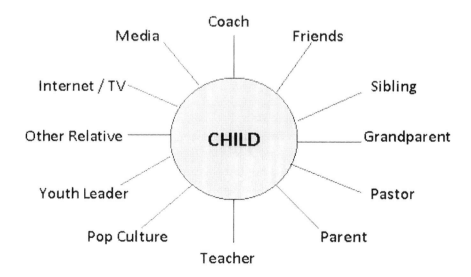

A Barrage of Influence

Obviously, whoever spends the most time with your children has the most opportunity to shape them. Not all socialization is good for that shaping. There is "positive social interaction—fertilizer" and "negative social interaction—muriatic acid." Is your child getting more fertilizer or more muriatic acid? In aggregate, the family unit has the most opportunity to influence and shape a child. Although it might not be an integrated family unit like it once was, we can return to a solid family unit once again. Parenting is one's highest, noblest calling. Likewise, a successful marriage can often lead to successful children, and successful marriages are hard to find. It is hard work and one of the hardest things to achieve in life.

The family unit is a powerful thing. An intact, traditional, worshipping family has a significant impact on our nation's future. Consider some statistics from the Marriage and Religion Research Institute.[128]

- Elementary school children from intact biological families earn higher reading and math test scores than children in cohabiting and divorced single and always-single parent families.
- High school students who live in intact married families have a higher average GPA in English and math than those in married stepfamilies, divorced families, or other families.
- More than 57 percent of children who live in intact biological families enter college compared to 33 percent in stepfamilies, 48 percent in single-parent families, and 32 percent for those children with no parent present.
- Eighty-five percent of adolescents in intact biological families graduate from high school compared to 67 percent in single-parent families, 65 percent in stepfamilies, and 52 percent who live with no parents.
- Children in intact married families are more likely to worship regularly.
- Adolescents who attend church regularly tend to complete more years of school.
- Intact married families are stronger economically.

Even if you are part of a broken or blended family, do not be dismayed. You, too, can have a strong family. It will take an intentional, purposeful effort on the parents' part, but it is possible! Find successful families to hang around with and model yourself after. Be wary of looking to Hollywood for values to mimic. It used to be that they would reflect somewhat the values of our society, but now the minority is trying to influence us all. Cameron Diaz, for example, says that the institution of marriage is dying. *"I think we have to make our own rules. I don't think we should live our lives in relationships based off old traditions that don't suit our world any longer."*[129]

Or look no further than the movie *Wedding Crashers*: "Guys, the real enemy here is the institution of marriage." The model families that Hollywood portrays as "normal" are *The Simpsons, Family Guy, Modern Family,* or *Desperate Housewives.* A far cry from *The Walton's, Eight is Enough, Ozzie and Harriet, Leave it to Beaver, Little House on the Prairie,* or *Cosby.*

Hollywood not only degrades and mocks traditional marriage and biblical family roles but also promotes sexual promiscuity, alternative lifestyles, infidelity, weak men, and promiscuous women, and rarely promotes positive moral values or demonstrates Christianity in a positive light. This, however, is not an "American" problem. It is a societal problem and a family problem. It is a problem for Christian families as well as those who are not believers. The statistics are stunning in that nine out of ten children leave the church when they leave home, and we will explore more why that is, why it should be of concern, and how to fix it.

What actions can you take to put Family First and better influence your children?

Already Gone?

England was once the cornerstone of Christianity in the West. The Protestant Reformation spread westward from the Continent and England. Today, the £10 currency and the £2 coin depict Charles Darwin. Darwin was honored by being buried in the floor of the Westminster Abbey. The man who developed evolutionary theory is celebrated on the pound and buried where the King James Version of the Bible was translated. "In a recent English church census, only 2.5% are attending Bible-based churches. Since 1969, 1500 churches in England have heard that final thud as their doors were shut after their final service after hundreds of years of active life. Former places of worship have been turned into museums, restaurants, offices, cottages, clothing stores, music stores, liquor stores, nightclubs, rock climbing centers, theaters, mosques, and tattoo and piercing studios.[130]"

Is this scene coming to America soon? It might already be here. According to George Barna, "61% of today's young adults had been churched at one point during their teen years but they are now spiritually disengaged"[131] and only about 6% of people in their 20s and 30s can be considered "evangelical." In *Already Gone*, Ken Ham and Britt Beemer cite statistics and surveys that show a mass exodus is underway. Most youth of today will not be coming to church tomorrow. The next generation is calling it quits on the traditional church.

As parents and spouses, it is time to stand up and be counted; roll up your sleeves and take action! A lack of a map (family goals) or a lack of gasoline (family time) is normal. That does not excuse us. It just shows us that we need a better plan. I recall being a new husband and new dad and realizing how clueless and confused I was. I knew that I was at a crossroads, but I didn't know where to turn. I feverishly began to read books about family, attended classes, and learned and educated myself as much as possible. I began to create my own family destination. I made many wrong turns, ran out of gas a few times, and failed often, but I dusted myself off and moved forward. The good news was that I wasn't driving alone. My wife was my passenger on this journey called "Family."

Who is your family modeling? Do you have a family roadmap? Which way will you turn at the crossroads?

"Example is not the main thing in influencing others. It is the only thing."
—Albert Schweitzer

Legacy Lesson: Our families are at a crossroads. Who will be the main influencer in your children and grandchildren's lives? All families struggle. All parents fail. Now is the time to make some changes in your roadmap.

CHAPTER 18

ELEGANT DECAY: A CRISIS AT THE CROSSROADS

"No church, community, or nation will rise higher
than the spiritual condition of its families."
—Dennis Rainey

*N*ations rise and nations fall. The United States of America has been on the center stage of world economics and strong moral values for centuries. However, history shows us glimpses of influential societies that were soon replaced by others. The state of decline in our society is evident. You can feel it, sense it, and hear it daily just by picking up a paper, flipping on the television, or browsing the internet. Our moral and social structures are decaying.

I recall our first international trip with the family in 2009. It took much sacrifice, saving and planning to pull off a trip to Europe. It was surreal to walk the historic streets and sites of Rome and visit the once thriving Venice and in parallel to study the rise and fall of the great societies of the past. These falls did not happen overnight. Just as tooth decay sets in, it often takes years to see the results of that hard candy or the lack of discipline in brushing or flossing the teeth.

Although I am not a doom-and-gloomer, our nation is no longer on the rise—economically nor morally. It can rise once again, but the evidence of decay cannot be brushed aside. The statistics are simply numbers but they are ever increasing evidence of this decay. The results of this decay are already affecting our children, and future generations will suffer even more if we don't start that root canal on our own families or, at a minimum, start or revive a few habits of spiritual discipline in ourselves. Often, we rely on other influencers, including the church, to do what God designed the family to do.

Detailing "The Fall"

Obviously, the reasons for the decline of the Roman Empire have been analyzed and debated for centuries, but Pitirim A. Sorokin of Harvard University cited that "the growth of sexual anarchy, divorces, the masculinization of women, the effemination of men, and the decrease in birth rate" were increasingly evident in Roman society and law. The lack of a strong, cohesive, and spiritual family unit was evident.

A spiritual family is the foundation for a strong society. All of the spiritual, civil, economic, political, and social roots for the West have been in the family. Some common patterns have been evident in societies in decline in many nations. The patterns in ancient Greece, the Roman Republic and now America have some common threads according to Carl W. Wilson in *Our Dance Has Turned to Death.*[132]

1. Men ceased to lead their family in worship. Spiritual and moral development became secondary.
2. Men selfishly neglected care of their wives and children to pursue material wealth, political and military power, and cultural development. Material values began to dominate thought.
3. Men, being preoccupied with business or war, either neglected their wives sexually or became involved with homosexuality.
4. The role of women at home and with children lost value and status. Laws regulating marriage made divorce easy.
5. Husbands and wives competed against each other for money, home leadership, and the affection of their children. Many marriages ended in separation or divorce.
6. Selfish individualism grew and was carried over into society. The nation was weakened by internal conflict. The decrease in the birthrate produced an older population.
7. An unbelief in God became more complete. Parental authority diminished. Ethical and moral principles disappeared, affecting the economy and government.

I see a theme of selfishness and a departure from God's roadmap. Sounds a little like the fall of Adam and Eve. Is the same decline occurring in modern day Europe and America? Are we in surgery, in the intensive care unit, or in the recovery room?

> *"Blessed is the nation whose God is the Lord."*
> —Psalm 33:12

In Recovery or in ICU?

Although I think most of us "feel" and "see" the decline, I think it is necessary to look at historical precedence as well as statistical evidence to assess our condition. The results of my research did not make me feel that we were out of Intensive Care. "British anthropologist J.D. Unwin studied 80 societies, analyzing their cultural beliefs and practices, especially as related to sex and marriage."[133] He included primitive societies, societies of his own time, and ancient cultures, including Babylonians, Greeks, Romans, and others. He looked at the "cultural condition" of those societies, and one strong piece of evidence he cited was that "absolutely monogamous cultures were the strongest." However, "when a people began to transgress its own moral codes—when sexual opportunity began to be extended in both pre-marital and extra-marital sexual freedom, across the board—such cultures began to decay."[134]

In the *American Sex Revolution*[135], Pitirim A. Sorokin examined this subject as well. He noted that the greater society's debauchery, the graver the consequences were for the entire society. Again, a common theme of self-focus and self-gratification were evident. "Sorokin stated that in the decline of ancient Egypt, sexual anarchy spread through a large part of the population." One historian said that homosexual love entered the morals and manners of the population at the time of this Egyptian decline. In 5th century Athens, old customs had disappeared and divorce became easy and common, homosexual relationships, and affairs became more common and three generations later, this once vigorous city was subject to a foreign master.

> *"When a society gives way to a sensuous culture, when it distorts the male and female roles and indulges in sexual anarchy, it is nearing collapse."*
> —Harvard sociologist Pitirim Sorokin

The 1950s brought the sexual revolution that has had a major impact on our culture. Traditional marriage and family began to suffer, and that slippery slope continues to steepen. On June 25, 1962, the Supreme Court ruled that the following simple official New York public school prayer was **unconstitutional**:

> *"Almighty God, we acknowledge our dependence on thee and beg thy blessing over us, our parents, our teachers, and our country."*

Secular humanism began to permeate college campuses in the 1960s and 1970s. Women were seeking the "right" to abort pregnancies, and homosexual groups were demanding employment and housing "rights." The ACLU began taking aggressive stances; evolutionary teachings became bolder; and Planned Parenthood's role in condom distribution, sex education, and abortion counseling took a more prominent place in education. In 1973, the Supreme Court legalized abortion.

David Barton did an excellent study in *America: To Pray or Not to Pray.*[136] Barton's research shows that some remarkable things have happened as a result of the Supreme Court ruling to ban prayer in 1962. Massive cultural change has followed since that decision to remove the acknowledgement of God from our classrooms. That change has been to America's detriment. The resulting cultural changes during just one generation have indeed been startling. I have combined seven graphs into one graph depicting the results. No Y axis is detailed because each of the items has a different measurement. Dr. Donald R. Howard, founder and president of Accelerated Christian Education and author of *Crisis in Education*, also provides a thorough commentary on the moral decay as a result of this and other factors. The black line indicates June, 1962 when prayer was removed from our public schools. The trends speak clearly for themselves.

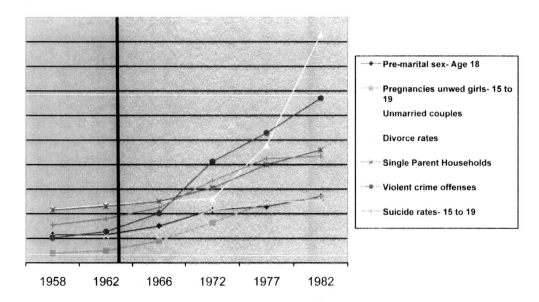

Data from *America: To Pray or Not to Pray* by David Barton

Is it a coincidence that nearly all of the vital statistics, including crime, out-of-wedlock births, welfare dependency, divorce, abortion, cohabitation, and pornography have climbed dramatically since we took God out of the classroom?

 "America Again," Carman

Erosion Explosion

The family structure is eroding, and that is leading to an insecure social and financial future for the next generation. More and more childbirths are occurring outside of a normal marriage. According to the U.S. Department of Health and Human Services,[137] nearly 4 in 10 U.S. births were to unmarried women in 2007. This percentage has increased nearly ten-fold, from only 4 percent in 1940 to 40 percent in 2007. This has doubled over just *one* generation, from 18 percent in 1980 to 40 percent in 2007. These statistics are not unique to the United States; we are in the middle of the pack, and the worldwide trend is even more alarming.

- Sixty-six percent of all births in Iceland are to unmarried women.
- Fifty percent of all births in France are to unmarried women, up from 11 percent in 1980.
- A stunning 86 percent of births to United States teenagers are nonmarital.

According to the United Kingdom Office for National Statistics[138], trends are similar to those in the United States. "Increasingly couples may have a child together prior to marrying," and cohabitation before marriage is also a trend. Of the approximate 600,000 births per year in England and Wales in 1941, less than 50,000, or approximately 7 percent of births, occurred outside of marriage. In 2000, approximately one-third of births, 200,000 of the 600,000 annual births, occurred outside of marriage in England and Wales.

Who's Your Daddy?

I watched in stunned amazement as Dr. Walter Williams, an African-American professor at George Mason University, made a compelling case as to the troubling trends in black families in America.[139]Although this is not strictly a black or white issue, Williams based his conclusions on facts. "Today, just slightly over 30 percent of black kids live in two-parent families. Historically, from the 1870s on up to about the 1940s, and depending on the city, 75 to 90 percent of black kids lived in two-parent families. The illegitimacy rate is 70% among blacks where that is unprecedented in history. This is also seen in European welfare states as well. "Illegitimacy in Sweden is 54%."

I recall serving in an inner-city ministry, Dallas Metro Ministries, and rarely seeing a father in the housing project household. The child and family suffer with no father present. Williams states that "the government has said to many young women, 'I am the father.' That is a heck of a start in life, to be born—you don't know who or where your father is." What a shame—*for the child*, who is missing out on the love, care, provision, and discipline of a father, and *for the father*, who has gratified selfish desires and passed the baton of marriage and parenting to the government. Williams went on to state a compelling case about programs that are designed to help the poor, "like welfare payments, have wrecked the lives of millions of black people." He likened the welfare state to a drug pusher that keeps people dependent and in poverty.

John Stossel's interview[140] gave compelling evidence that government aid is hurting families, not helping them. Government has spent "trillions of dollars on poverty programs, and the poverty level stayed stuck at about 12 percent of the population. It's stayed there for about 40 years."

The welfare system discourages marriage, and discourages parents from getting a job. Although government intentions were good, it is causing and feeding behaviors that are creating dysfunctional families, not to mention government debt we cannot afford.

Fatherless?

The facts[141] stated in this interview were so stunning and compelling that I needed to do my own "fact check" on them, and I wanted to see if this was affecting *all* families (black, white, brown, etc.) as significantly as stated. Sure enough. "Daddy DC" is a reality.

	Number Live Births	Number Illegitimate	% Illegitimate
1917	2,944,000	20,464	1%
1947	3,817,000	98,677	3%
1972	3,258,411	403,200	12%
2008	4,247,694	1,726,566	41%

We have gone from 1 percent to 41 percent of children born outside of marriage in less than a century! In fact, just as this book was going to press, the latest statistics showed that for the first time *more than half* of mothers under 30 are unmarried. It used to be called illegitimacy, now it is the new normal."[142] The specific causes and effects are always up for debate; once again, however, the data validate both the slipping morals of our society and a radical change in how children were raised in the last one or two generations. The traditional family approach is disappearing.

Many governments around the world are now feeling the need to take on the role of Daddy, of provider, with programs and money that are not fixing the heart of the problem— a man's heart. What is going on in the home is the leading indicator. Government's trying to fix the problem is a lagging indicator. The heart of the matter is a sinful, selfish heart. That is what needs fixing more than a financial program.

Warning: PG-13/R-Rated Material

Our moral barriers continue to erode. For those of you who are into words more than numbers, grab your iPod or just read the very simple lyrical content below. It illustrates this erosion. American Family Association[143] did a brief lyrical comparison of the moral barriers that continue to get broken down by decade. One area in which this is true is our music. Here is a sampling of some of the racy lyrics that have broken down barriers in our society:

- 1964—*I Wanna Hold Your Hand,* The Beatles—the lyrics suggested a new "physical aggressiveness" without emotional commitment.
- 1967—*Let's Spend the Night Together,* The Rolling Stones—this song was such a major leap that Ed Sullivan made them change the lyrics to "Let's spend some time together." "*I would know you'll satisfy me. I'll satisfy your every need.*" This launched the onslaught of suggestive songs, but it still seems so tame compared to this century.
- 1976—*Tonight's the Night,* Rod Stewart—A song about giving up virginity was now acceptable. "*Draw the blind. Loosen up that gown. Don't deny your man's desire. Spread your wings and let me come inside. Don't say a word my virgin child.*"
- 1981—*Let's Get Physical,* Olivia Newton John—The girl next door could now be as aggressive and physical as any man could. Another barrier broken down. "*Nothing left to talk about unless it's horizontally. You bring out the animal in me.*"
- 1987—*I Want Your Sex,* George Michael—All forms of subtlety have now been dropped. Later, George Michael admitted his homosexuality: "*I don't need no Bible, just look in my eyes. . . . I want your Sex.*" I will spare you more details.
- 1991—*I Wanna Sex You Up,* Color Me Badd—"*We can do it til we both wake up. . .let me take off all your clothes. . .lay back and enjoy the ride*". . . .
- 1994—*Closer-* Nine Inch Nails—"*I wanna fxxx you like an animal. Let me violate you. Let me desecrate you. Let me penetrate you. I've got no soul to sell. You get me closer to god.*"
- 1998- *Tonight's the Night,* Janet Jackson-—First popular song about lesbian sex. I will spare you the lyrics.
- 2000's- *I Kissed a Girl-* Katy Perry, Pastor's daughter, sang in local church growing up, married a Hindu "*I kissed a girl and I like it. It felt so wrong. It felt so right.*"

- 2010's- *Every Girl In the World*- Lil Wayne- *"I wish I could fxxx every girl in the world. . .open up her legs. . . .that pxxxx. . . .I got that dxxx".* . . .

I have more depressing examples than these, but one thing is blatantly obvious: We have spiraled a long way in one or two generations—and we are still spiraling. Just ask your kids. If this doesn't sadden you or cause your heart to ache, you need an EKG!

Eye Candy

Pornography is now brought into almost half of all homes via the internet. There are more than 4.2 million pornographic websites and more than 100,000 websites offering child porn. "The Grecian government just expanded their state-recognized disability categories to include pedophiles. Pedophiles are now awarded a higher government disability pay than some people who have received organ transplants."[144]

Porn is a world-wide problem, but the United States is leading the way in polluting our world as the #1 producer of pornography around the world.[145]

- U.S. porn revenue exceeds the combined revenues of ABC, CBS, and NBC.
- U.S. porn revenue exceeds the combined revenues of the NFL, NBA, and MLB.
- The U.S. has 244,661,900 porn web pages. This is 89 percent of the world's porn web pages.
- The U.S. releases about 13,000 new hardcore porn titles a year. This has grown by ten times since 1988 and is twenty times more releases than normal movie titles each year.
- U.S. adult video sales have doubled in the last thirteen years, now at $3.6 billion a year.
- Ninety percent of 8- to 16-year-olds have viewed porn.
- Forty-seven percent of Christians said porn is a problem in the home.

STOP How much of the decay and pollution (music, porn, movies, shows) is allowed into your household via TV, internet, or iPOD? Do you need to make some changes? Set some boundaries? Get some filtering software? Get some help? Stop the erosion in your home now.

Fatness

Another symptom of the erosion is something we are all guilty of—a focus individually and corporately on self. We have an *inward* focus. Selfishness. Whether it be in our marriages, with an imbalanced emphasis on recreation and entertainment, or a money- and power-focused life, we are a self-focused and success-driven society.

"When success is achieved in a culture, the process of outward expansion can begin to wane. The fruits are enjoyed, and now more energy is expended inwardly on self-gratification, and the culture becomes self-centered and weak"
- Ed Vitagliano

In many cases, we are living lives of fatness and luxury. We have a pleasure-seeking, entertainment, spectator culture. Neil Postman wrote about this in *Amusing Ourselves to Death*. I often wonder as I drive by some of our materialistic monuments to self if one day our giant shopping malls, athletic stadia, and government buildings will be toured like the Roman Coliseum and Doge's Palace in Venice are today—museums of emptiness, monuments of self-gratification and fatness, proof of decay from years gone by.

The Fate of an Empire

We learn from our past experiences or our family's experiences. As this book has detailed, sometimes we learn and act. Sometimes we don't. Solomon said there is "nothing new under the sun". As a human race, patterns tend to be repeated, and the history of the human race has been documented for all to see. Unfortunately, most of the time we don't think generationally and only look to our own nations history. Sir John Glubb, born in 1897, grew up in England and Switzerland. He did an exhaustive study on the rise and fall of empires, those countries that were a great power or superpower. The average empire has a period of ~ 250 years of national great and worldwide influence. This average has not varied for 3000+ years. Normally an empire had a gradual period of expansion and then a period of decline. It was also the norm that great nations would fall due to "internal reasons".

In his paper called "*The Fate of Empires and Search for Survival*" John Glubb discusses the decline of courage and a sense of duty during its final stages of intellect and decadence. He talks of wealth injuring a nation morally. Ambition and pursuits are focused on wealth and academic acquisition for the sake of riches rather than honor and service. He shows the rise of frequent frivolity and pursuit of entertainment and athletic events. We have more than 1 Roman Coliseum. We have a handful it seems for most major cities! He mentions the hero's of a declining nation being athletes, singers, and actors. You don't find too many celebrities that hold public office, are statesmen, generals, or authors. History also suggests that a "welfare state" is another key milestone in a decrepit empire.

Have we had too much wealth and power for too long? Do we take it for granted and not attribute it to God anymore? Are we suffering from moral disease and entertainment/idleness overload?

"I sought for the greatness and genius of America in her harbors and her ample rivers, and it was not there; in her fertile fields and boundless prairies, and it was not there; in her rich mines and her vast world commerce, and it was not there. Not until I went to the churches of America and heard her pulpits aflame with righteousness did I understand the secret of her genius and power. America is great because she is good, and if America ever ceases to be good, America will cease to be great."
—Alexis de Tocqueville, French historian, in *Democracy in America*, 1835

Legacy Lesson: Our decay can only be reversed if the spiritual condition of a family is reversed. Lead your spouse. Lead your children. Lead by example. Your self sacrifice will impact a nation and generations to come.

CHAPTER 19

FAMILY MATTERS: THE HEART OF THE MATTER

"No nation has ever been more clearly born in the womb of providence and grown to such great beauty, strength and prosperity as the United States of America."[146] Seventeen of the first eighteen universities and colleges were founded by a church or a church and the state combined, and 85 percent of our institutions of higher education were still guided by the light of Christian philosophy until after the Civil War.

The wealth of America transcends that of any other place or time in history. Yet, we have taken that for granted and no longer give God glory for those blessings. We have shared our wealth with others. In fact, the Marshall Plan helped Europe to rebuild after World War II. We have helped free people and countries from evil leaders numerous times since World War II. Our gifts and loans have helped many poor nations over the centuries. Christian missionaries have taken the Christian truth around the world. Our nation has enjoyed more freedom than any other country on earth. Our coins bear the official motto "In God We Trust." We have a strong Christian foundation as a country for which we should be grateful.

- On July 12, 1775, Congress said that "taking cognizance of the critical, alarming, and calamitous state of these colonies," it is resolved that day of "public humiliation, *fasting and prayer*, be observed by the inhabitants of all the English colonies on this continent. . . that we may *confess and deplore our many sins*, humbly beseeching Him to forgive our iniquities."
- In 1782, the U.S. Congress passed a resolution by which it "*recommends and approves the Holy Bible for use in all schools.*"
- In 1784, President George Washington proclaimed "*a day of public thanksgiving and prayer to the great ruler of nations.*"

Abraham Lincoln proclaimed a day of fasting. Imagine a public leader doing that today! Our country is sick with a cancer of sin and a hardness and pride of a self-sufficient heart. Stable and strong families are an endangered species. As our social fabric unravels, we continue to pursue wealth and chase materialism, and are selfish and rights-focused.

143

There is a dearth of strong Christian leaders—the Elijah's, the David's, the Paul's. We are unrepentant as a nation and as families.

The founding fathers had a strong commitment to God, and worship was centered in the home. The Great Awakening led to a revival of repentance and church membership. Today, much of the church is trying to fill a void left in the home. The Sunday school and youth groups are trying to shore up sinking sand and have also given fathers another excuse to shirk their responsibility to teach and train their children. These church programs should augment and compliment, not replace, spiritual leadership in the home. Men have been preoccupied with providing and moneymaking. This is a matter of personal responsibility.

> *"**YOU** shall teach them diligently to your children, and shall talk of them when you sit in your house, when you walk by the way, when you lie down, and when you rise up."*
> —Deuteronomy 6:7 (emphasis added)

A Shift

Note, it is not the church, the youth pastor, the sociology professor, the English teacher, or Uncle Sam. It is you and I who are to instruct our kids—and we are to do it *often!*

The problems we face are not political problems. Our recent leadership in Washington, D.C., is simply reflecting our transition to a secular society. Just as the Israelites rejected God and requested a king "like other nations,"[147] so are elections a reflection of the hearts of the people. God will "heed the voice of the people" on some occasions. The shift has occurred not with one president or one political party but rather gradually over generations. That was not the intentions of the founding fathers.

> *"You do well to wish to learn our arts and our ways of life **and above all, the religion of Jesus Christ**. These will make you a greater and happier people than you are. Congress will do everything they can to assist you in this wise intention."*[148]
> —George Washington, speech to the Delaware Indian Chiefs,
> May 12, 1779

> *"It is impossible to rightly govern the world without **God and the Bible**."*
> —George Washington

> *"The Declaration of Independence laid the cornerstone of human government upon the first precepts of **Christianity**."*
> —President John Adams, First Vice President,
> Signer of the Declaration of Independence,
> Signer of the Bill of Rights, and Signer of First Amendment

> *We recognize no sovereign but God, and **no King but Jesus**.*
> —John Adams and John Hancock

It cannot be emphasized too strongly or too often that this great Nation was founded not by religionists, but by **Christians;** *not on religions, but on the* **Gospel of Jesus Christ.**
—Patrick Henry

"Whatever we once were, **we are no longer just a Christian nation***; we are also a Jewish nation, a Muslim nation, a Buddhist nation, a Hindu nation, and a nation of nonbelievers."*[149]
-—President Barack Obama

The shift has already happened; syncretism is upon us! However, there is a remnant of Christian parents in America and Europe and around the world that are not throwing in the towel. It is our job to train up children in the way they should go, so when they are old they will not depart from it.[150] We will not rely upon a government or a secular society to do our jobs! The heart of the matter rests with us as parents and grandparents.

Generational Giant

A woman named Susanna Wesley[151], born in 1669, in London, England, was the twenty-fourth child. At age 19, she married Samuel Wesley. They spent their nearly fifty years of marriage barely getting by financially. Middle-class women did not work outside the home then. She had more than a full-time job at home caring for her family. She managed the money, ran the household, and oversaw the farming. She had nineteen children, only ten of whom survived. Her most important task was to educate her ten children, for six hours daily, six days a week. She "devoted more than 20 years of the prime of her life in hopes to save the souls of their children." Her sacrifice, her self-denial, her laying down of her life, led to a multigenerational impact. One son, Charles Wesley, was one of the greatest hymn writers of all time. Another son, John, helped to shape England more than anyone in his generation, and his impact on Christianity is enormous.

Legacy Lesson: Teach and Train your children and grandchildren. Invest your time and money in them. Start with your family priorities. Your influence will multiply more than you know! Commit to the Lord whatever you do and He will establish your plans (Prov. 16:3)

CHAPTER 20

SHIFTING TIDES: A FAMILY REFORMATION

"Revival is God's invasion into the lives of one or more of His people in order to awaken them spiritually for kingdom ministry."
—Alvin L. Reid and Malcolm McDow

Can the decay be reversed? I address this question more in the fourth section of this book, but the simple answer is *yes*! However, the odds are against us. Past societies have "rarely succeeded in stopping the catastrophic drift, *however*, the key to success, seemed to lie with a small portion of the decaying society that stood firmly against the tide. . . a *minor part* of the population tends to become more religious, morally heroic, and restrained sexually in the periods of disorder and calamity."[152] It is up to us—the "few," not the government, and not the "visible many."

We must 'fess up to the decay. That doesn't make you a "doom-and-gloomer." It makes you a realist. However, instead of dwelling on it, we must seek a family reformation. A rebuilding. Rebuilding you. Rebuilding the family. Rebuilding the church. Rebuilding our government. Sorokin warned "most people and leaders of decaying societies were unaware of their cancerous sickness. They continued to live cheerfully in a fool's paradise. Their leaders attacked all honest appraisals of the situations, and called them false prophecies of doom and gloom."[153]

Will you be that hero for your family? Will you be that remnant? Will you begin to make a "second-half" impact now? You have the potential to be a game changer and a history maker. Stand firm. Rise up. Be a hero. Be salt and light. Start with your family.

Take two minutes and weigh the incredible importance and urgency of your role in this reformation.

1) Read Haggai 1:12-14 and 2 Chronicles 16:9. God is with you. Ask Him to stir you to action.

2) Read Jeremiah 42:1–3. Ask God, "Where should I go?" "What should I do?" Start with what is in front of you now; start with your family.

3) Read Amos 5:14–16. Perhaps God will relent—
if enough of His children respond.

4) Read Matthew 5:13–16. Be salt and light.

5) Sometime this week, pray and repent for our country. Use Daniel 9:3–19 as a model to help you with specifics.

The government will not reform our country, our morals, or our families. A focus on improving the statistics or funding more programs will not change our world. The influence on the next generation starts at home.

A national survey was conducted to determine the factors that most influenced teens in their faith.[154] The list of twenty-eight items included a wide range of significant influences, including coaches, camps, books, youth groups, movie stars, and friends.

> ➤ The most significant religious influence for teens today is **Mom**.
> ➤ The second most significant religious influence for teens today is **Dad**.
> ➤ The third most significant religious influence for teens was a **grandparent**, followed by friends and siblings.

The youth group leader, church school, and educational influences were way down the list. It starts at home. A reformation will occur one family at a time. Don't wait for the next Martin Luther or Billy Graham to revive the nation. You are it!

It is our responsibility as parents to give them these assets, traits, and opportunities. We must show them, impress them, and teach them. Search Institute's[155] survey results show that we aren't doing very well on the spiritual end of this.

- Teens that have a regular dialog with their *mother* on faith/life issues 12%
- Teens that have a regular dialog with their *father* on faith/life issues 5%
- Teens that experience a regular reading of the Bible and devotions at home 9%
- Youth that have experienced a service-oriented event with a parent 12%

Add up the time that someone has your child on an average week, then toss in sleep. It might end up looking something like this:

Church leaders/teachers	4 hours
Extracurricular teacher/coach	6–8 hours
Friends	8 hours
School teachers	40 hours
Home (Mom/Dad/family/self)	50 hours
Sleep	60 hours

Your influence is significant. Only sleep gets more attention! Who is developing your child's worldview? Be a hero to your child! There is no particular one correct style of parenting. I think of people who coach winners, and I see quite a different leadership style: Tom Landry, Tom Izzo, Billy Martin, Phil Jackson, Sparky Anderson. You are unique; let God use you.

 Read Psalm 78:1–8, Proverbs 22:6, and Deuteronomy 6:5–9.

 "Shade for the Children," Steve Camp

Teach your children by modeling, by demonstration. Leave footprints in the sand for your children. It is actually more like footprints in fresh cement. These imprints last much longer than those made in the sand. I like the quick summary of how to do this from *Dad the Family Mentor*[156] by Dave Simmons. It is based on a biblical method from Deuteronomy 6:6–9:

Method	Verse	Reference
1. Modeling	v. 6	"on your heart"
2. Discussion	v. 7	"teach diligently"
3. Daily Events	v. 7	"talk in your house"
4. Object Lessons	v. 8	"bind them as a sign"
5. Creative Projects	v. 9	"write on your doorposts and on your gates"

Generational House

Think of yourself as the foundation of the generational house you are building. There will be second and third floors someday. The cement and mortar are God's Word and God's Spirit. Each room is a child. They are different sizes, different colors, have different lighting, and a different feel. The hallways are the actions and your connectedness to them. Each of our basements and attics need a thorough and regular cleansing. We all have areas that are not visible to others but are visible to God.

In building a house, the first step is excavation and site preparation—our lives, ourselves. I have had some painful excavation in my own life, but looking back now I see that it made for a firmer foundation. God might be whispering to you to change some things, to start doing some things, or to stop doing some things. Sometimes He speaks louder and clearer, and many times He speaks through multiple voices. You are that foundation upon which your children's future will be built. Don't skip the important step of excavation in your own life.

For about eight years early in our marriage, God did some serious spiritual excavation and pruning in my life. He used that time to lay a foundation spiritually and to build a strong family focus. I was able to pour into my family and three children. My wife Dana obeyed the call to quit her job and stay at home to raise and train our children. I obeyed the call to focus on my family. We often don't know if God is asking us to make permanent changes or if those changes are for only a brief season. That is where trust comes into play. Did I trust Him? Ultimately I did.

I soon began to see the results of why God wanted me to lead my family and to make some of the tough earlier decisions. Some of them were big decisions; others were not so big. But all of them required change and obedience. Some behavioral/obedience changes that seemed so small at the time are now so very large in the rear-view mirror. Don't underestimate the power of taking a little action, a baby step.

 Read James 4:4–10, 13–17.

What is separating you from God or from your family? Do you have any excavation areas that need some work done on them? Do you have any time-killing habits you need to throw on the bonfire? Confess your sin directly to God. You also might need to confess some sin directly to someone, pray with them, and let the healing begin.[157]

Our life is but a vapor, and sometimes our friendship with the world separates us from God. As He speaks gently to us about our priorities and our heart condition, knowing to act but not acting is sin. God is jealous of our idols and friendship with the world, but He never strong-arms us into a relationship with Him. If you submit to God and draw near to Him, He will lift you up.

Modeling

I recently polled my Facebook friends and asked them who was the most influential person in their lives. A couple mentioned a pastor, teacher, or friend. But the majority listed a family member. We have a great opportunity at hand, whether it be as grandparent, parent, child, brother, or sister to influence our family for generations to come. We have had an interesting discussion in the past with my children when I asked, "Who is your role model?" It is never a quick answer, and my kids have struggled to answer this question. Thankfully, they did not answer with the latest rapper or pop culture icon. One time my son answered, "Josh Hamilton," not only because of his great baseball-playing abilities but also because he has been vocal about his faith. Another time the answer was "Tim Tebow" for similar reasons. Other times they have answered "Mom" or "Dad."

Often, kids will not admit it until they are older and raising a family of their own, but *you* are that role model. Often, children cannot have candid discussions with friends about their struggles. They also might be getting bad relationship advice and struggle with teen temptation areas from others in their circle of influence.

Even if you don't consider yourself a role model, you are. Kids look to you as a family mentor and family leader. Children were asked, "If you had to pick one person as a role model, in which of the following categories would that person be?"

1) Family member 57%
2) Friend/family friend 11%
3) Entertainer 9%
4) Teacher 9%
5) Sports figure 4%
6) Religious leader 4%

When asked specifically to choose a family member as their role model, mothers are the most popular choice:

1) Mother 36%
2) Father 28%
3) Brother/sister 16%
4) Grandparent 10%

You have a great opportunity to lead your children! You are raising the next generation, and that is not easy.

The challenge is not just to give our time and love, although that is extremely important. In the book *Raising a Modern Day Knight*,[158] we are challenged to give our children the "best things." These best things will vary by age, but they aren't usually material things. How are you doing?

Give yourself a grade from A to F for giving away the following areas. I gave myself a "letter grade" from A to F when my kids were younger and barely gave myself passing grades in a few of these categories. It spurred me on to be better. Go ahead; score yourself!

1) Involved in your child's activities

2) Helped with homework

3) Teaching them specific noble, godly values

4) Training them to relate to the opposite sex

5) Imparting a biblical vision/worldview to them

Don't be embarrassed; those who were surveyed seemed to do well in #1 and some in #2. But most men are failing at #3–5. Are we giving our children good things—or the *best* things? Are we providing them a roadmap for life or just the minimum to get by?

Under Construction

"You shall raise up the foundations of many generations."
—Isaiah 58:12 (NKJV)

Take a quick look at the logo above and on the back cover.
We are all under construction, just as this house is. Our hearts, our families, our relationships. When you look at this house, despite seeing unfinished construction, you also have a secure feeling. Why? Because of the solid rock on which it is being built. Yes, our rock is God. It can also be our spouse at times, but in the scripture below, read carefully how you can ensure that your house is built on the rock. The answer might surprise you.

"Therefore everyone who hears these words of mine and <u>puts them into practice</u> is like a wise man who built his house on the rock. The rain came down, the streams rose, and the winds blew and beat against that house; yet it did not fall, because it had its foundation on the rock. But everyone who hears these words of mine and does not <u>put them into practice</u> is like a foolish man who built his house on sand. The rain came down, the streams rose, and the winds blew and beat against that house, and it fell with a great crash."[159]

The house that survives and thrives is one of action and of obedience. It is one of alignment and obedience to God's Word. Build. Do. Act. The rains and storms will not stop. Be strong. Build on the rock. God is that rock. It is easy to be a hearer. The truly blessed person hears and then *acts!*[160] Teach your children about the rock, the refuge, the strength in your life. Sometimes you will feel like the foundation/the rock is nowhere to be found. However, when the storms subside, if you have been obedient and put God's Word into practice, you will return to that solid foundation—OBEDIENCE and ACTION. Obey! Act!

Be the DOT

When children become parents, they become part of a three-generation chain. A link is now formed between ancestors and posterity. *You* are that link! You are transferring genetic inheritance, taught inheritance, and financial inheritance. You are passing a baton loaded with your social, spiritual, personal, and material life. In a relay race, it is not carrying the baton or running with the baton that brings the potential rewards and risks; it is the *passing* of the baton. Pass it well!

We have a plan for our job, for our health, and for our finances. We need a plan for our family, too. It will help you to leave a legacy, but more importantly a plan puts some meat on the bones of a vision. How can we accomplish this vision?

You must be purposeful and intentional in planning family time. Family doesn't become a priority by wishing for it. You might need to start calendarizing things to plan family time better. The next section is about how to practically connect with your kids. Giving them your time is one of the best things you can do. The more time you give them, the greater your influence will be. In addition to the connection between you and your parents, you are the greatest influence in your child's connection with God. You are the teacher, the family leader, the instructor. Be a large, visible connecting dot. It will take work and a purposeful plan.

Younger children or grandchildren

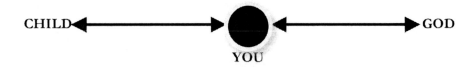

As the kids get older or leave the nest, you will still be an influence, so you must nurture the one-on-one relationship with God and allow that to grow.

Legacy Lesson: Your children and grandchildren are your greatest asset. They are your greatest way to leave a legacy. Start a family reformation! Relate. Communicate. Mentor. Model. Build. Teach. Pray.

CHAPTER 21

FAMILY DRIVEN: BUILDING A STRONG, SUCCESSFUL FAMILY

I sit in Jiffy Lube with my eleven-year-old son. I am enjoying *my* book and *my* cup of coffee. Two of my staples in life—a little mud and a little peace and quiet. Don't expect any small talk from me for the next forty-five minutes. My flesh is wanting to indulge myself in a little "rest and relaxation." I glance over at my son as he bounces a tennis ball trying to keep himself entertained. That quick nudge of the Holy Spirit whispers to go throw the ball around with him and talk. I wrestle a little, look down at my book and cup of filth, and then look at the Jiffy Lube logo and chuckle as I remember the movie *The Rookie* in which Jim Morris (Dennis Quaid) wears that Jiffy Lube baseball cap and lives out his childhood dream of playing big league ball. The movie poster hangs in our home, autographed by Jimmy Morris himself. My mind then races quickly back to the scene in *Field of Dreams* in which Kevin Costner "has a catch" with his dad. I wrestle a little more, then realize that time is fleeting. The clock is ticking, and I have only a few years left with my son. The hourglass/baton angel wins out over the mud angel, and I ask my son if he wants to go throw the tennis ball around. His eyes light up and we head outdoors for a great time of talking and just having fun. A silly little forty-five-minute window that turned magical. Those windows get more precious as the years whisk by. While throwing ground balls, I told my son of my mental gymnastics and the choice that I had just made, and that he would have similar choices when he was a husband and dad. It was a teaching moment about priorities. Time and talk. You will get plenty of opportunities in your daily routine. Don't ignore the whispers.

Swimming upstream is hard. Having family time is swimming upstream. It is also a *main thing*. Quality time and quantity time with family are not accidental. They will have to be intentional, purposeful, and scheduled. Quality family time is not just showing up and being a spectator at a sporting event or recital. That is easy. The hard part is being an influencer, example, instructor, and teacher. It is not just quality, but it is quantity. A great collection of wisdom quotations for life can be found in *Along the Road to Manhood*[161] by Stu Weber. One of my favorites is

*"Quality times will arise spontaneously
out of the great deliberate quantities of time
spent in relationship."*

You never know when quality time will grow out of some of that deliberate quantity time you have invested. You will not be able to plan or calendarize some of those magical moments or bonding that will occur when you give them quantity time.

Look for opportunities to engage. I remember when my kids were younger and I was asked to help coach soccer. Soccer? Are you kidding me? I don't even know how many kids are on the field. Is it even called a field or do they have a more English name for it? I helped "coach/cheer" for a few seasons. The kids didn't care about my expertise; they cared about by presence. I coached both of my boys baseball teams as they grew up. Life is too short. They will be gone before you know it. Time is precious and we only get one chance to raise our kids. No "do-overs." Engage!

Mentor

As your kids grow and you add ever-increasing titles to your parental arsenal (taxi driver, cook, maid, doctor, coach, teacher, spouse, cleaners, accountant, disciplinarian, and counselor) do not forget *spiritual mentor*. *Family time is great, but it is not just about* family "time." Vacations are great. Enjoying a movie together is great. But we need to go deeper with our kids—quality communications, spiritual events, church together. Shipping them off to a youth group is not enough; church activities can actually sometimes divide a family. You need the family times together and you need *spiritual* family times together.

I love the Rainey's[162] simple advice on three important things we need to give our children and our spouse:

- Your Time
- Your Touch
- Your Talk

Repetition is key! Regular hugs, cuddling, date nights, and family communication. Consistency early on makes it easier when the kids get older. This will get more difficult as they are teenagers, but *do not quit*. Continue to pursue them. They might act as though they don't need you, or it might feel awkward, but they need those three T's more than ever, or someone else will give it to them!

How in the world can we effectively give them *more* time, touch, and talk with our busy, hectic lives? I love Mark Holmen's simple way to remember this via the acronym T.R.A.I.N:

T—Time: This will vary with location, and from day to day—Car Time, Bed Time, Meal Time, Vacation Time, Memory-Making Time, and one-on-one Time. Be intentional. Be creative. Brainstorm with your spouse.

R—Repetition: This goes back to forming new habits and having someone hold you accountable for doing so.

A—Acceptance: Listen. Receive. Love. Accept them for who they are and how God made them. They are unique. They are the acorn near the tree, but they are not a duplicate of you.

I—Intentional: This will take work and a strong backbone. It will not be easy and will require you to give up some of your most treasured time, and desires. It might require a radical change in who you are.

N—Never-ending: This is not a twenty-one-day journey but a life-long effort. You won't stop getting on the TRAIN when the kids move away or start their own families. You are always a parent! You may be a grandparent! You are making a generational impact!

STOP Quickly grade yourself from A to F on how you are doing in these three areas with your spouse and kids.

	Spouse	Kids
Your Time		
Your Touch		
Your Talk		

Fears and Failure

No matter how much you prepare for parenting, you're not prepared. You just don't have a clue until you go through it. Along with the many new responsibilities comes fears— fear of failure, fear of inadequacy, and a multitude of other fears. The good news is that your children don't expect your perfection, but they do desire your presence. They will watch to see if you follow through on your great plans! You are putting generational habits into motion.

Some encouraging findings were published recently in the *"The State of our Nation's Youth"* report[163] that suggests our children are yearning for your involvement and your time. Children were asked, "If you had only one wish, which of the following would you wish for to create a better life for you and your family?" Here's how they responded:

1.) More time spent with your family   46%
2.) More money to buy material things   27%
3.) Living in a bigger house   14%
4.) More time spent on spiritual pursuits   7%

They might not *ask* you for your time, but they need it. The evidence and data show that they want your time and they need your time.

> *"Excellence in childrearing does not evolve from making fewer mistakes than everybody else. It evolves from making plenty of mistakes and learning from them."*
> —Dr. Ray Guarendi

In a Family Life Family Needs survey, "66% of parents agreed with the statement 'I don't have much confidence in my parenting skills." Join the club, but don't let that excuse you. We will seek help with investment advice, our golf slice, or career growth. It is time to take responsibility for our children and marriages, to be aggressive, take an offensive stance, obtain those skills we lack and develop a plan of action. Even more important than a plan and man-given knowledge is to seek God's wisdom.

> *"The righteous man is the one who lives for the next generation."*
> —Dietrick Bonhoeffer

Family Behaviors and Priorities

Most spouses and parents know that they have much to improve on, so what specifically can we work on with our spouse and children? There are many characteristics of a strong family. Here are a few:

STOP Prioritize from 1 to 10 the behaviors that need work, with 1 being the most critical and 10 being the least critical or that you might have already conquered.

	Spouse	Children
- Open and regular communication	_____	_____
- Time together—quality time and quantity time	_____	_____
- Openness/honesty	_____	_____
- Trust	_____	_____
- Feeling loved/cared for	_____	_____
- Feeling safe/secure	_____	_____
- An environment of forgiveness	_____	_____
- The fruit of the Spirit is evident—Galatians 5:22	_____	_____
- Strong spiritual atmosphere—seeking God	_____	_____
- Touch	_____	_____

Ninety percent of high school students say that "they can confide in and talk to at least one family member about things. As students struggle with problems, they find that they can talk to their families. Is that true in your family? Why or why not? It could be that one child is more candid with one parent, and a different child is more open with a different parent. There is not a right or wrong answer, but the fact that they can share struggles and issues with you is important.

 Read Matthew 10:39; John 13:12–14; and 1 Timothy 5:8.

How do these passages relate to the time and money that you spend on your family?

The Challenge

It is not easy to build a strong family, just as it is not easy to become physically fit. It takes discipline and time. Our family should be our primary focus, our primary career, our primary project. We are affecting history with this selfless decision. Time and money have one thing in common—once spent, they are gone forever. There is a shortage of future, so don't waste any time and don't wait "until you have time." It will never happen. You must *make* time.

The road to selflessness starts at home. When coming home from my first job, I knew that I must focus on my *most important* job—my family. The rationale comes easy for plopping in front of the television, unwinding, or just plain having some "me" time. Edith and Francis Schaeffer founded an international study center and Christian community in Switzerland. Edith's plain analysis of the family makes it all so simple: "*How precious a thing is the human family. Is it not worth some sacrifice in time, energy, safety, discomfort, and work? Does anything come forth without work?*"[164]

For many parents, the challenge is to balance "work" and "family." It is possible that they can be in balance and even complement each other if you work at it. For particular life seasons, it might be harder than for others, and you might have to make some adjustments. It also might be that you just need a heart or mindset change in how you view your work and how you view your family. You might need to value one or both more. Many of us have become so used to a life of imbalance that we do not know another path. Balance is key, and this might mean some tough decisions—turning down a promotion, not moving, or taking a hard look at priorities.

It might be that a mother needs to transition back to the home. It might be that the greatest generational impact you could make is to have a full focus on raising and influencing your children, or you might find a compromise part-time job working from home. Listen to your gut, your spouse, and to your God. Seek God with your spouse. That dual income might not be worth the stress on the family and the missed teaching moments. It also might not be producing the financial advantage you think. There is much pressure to focus on career, when your family might need you more.

I remember needing to go into work on a Saturday and I thought it would be a great opportunity to explain to my kids what I do for a living. They were so young that, more than my stories or the pictures on the wall, they enjoyed coloring on the whiteboard in my office.

For years, I have not erased that small corner of my whiteboard as a memory of my kids. It also doubles as a reminder of a need for balance. My walls and shelves at work also are framed with many family pictures and coloring pages as a constant reminder.

 Do you need a tune-up in how you view your current job or your family?

"Do not prepare the path for the child; prepare the child for the path.
—*Brad McCoy, father of Colt McCoy*

Legacy Lesson: Building a strong, successful family will take WORK! The hardest part will be laying down your desires and priorities for God's and for your family. Give them your Time, Touch and Talk. It will impact generations to come!

CHAPTER 22

FAMILY LIFE: THE MAGICAL FEAST

*T*he *Walton's. Eight is Enough. Little House on the Prairie. Happy Days. Leave it to Beaver.* All idealistic families and traditions from yesteryear. You can still picture the smiling faces, the meat and potatoes, the weighty subjects being discussed. Dinner used to be the centerpiece of a family's day. Robin Fox, an anthropologist who teaches at Rutgers University, states that "food comes so easily to us now, that we have lost a sense of its significance." In the olden days, "when we had to grow the corn and fight off predators, meals included a serving of gratitude. Fast food has killed this. We have reduced eating to sitting alone and shoveling it in. There is no ceremony in it."

Finding the time for a family meal together, especially a five-course feast is certainly no easy task. It will take some radical change and possibly some arm twisting, especially with the already overcommitted family—jobs, travel, school, sports, music lessons and other extracurricular activities. These are all good things, yet they pull us away from family. Finding time for a regular family feast will not be easy. Each generation has less and less discretionary time, but it will be so rewarding. I can guarantee that you will not always succeed, but if the family meal is the rule rather than the exception, you will see results.

Studies have shown that families who eat together eat healthier and raise better adjusted kids who avoid smoking, drinking, drugs, depression, teen issues, and eating disorders. They also learn and expand their vocabulary because of discussions with adults. There are many other benefits. It creates intimacy, creates a secure environment for kids, fosters sibling connections, and provides an opportunity for genuine discussions about tough days, stress, or the joys of life.

I cannot overemphasize the power of the family meal, especially as the children get older and your time together is more limited. The experts in adolescent development emphasize the payoff and dividends being the greatest in the teen years. They will actually talk, engage, listen. Books have been written on this subject alone. For us, the only meal a day we have a chance to be together is dinner. This time can truly be an anchor for your family. Obviously, this one common mealtime will not transform your family. A smorgas-bord of habits and values is necessary for a strong, successful child.

A recent article in *Time* magazine[165] referenced a study that collected family data over a 10-year period. The families with the least educated parents eat together the most. This could certainly be due to all the many activities that some children are involved in, which might splinter the family. Kids who eat most often with their parents are 40 percent more likely to get A's and B's than kids who have two or fewer family dinners per week. The article goes on to state that "laziness and leniency are enemies of the common meal. Sometimes we treat our kids as customers who need to be pleased. We have a food-court mentality: Johnny eats a burrito, Dad has a burger, and Mom picks pasta." The CASA study also found that a majority of teens who ate three or fewer meals a week with their families wished they did so more often!

Because you might experience some resistance with older children, start when they are young, and if you are starting late, then "beg, bribe and bargain."[166] Do whatever it takes, or ask them to try it for two weeks. In might be difficult to pry a lengthy discussion out of their mouths, but try the "rose-and-thorn" approach. Everyone talks about one good thing (rose) and one bad thing (thorn) that happened during the day. Sometimes it facilitates a good discussion.

I was told as a young father to make this a priority and that we would be greatly rewarded. It was not only tougher than I thought but also more rewarding than I thought. We rearranged our schedule for nearly three years to eat dinner at 7:30 instead of 5:00. It was the only time we could all be together. We still don't eat together every night, but we do the majority of the evenings. It is the glue that holds our Family Vision together and keeps the communication lines open.

More than half of students (51 percent) already eat a family meal together every day, and 85 percent say that they eat with their families at least a few times a week. Surveys show that they are looking for even more! Seventy-one percent[167] of students say that when they think about a good meal, they would prefer to eat a home-cooked meal.

We have heard the adage "The family that prays together, stays together.". This is so true, but you might want to add "the family that eats together, stays together." Dust off those pots and pans. Turn off the TV. Gather the kids around. Have a magical feast.

I am not exactly sure why, but I am inspired enough to write my own Seuss-like rhyme:

Not in a car, not from a bag.
Not from a jar or grease that makes you gag.
Not in a bar, or from afar.
Not from a can, or with half the clan.
But with a pot and with a pan.
At the table, all were able.
With manners plain, and kids all sane.
Good talks just the same, not with great pain.
Life shan't be a rush, but talks that gush.
No time for fuss, but to discuss.
Our Time Together.
The Magical Feast.

Legacy Lesson: Taking the time to bring the family together for a meal and purposeful conversation will have a greater impact than you know. Show your family they are a priority.

CHAPTER 23

FAMILY BY DESIGN: A DNA TRANSFORMATION

*F*amily times should be designed and purposeful. Although we fail often, Dr. Richard Ross gave us a target to shoot at, and it sticks to this day:

1) **Daily** prayer together
2) **Weekly** family Bible/worship
3) **Monthly** family service/volunteer
4) **Yearly** missions trip

The *Daily*

Probably the most rewarding time that we have had with our children—and I also see it with my grandparents and grandchildren—is reading time. In the preteen years, nothing was more rewarding than to read a book and the Bible and pray with each of the kids by their bedside and sing them to sleep. We often also had times of worship as I walked around the house holding them. Precious memories and a foundation built. These were designed times. They were planned; they were not accidental.

When the kids were younger, it was a nightly habit to read to them together and then adjourn with them to each of their bedrooms for a book, prayer, and Bible-reading time. After a few weeks of it, they would not let us miss a night! We visited the library weekly when the kids were younger. Our friends, the Postemas, have always made a priority of reading. They reward their kids with an hour of video games for every hour they read. We have learned to be flexible over the years and modify our approach to Family Times. What works for one family might not work for another. What works in the elementary years will not work in high school years.

Now that the kids are older, we head directly from the dinner table to the living room, and I read a short Bible story from *Egermeier's Bible Story Book*. After reading, we then recite a scripture verse of the week, and then each prays. For busy teens, this is not overwhelming, taking ten minutes total, but it provides a spiritual anchor, and it also provides a forum for discussions and laughter. We have to squelch the humor quite often.

We don't accomplish this daily, but it is an important building block to ensure that we don't have just a compartmentalized Sunday faith. These are good bonding times and fond memories, but on top of that it introduces them to an intimate one-on-one time with God (you are the dot!), slows both of your worlds down, teaches your child to listen, and helps to build their vocabulary. We have had the privilege of leading all three of our children to Christ in our homes because of this foundation that was built and then strengthened by strong teaching at church.

> *". . .I have no greater joy than to hear*
> *that my children are walking in the truth. . . ."*
> —3 John 4

 What top three "Time Drainers" in your life
are limiting time with your family?

The *Weekly*

When the kids were younger, we had once-a-week "Family Fun Nights." Instead of just plopping in front of a Disney movie (although we did that too occasionally) every week, we would try to do a regular Family Fun Night. Heritage Builders has some incredible materials that will help you build a great family night. The *Introduction to Family Nights Tool Chest* is a great place to start.

Begin to find out what your children's "bents" are and get into their world. I cover this in more depth in *Ease the Squeeze*, but here are some ideas:

- Ride bikes together.
- Walk together.
- Play sports together—throw a baseball, shoot some hoops, play ping pong.
- Do yard work together, but make them games and races.
- Do chores together.
- Play board games.
- Talk.

Family Time
Your Zip Code

Some of the best quality times you will have in our busy society is in the car. These "drive time" talks will vary depending upon the age of your kids. If you struggle to know what to talk about, come up with some fun things you can all participate in. What is your favorite vacation memory? What was the best thing about school today? On a scale of 1 to 10, how are your teachers? My favorite (the kids get sick of it) is "penny for your thoughts." When they were younger, I stashed pennies and handed them out after they shared something. Now they get nothing but still play along since that is built into them.

Breaking the ice and finding common ground is the hard part. First, talk about something they are passionate about. Never start with the grades, chore list, or homework discussion. Sometimes you do the talking and share what you did at work today, why you do it, how you ended up at this stage of your life, what God is teaching you or challenging you on, share the stories of your youth, and preserve some other memories. They make for a powerful generational impact.

In our men's small group, one of the men[168] shared emotionally about how God opened a door for him to have a deep discussion with his son while on a long drive to college. He took advantage of the opportunity. If an opportunity presents itself, don't run from it. Share your challenges and failures as the Lord leads and at the right age. Share your struggles and how you are dealing with them. Confess your shortcomings. Build your children up.

Date Nights

The most powerful thing I determined to do when the kids were younger was to have a "date night" with each of my kids. I would rotate and take a different one each week. The quality time we had in discussion was invaluable. Build this tradition early when they are young so your seventeen-year-old doesn't roll his or her eyes when you say "date night." He or she knows that this is "dinner with Dad." What they don't realize is that it is a disguised as a "connection time." It is something the kids have always enjoyed. It is amazing how they open up and talk when they are feeding their faces! When they were younger, I would take them to eat and then to the park or for a hike. As the kids got older, it was more just eating and talking and then maybe an ice cream after. Keep it real, and have honest conversations. It is amazing what a meal will do!

Other things to do in your zip code:

- Museums
- Concerts
- Plays
- Church
- Volunteer work
- Date nights—walks, hikes
- Participating in your child's activities—practices and games

I recall a season when my son was wrestling with the decision to continue to play competitive tennis and whether he should leave his tennis academy. We were driving home one day having a deeper talk than usual, so my antennae were up and ready. He said, "Dad, I think my priorities have been in the wrong order. I think my ranking has been (1) Tennis, (2) God, (3) Family, and (4) Others." We had a good talk about idols and what it meant that Jesus was Lord, how I had to give up some things at different times in my life for similar reasons. We prayed and talked about this for several weeks. He ended up making his own determination to shift his priorities.

Family Time
On the Road Again

Probably our best quality and quantity times as a family are the uninterrupted times away from home. The family vacation is priceless. We have done almost all of these as driving vacations. First, because I am cheap; second, because it gives us more flexibility in where we visit and when we visit; and third, because it bonds us together. Although the teen spats happen once in a while, the rest stop visits, the many side visits, the constant family time, or the hotels or campgrounds en route were always great times and memorable. Camping was a wonderful time when the kids were younger. We have some great memories that are now in our family memory museum, but more on that subject later.

Now that our family times at home are more scarce, we also made a commitment when the kids entered their teen years that we would attend youth and family conferences together more often. A generational tradition is a visit to Camp of the Woods—a vacation with purpose. It ties together a vacation, beach, hikes, outdoors, family times, fun times, teaching times, and some great family feast times.

We also try while on vacation to visit different churches that are outside of our denominational comfort zone. Some of them have provided great teaching moments after the service. Others pleasantly surprised us and even convicted us a little because of our denominational walls that we had built up.

We have also visited prayer conferences and youth conferences as a family. With no youth group or other distractions, the kids sought solely after God. The kids might sometimes battle these times. I recall recently taking our family to a Youth Prayer and Worship Conference, albeit with a little kicking and screaming, some louder than others. We knew that God had planted a seed in my wife and me to have our kids see other kids who were "on fire" and passionate for God in their worship. Planning this and executing it were not easy. It took time away from the kids' plans with friends. It affected our to-do lists and all of the many things we needed to get done. It was a Mary-and-Martha tug of war, but I was resolute. Resistance was plentiful, and numerous opportunities presented themselves as an "off-ramp." I nearly caved multiple times, and my wife and I were just flat tired of the push-back we were receiving. We had so much to do, the weather was horrible, we had already had plenty of family time, and we couldn't afford it. But I stuck to my guns, and it was a rewarding spiritual milestone in our kids' teen lives. It also blessed the adults!

Legacy Lesson: Family time will not happen by accident nor find its way into your busy calendar. You may need a DNA transformation to get that time together. More importantly, the spiritual times you spend with them in prayer, the Bible, church and service.

CHAPTER 24

FAMILY DOWNLOAD: GET CONNECTED

"The problem with a family is that is so daily."
—Dennis Rainey

The best "connection" moments will come unplanned and unscripted. These are powerful moments. Don't be so pre-occupied with your own day or own challenges that you miss them. A communication time might start with a news story on the radio or TV. It might start with a feeling that you have and that you make public. It might start with a feeling or emotion that your child has. This thirty-second teaching moment or relation-building connection might stick for life and is better than a thirty-minute pulpit-pounding message by Mom or Dad in the living room, although there might be times for that, too.

Never say No. Stop, Drop, and Roll.

Here I sit, in the thick of writing this book, forty things on the to-do list, many things lingering from carry-over lists from weeks and even months earlier. A critical deadline looms with only ninety minutes until I have to get in the car. My 14-year old wanders into my office and says, "Dad, wanna shoot some hoops"? I open my mouth ready to give him an impressive lengthy summary of "the list" when I realize my vow from years back.

Never say "no" or "not now."

On this occasion, it became even more important as our relationship had recently had some struggles and recent discipline has left him questioning our love or care for him. No matter what I am in the thick of, if one of the kids asks me to do something, stop, drop, and roll. I stop what I am doing and give them my undivided attention. I drop my self-focus and roll with the request. Am I always successful? No. Sometimes I am in the middle of a call or text and have to say, "Sure, give me a minute," but as I realize the shortage of future, rarely do I miss those opportunities or key events or activities with my children. No regrets. There is a shortage of future with your children. Don't miss it.

Seize the Minute

I remember making a vow many years ago that when my kids said, "Can I ask you something?" or "Can we play basketball?" or "Wanna play ping pong?" or "Wanna go on a bike ride?" that my answer would be "sure" instead of "I'm too busy" or "not now." "Just a minute" would only be acceptable if I really was in the middle of something critical or with a deadline and I had to conclude a thought. For the most part, this vow has been fulfilled.

The computer is my big challenge in this area. For some people it might be television or relaxing while reading a good book. If we really give this some thought, what could really be more important than the words of those near us, or that time wrestling on the floor, or reading with our kids. You cannot get that time back. Seize the moment. Get connected!

"Seize the minute" rather than "Just a minute."

The e-mails, the social media, the good book, and the sitcom can all wait. Our time is so short with our children. I have purposed to focus on uninterrupted time with kids and God by periodically conducting a "Media Fast." No television, no radio, no newspaper, no social media, no magazines, no advertisements, or any of the barrage of other distractions. Be fully focused on God and family. Don't be a "Cat's in the Cradle" victim.

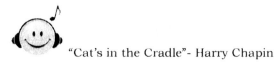

"Cat's in the Cradle"- Harry Chapin

Connection Points

Though it is not Biblical, I like this line from *Evan Almighty:* God will not give you "patience"; He will give you "opportunities for patience." Ditto for "communication and quality time opportunities." Ask for and watch for those "opportunities to talk and teach." Warning: They might not always come when you feel like it! It still takes our action and follow through. Take advantage of those little opportunities that come your way. A simple practical discussion can connect you with your child and can also connect them with your God. Here are some of the best opportunities you will have for a "Family Download" connection with your kids.

Passion play: One of the absolute best ways to get plugged in or connected is to join their world, their passions. My daughter's is photography. One of my son's is tennis—traveling with him, being there. The latest video game, song, art contest, project, etc., are others. We spent a whole weekend once working on my daughter's photography contest entries. I have watched my sons prepare You Tube videos, play a video game, etc. We have built models together, played ping pong, and shot baskets. Their passions change; change along with them. Then they will listen to your five-minute pulpit message. Without the relationship, forget it.

Fishing: Seize the moment. I am not a fisherman, but I have heard the saying "The best time to fish is when the fish are biting." Hmmmm. That was not a rocket scientist they were quoting. But when it comes time to connecting with the kids, you cannot always calendarize a good discussion. When you want to talk, they often are tired or worn out, and vice versa. If they are talking, you better get to fishing!

Get God Times: Get God in the middle of your connection times. You will find common ground there most of the time. This is easier if you start it when they are young, but the kids know that several times a week we will get out the Bible, read a devotional, memorize a verse, and pray. This shows the kids what is important in life.

Hostess with the Mostest: Let your house be the one where kids want to hang out. Pay for the pizza, the donuts, the movie, etc. Get to know their friends. This is a tougher one, but again, the earlier you start, the more they will understand it is not an option but rather an expectation. This goes beyond social media stalking (although that doesn't hurt), but our kids know our home is a safe environment for inviting friends over for a sleepover, having birthday parties, etc. Invite them out to a ballgame or family event. You need to make a connection early. My daughter's first "friend that is a boy" has probably spent more time with our family members than the two of them have spent alone! Although he is not a part of our family, we are treating him as such. You get to know people when you spend time with them. If you think of your high school and college friends, you were probably *greatly* influenced by who you hung around with. It is an imperative to get connected with their friends.

Have a sense of humor: As parents, we often get so focused on the to-do list, the homework, the chores, and the discipline. Levity is a good way to connect. I am not talking about a "best-friend-buddy" approach, but ensure you smile and add some humor to lighten the tension and stress. Work on the relationship before working on the "list." Listen. Engage. Laugh. *Then* talk about the hard stuff. Be creative, and be yourself in how you do that. For me, that is my "morning alarm wake-up call." The kids never know how I am going to wake them up in the mornings. It is usually most obnoxious and involves my singing, poking, or exploding. Although it is extremely annoying it gets 'em chuckling.

Be There: Often, a word doesn't even need to be spoken. Be in the crowd. Don't miss the game or the performance. Smile and wave from the stands. No matter how small or big it is, it is important to them—even if they say it isn't. Sometimes you might have an issue arise that prevents your being there, but attend as many events as you can. Take a picture. Capture the moment. Smile!

Teddy Bear: Even if you are not the hugging type or never received affection as a child, giving a hug is so very important. It is an unspoken form of communication that is so critical between a parent/child and spouse/spouse. Human beings thrive on appropriate touching, and it definitely affects your relationships. Numerous research studies show that we all need "touch" and that regular touching leads to better emotional health and even more positive intellectual and physical ability and growth. A hug is good medicine! I ensure that my kids and wife get an overdose.

Say it!: Go ahead say it if you dare. It is amazing the number of adults who can't recall their father's telling them "*I love you*" very often. I have made the commitment to tell my spouse and children every day that I love them. Even if we have had a disagreement, I find that hearing the words verbalized helps me process the fact that I love them regardless of the struggle we might be going through. Say those three words, and say them regularly!

Affirm: I know that this one can be a mixed bag. I recall my son's playing on a baseball team when we won the league championship and year-end tournament and yet every team received the same trophy. This might be an extreme example where we are afraid to affirm success and don't want to alienate the "loser." That might be appropriate at a young age, but reality is that in life that will not always be the case. Although everyone likes a winner, the most important time you can personally affirm your children is when they are struggling, when they have just failed, or when they have lost. Affirm your love for them. Affirm your belief in them. Nurture and support them.

Teach: Everything we learn should be given away. As a parent, you have a unique opportunity to teach and train your children. You have a short window of influence, and that foundation is mostly built before your child becomes a teenager. The focused, prioritized time you spend with younger children or grandchildren is monumental. Teach them morals, teach them God's Word, teach them to pray and worship, teach them obedience, teach them a disciplined life, teach them a strong work ethic, teach them priorities, teach them right and wrong. *You* have that responsibility, not a school teacher, not a children's pastor, and not a youth leader. Certainly friends, Hollywood, and social media could be battling you all the way, but if *you* aren't teaching them, someone else will.

Serve: As I stroll through the cavernous Dallas Convention Center, I am in shock. I am stunned. Speechless. We are only thirty minutes from home, yet we're in another world. Two different worlds on a collision course. It is the Dallas Homeless Christmas Party, and volunteers are giving haircuts, foot washing, and toys and clothing to needy kids. Plenty versus need. I see it all around. When is the last time you chose a purposeful head-on collision? We are safe. We have a full stomach, heat, and a coat. We are busy. We are secluded. We are stressed and broke and can't afford the time, yet this collision meeting results in seeing the joyful faces and ear-to-ear smiles with a simple stocking with someone else's leftovers, or a generic-brand basketball. Serving is so rewarding. Back in the car, as we drive toward home, we pass the homeless man with a grocery cart, usually empty. This time it is filled with a bag of Christmas love. Give your time away. It is a dual benefit—to you as a parent, but also the connecting with your kids in a common serving action. You are downloading a life priority and giving to a bigger cause together as a family.

The importance of giving is the benefits it brings not only to the receiver but also to the giver. Research indicates that it might indeed be healthier to give than to receive. A recent study[169] found that "mortality was significantly reduced for individuals who provided support to friends, relatives, and neighbors." During this five-year study of older married adults, those who gave their time and support to others lived longer than those who didn't."

Often, we do the easy volunteer work: the local school or local church work. We often don't get out of our comfort zones, our local boxes. We can come up with a lot of excuses for not engaging in "higher-risk" volunteer work or a missions trip: our kids won't be safe, we can't afford it, etc. When our kids see us give of our time and money, they will do the same. Action and not just talk is key to this.

I was asked in our Sunday school class[170] to participate in a very humbling activity. I adapted the following from that exercise:

1. Read Matthew 25:31–46.
2. Grade yourself—circle your grade for that activity below.
3. Come up with a plan to get a passing grade.

Hang on—don't skip this! I'll confess. I failed miserably when I graded myself, but it spurred me to make a few changes.

Feed the hungry	A	B	C	D	F
Give drink to the thirsty	A	B	C	D	F
Sheltered strangers	A	B	C	D	F
Clothed the needy	A	B	C	D	F
Cared for the sick	A	B	C	D	F
Visited those in prison	A	B	C	D	F

Read Proverbs 14:31; Philippians 2:3–4; James 4:17; and 1 John 3:16–18.

1. What is one local ministry activity you can participate in as a family?
2. What is one missions trip you can start praying about and saving money for?

Legacy Lesson: Finding ways to get connected with your kids and grand-kids shows them you care and love them. Seize the time. Get into their world. Find those connection points. You are creating a generational chain of connection points.

CHAPTER 25

REAL FAMILY VALUES:
A FAMILY AWAKENING

*D*on't expect your children to listen to your advice and ignore your example. Some good counsel in making family a priority is to get God's help in doing so! Beginning some new spiritual disciplines (e.g., church, Bible reading, or prayer) will be a challenge. We have talked some about church and Bible reading. Reading the Scriptures alone and with family will help you grow together and will help you pass the baton more effectively in this generational relay race. There are many different ways to do this.

Connect with God and your families by prayer. Prayer is a topic that most people can always use some ideas on. We have a chalk board near the kitchen table that has prayer requests, and we ask the kids to pick one off the list and pray for it during our meal time.

 Read Ephesians 6:4.

We have the responsibility as parents to raise and train our kids. Prayer is tough for kids. In fact, talking to someone who is not visible is tough for everyone. Do not let fear or feelings of inadequacy rob you of the joys and the responsibilities of leading your family. It is difficult to know what to pray for and how to pray. A child's innocent prayers can be fun to listen to, but they also reflect the beginning of a "real relationship" with a distant God. Teaching them that prayer is not just one-way communication or a rote formula is important. Teach them to be themselves. I had a mid-life epiphany when someone stated, "Pray the Word." I had heard it many times but I had seldom taken my Bible into my prayer closet and read it out loud and changed some of the verses into prayers. "Praying the Word" often provides a jump start and gets the juices flowing in a dry prayer time. It also actually gives you ideas for something to pray for other than the dinner meal, Aunt Gert's hip, Uncle Vern's foul language, or your dog's constant barking.

I had the kids try it with our memory verse for the week during our prayer at dinner and asked them to turn their scripture into a prayer—no plagiarizing. Just make it a real, authentic talk with God. It felt pretty weird practicing prayer with the kids but it helped them to understand it. I turned the scripture "*I want to know Christ and the power of*

His resurrection and the fellowship of sharing in His sufferings, becoming like Him in His death"[171] into a prayer that gave the kids some ideas for how they could turn this scripture into a prayer. It went something like this: "Lord, I want to know you better. Sometimes I don't feel like I give you enough time. I am sorry for that. Help me to know you more and become more like you, so kids at school can see you and know you, too. Thanks for dying on the cross for me and for rising again. Help me to share that with others and know the power of that love. Sometimes I feel like I suffer at school. Help me to look to you when I feel that way. Thanks for always loving me. Help me to be more like you and give my desires and selfishness up for my family and friends. I love you. Amen.

This was obviously my adult version; the kids' version was much simpler. In reality, it might go more like this. Our scripture for another week was *"You will seek me and find me when you seek me with all your heart."[172]* When I asked the kids to try and pray that scripture, it went something like this: "Lord, help me to seek you with all of my heart. Amen." No doubt a little shorter than the example above, but nevertheless a good prayer.

Model Prayers

You might look at the following scripture passages to give you ideas in how to teach your kids to pray: 1) John 17—Jesus' prayer, 2) Daniel 9:1–19—Daniel's prayer, and 3) Matthew 6:9–13—The Lord's Prayer

ACTS

We started using the ACTS model of prayer. ACTS stands for Adoration, Confession, Thanksgiving, Supplication (Ask List).

> **A—Adoration:** Worship God for His love, for His grace, for your family
> **C—Confession:** Confess your faults to each other and to God.
> **T—Thanksgiving:** Thank God for your family, home, job, for His Son
> **S—Supplication:** This will usually be the longest section! That is okay! Ask God for help with struggles, children, weaknesses, decisions, finances, etc.

The ACTS formula can be helpful, but too much of it can get "religious" and add to the dryness at times. You might have other prayer traditions that you pass down from generation to generation. One prayer we learned from grandparents and great grandparents was the singing of a "God is great" prayer we all learned at Camp of the Woods. We still sing it together every Sunday just as a reminder of the generational baton that was passed on to us. Lighten up! Take some risks and enjoy the journey!

Fasting, Fear, and Faith

Days of fasting and prayer were common in early America. Abe Lincoln called on Americans to fast multiple times for multiple reasons. Fasting is something we started when the older kids moved into their teen years. We had the entire family fast and pray together when they/we faced bigger decisions, bigger distractions, and bigger temptations.

There are times in life when we all have milestones that will require major tests, major decisions, or monumental launches of faith. I look back at some of our major moves and know that prayer and fasting had much to do with making the right decisions: marriage, having kids we couldn't afford, buying a house, writing a book, moving to a new job, and starting a school to name a few. My biggest fear was usually not the "risk of loss" associated with those decisions, loss of income, loss of credibility, or loss of relationships but rather ensuring that this was "God's will." My sensitivity to "the Ishmael moment" (forcing God's will, impatience, see Genesis 16) always loomed large. I didn't want my will to overshadow God's will. I remember when a job opportunity opened that required a major uprooting. I did the practical things one should do—made a pros-and-cons spreadsheet; sought counsel of others; and researched the position, leaders, and region.

But the most important thing I did was have a season of fasting and prayer with my family. My prayer was that God would open the door or close the door. It was a great opportunity to teach the kids to "inquire of God" and to try and hear His desires for our family. The "process" is the key. Getting your heart and mind to a place that is open to "any" decision. We moved through the process together—praying daily together, talking about pro's and con's, and fasting. It taught us each a number of things, especially to lay down our own desires and see what God wanted and how our decisions affect those around us.

 Read 1 Corinthians 16:9 and 2 Corinthians 2:12.

The power of open doors and closed doors!

Faith Calls, and Ishmael Halts

Although some choices will seem massive in our own lives, they pale in contrast to some of the steps of faith of the biblical characters we grew up reading about: Noah building an ark, Joshua crossing the Jordan, Moses returning to Pharaoh or crossing the Red Sea, Abraham leaving his country, Abraham's test of faith with Isaac, Peter walking on the water, or Jesus Himself preparing for His final mission, the Cross.

Seeing God's faithfulness in the rear-view mirror provides a buildup of faith that makes some of the tests, trials, and fear of life's issues seem trite. That root canal, EKG, MRI, pacemaker, or major life decision or faith test gets easier the more you can see God's hand and plan. Fasting helps you see His will and trust in Him. Imagine the fear-and-faith battle of some of those Bible characters listed above. Don't leave some of your major decisions to chance. Before you or your kids embark on them, pray and fast. My prayer is that each of us is open to the "faith calls" as well as the "Ishmael halts." Let God do heart surgery on you during this process. Search my heart, oh God!

We have had decisions about colleges, school changes, house and job moves, and preparing for missions trips. On each occasion we have used media fasts, snack fasts, social media/phone fasts, or food fasts. (See the fasting scriptures and books I've recommended.) It teaches not only us but also the kids that certain times and seasons require a more intense focus on God. Fasts help provide a clear line of sight and sound to God.

If you have never tried fasting, it can be very rewarding. First and foremost, it brings you closer to God. You will hear His voice and sense His presence. If your spiritual life has become routine and ritualistic and you need a refreshing, this rekindles the fires. We need to develop a fasting lifestyle. I remember that advertisement from 30+ years ago: "*Calgon, take me away!*" Make this your prayer as you fast and separate yourself from temporal things: "Jesus, take me away. I want more of You. I want to know You." Even fasting about what changes you need to make with your family is a great way to start.

> "*A family without prayer is like a house without a roof,*
> *open and exposed to all the storms of Heaven.*"
> —Arthur Pink

Bible Bucks?

Teaching your children to read the Bible on their own is important. There are many practical ways to do this. Some of you will choke on this next idea buffet. If so, skip over it. It is not for everyone. Just as some parents choose to give an allowance, some also choose to provide incentives for book or Bible reading for their kids. I know not everyone will agree with it. We don't use it often, but to some it might be beneficial. Maybe use incentives other than money. Participate with them. Model the behavior you want to see.

- Pay them to memorize a particular chapter of the Bible. One dad offered his son $50.
- Pay them for each verse they memorize from a list provided by parents.
- Pay them to read their Bible daily. One dad offered his children $100 if at the end of the year they had read their Bible each day. If they missed a day he deducted $10.

We personally have not used such incentives and prefer to make reading and memorization a part of the kids regular disciplines. However, do whatever it takes!

 Read Psalm 19:7–8; 107:19–20; and Matthew 4:4.

Your Family Values

You might not know where your child stands on the family values you are trying to instill. You might believe that they have a biblical standard when in fact they have a secular or humanistic standard. I developed the following survey to help you discover any gaps or concern areas. Photocopy this section and have your child complete it, and discuss it with him or her. It will be a good tool in helping determine what needs work.

STOP For Questions 1 through 23, have the child pick one of the 4 answers and mark with an X. For Questions 24-36, have them circle the number that best reflects the answer.

Discussion Survey

	Yes	No	Maybe/ Some- times	Don't Know
1. Do you believe if you died today you would go to heaven?				
2. Do you regularly attend church (more than twice/month)?				
3. Do you regularly attend a youth group (more than twice/month)?				
4. Do you read your Bible regularly (several times/week)?				
5. Do you pray regularly (daily)?				
6. Do you have a Christian friend you talk to?				
7. Do you plan to attend church regularly when you are in college?				
8. Do you plan to attend church regularly when you have a family?				
9. Do you believe all accounts and stories in the Bible are true?				
10. Do you listen to Christian music regularly?				
11. Do you believe abortion, homosexuality, and premarital sex is sin?				
12. Do you believe lying, stealing, and cursing is sin?				
13. Do you believe God used evolution to create human beings?				
14. Do you talk about God and your faith with friends weekly?				
15. Do you talk about God and your faith with family weekly?				
16. Do you believe the way to achieve heaven is to be a good person?				
17. My school helps me give me stronger belief that the Bible is true?				
18. "Right"/"wrong" might be different from person to person				
19. The Bible determines what is "right"/"wrong" for all people				

20. Do you live your life according to the Bible?   _____   ____   _____   _____

21. Do you believe God created everything in six days?   _____   ____   _____   _____

22. Are alcohol and drugs a sin?   _____   ____   _____   _____

23. Have you been taught something different from what the Bible or your parents have taught you about God or your faith?   _____   ____   _____   _____

	Zip Poor	Little Okay	Some Avg	Lots Good	Tons Great
24. How relevant/useful is your church to your spiritual growth today?	1	2	3	4	5
25. How relevant/useful is your youth group to your spiritual growth?	1	2	3	4	5
26. How useful/influential are your parent(s) to your spiritual growth?	1	2	3	4	5
27. Do you believe in creation as stated in the Bible?	1	2	3	4	5
28. How useful is the Bible to your needs today?	1	2	3	4	5
29. How useful is prayer to your needs today?	1	2	3	4	5
30. How is your relationship with God?	1	2	3	4	5
31. How is your relationship with your Dad?	1	2	3	4	5
32. How is your relationship with your Mom?	1	2	3	4	5
33. How is your relationship with your siblings?	1	2	3	4	5
34. Do you believe the only way to heaven is Jesus Christ?	1	2	3	4	5
35. How confident are you to talk about your Christian beliefs?	1	2	3	4	5
36. How confident are you in answering what and whys about faith?	1	2	3	4	5

If you are not teaching your children, someone is.
Be shade for your children

Legacy Lesson: Instilling family values is a parent's main job. Prayer will help you with that. Prayer will also change your attitude towards others and it will change you. Prayer and study of God's powerful word will lead you to a Family Awakening.

CHAPTER 26

GROWING A STRONG FAMILY TREE: THE FAMILY FARMER

Sow a thought and you reap an action. Sow an action, and you reap a habit. Sow a habit, and you reap a character. Sow a character, and you reap a destiny.
—Ralph Waldo Emerson

As we visited the many art museums in Europe—The *Louvre, Musée d'Orsay, Uffizi, Accademia,* and others—we were struck by how many Christian and biblical figures appeared in the paintings and sculptures. Scriptural references were everywhere. I was deeply moved seeing the work of artists who used their gifts for God. God has gifted every believer with unique abilities, skills, and callings. We have discussed how we can begin to prepare for our "Second Half." Just as important is how we prepare our kids for their "First Half". Nurturing their gifts is a big part of that. Helping them to understand their gifts, teaching them how to contribute to society and how to grow spiritually is not an overnight process. We are in the planting business.

One generation plants the trees and another gets the shade.
—Chinese proverb

The Teacher

Things tend to happen in bunches when God is trying to get your attention. An old marketing adage is "the rule of seven." The data show that you need to see and hear something seven times before you will take action and buy it. My wife will tell you that the same principle applies with me in our household. My thick headedness: I need to hear things multiple times before they *start* to sink in. This planting-and-nurturing business is hard stuff.

I walked my son out to the mower, gave him some *brief* instructions, and then said that I would check his work out when he was done. Later, as I surveyed his work, I realized that maybe it was not worth all of the trouble. My report card on his work was a D+ and I thought this was a good time for teaching thoroughness, work ethic, and diligence. I tend to be a perfectionist, Type-A papa bear—do it right or I will just do it myself. The

Holy Spirit gently nudged me and reminded me about a teaching from our Sunday school class[173] about what discipleship or training really is. Our society doesn't really practice it much anymore, but we used to see more "apprenticeship." Teaching needs to be repetitive, but it is also a multiple-step process. Maybe that is why I personally need seven reminders about things.

The old concept of apprenticeship applies well to how we should instruct our kids—and that's what I should have done before I had my child mow for the first time. Apprenticeship is

1. I do; you watch.
2. I do; you help.
3. You do; I help.
4. You do; I watch.

The term *modeling* is also used. We should model behavior before we expect good results. You could further explain it as

1. Explain—tell
2. Demonstrate—show
3. Supervise—do
4. Affirm—go

My mowing apprenticeship effort had skipped steps 1 through 3 and moved directly to step 4. Actually, I had rescoped #4 to "You do; I'll critique your work later." I am reminded of God's patience with me as His child. As a parent, I have drilled "Children, obey your parents. Honor your father and mother"[174] into my child's heads. As I read the rest of that passage, it says, "Fathers, do not exasperate your children; instead bring them up in the *training and instruction* of the Lord." As I wrestled with my laziness in "training" my child to mow straight rows, I realized that maybe I am often not honored or obeyed because I have not taken the time *I* need to in partnering with my child, in mentoring and teaching them.

Plant a Tree

I was watching my son play in a national tennis tournament. I was utterly amazed as he hit an incredible shot called a "tweener." Roger Federer hit this type of "trick shot" in the U.S. Open in Flushing Meadow, New York on September 13, 2009, and we were there to see it live. It was called the greatest shot of all time. It is worth YouTube viewing. My thirteen-year-old son had just decided to execute the shot on the biggest point of his match. It was a third-set tiebreaker and his opponent was ranked in the Top 10. My son swung his racket back, with his back to the net and his back to his opponent. The ball went backwards through his legs, past his opponent and landed in by a foot! He went on to win the match! It was great fun to watch!

What I didn't understand was that his opponent yelled out "TREE" right after the big shot. I thought that was a compliment as the kid smiled and shook his head just like Federer's opponent did after his shot. Turns out that "tree" means "come on dude, that was a ridiculous shot and lucky as heck." You won't find that definition for *tree* anywhere in Webster's dictionary. I closed a generational gap with my son that day by learning a new definition of the word *tree*.

I did not teach my son the "tweener" between-the-legs-backwards tennis shot. Nor did his coaches. He learned it on his own. In one sense, his tennis training parallels his life training. We instruct him in certain areas: behavior on the court, his independence, his work ethic, the value of money, whom he is practicing and playing for, etc. His coaches teach and influence him in other areas: stroke technique, technology and equipment, strategy, etc. He also makes some choices and decisions on his own: he learns from modeling himself after other players, learns from friends, and makes choices on his work and practice ethic, and even when he opts for the "tweener" trick shot. All have an influence on this growing "tree."

Although we enjoy sports and the arts as a family, those are not our primary teaching responsibilities as a parent. The "tree" we are focused on is not a trick shot but rather our "family tree." As a parent, I am responsible for the roots, and the pruning. I love Martin Luther's reply when asked what he would do if he knew he was going to die the next day. The great reformer said, "*I would plant a tree.*" Luther thought and acted generationally. Luther's influence is still being felt nearly five hundred years after his death.

Before you plant a tree, you must prepare the soil. Sometimes the ground is hard and needs to be broken up and prepared for planting.

 Read Jeremiah 4:3 and Hosea 10:12.

Ensure that you are not sowing thorns but righteousness in your child. You are the Arborist.

The Arborist

As a parent, most of us believe it is primarily our responsibility to teach, train, and raise our children. In a recent survey and article by George Barna Research,[175] Barna wrote that "96% of all parents of children contend that they have the primary responsibility for teaching their children values. 85% believe they have the primary responsibility for teaching their children about spiritual matters." Yet research reveals "that a majority of parents do not spend ANY time during a typical week discussing religion matters or studying religious materials with their children."

The survey data indicated that "parents generally rely upon their church to do ALL of the religious training their children will receive." It was positive to see that "about two out of three parents of children 12 or younger attend religious services at least once a month and generally take their children with them." Yet the troubling thing is that "the very people who claim responsibility for the spiritual growth of these children are doing little about it beyond dropping their kids off at church." The sad thing is that Barna's research indicates that often parents are struggling with their own faith development and they feel ill-equipped to do any training. It is not so much that parents don't desire to do the training, they just do not feel capable.

I know that I felt that way as a new parent. I received training for my career, training to drive a car, balance a checkbook, do a math problem, spell a word, construct a sentence and learn about our country's history. I wanted to be a good parent, but my shelf of life learning was empty when it came to instruction to be a good husband or a good parent. Hence, I forced myself to read, read, read. Some helpful resources are noted at the end of this section and www.futurefoundationbuilders.com.

Barna sadly proclaimed the adage "You can't give what you don't have." The bottom line is that we are responsible first for our own spiritual growth and second for our children's spiritual growth. Not the school. Not the church. Not a coach, relative, or neighbor. It is *our* job to "get equipped" and then "equip our children."

Back to the "tree" analogy.[176] You might relate to the proverb "The best time to plant a tree was twenty years ago. The second best time is now." It is not too late. Cultivate. Prune. Nourish. Do what you can. It might be several years until you see fruit. You might not see the fruit at all. Many times your investment will yield fruit with people you never meet. Do not underestimate the power of your impact. You might be a relative, educator, or youth worker. You might be a grandparent, a teacher, a coach, or an instructor. You have the great opportunity to influence a child. Bill Wilson said "It is easier to build a child than to repair an adult." George Barna noted the needs of millions of children. He said that "of the 51 million children under the age of 18 who live in the United States, more than 40 million of them do not know Jesus Christ as their savior."

Teaching our children biblical values when they are young builds a foundation that increases the probability that a child will be a follower of Jesus Christ. *World Relief Magazine*[177] quotes some eye-opening statistics from Barna Research Group:

- Children in the United States between ages 5 and 13 have a 32 percent probability of accepting Jesus Christ as Savior.
- Children in the United States between ages 14 and 18 have a 4 percent probability of accepting Jesus Christ as Savior.
- Adults and teenagers older than age 18 have a 6 percent probability of accepting Jesus Christ as Savior.

I hesitate to quote these statistics, as they are only numbers; and God is not limited by statisticians or historical probability. However, I quote them simply to show that teaching our children early does have a major impact, not to mention that the Bible instructs us to do so.

 Read Psalm 1:3.

Meditate on God's Word. It makes us fruitful.
Make this your prayer for your children.

Where Is that Perfect Family Tree?

We all have seen that "perfect family." That Sunday-smile-got-it-all-together-grin family walks hand in hand into church or that social event. Is it real? People let you see what they want you to see, and not too many people I know display their private failures or shortcomings for the world to see. Do not dwell on their visible and perceived success. *Every family is dysfunctional.* That needs to be said a second time: *Every family is dysfunctional.* Being married and parenting is hard work! After nearly twenty years of marriage, sending one off to college and surviving the parenting of two teens, we know a thing or two about the challenges, bumps, and bruises of raising a family.

I remember my parents telling me to "bloom where you are planted." I always thought that to mean "don't move every two years and take every new opportunity that comes along." As I get older, I tend to think of that saying in spiritual terms as well. I am thankful that for multiple generations we have had relatively strong spiritual roots to help me bloom. The roots that matter are not picture-perfect parenting or relational romance stories that last but fleeting moments but rather a strong faith.

You could think of your family tree as being made up of four parts:[178] (1) roots, (2) trunk, (3) branches and leaves, and (4) fruit. Historically, the roots might be your parents and grandparents. Looking to the future, we need to work wholeheartedly in creating a strong root system for our children. Those roots are established by you in building, teaching, instructing, and training your children. You are the trunk. Your children are the branches and leaves that are budding or will bud at different seasons of their lives. They will also need pruning. You will never see all the generational fruit, but know that it is coming. Start with good soil (God's Word) and water it regularly.

It is the responsibility of both parents to create a strong root system, to create an atmosphere for a strong family life, to instill values, to teach and to train. It is easy to rationalize that one spouse should do more because of the other spouse's lack of availability or time. It is also easy to delegate or outsource this "arborist" role to others.

 Read Proverbs 1:8 and Proverbs 6:20 and Proverbs 22:6.

The best thing you can do for your family is to address your own root system. The inclination often is to work on our spouse's root system. That is a tad easier. Working on one's own root system will eventually help your family become an "oak of righteousness."[179] Maybe your past family tree resembles a weeping willow more than a strong oak. Maybe you have inherited some bad root system DNA. You might need to do some pruning. Don't let that stand in your way. It will not be easy. It will take time. The best way to do that is to start now.

The obvious fertilizing of your root system will be a strong Bible-believing church, family spiritual leadership, and positive educational instruction. We must know "what" and "who" is watering our kids and choose the very best, most effective fertilizer for our family.

Some very powerful fertilizer is prayer. "Less than 8% of all couples pray together regularly, and less than 3% of all Christian couples have daily prayer together.[180]" Praying with your spouse and children might be a very humbling experience, but it is so rewarding.

Having spiritual intimacy really is the best fertilizer in both your relationship with God and your spouse. We stopped praying together for several years because of busyness, but we realized a gap and an emptiness when we missed those prayer times. It is helping us to be a stronger trunk for our children.

STOP   Read John 15:1–8, Romans 11:16–24 and Ezekiel 36:26. First, think about your heart, then the roots, trees, and vines and how they apply to you and your relationship with God. Next, think about you and your children. Does a tree yield fruit all of the time?

Think generationally! The seeds that you are planting that will yield either a weeping willow or a booming oak tree! Plant some seeds of prayer, and be earnest about it. The clock is ticking.

"Prayer seemed to be as natural to me as a breath by which the inward burnings of my heart had vent."
—Jonathan Edwards

STOP   Where can your prayer life improve? Confess; tell God—He will help you. Make a commitment and tell your spouse that beginning today you will pray together every day. Be real and authentic in your prayers. Relax in knowing that there is no perfect prayer!

Generational Giant

Mordecai Ham/Edward Kimball. These two men are part of Billy Graham's spiritual family tree. Graham came to know Christ after attending revival meetings led by Mordecai Ham. You can trace this generational spiritual tree back to a gospel crusade by the famous D.L. Moody. But who won D.L. Moody to the Lord? A Sunday school teacher named Edward Kimball who took a personal interest, one-on-one with Dwight Moody, and led him to the Lord. An ordinary man. Billy Graham preached the gospel to more than 80 million people in person and to millions more on the airwaves and film during his life. Three million people responded to his simple message and invitation to "Come as you are" and receive Jesus Christ." Just like David was an ordinary shepherd, so were Mordecai Ham and Edward Kimball. Jesus was born in an ordinary manger. Noah was a normal father. Nehemiah was a cupbearer. God used ordinary, unschooled men to make a generational impact. You are that oak tree in your children's lives and in others' lives. Those seeds you are planting will in time have a generational impact.

*"Our death is not an end if we can live on in our children
and the younger generation. For they are us, our bodies are only wilted leaves
on the tree of life.*
—Albert Einstein

Legacy Lesson: You are a Family Farmer. It is your responsibility to plant, prune, fertilize and water your children. Sow good seed in the hearts and minds of your children and you will reap a great generational harvest.

CHAPTER 27

PARENTING PURPOSEFULLY: EFFECTIVE DISCIPLINE AND NAVIGATING THE HIGH SCHOOL YEARS

 Read Hebrews 12:5–11.

I remember being a young teenager and having my Dad bring out that big stick in the bathroom. I knew the drill pretty well. Lean over and keep your hands in front of you. Then the spanking came. Sometimes real tears came; at other times they were fake tears. The fake tears were always prudent so he knew it *really* did hurt, and the next time the paddling wouldn't be any harder. I remember one time having enough time to run upstairs and put on three pairs of corduroys before the spanking. That was a fake-tear-acting moment second to none.

I hate discipline. I hated being on the receiving end as a child, and I despise putting my child through a similar experience. It is often drama filled and would just be easier to turn my head and shut my ears to the arguing or disrespect being shown. I admit I am not as consistent as I need to be. Much of that is due to a soft heart and loving my kids. But the fact of the matter is that God disciplines those He loves,[181] and it is my job as a parent to do the same. If you are early on in marriage, ensure that you have discussions with your spouse about your approach to discipline. We are often products of our parents and their discipline approaches. My parental tendency in discipline is similar to how I was raised.

Many parents might not see eye to eye on this. Don't let it be a source of disagreement, but study and discuss and don't just go with the mainstream flow. Most kids today do not get disciplined adequately.

A Heart Issue

Our culture tends toward either the John Wayne/military approach of parenting or the wimpy "be-my-friend" approach. The best approach might lie somewhere in between. You must exercise authority. You must require obedience. You must discipline. But according to Tedd Tripp, you must *Shepherd a Child's Heart*[182] in love. This process is harder and requires a richer interaction with the child, a real investment of showing them "the whats and the whys" of life. Tripp talks of the key issue not being the behavior but what is going on in the heart. The behavior reflects the heart.

It is difficult to remember that our children's future is so much bigger than their test or quiz that week, the failed relationship, or the lack of respect at that moment. Our prayer this year has been one from *Shepherding a Child's Heart*: "Lord, change their heart, not just their attitude." We also added, "Lord, change *my* heart! I cannot do this parenting thing with a smile and a deep love in my heart right now. I need Your strength and power! Help me to have the strength to discipline." Or it might be, "Help me, Lord, to have a softer heart, a gentler heart, and less anger toward my child. Help me to have a love for my child right now, a peace and a calm in my tone."

It is not the mouth, the attitude, or the disobedience that is the real root issue. Those are symptoms. The heart is the issue. Out of the heart everything else flows.

 How should we respond to those realities?

	Reality	Response
Jeremiah 17:9–10	The heart is deceitful and wicked.	Say, "Lord, search my heart."
Proverbs 4:23	Out of the heart flows everything.	Guard your heart.
Luke 6:45	The mouth speak what's in the heart.	Fill your heart with good things.
1 Chronicles 21:8	We all choose to sin.	Confess our sin to God.

Discipline is also about the parents' heart. I know that at times I have had to apologize for my anger during discipline. That is humbling, but it also holds me accountable when I tell my child that I should not have spanked them in anger. Sure, they stirred up that anger most of the time, but that is only part of the point. What is God teaching me through this discipline process?

In our child training we tend to use a lot of incentives and boundaries: allowances, contracts, and other motivational tools. These are okay, but they can be superficial if we are not also training the heart and the "why" we need to work hard, the "why" we need to stay pure, etc.

We also used spanking as the primary discipline method until they were teenagers, and then we used grounding as they got into high school. Again, these methods might be okay, but are the heart issues being addressed? Interaction and discussion are sometimes harder than quickly yanking a phone away. Some teen rebellion is a result of their trying to establish independence and obtain freedom. Some of it might be due to a deeper reason— new friends, music, anger at a parent, etc. We need to understand the heart issues that are going on. This requires constant attention and on-going discussion—communication. We all need "heart surgery," not some external makeup.

Tripp says that our child should obey "*without challenge, without excuse, without delay.*" We have always asked our children to obey immediately, without delay or excuse. That means the "count-to-three" approach is not acceptable. If you accept any other response, you are training your children to disobey. Consistency in discipline is key. They should know that they aren't going to get eighteen warnings, or they will keep testing the boundaries. Discipline should be immediate and consistent. If we come out of left field and spank them one day for disrespecting a parent, and then we don't say a word when they are disrespectful the next day, we will confuse the child.

You can read many, many books on discipline from a different perspective. I would prefer to start with the Bible and do a quick ten-minute study on correction and discipline.

- We all despise correction: Proverbs 5:12.
- Refusing correction leads to a going astray: Proverbs 10:17.
- He who hates correction is stupid: Proverbs 12:1.
- Poverty and shame comes for those who disdain correction: Proverbs 13:18.
- He who receives correction is prudent: Proverbs 15:5.
- A father and a mother are involved: Proverbs 1:8–9.
- It is our responsibility to train our children: Proverbs 22:6.

What about Spanking?

Again, I would prefer not to give you my opinion but rather ask you to take five minutes and review what the Bible has to say about it.

 Read Deuteronomy 8:5; Proverbs 10:13; 13:24; 19:18; 20:30; 22:15; 23:13–14; and 29:15, 17.

The Bible seems to be clear on the value of the rod. The key is to not use it in anger and to do it promptly.

> "*He who spares the rod hates his son,*
> *but he who loves him disciplines him promptly.*"
> —Proverbs 13:24 (NKJV)

Love

Our kids need to see and feel our love as much as they need to feel our discipline! One thing I always force, and often they might not want to receive it right away, is big hugs and holding them after spanking. This time of touch-and-love is not just for post-discipline. It should be a normal way of life.

Jesus took time to "just relate," to just slow down and bless the children. He took time with large groups and multitudes and his disciples, but He also just slowed down, grabbed the kids, and loved on them.[183]

"He took the children in His arms." He took the initiative.
He made time for them. He slowed down.
"He placed His hands on them." Our kids need hugs.
They need love. They need our touch
"He blessed them." His words were encouraging and positive.
He blessed them.

As parents, if you partitioned the amount of time we spend correcting, teaching, challenging, for most families it is a very high percentage of time. I am very convicted that I need to spend more time just loving my kids. I recently just grabbed my youngest son and bearhugged him down next to me and told him I loved him. He was surprised but loved the moment. I remember spanking him another time and then having him come cradle in my arms while we talked through the "why" of the discipline. We spent the first five minutes talking about his anger from the discipline and whether that was the right response or whether a broken, repentant heart was the correct response. One time recently, my son's response was, "Jesus never spanked the disciples." We then spent the next ten minutes just talking about discipline's purpose, going through the scriptures above, and then my loving on him.

Older kids might not seem to express their appreciation for a good hug as much, but deep down inside they need it. Most of their teenage lives are surrounded by sarcasm and tearing down. Yes, they need the instruction and the correction, but they also need that positive word of encouragement. I made a commitment to hug and bless my kids and wife every day. I had always hugged them and said "I love you" sporadically, but now that my kids were in high school I knew this was even more important and necessary. It was a more consistent habit, but now the kids have come to expect it.

Kids today deal with texts better than with a phone call. I recently sent my teenage son a text that said, "I just want you to know that I love you and I am proud of you." His response back was "?". I am sure he was conflicted. I am certain he was thinking, *Who replaced my Dad and sent this text from his phone?* Deep down he needed it and appreciated it. When I got home from work, he asked me more about why I sent the text, so we had a chance to talk. (The talk was brief. He is still a boy. And still a teen.) I just told him that I was sorry that I didn't praise him more, that I was proud of him for making good choices, and that I loved him. Influential.

The Hourglass

The very last chapter of the Old Testament sounds a lot like the fiery furnace of judgment that we might be dealing with in our world today. The final admonition is to *"turn the hearts of the parents to their children, and the hearts of the children to their parents.*[184] We need to feel the urgency of that because of the days with your children are short, but also because the days we live in are evil. One of the most challenging words for me as a parent is "Be very careful, then, how you live. . . making the most of every opportunity, because

187

the days are evil."[185] We must redeem the time. Make up for lost time. The sand in the hourglass of life is running down. Do not delay. Get to know your child and his or her heart.

Teach, train, correct, rebuke, discipline,
but encourage, love, bless, and touch!
Don't delay—take the initiative!

Legacy Lesson: Parenting purposefully includes discipline and correction. Though difficult, it is an act of love that trains a childs heart. The fruit of that training will carry on to future generations.

CHAPTER 28

PARENTING: CONFLICT, PROBLEMS, AND TOUGH DISCUSSIONS

My wife and I were recently in a high school orientation meeting for our new high-schooler. The principal made a statement that caused me to take inventory. He said that many parents tend to relax and disconnect as the kids get older. "Ahhhh! What a relief! We finally got them into high school." He stated that they actually need us more than ever and definitely more than they think as they face the pressure cooker of life during the high school and college years. Our role might change to one of protector and partner, and our role in the prayer closet ought to intensify during these years.

Our kids are engaged daily in spiritual warfare. They might not realize it and we may not see it, but a battle is raging. The tempter stalks. He seeks to destroy our children, lead them to compromise, and fill their minds with lies. We are needed more than ever during these years! One of the men in my small group was studying the Book of Acts and contrasting it with the modern church. He shared Acts 20:28–32.[186] We are the shepherds watching over our "flock of kids." When we aren't with them, they face savage wolves. Be on guard. Communicate. Lead.

I recently took a few highlighted pages from a book by Dr. James Dobson titled the *Strong Willed Child*[187] and had a long talk with one of my strong-willed children (they each have had their strong willed seasons). The talk centered on the transition and adolescent changes that were transpiring right before our eyes. These were some turbulent times, where we were jointly having problems understanding each other. During these teen years our children can seem literally to change overnight—both physically and emotionally. Sometimes the parents have just as much trouble adjusting as do the children. We were finding ourselves raising our voices more often than in earlier years, and our high school "transitioning kids" seemed to be sharpening their legal discourse and debating skills. Amazingly, no one seemed to be winning any arguments!

I took my child to a park and we just sat under a tree and talked. The discussion focused on the changes that were transpiring. We talked about some of the heart issues discussed earlier and the lack of respect and honor for parents. We discussed the failure on both ends to be "quick to listen, slow to speak and slow to become angry."[188] The reality is that the adolescent years are different; this is the final curtain call for childhood. Unfortunately, these curtain calls can seem to last an eternity instead of a quick bow, and oftentimes they are not so pleasant, but this will vary by child. We talked about the pressures our teen was facing, the freedom and independence he longed for, the necessity of responsibility that comes along with those freedoms, and what our roles were as parents and child. Your child might be going through a number of things you are not even aware of. Have a discussion with them.

According to a recent survey of teens, the top social and family pressures[189] that your kids are dealing with include the following:

Financial pressure	56%
Family problems/getting along with parents	56%
Concerns about personal safety	53%
Pressure to look a certain way	50%
Health concerns: cost and availability	49%
Loneliness or feeling left out	43%
Pressures to do drugs or to drink	39%
Pressure to engage in sexual activity	38%

Discuss these issues with your teen, and find out what pressures they are feeling.

During our park discussion, I asked my child open-ended questions about what was going on and why we weren't seeing eye to eye. It was a good chance to listen instead of lecture. When it was my turn to talk, I interspersed reading some of the highlighted sections from the Dobson book, along with some commentary and heart-felt emotion as I felt able. It was not a comfortable session for either of us. The challenge was to discuss the largeness of our responsibility as parents and couple that with a genuine love for our child, despite the challenges and feelings that were being experienced. We discussed the fact that God was going to hold us accountable for how we were raising our child. I read portions of the sobering Bible story of Eli[190] and his failure as a parent. I told him, "I will not be an Eli." The buck stops with me as Dad. My role in disciplining would be more consistent going forward and my expectations would be more honor, respect, and obedience. We, as parents, in turn, would also try to be more sensitive and more measured in our anger and tone. I asked if discipline should be inflicted upon someone who murdered someone or committed adultery (Commandments 6 and 7). The obvious answer was "yes." Then I asked if one should be disciplined (by God and Dad) if Commandment 5 (Honor your father and mother) was broken? Again, a less emphatic and mumbled "yes." Thus, it is my job as Dad to correct and discipline. The park discussion was not a magic pill but rather a connection time, a time to be sensitive to each other's feelings and a time to clarify our roles.

Sometimes it is easier *not* to deal with a problem and to let it fester than actually to address it. I recall a recent struggle between my two boys. When we inquired and they were confronted about the "disagreement," they both had a good defense and emotions were running high. I asked them if they both were wrong, and they quickly pointed the finger but did not admit any wrongdoing. We told them to go to a room together, and I asked each of them to read 1 John 3 to each other, out loud, and discuss whether they felt loved by the other. The second part of the assignment after discussing together was to make up, hug, and pray for each other. This second part was a toughie for two boys! The whole process sounds simple but, in fact, it took almost two hours to complete in this instance!

Glimpses

Sometimes your house might feel like a war zone. At other times, you might feel as though you are that warped or scratched LP record spinning around and around the same issues with little or no impact. Your kids might be the needle scratching that record! We had been through some rocky times with "respect" issues, and it had been frustrating for all parties involved. Groundings. Spankings. Speeches. We wondered if any of this was sinking in.

I was on a business trip recently and texted my kids just to tell them I love them. Kids don't use phones to talk anymore, they are simply for texting, you know. Imagine my amazement when my daughter actually called me and asked, "When you gonna be home?" I was 1500 miles from home driving on the highway, and it was all I could do to keep the rental car on the road. She went on to say, "I miss our family dinners together." Wow! Once in a while you get glimpses that you are, indeed, making an impact. Another time I over-heard my child having an intense discussion about a major decision with God, seeking His will. It brought tears to my eyes. Glimpses.

Before you put our family on a pedestal, though, be certain to know that does *not* happen every day, but it was a nice glimpse into knowing that maybe portions of our investment—in time, in discipline, in transferring our faith—*will* stick! Hang in there. Similar to that great golf shot that brings you back to the links again—keep it up!

Dealing with Problems

My teenage son and I entered the jammed parking lot outside the massive church with the big steeple. We were in Atlanta, Georgia, 800 miles from home. Previous trips to Atlanta had resulted in great memories, and I felt very much at home there. I had spent a weekend at Callaway Gardens at Pine Mountain with my daughter at a Vision Forum daddy/daughter date weekend, where we enjoyed a bike ride through the world's largest azalea display and a tea party for two. I had been a guest on Larry Burkett, Howard Dayton, and Steve Moore's Crown Ministries talk show to discuss *Ease the Squeeze,* and then I returned another time to conduct a seminar at the oldest African-American church in Metropolitan Atlanta, the historic Big Bethel Church, where President William H. Taft had spoken and half a mile from the childhood stomping grounds of Martin Luther King Jr. We also had great family memories of Stone Mountain and the Coca-Cola factory.

So, being in Atlanta again made me a little nostalgic, but as we approached the building, the nostalgia was turning to butterflies and a nervous gut. My son and I had a great weekend. He had just finished playing in a National Tennis tournament in Norcross. I wasn't nervous because we had shorts and sweats on and people with suits, dresses and top hats were walking by us with one eyebrow raised. I was nervous because I was getting ready to see *"the man."* The TV preacher with a southern drawl who helped reel me in nearly twenty years ago. Late, late nights, as I channel flipped in a daze, a welcome, soothing voice always seemed to greet me, a total stranger, with compassion and care. He and another fire-and-brimstone preacher, Dwight Thompson, always seemed to be speaking directly to me as I lay on my couch of compromise.

That was then. This is now. We were a tad out of place. This place was made for TV. The marching cadence of the glitzy robed choir. The elevated orchestra pit. Every move seemed orchestrated as cameras moved along the catwalks. As I joined in worship, the generational differences and traditions were multisensory. The dress style. The well-coifed hair. The worship style. The liturgy and tradition. It was foreign to my worship experience, but it mattered not. Pride is the main reason, I believe, that one generation rejects another's wisdom. Although I was distracted by the differences in my worship preferences, I was intently focused on ensuring that this time was not wasted.

Generational Giant

The media team wheeled out a small table and chair as *the man* moved slowly with an uneven shuffle toward the center of the stage—the 78-year-old Charles Stanley: a generational giant. With a golden voice that only Ernie Harwell could compete with, Dr. Stanley began to speak, and it was music to my ears and to my soul. In his smooth drawl he said, "*Out of every problem something beautiful is there.*" I was overcome by a sense of gratefulness to God for sending this man of God into my life. There are enough TV preacher horror stories to go around, but I had two of them who spoke into my life. This was a generational impact playing out. My son was sitting next to his dad, listening to a man talk about his father and grandfather and their influence on his life.

After we sang "*God in three persons, blessed Trinity*," Stanley related a story of how his grandfather had been thrown out of the Methodist church for believing in the Holy Spirit. The message was based on 2 Chronicles 20:1–31 and covered a topic that all can relate to: "how to respond to problems." Jehoshaphat was in a battle, experiencing problems, and he was outnumbered. You will have problems and conflict with your children. Guaranteed. I share with you a few golden nuggets of inspiration[191] in understanding and dealing with your problems:

- God is interested in your problem. He is ready to bear your burdens. Cast your cares on Him, for He cares for you.
- Seek the Lord. Proclaim a fast. You will get plenty of opinions in how to deal with the problem, but start with God, not all of the "generals'" opinions. Don't go to God as a last resort.
- God is greater than your problem. Nothing is too difficult for Him. He knows the number of hairs on your head (easier with me than with others). He will see you through it. The battle is the Lord's.
- He might want to involve other people. Who do you trust? Who do you treasure? Use these times as examples for your children to pray and see answers to their prayers.
- God is more interested in what you are becoming than in the solution. James 1:2–4 talks of maturing, developing, growing. Let this temporary time of trial be an opportunity to do some self-examination, and ensure a pure heart.
- Know that this time of trial is temporary. Know also that although the enemy might be involved, God will use this time to perfect, establish, and strengthen you. (See 1 Peter 5:8–11.)

- Make your prayers God-centered, not self-centered. The problem will get smaller with this approach. In 2 Chronicles 20:6–9, Jehoshaphat looks to God twelve times!
- God's solution will require an act of faith. Are you willing to trust Him? Even if the solution is not what you desired? Do not waver in faith. (See James 1:6–8.)

Experiencing problems is not a waste of time. Failing is not a once-in-a-lifetime thing. Problems are not a once-a-year event. Growth, maturity, and trust are the ultimate results of problems. My son lost his tennis tournament that weekend. My wife and I and he could all sense that his focus was shifting more to academics than to tennis. He had plenty of state and national tournament wins under his belt, he was ranked #14 in Texas and #166 in the nation. As a parent trying to nourish and fertilize your child's dreams and juggle your expectations and desires versus your child's, some of the seasonal transitions will be bittersweet. Some of the problems with your children or living through the teen years are a great example of difficult seasonal transitions.

We realized that that weekend was about so much more than tennis. The journey through competitive tennis was not so much about the wins and losses as it was about the man he was becoming. To my son, it could have been a two-hour service with too much organ, too little guitar, too many lights, too much hairspray, and sulking after a loss. Instead, it was about being together, sharing a generational mile marker, and transitioning to manhood. We both knew that season, that time, that weekend wasn't about the wins and losses but about the process and how it would help him in his life—the problem solving, trusting of God, dealing with competition, managing emotions, responding to the influence of outside forces and people—both positive and negative. He was becoming a man.

By the way, Dr. Stanley stood for the entire message; he never once used the chair that had been wheeled out for him.

"Do not be afraid or discouraged, for the battle is not yours, but God's."
—2 Chronicles 20:15

 "Rest"—Dennis Jernigan

Tough Discussions

Ensure that you have the tough discussions with your kids earlier rather than later. We used the *"God's Design for Sex"* series about the "birds and the bees" over a number of years. Reading these books aloud to the kids helped with the awkward moments. I would highly recommend you address this tough discussion before your child's friends teach him about sex. Most kids learn of these critical life issues from friends and it is usually PG-13 to R-rated. Talk to your kids about drugs and drinking. According to Mothers Against Drunk Driving, "74% of teens say parents are their No. 1 influence in their decisions about alcohol."[192] MADD recommends starting these discussions at the fourth grade.

Your actions and your habits will speak louder than any words. Practice what you preach. Talk and listen. Often, parents are embarrassed or fearful about talking of these things, but it is important to let your kids know the difference between right and wrong and your opinions and ground rules on key subjects. We have a "contract" and a yearly reward offered for every year of purity for our kids. The rewards grow as they age. A down payment on a house is the ultimate carrot. We also bought a purity ring with our daughter when she started high school.

We have not allowed dating during the middle school and early high school years. While the kids are in high school, it might be good to create a list of qualities you desire in a spouse. Knowing that no perfect individual is out there, and that it will be impossible to find someone with all of the traits listed, at a minimum it will force them to consider what they are looking for. Having some key "musts" and some "shoulds" will help narrow down the non-negotiables. Following is a comprehensive list that was inspired and adapted from a list by Christy Farris.[193] I gave it to my children and asked them to consider making their own list when it was time.

Characteristics of a Future Relationship/Spouse

- **Must** be a born-again Christian, able to give a testimony of his or her salvation
- Should be patient and kind
- Should not be envious
- Should be humble
- Should not be easily angered or hold a grudge
- Should not delight in evil, and should rejoice with the truth
- **Must** be a protector (man)
- Should be trusting
- Should have hope
- Should persevere
- Should be loving
- Should be joyful
- Should be good
- Should be peaceful and gentle
- Should be faithful
- **Must** have self-control
- **Must** be a hard worker
- **Must** love the Lord with all of his or her heart, soul, mind, and strength
- Should walk in all God's ways
- **Must** hold fast to the Lord
- Should not worry but turn to God in prayer
- Should build others up with words
- **Must** not even hint at sexual immorality or impurity, living a holy life
- Should not joke coarsely or say inappropriate things
- **Must** not be greedy
- **Must** not be yoked with unbelievers
- Should be the salt of the earth and the light of the world and obey the Great Commission
- **Must** like children
- **Must** be committed to attending church regularly
- Should keep his or her priorities straight

- Should have a sense of humor
- Parents **must** get to know them and approve of them
- **Must** have a strong family life
- **Must** be prepared to support and provide for a family (man)
- **Must** be prepared to be the spiritual leader of the home (man)
- **Must** be committed to staying out of debt
- **Must** understand the priority of a homeschool or Christian education
- **Must** support the option of a mother's staying at home to raise the kids (man)
- Should be attractive to me
- **Must** have daily quiet times with the Lord
- Should be willing to sacrifice his or her own comfort for the needs of the family
- Should be willing to love and serve the poor
- Should be strong and dignified
- **Must** love the Lord more than me—and make it obvious!

> *"Modern American dating is no more than glorified divorce practice."*
> —Voddie Baucham Jr

Media Influence/Boundaries

The average teen has a lot of plates in the air, which can lead to stress, turmoil, and family challenges. It also leads to little time for teaching, instruction, or just hanging out.

Teenage Average Activity (hours per week)[194]

We have made the decision that our children would not work during early high school. That might not be the right decision for every family, but the homework they have is staggering. Our homework numbers are probably three times the average shown in the preceding graph, and we chose to add a priority of spiritual emphasis that takes up additional time. It is interesting that if you add up the time for media/technology, it is nearly one-third of the time, between internet, cell phone, and television. That is a great opportunity area to shift more time to relationship time, spiritual emphasis, and volunteer/ministry time, or work if necessary.

Media Barrage

Media are probably the most powerful influences in a young person's life today. According to a Kaiser Family Foundations study, "8 to 18 year olds spend more time with media than in any other activity besides (maybe) sleeping—an average of more than 7½ hours a day."[195] When I was a new parent, we were counseled to ensure that we knew about the friends our children hung out with. I think it is now just as important to know what media our children are interfacing with. They are now communicating with children in other countries with different beliefs and value systems. "The TV shows they watch, the video games they play, the songs they listen to, the websites they visit are an enormous part of their lives, offering a constant stream of messages."[196] This will influence their values, their spiritual compass, their peers, their relationships, and many other things.

Over the past five years, young people have increased the amount of time they spend consuming media by an hour and seventeen minutes daily, from 6:21 to 7:38![197] That is a full-time job for most adults! Yet they only spend an average of only one hour and forty-six minutes engaging in physical activity. Youth who spend more time with media report lower grades, do not get along with parents as well, are not as happy at school, get into trouble more, and are more sad as a group."[198]

We adults are not discouraging the media magnetism. Parents usually make the decisions about their children's media environment. "The typical 8 to 18 year old home contains an average of 3.8 TVs, 2.8 DVDs, 2.2 CD players, 2 computers, and 2.3 video game players.'[199] Most of these were purchased by us adults.

Drown out the Noise/Boundaries!

If parents do not set rules, the kids will make their own rules. Hardenbrook reported that "64% of youth say the television is on during meals, 45% say the TV is left on most of the time, even if no one is watching, 52% say they have rules about what they're allowed to do on the computer, 46% say they have rules about what they're allowed to watch. 30% of parents regulate video games and only 26% regulate music."[200]

Maybe make a media resolution and lay down some boundaries. You should come up with your own rules, but here are some suggestions to start:

- Allow no media in kids' bedrooms.
- Allow no television during meal times.
- Turn off the noise.
- Limit the amount of video-game play daily (use the timer).
- Reward media time according to the amount of reading time or outside activity time.
- Add timers to the computer.
- Add filters to filter certain sites.

Legacy Lesson: Parenting is the most difficult job you will face. How you deal with family problems and conflicts will determine much about their future. Don't run from the tough discussions and issues.

CHAPTER 29

PASSING THE BATON: GENERATIONAL BLESSINGS

Two instrumental men challenged me to "bless" my kids daily. Although it might seem a bit weird or "priestish" to you, there is plenty of biblical precedent for this action, and a great book on it is *The Blessing* by Gary Smalley and John Trent. In their book, they say that a blessing encompasses five things: meaningful touch, spoken words, high-value messages, a vision of a special future, and active commitment. These are ways to pass your generational baton regularly.

When I hug my kids daily, I ask them if there is anything specific I can pray for them for that day. It is usually a chemistry test or an algebra test, but sometimes they will share other things. So after the hug I pray a "drive-by" prayer and then add in a quick blessing. I have memorized the following two scriptures, and I improvise a prayer or blessing for my kids. Sometimes I will pray or speak this blessing over them while they are sleeping if I arise earlier than them.

STOP Read Romans 15:13 and Numbers 6:24–27.
Consider praying these blessings over your kids or grandkids,
blessing them verbally with them.

One of the men in our small group[201] shared how he had "passed the baton" to his kids. Because his kids were little, his wife and he have a few key "life verses" with which they saturate their kids' lives. To this day, now that they are grown and off to college, they still use these verses as a reference point: Proverbs 3:5–6, Romans 12:1–2, and 1 Corinthians 10:13.

Another man shared how he had documented and laminated "10 Guideposts for Life[202]" scriptures for his child before they went off to college. Another friend shared an example of "a blessing" for their daughter that they prayed over her and then framed for her. It now hangs in her college dorm room. These are all great creative ways to pass the generational baton. Use your own creativity to bless your child.

I just finished a hardcover, sixty-page photo book for our daughter to present to her as she goes off to college as part of a "treasure chest." It included our favorite family pictures and memories as well as twenty Guideposts for Life for her. (See the appendices for an example.)

Rite of Passage

"Boys become men by watching men, by standing close to men. Manhood is a ritual passed from generation to generation with precious few spoken instructions. Passing the torch of manhood is a fragile, tedious task. If the rite of passage is successfully completed, the boy-become-man is like an oak of hardwood character. His shade and influence will bless all those who are fortunate enough to lean on him and rest under his canopy."
---Preston Gilliam

Most boys, including me, just drift into manhood. When did I "become" a man? When I noticed the peach fuzz under my arms? When my voice starting changing and cracking? My first kiss? The first day of high school? The last day of high school? When I had my own address? Or my own car? This is true of girls as well. When do they become women? Most of us really never had that defining moment when expectations changed and roles started to transition.

Many societies throughout history have manhood ceremonies that signify that "coming of age," an acknowledgement of the transition from boy to man. Many of these are survivor-type warrior events (boy kills lion, boy spends night blindfolded in wilderness, etc.) that probably wouldn't sit too well with the average teen. Most of us hold no rite of passage, celebration, or ceremony to mark the official entrance into manhood. One size might not fit all. I would recommend Jim McBride's book *Rite of Passage*. Here are a few examples of what we did with our kids.

Prayer Passage

One of the things I had planned for our boys was to have a "Prayer/Blessing Passage" event when they reached the age of adulthood. We couldn't decide whether to call it a "Prayer passage" or a "Blessing passage," but we wanted him to look back on this event as a passing of the baton of sorts. I asked a small group of individuals, "generational giants" or "prayer warriors" in my life, to pray about his future and what God might want to impart or speak to him about. They spent time in prayer and seeking God and sent a written blessing or prayer. About ten responded. My wife and I each wrote our own. (Mine is included in the appendices.) So our simple event was he and I alone together for less than an hour:

1. I read/prayed my friends/people of influence "blessing letters/prayer passages" over him.
2. I read my personal blessing and prayer to him and over him.
3. I read my spouse's blessing and prayed over him.
4. We celebrated at Starbucks.
5. Went to church.

I bound all the letters and my wife's and my blessings in a folder with the specific date and time referenced. Others choose to have a more public ceremony, but this fit our son the best. My friend had six close friends/influencers of his teen son to dinner, and they each read him their letter and we prayed over him. It is never too late. If your child is out of the house, do a video tribute, a blessing letter, or anything that fits you and your child. You can present it to him or her during a get-together. This would also be a great exercise for older grandchildren.

A Cherokee Legend

I came upon the following Cherokee legend about the Cherokee Indian youth's rite of passage:

> His father takes him into the forest, blindfolds him and leaves him alone. He is required to sit on a stump the whole night and not remove the blindfold until the rays of the morning sun shine through it. He cannot cry out for help to anyone. Once he survives the night, he is a MAN. He cannot tell the other boys of this experience, because each lad must come into manhood on his own.
>
> The boy is naturally terrified. He can hear all kinds of noises. Wild beasts must surely be all around him. Maybe even some human might do him harm. The wind blew the grass and earth, and shook his stump, but he sat stoically, never removing the blindfold. It would be the only way he could become a man! Finally, after a horrific night the sun appeared and he removed his blindfold.
>
> It was then that he discovered his father sitting on the stump next to him. He had been at watch the entire night, protecting his son from harm. We, too, are never alone. Even when we don't know it, God is watching over us, sitting on the stump beside us. When trouble comes, all we have to do is reach out to Him.

"Inviting a teenager into adulthood on purpose is better than letting it happen by accident."[203]

Off to College

Our daughter is going off to college this year. Here are some ideas for such a monumental event for your child.

- Create a Treasure Chest of Memories
    - o Two letters of blessing, one from each spouse
    - o Photo book with family memories for the dorm room
    - o Guideposts for Life—key spiritual truths—laminated
    - o A written blessing framed for the college dorm room
    - o A family picture framed
- Prayer walk together the day before—no stress or time pressures
- Establish a tradition when visiting the campus—restaurant, church, etc.
- Create or document any financial agreements or contracts as reminders

Generational Blessing

Earlier in the book, we discussed the reality of genetic traits. We can inherit our father's nose, our mother's eyes, or the hairline of a grandfather. We also can look at our family through the generations and see that we have picked up a character quality or two as well along the way. You might have joy, a heart for giving, and a positive outlook on life, or you might struggle with worry, depression, pride, a bad temper, an addiction, or possibly an inclination to lie.

Some of these features might just be learned traits, but some of them might also have a spiritual root. A particular family might have a tendency toward habits or sins such as alcoholism, divorce, addiction, or suicide. Rather than just write these off as "learned" or "genetic," it might be wise to take them to a mighty God in prayer. We even went so far as to have a three-generational male bonding prayer time in March 2010 with my dad and my two sons. This was a time to confess sin and pray that any generational bondage would not carry on. We had a few key areas that my dad and I identified that might have a spiritual root. It's better to pray over them than not to, was our philosophy. God's Word, prayer, and the power of God's Spirit are enough to destroy anything and bring liberty to a family.

STOP Read Psalm 22:30, Genesis 17:7,
Exodus 20:5, and Jeremiah 32:18.

This was a memorable time seeing three generations pray together. It might seem a little hokey and awkward, but it was a great time together. I prepared a few key scriptures that we read together and prayed together. We laid hands on the two boys and prayed that they would live holy lives and that any generational sins or spiritual attacks would be broken and cut off, not transferred. We confessed our sin areas (generically) and the sins of father and grandfather, and asked that they be stopped now with this bloodline. We prayed that any ancestral roots would be destroyed—physically, genetically, psychologically, and spiritually. Finally, we prayed that generational blessings and favor would pass to future generations. We read and prayed the following Scriptures over them:[204]:Isaiah 61:1; 2 Corinthians 5:17; Galatians 5:1; Colossians 1:12-14; Titus 3:3–7; and 1 John 1:9.

You might need to cleanse your family root system of past iniquities—certain behavioral characteristics that can't seem to get broken—alcohol, divorce, rebellion, fear, abuse, health, anger, violence, or sexual sin. We took about thirty minutes to read the scriptures and pray together. You could also use a simple prayer such as this:

"Father, I thank you for your Word which is a lamp unto my feet and a light unto my path. I thank You for redemption through the blood of Jesus. I give myself to you. I ask You to cleanse me from all sin and iniquity. I confess the sin(s) of _____ that has been in my family for generations. Forgive us—myself, my parents and my forefathers—of all unrighteousness. Cleanse me and my children now by the blood of Jesus. I believe that You are breaking the link of sin and delivering me, my children and future generations right now from the bondage of hereditary weaknesses, sins and curses. We pray that it will stop now and forever with my bloodline, in the name of Jesus Christ, and through His blood shed on the cross. We accept Christ's forgiveness for the sins of the past and ask that You destroy

and curse any generational roots that might be left in my family and our children. I ask that You rebuke the evil one and that You cleanse and protect me and my children (by name): _____, _____, *our minds, emotions, wills, and bodies. In Jesus name I pray. Amen.*

Legacy Lesson: Be purposeful about how you can pass the baton to your children, grandchildren, or others close to you. It might be a ceremony, a blessing, or special get together. You are impacting generations to come!

CHAPTER 30

A SUCCESSFUL MARRIAGE

"Married life is a marathon, not a sprint. It is not enough to make a great start toward long-term marriage. You will need the determination to keep plugging on, even when every fiber of your body longs to quit."
—Dr. James Dobson

 I would highly recommend you take a couple minutes and view the video Johnny and Chachi "Killer Marriage Tips".

I hope I am not as bad as that video depicts us men to be. I am dysfunctional but hopefully not to that extent. Marriage, however, is indeed "a great mystery."[205]

Dysfunctional Adventure

February 2, 1991—our first date: the adventure begins. We had many adventures during those dating years, but it often feels as though they were a lifetime ago. My wife knew that she was in for yet another adventure when I picked her up from her apartment in Lewisville, Texas, and instead of proceeding to our planned destination in San Antonio, I surprised her and swept her off to Key West, Florida. A man ought to know better than to give a woman ten minutes notice for a change in destination so drastic. She should have seen the red flag regarding my "marriage intelligence" at that point. The next surprise was my proposal on a sunset dinner cruise. I still recall clearly getting on one knee with the sunset as my backdrop and starting my proposal with a paraphrase of Romans 15:5: *"May God, who gives endurance and encouragement, give us a spirit of unity among ourselves as we follow Christ Jesus. Dana will you marry me?"* It was all bliss, emotion, love, and passion.

It was the first of many, many surprises for the young Hag couple. She might have had second thoughts when my best man handed me her wedding ring in a Cracker Jack box. The pastor wisecracked, "Knowing Doug and these guys, I am glad it was a Cracker Jack box." She continues to stomach my surprises, puts up with my warts, and loves me for

202

who I am despite my dysfunctions. Those dating and honeymoon years can awaken all of our senses but blind us to the other blind spots. Actually, you don't see many blind spots at all early in a relationship.

Every family and couple is dysfunctional in one way or another. Our family is not *The Waltons* or the Cleavers, but neither are we *The Simpsons* or *Modern Family*. We do not have the perfect marriage, and although we might be dysfunctional at times, we know the God-established boundaries and live within them. We work hard at our marriage. Every marriage gets tested. It is how you respond to those tests that make or break it. You will really find out who you are (your spouse might figure it out before you do) deep to the core as the years in a marriage pile up. As a new spouse and a soon-to-be-new father twenty years ago, I had no plan, no education, no goals, no role model and no accountability. What were our odds for success? A successful marriage is a rare find in today's world despite the fact that our country was built on the foundation of strong marriages. Maybe you have failed in marriage. Be doubly purposeful in ensuring your next relationship is successful.

Family Foundation—The Power of Marriage

The best gift children could receive is a loving, respectful, lasting marriage between a man and a woman. In *Reynolds v. the United States* (1878), the Supreme Court called marriage a "sacred obligation." According to *Murphy v. Ramsey* (1885), the states of our Union were established "on the basis of the idea of the family, as consisting in and springing from the union for life of one man and one woman in the holy estate of matrimony." We are seeing the erosion of the priority of the traditional marriage and its permanence and exclusivity. We must be countercultural. Timothy Dolan, Archbishop of New York for the Roman Catholic Church, spoke of the battle being fought for traditional marriage:[206] *"The Church is 'counter-cultural,' like Jesus, often at odds with what passes as chic, enlightened and progressive. We have been bloodied, and bruised, and yes, for the moment, we have been defeated. But we're used to that. So was the Founder of our Church."*

That Sacred "Obligation": Commitment

During nearly twenty years of marriage, my wife and I have had our good days and our bad days and days where we have "loved each other" but maybe not "liked each other." One thing that we have endeavored to do is to remind ourselves of our vows. We made a commitment, a covenant. After our marriage ceremony, I typed out our vows and we signed them and framed them. On particular milestones, we refresh and recite them again publicly. On our ten-year anniversary, I was able to get access to the church where we were married and had a horse and carriage waiting for us just like on our wedding day. Our pastor and his wife publicly witnessed our vows once again at the altar and signed them with witnesses. A little corny? Yeah, but an effective reminder that this was a life-long commitment. I even ordered a replica of our wedding cake and had a surprise "mini-reception" at Traildust Steakhouse where we had invited friends ten-years earlier. At the fifteen-year mark, we publicly read our vows and then signed them again with family members.

As young newlyweds, we had attended Dennis Rainey's Family Life Marriage Conference and I had read his book, *One Home at a Time*, and that had encouraged me to frame our vows. Love isn't just a feeling, like it was in the dating years and honeymoon years.

Love is a commitment. It is a verb. It is sticking it out in your marriage when things are rough. Love is giving without expecting anything in return. Love is not focusing on getting your needs met. Love is being a peacemaker and not battling for a "win" in argument, even if you are right. No marriage is perfect. Take the following "marriage check" to see not *if* you need a tuneup, but *where* you need a tuneup.

Marriage Check-up Questionnaire[207]

STOP This will help you determine your marriage strengths and areas for improvement. I would encourage you to have your spouse take it, too. It can help you identify those blind spots that need work.

Score you and your marriage from 1 to 5 with 1 being not doing well, not effective, not satisfied; 2 being rare, but occasional effectiveness and satisfaction; 3 being average, spotty but somewhat effective, satisfied; 4 being good, do pretty well, fairly satisfied, strength; and 5 being the best, doing well, very satisfied, a real strength area.

We make decisions together and are in unity.	1	2	3	4	5
Communication is a priority and we communicate well.	1	2	3	4	5
My spouse trusts me, and I trust my spouse.	1	2	3	4	5
We have a good sexual relationship.	1	2	3	4	5
We show affection and make time for romance.	1	2	3	4	5
We have daily personal interaction and involvement.	1	2	3	4	5
We manage money effectively and together.	1	2	3	4	5
We are involved together at a church.	1	2	3	4	5
We have positive spiritual interaction at home.	1	2	3	4	5
We support each other's careers/callings.	1	2	3	4	5
We support each other's hobbies.	1	2	3	4	5
We support each other during bad times and struggles.	1	2	3	4	5
We interact with friends together more than apart.	1	2	3	4	5
We spend quality free time together.	1	2	3	4	5
We have learned to resolve conflict together.	1	2	3	4	5
We have learned to adjust to each other's differences.	1	2	3	4	5
We have positive interactions with our relatives.	1	2	3	4	5
I listen attentively when my spouse is talking.	1	2	3	4	5
I do not interrupt my spouse.	1	2	3	4	5
I express appreciation for my spouse.	1	2	3	4	5
I can disagree without losing my temper.	1	2	3	4	5

I serve my spouse above my own needs.	1	2	3	4	5
I work to understand my spouse.	1	2	3	4	5
I encourage and validate my spouse.	1	2	3	4	5
I give my spouse quality time daily.	1	2	3	4	5
We have a daily undivided attention communication time.	1	2	3	4	5
We read the Bible together daily.	1	2	3	4	5
We pray together daily.	1	2	3	4	5
Family time is a priority for both of us.	1	2	3	4	5
We have an honest and open relationship.	1	2	3	4	5
We have 5 times more positive moments than negative.	1	2	3	4	5

 Take some time to reflect on your responses to these questions. Discuss them with your spouse.

*"A lasting marriage results from a couple's ability to resolve
the conflicts that are inevitable in any relationship."*
—John Gottman

Why Marriages Succeed or Fail

The book *Why Marriages Succeed or Fail*[208] by John Gottman discusses how we grow in our relationships when we learn to resolve conflict. Just because "you never fight" doesn't mean that you have a happy, successful marriage. In studying 2000 married couples more than twenty years, he was able to predict with 94 percent accuracy which couples would stay together and which would divorce. The data showed that it wasn't how much you fight, how much sex you have, or how much you are struggling with finances, rather it all boiled down to a "simple mathematical formula":

*"You must have at least five times as many positive
as negative moments together if your marriage is to be stable."*

I have "5:1" written on our prayer board, plastered on my Daytimer, and taped to all of the computers in our house as reminders to us. Maybe the negativity has been building in your marriage. Maybe the laughter is gone and the validation and support are gone. Quite possibly the criticism and arguing are more prevalent. For some people, negative thoughts and feelings abound, and the romance is gone. Maybe criticism, defensiveness, and withdrawal are the norm. Obviously, starting with prayer and communication is key, but Gottman offers a number of self-tests and other helpful advice in the book. He recommends that you can start four things immediately to help you get to 5:1:

- Calm down.
- Speak non-defensively.

- Validate your spouse.
- Overlearn—try again and again.

Are you seeing a "5:1" positive-to-negative ratio? Or is it more like "1:5"? It might make sense to make this a matter of prayer and of joint discussion and hard work. Differences need to be aired and worked through.

Answer the following questions and then, if appropriate, do something intentional to appreciate your spouse.

1. How much time do you spend together alone as a couple?	
2. Describe three things your spouse does that you appreciate.	
3. What are three personal qualities of your spouse that you appreciate?	
4. How often do you recognize or appreciate these things or personal qualities?	
5. What do you do to show that you love your spouse?	

STOP Read Proverbs 17:14,28 and Proverbs 29:11—
Are you listening? Are you controlling your tongue?

Divorce Factors

Divorces are now accepted as the norm. The sanctity of marriage is being attacked, and broken marriages are as near normal as getting a marriage license.[209]

1867: one divorce for every thirty-six marriages
1900: one divorce for every thirteen marriages
1945: one divorce for every three marriages
1998: one divorce for every two marriages

Likewise in Europe, the number of divorces per one hundred new marriages continues to grow. In the United Kingdom, fifty-three divorces per hundred marriages occur. In France, forty-one divorces for every hundred marriages. Italy is the exception with only thirteen divorces per hundred marriages.[210]

Forty percent of all divorces occur in the first five years of marriage. People quit after the romance is gone and the "real you" comes out. We have heard over and over again the statistics that one in two marriages will end in divorce and that Christian families don't fare any better. Rarely do you see any data on the thought process that led to those divorces. A recent survey[211] gives insight into contributing factors in why people decide to call it quits.

- Growing apart (55 percent)
- Unable to talk together (53 percent)
- How spouse handles money (40 percent)
- Spouse's personal problems (37 percent)
- Not enough attention from spouse (34 percent)
- Infidelity (34 percent)

Act Now

It is natural to experience these things in a marriage. What will you do to go on the offensive to battle some of these factors and fight for your marriage? Carve out times to talk; attend a financial class together; treasure, love, and respect your spouse; read a book on being a better spouse; or do a Bible study on how to be a better spouse. We expect so much out of marriage, but we don't equip ourselves with the skills necessary for a successful marriage. Make a choice to develop a battle plan for your marriage.

Author Rick Warren says, "*He thought he had married a gentle, quiet, young woman when, in reality, he had married a cleverly disguised volcano.*"[212] They were too embarrassed to talk about their marriage problems with family and friends and too proud to seek counseling initially, but they finally went to therapy, and he discovered that he had some attitudes himself that were perpetuating the problem. You might need some counseling. Don't let pride get in the way.

The "D" Word

We made a commitment on Day 1 of our marriage never to utter the D word—*divorce*. It was not an option. We might argue, fight, quarrel, or battle, but we have never discussed or threatened each other with that option. We have never used the "D" word. Not as a threat. Not as a joke. The damages to our children or future generations would be significant. For those of you in a broken or blended family or who lived through your parents' divorce know the truth of this. "After a divorce approximately half of all children do not see their fathers! The top three problems for blended families are discipline, resolving conflict and division of responsibility."[213] Blended families bring extra challenges, and the parents often have to work doubly hard. But it is worth the battle! As Max Lucado said, "Lock the escape hatch and throw away the key."

Legacy Lesson: Your marriage is worth fighting for. Remember you are battling for your children and grandchildren as well. Be a good example to follow. If you have already failed, then start now! Commit or recommit to making your marriage a top priority.

CHAPTER 31

YOUR MARRIAGE: LOVE, RESPECT, AND NEEDS

I can remember the year I bought my wife Dana a big ghetto box for her birthday when we were dating. A dream gift, wouldn't you say? Let's just say that I have learned to do a little better over the years in meeting her wants and needs. Electronics just doesn't quite cut it. It is not good kindling for romance, that is for sure. Speaking of romance, most couples wonder, *Where did romance go?* It might seem like a foggy memory if you have young children or teens in high school. Instead of moonlight walks and candle-lit dinners, it is changing diapers, helping with a science project, washing mounds of laundry, breaking up a fight, or putting endless miles on the minivan for yet another extracurricular trip. Parents are exhausted and overwhelmed and are usually happy to get into bed, but it is for the primary purpose of collapsing in it. Caring for children usually becomes the primary priority of the parents, and over time they lose those feelings of love. Most couples don't redirect that cruise ship back toward beaches of love, care, and romance for each other. There are not enough hours in the day realistically to do both adequately—shepherd the kids and love your spouse!

Often, recreational activities or spare time hobbies do not include each other, and spouses begin to neglect each other. Although it is important to keep your unique personality and interests, you also need each other. Romance may seem like a distant memory and now a chasing after the wind. William F. Harley Jr. writes like none other on keeping romance alive in *His Needs, Her Needs for Parents*. I think that this book and a book called *Sacred Marriage* by Gary Thomas have challenged me more than any other books on marriage. Harley is very convincing in the dire necessity of meeting each other's intimate emotional needs. He writes of the differences between a romantic love and a caring love—one is feeling based whereas the other is decision based. He invented the concept of the Love Bank that each of us has. We deposit love units and withdraw love units based upon how we treat our spouse. There are also Love Busters that most married couples have that seem to make each other miserable: "selfish demands, disrespectful judgments, angry outbursts, dishonesty, annoying habits, and independent behavior."[214]

Love and Respect

I always try to ask my spouse regularly what I can do better to meet her needs. Often, the answer stays the same as I try to chip away at improving upon how well I am addressing it. Spouses need to feel loved. They need to feel respected. They need to be treated as intellectual equals and valued. This starts with open and frequent communication. We recently attended a "Love and Respect"[215] marriage conference with Dr. Emerson Eggerich. He asked seven thousand people, "When you are in a conflict with your spouse or significant other, do you feel 'unloved' or 'disrespected?'" Eighty-three percent of the men said "disrespected." Seventy-two percent of the women said "unloved." Eggerich says that "we are as different as blue and pink, but. . . .love best motivates a women and respect best motivates a man." (See Ephesians 5:33 for the link.) For us, it is the opposite. Regardless, find out what motivates your spouse and what could make for a better marriage.

What one or two things would make you the happiest
and improve your marriage and home life?

His Needs, Her Needs

When Harley asked, "What would make your marriage happier?" almost all of those interviewed answered with one or more of the same emotional needs: affection, conversation, recreational companionship, sexual fulfillment, honesty and openness, physical attractiveness, financial support, domestic support, or family commitment and admiration. You can guess which fall on most of the men's ledger side and which on the women's side.

You must resolve to work on your spousal intimacy. It is my top resolution. This means dealing with weaknesses or issues that you might have assumed to be normal or at a minimum you are not dealing with—selfish demands, anger, disrespect, dwelling on negatives or mistakes, or half-listening. You might start with little things, such as a hand squeeze, a daily hug, daily prayer together, or scheduling a daily communication time. Harley says that spending time alone with each other—with undivided attention—is to be your top priority. I hesitate to conclude with the major challenge of his book. It might seem like an impossibility, and you might need to set a smaller goal.

He says that you and your spouse need fifteen hours each week of alone time together to regain your love!

Shall I repeat that again just for emphasis? You might need to be creative to get fifteen minutes per day! Work together, clean together, shop together. You might need to make a list of household responsibilities and split them or combine them.

What is your spouse's *one* most important *need*
he or she wants met? How are you doing?

Small Beginnings and Stepping Stones

This book is about stirring you to small beginnings. Which activities on your calendar must change to start some intimacy stepping stones? How much time per day will you commit to "alone time" with your spouse? Ask God to help you find your blind spots and admit your faults to Him and to your spouse. That will take *much* courage, but it will also humble you and help you do better in the future.

Serve

This past Christmas was like no other in our household. We had to cancel our vacation plans due to my health problems. During this near-month at home I watched as my wife slaved over our house and saw all the detail of how she served us every day. I had taken it for granted. The washer was broken so I watched in amazement at the mountains of our stinky laundry that she washes every week. I watched as she cleaned, cooked, drove, and served, served, served.

I call myself a Christian, but I felt convicted watching her in action. I was seeing self-denial in action. Just as all of the scriptures on trusting God, peace, and worry came to life, the one that struck me most was the words from Jesus to His disciples: "Whoever wants to be my disciple must deny themselves and take up their cross and follow me. *For whoever wants to save their life will lose it, but whoever loses their life for me will find it.*"[216] None of us is a perfect spouse, and it is good to admit so. I had to confess my taking her for granted. I thanked her and thank her much more often now.

> *"[H]e did not come to be served, but to serve,*
> *and to give his life as a ransom."*[217]

 How are you serving your spouse? Is your motive pure?

A Happy Marriage?

Everyone wants a happy marriage. You see it on TV, in the movies, and through your neighbors' fine acting abilities. However, the book *Sacred Marriage* took me out of this thinking pattern and challenged me like no other. The premise is that maybe marriage isn't to make you happy, but to make you holy.

As I read this in the context of my own marriage, I reflected that as the years raced by my level of sacrifice for my wife, my acts of self-denial became more absent. It wasn't purposely, but I began to take for granted all that she does for me and our family. The laundry. The cooking. The taxi service. The cleaning. The toilets.

Toilets? Uh-oh. God seemed to stop me as I contemplated all that she did without a thank-you. When was the last time I cleaned a toilet? Ummm. Er—What's your point, God? I began some debating and thought of other areas in which I was not denying myself. Times that I spent on the computer rather than communicating or praying with my wife. The Lord has been taking me through times of challenge. For too long we have been satisfied with "good enough," with the status quo. I felt impressed to clean all of the toilets and not do it for a pat on the back. Not to even tell her. My flesh wanted to scream out and make sure that she knew of my great sacrifice. As I scrubbed each toilet, I was convicted that this was hardly a sacrifice. My one-time toilet-cleaning adventure versus her week-in, week-out sacrifice.

The last few years, God has really challenged me to step it up in my marriage and deny myself. Giving her more of my time. Following the Holy Spirit's lead when He nudges me to do something very little. Shutting the TV off. Putting the newspaper away. Turning off the computer. Giving my wife my *undivided attention.* Losing my life, my desires, my wants.

Life is really about a series of choices. How we serve our spouse is a daily choice. If you haven't seen the movie *Courageous,* I would highly recommend it. Five families make choices in how they will serve each other. It is inspiring. Today I choose. As for me and my house, we will serve the Lord. You must choose to fight for your marriage. Long after the honeymoon stage and the moonlight-romance emotions are gone, love becomes a verb. Action. Sacrifice. Self-denial. Communication. Treating others better than yourself. Love. Respect. Time. Serving.

STOP Read Mark 8:34; 10:31, 43–45; Luke 9:23; 22:26–27; Romans 12:1–2; and 1 Corinthians 15:31. How can you practically deny yourself and lay down your life in your marriage? Ask your spouse how you can better serve, love, or respect him or her. You might get a few new things for the "to-do" list.

Lead Me- Sanctus Real (Courageous Soundtrack)

Christ's view of greatness is different than ours:[218]

"The world's idea of greatness is to rule, but Christian greatness consists in serving. The world's ambition is to receive honor and attention, but the desire of the Christian should be to give rather than to receive, and to attend to others rather than be attended on himself. In short, the man who lays himself out most to serve his fellow men, and to be useful in his day and generation, is the greatest man in the eyes of Christ."
—J.C. Ryle

STOP Read Ephesians 5:21–33 and Ecclesiastes 4:9–12. How are you doing at obeying these challenges? Do you see your spouse as someone who can help you improve? Assess your progress below with a grade from A to F. Then ask your spouse to do the same. Sorry, guys, for the imbalance, but I guess we are expected to do more.

Husband		Wife	
	Submit to your wife.		Submit to your husband.
	Love your wife.		Be subject to your husband.
	Give yourself for your wife.		Respect your husband.
	Wash your wife with the Word.		Lift your husband up.
	Love your wife as your own self.		
	Lift your wife up.		

Prayer

One of the biggest challenges for a couple is to pray together. Many men were never taught to pray. Women might be too busy or be fearful to take this step. I remember being challenged with this twenty years ago and not knowing what to do. I knew that I was to lead spiritually, but I was fearful and didn't want to be rejected or ridiculed. Praying publicly and praying aloud was for preachers. What should I pray? How should I pray? Some practical helps are included in the Faith section, but just step out and begin.

If we acknowledge God only in words and in a quick prayer before dinner or breakfast, that is not enough. He wants to help us with our marriages. Sometimes it is difficult to know how to pray. Ask for the Holy Spirit to guide you. Here are some helpful scriptures that you can easily turn into prayers and blessings for your spouse and family:

- Galatians 5:22–23
- Ephesians 1:16–19
- Ephesians 3:14–20
- Colossians 1:9–12
- Romans 15:13
- Numbers 6:24–27

Obstacles will always present themselves. One spouse might be tired or grumpy. One spouse might have work to do or kids to drive. One might be out of town. One might not be open to this. Maybe start to pray for each other silently. Hold hands and pray for each other. Start with a list and each pray a sentence. Have a subject for each day. One day it will be thankfulness. Then next it will be needs. The next it will be to ask for forgiveness. You can keep a prayer journal, a prayer jar, or prayer request basket. I have a prayer list in my Bible. My wife and I pray every evening for *one* thing for each of the kids, depending upon what is going on. Start a prayer board. We have a chalk board in our kitchen that is near the dinner table so we can pray together as a family for things. It might be difficult to find a regular time to pray with your spouse or family because of schedules. Look and pray for opportunities when you are together—after a meal or at bedtime. Here are a few models to help you:

1) Use John 17 as a model. Start with a focus on God (vv. 1–5), then on those around you (vv. 6–19), then for other believers (vv. 20–23), and then for your community,

circle of influence, and the people in the world around you who need God (vv. 20–24). Insert phrases about your family or needs as you read.

2) Use the Lord's Prayer in Matthew 6:9–13 as a model.

3) Use Daniel as a model for humbling yourself and changing (Daniel 9:1–19).

4) Pray the Scripture.

Consistency

> *"Now when Daniel learned that the decree had been published, he went home to his upstairs room where the windows opened toward Jerusalem. Three times a day he got down on his knees and prayed, giving thanks to his God, just as he had done before."*[219]

Repetition. Repetition. Daniel started a habit and then was consistent in that habit. Daniel took responsibility for his people and his country. We as spouses should take care of owning up to our family's issues. Although repentance is personal, read Daniel's prayer in Daniel 9:1–19. He personally prayed, repented, confessed his faults, and fasted, then he turned to a broader prayer. He used the word we fifteen times in fifteen verses.

"*We* have sinned and done wrong. *We* have been wicked and have rebelled. *We* have turned away from your commands and laws. *We* have not listened to your servants the prophets. *We* are covered with shame, *we* and our kings. *We* have sinned against you. *We* have rebelled against him; *we* have not obeyed the LORD our God or kept the laws he gave us through his servants the prophets. *All Israel* has transgressed your law and turned away, refusing to obey you. *we* have sinned against you. *We* have not sought the favor of the LORD our God by turning from our sins and giving attention to your truth. Yet *we* have not obeyed him. *We* have sinned. *We* have done wrong."

STOP Is there anything you need to confess to God and then to your spouse regarding your marriage?

> *"The family you come from is not as important as the family you are going to have."*
> —Ring Lardner

Legacy Lesson: Love, Submission, Sacrifice, Serving, Encouraging. Prayer. Love. Respect. These are all actions that are necessary for a marriage that flourishes and that has a multi-generational impact.

CHAPTER 32

FINISHING STRONG: A MARATHON FOR MEN

*"Concerning the spiritual state of his family;
the father ought to diligently and frequently bring before his family
the things of God, from His Holy Word."*
—John Bunyan

Men have been portrayed throughout the past few generations as spiritual misfits, world-class wimps, lazy, and with no leadership. From the Archie Bunkers to *Married with Children*'s Al Bundy to Homer Simpson, men are portrayed as couch-potato idiots. Dads are going through an identity crisis. Even the feminist leader Gloria Steinem said, "Most American children suffer from too much mother and too little father." Today, four out of ten American children do not live with their fathers.

In *From Faith to Faith*,[220] Bill C. Dotson focuses on *abiding* in the home instead of *absence* in the home. He quotes some alarming statistics:

- 63 percent of youth suicides are from fatherless homes.
- 90 percent of all homeless and runaway youths are from fatherless homes.
- 71 percent of high school dropouts are from fatherless homes.
- 71 percent of youths in state institutions are from fatherless homes.
- 75 percent of adolescent patients in substance-abuse centers are from fatherless homes.
- 85 percent of rapists motivated by displaced anger are from fatherless homes.

It is a personal decision to turn the tide. I made the decision early in my marriage that my most cherished titles are husband and father. The decision is only the first step. When we constantly hold up the mirror and assess how we are doing as a husband and father, it can be humbling—maybe even downright depressing. We see flaws and past failures. We must act now to change and finish strong.

Finishing Strong—A Marathon

Bron Clifford, Billy Graham, and Chuck Templeton. "In 1945, three young men with extraordinary gifts were preaching the gospel to multiplied thousands across this nation. Within 10 years, only one of them was still on track for Jesus Christ. It's not how you start that matters. It's how you finish."[221] Five years later, Templeton no longer believed in Jesus Christ, and five years after that Clifford lost his family, his ministry, and eventually his life as alcohol and financial failures did him in.

It is not easy to finish strong. In fact, the odds and the world are against you. Coasting into the finish line will just not cut it. You can read the story of Joshua and Caleb and be encouraged. Two out of twelve finished strong. Life is not a sprint but a marathon. We must run with endurance. None of us knows when our finish line is, but we can be certain that none of us will finish perfectly. However, we can finish strong. We make the choices that will allow us to finish weak, finish average, or finish with a flourish.

 Read Hebrews 12:1–2.

In his book *Finish Strong*, Steve Farrar discusses being ambushed. We can be ambushed by money, greed, sexual temptation, or many other things. What are you doing to anticipate and protect against the risks to finishing strong? How are you going to avoid the ambushes?

Do You Have Insurance?

We have every sort of insurance available to mitigate our risks: health insurance, dental insurance, car insurance, travel insurance, malpractice insurance, property insurance, mortgage insurance, life insurance, disability insurance, and the list goes on. What about marriage insurance? How are you protecting your marriage?

Farrar mentions a study by Dr. Howard Hendricks of 246 leaders whose marriages failed and derailed. Of the 246,

- none was involved in any personal accountability group
- all had stopped investing in a daily personal time of prayer, scripture reading, and worship
- each of the them had been convinced that moral failure "will never happen to me"

How are you doing in these areas?
Give yourself a grade from A to F.

Involved in a personal accountability group	
Have a daily time of prayer, Bible reading, and worship	
Recognize that moral failure could happen to me	

Who's on First?

One of my favorite humor sketches growing up was Abbott and Costello's "Who's On First"? As much as I tried, I just couldn't memorize or re-enact it. I gave up. It was too much work. Getting started in some of these spiritual disciplines is similar. The bar might seem too high. Many men never seem to get beyond 1st base spiritually. These things will take discipline and personal responsibility. Not easy by any stretch. Yale sociologist Stephen B. Clark says rather plainly, "Men have a natural tendency to avoid social responsibility." This seems to be more and more normal in our society. Families are crying out for men who will engage, who will accept responsibility, who will help, who will be a voice in their lives, who will lead spiritually and provide direction for the family. Our families and our nations are depending upon us. It is time for us to "man-up." It is important to do the following things.

1) Recognize the responsibility that is ours as men.
2) Recognize that we are ill-prepared and inadequate to do it on our own.
3) Learn; get the training to lead.
4) Start small; start now.

Don't get to the destination of empty-nest country and find it full of emptiness and regret. Dr. Richard Halverson, former chaplain of the United States Senate, called it "Destination Sickness."

> . . . *the syndrome of the man who has arrived*
> *and discovered he is nowhere*
> . . . *he has achieved his goals and finds they*
> *are not what he had anticipated*
> . . . *he has all the things that money can buy*
> *and finds decreasing satisfaction in all he has*

I recommend that every man read the book of Ecclesiastes at least once per year. It will give you proper perspective on your priorities. This spiritual leadership our families so desperately need is not a one-time seminar or a delegating of the duty to a church or an educator. It is lifestyle leadership. When you sit in your house, when you walk by the way, when you lie down, and when you rise up. It is in activity, in mealtimes, and every day. Quite often, we fail as men to lead, especially spiritually. We could be viewed as priest, prophet, and king of our households.

STOP Below is a Husband checklist.[222] I know some of these self-report cards are painful, but if you truly take an introspective look and then take some action, the results can be quite rewarding. You could ask your wife to help grade you.

Husband Checklist

Be on the alert, stand firm in the faith,
act like men, be strong. Do everything in love.
—1 Corinthians 16:13

Priest		
	Leading in worship	
	Prayer/intercession for your wife	
	Reminding your wife of God's grace and mercy	
	Building up your wife's spiritual walk	
Prophet		
	Hearing from God	
	Setting the doctrinal foundation for your home	
	Proclaiming God's truth	
	Confronting sin	
	Reminding your wife of God's love for her	
King		
	Visionary leadership	
	Sacrificial service	
	Providing for needs	
	Spiritually	
	Physically	
	Emotionally	
	Protecting my wife	
	Spiritually	
	Physically	
	Emotionally	

The main moral of this checklist is that we are miserable failures. Okay, maybe not miserable, but we certainly fall short, if not in a couple of areas, maybe in all of these areas! The consolation is that we can act! But we cannot do it in our own strength.

I was recently reading about King Uzziah in the Old Testament. He reigned over Judah. He followed the Lord and was a very successful king. Two verses[223] jumped out at me:

- As long as Uzziah sought the Lord, God made him prosper.
- But after Uzziah became powerful, his pride led to his downfall.

When he was successful, he did not seek the Lord or lean on him. He was self-sufficient. Pride always comes before a fall.[224] We tend to be the same way, and we often prefer isolation. We can do it without God or without other men. The enemy operates and deceives when there is isolation. Being isolated from godly influence or from others who will challenge you and hold you accountable is downright dangerous. Often, temptation will come knocking in the form of pride, or with career or financial opportunities, or in sexual temptation. David was a man after God's own heart and had an incredible first half, yet he did not finish strong. Max Lucado says of David, "*Mark it down. Compromise chills the soul.*" Farrar mentions how sin can shipwreck your life: "*Sin will take you farther than you wanted to go; sin will keep you longer than you wanted to stay; sin will cost you more than you wanted to pay.*"[225]

You might have had your share of mistakes along the way: Divorce, affair, ethical and moral faults, or parenting, spousal, or financial failures. God can use our failures to prepare us for our future. In what areas are you too isolated and need to make a change?

How to Get Accountable

1. **Find a small group or start a small group**. Do life together in a small group. We have done this on several different occasions in several different communities and churches and it is powerful. If your church or neighborhood does not offer small groups, find 2 or 3 people or couples and start one! These are not just times for surface socializing and small talk, although you will have some great times. It is a group you can go deeper with. You can lean on them during tough times and laugh with them during good times. It is great to share ideas with others and also encourage each other during life's challenges.

   I initiated a small men's group recently, and the results have been amazing. We all tend to wear many layers of masks and layers of protective "soul armor." They are layers we have put on over the years without even knowing it or how they now weigh us down. Layers added from failures, fears, rejections or embarrassments. Layers to keep up with the Joneses. Layers to ensure people know we aren't as bad as the next guy, or to show that we really love God, and have it all together. Rarely do we let people have a peek inside the "real me." Starting a small group and conducting studies on parenting and marriage was one of the best helps for a husband and father that I have experienced in 20 years of marriage. We are building relationships, sharing successes, sharing failures, challenging, encouraging and praying for each other. I think that is what "community" is. It is so easy to drop into church for an hour and stay at an arm's length.

Yikes. It might be stepping out of your comfort zone. Take a risk! It took guts for me, but if a closet introvert can do this, so can you! Start small and build.

"A soul which remains alone. . . is like a burning coal if left by itself;
it will grow colder rather than hotter."
—John of the Cross, Carmelite friar and priest, 1500s

2. **Accept a life-changing proposal**. I told you about my whirlwind proposal when I jetted off to Key West with my wife-to-be. Okay, so it was a puddle jumper that scared us to death. I didn't mention I had another proposal in the same time frame. Jesus was knocking on the door of my heart, and I made the most important decision of my life to follow Him the same week I met my wife. I went from living for myself to being sold out for God quickly. He filled an incredible void where stuff, stature, career, and fun had their empty place in my heart.

3. **Get Knowledge**. Read, read, read. Find people who are good at being a dad and father. Meet with them, and begin to model yourself after them.

Your decisions to make some changes in being a family man and a family leader might lead to rejection, and you might have failures along the way, but think generationally. You are leaving an incredible legacy for generations to come!

"Blessed is the man who fears the Lord, who finds great delight in his commands. His children will be mighty in the land; the generation of the upright will be blessed."
—Psalm 112:1, 2

 Courageous- Casting Crowns

Words of Wisdom

I tried to pick some of my favorite quotations from my years of research that tied directly to the topics in this book. For the topic of men, there were just too many good ones. A great source of many quotations is Stu Weber's *Along the Road to Manhood*.[226] Here are some of my favorites.

"No code of conduct ever compelled a father to love his children or a husband to show affection to his wife. The law court may force him to provide bread for the family, but it cannot make him provide the bread of love. A good father is obedient to the unenforceable."
—Martin Luther King Jr.

"A father—one of the easiest titles to get;
one of the most difficult positions to fill."
—Howard Hendricks

"If you take being a father seriously, you'll know that you're not big enough for the job, not
by yourself. . . . Being a father will put you on your knees if nothing else ever did."
—Elisabeth Elliot

"Everyday life must always be lived out against the backdrop
of eternity. . . my job as a parent is a temporary responsibility
with eternal consequences."
—Tim Kimmel

"Where a man belongs is up early and alone with God
seeking vision and direction for his family."
—John Piper

"Fathering is unpredictable, untidy and frequently confusing. That is why there are so
many fathers who have children, but so few children who have fathers."
—Tim Hansel

"The man who lets his family take second place to his work will live to regret it."
—Author unknown

"By profession I am a soldier and take pride in that fact. But I am prouder—infinitely
prouder—to be a father."
—Douglas MacArthur

"When the time drew near for David to die, he gave a charge to Solomon his son. "I am
about to go the way of all the earth," he said. "So be strong, show yourself a man, and
observe what the LORD your God requires: Walk in his ways, and keep his decrees and
commands, his laws and requirements, as written in the Law of Moses, so that you may
prosper in all you do and wherever you go."
—1 Kings 2:1–3

"When I was a boy of 14, my father was so ignorant I could hardly stand to have the old
man around. But when I got to be 21, I was astounded at how much the old man had
learned in seven years."
—Samuel L. Clemens

"The first man in every woman's life is her father. How she views the men she meets later,
how she values herself, depends to some extent on her relationship with her dad."
—Myrna Blyth

*"Experience has shown us that men who are the happiest
and most content in their masculine role today are those whose fathers
invested a great deal of time and energy in their lives."*
—David Stoop and Stephen Arterburn

Legacy Lesson: Leading our families is the most important job a man has. Seeking God in our lack of success or lack of experience will be life changing. He is knocking on the doors of our hearts just waiting to love us and help us.

CHAPTER 33

RAISING THE FUTURE: A GENERATIONAL IMPACT STORY

Raising and training your children and influencing your grandchildren is the biggest generational impact you will make in life. The decision of how to educate our children has been a weighty issue with each child as we realize the implications and the generational impact each of these choices made. Each child is unique, and each family is unique. There are different seasons and different needs for each child. It is important to understand each child: their weaknesses, their needs, and the educational approach that fits them best.

At the time of this writing, we have experienced all facets of education in our family with our three children. In cumulative total years at the time of writing, we have five years of public education, five years of homeschooling, and nineteen years of private, Christian schooling.

I encourage you as parents, as leaders of your family, and as the primary teachers of your children: do *not* weigh your children's education lightly. Do *not* make the decision solely on the financial considerations. Grandparents- your financial role could be very influential. Pray. Pray and fast. Read. Know what your children are being taught. Look at the textbooks. Be visible with their teachers.

The Great Adventure

I recall a series of discussions with my wife about our children's education in 2002/2003. Little did I know "the decision" that we were about to make would have a radical impact in our lives and hundreds of other families. Little did I know the spiritual battles that would take place: the loss of friendships, the loss of sleep, the loss of health, and also nearly the loss of our family.

We have made big decisions before. We had taken risks before. We had stepped out in faith before. I believe God tests us sometimes just to see if we will be obedient. Sometimes, He asks us to take major steps of faith—as He did with Abraham, asking him to leave his country, or when he was tested by God with Isaac. Sometimes He is convicting us to do some "little things." He always leaves us with the decision "Will I obey?"

With some of our memories and some of our traditions (i.e., "the good ol' days"), it is easy to look in the rear-view mirror of life. With other past experiences or events it may be ever so difficult to reflect on the past. For me, writing this next section of the book was bittersweet. It was akin to feasting on my favorite grilled steak and then being force-fed Brussels sprouts and sauerkraut in the same dining experience. Charles Dickens probably said it a little more succinctly: "It was the best of the times. It was the worst of times."

As you consider your "second half," as you prepare to take on a life-changing, generationally influential challenge, ensure that you do not enter into it lightly, and be prepared on all levels: spiritually, emotionally, physically, and financially. Although it will be a faith adventure and rewarding, there will no doubt be battles along the way.

The Early Years

Early in our marriage, we had decided that a priority for our future family would be having my wife stay home and raise our children. It was a major decision we made, and we knew it would be a sacrifice for her and a financial challenge for us all, but it would be a long-term blessing for the children. My wife has done an incredible job with our home and with our children. As new parents, we were troubled by the state of our country and had heard some horror stories from friends and acquaintances about some public school experiences, so we had determined when our children were barely walking that we would embark one year at a time upon a home-school journey. I loved reading to them, choosing curriculum, and spending time with them, while Dana did the heavy lifting—the teaching and most of the training. Texas had a very large home-school association support group and excellent curriculum choices. After experiencing this rewarding, yet challenging educational model for several years, we prayed about participating in a new model that had recently launched, a University Model School (NAUMS®). This model had recently been recognized by James Dobson and Focus on the Family. After much prayer, we began sending our kids to the UMS school. The concept was a nice match for our family; the model was a combination of private, Christian, and home-school approaches with three days in a small-class setting and two days at home with a Bible-based, disciplined lesson plan. The model was an incredible blessing to our family, and the children flourished.

Soon, however, the drive began to take a toll on my wife. She and a friend began to seek a UMS model closer to home and for God's guidance regarding other alternatives. But there was not one closer to home. We prayed together about God's direction for our family regarding our children's education. Although no specific, audible direction from God was evident, we believed that our restlessness and the desire that He seemingly had put into our hearts to consider a change was evidence enough to do additional research. We were living in the fastest-growing city in the county and one of the fastest-growing counties in the country. There was a real need for a UMS school locally, and we knew it would be an immense blessing to many families. As we sought out other families who might consider a UMS school close to home, many of them were interested in getting a ticket for the cruise, but just didn't want to captain the cruise or have a prominent deck officer position on the UMS ship. After much research, prayer, and reaching out to others about starting a school locally, it seemed that we could help facilitate the process and find four or five families who were like-minded and could assist with the process. We were warned that this was a full-time job for several years, so it was critical to find a good, solid group of "Founders."

In addition to Emily's currently attending a UMS school, Dana was embarking on our fourth year of homeschooling. Jacob was in kindergarten, and our youngest, Justin, was a toddler, so we knew that we couldn't get in too deep with any new commitments. Our plates were already overflowing. Emily was in competitive dance, Jacob was playing T-ball and soccer, and Justin was attending a Kids Day Out program. Dana was teaching Sunday school and children's church and was involved with homeschool extracurricular classes while updating Emily and Jacob's rooms in our new home. She definitely didn't have time for another full-time job. I was fully employed with a more-than-full-time job in a successful career while also serving on several nonprofit boards, coaching my son's T-ball, and ensuring that we had quality family times with a strong spiritual emphasis at the center of our home. We both made our kids' activities and performances a priority, not to be missed, so the plates were spinning!

A Change of Direction

I had finished writing *Ease the Squeeze* during late-nighters and all-nighters over the preceding fifteen months, and my hobby-time had turned into a broader success, thanks to God's favor, hard work, and opening of doors. *Ease* was nominated for Christian Living Book of the Year and had risen to #2510 out of over 1,000,000 books on Amazon.com. This led to several nationwide radio show interviews and articles with Marlin Maddoux, Kerby Anderson, Larry Burkett, Howard Dayton, Moody Broadcasting, and Charles Colson ministries, as well as conducting financial seminars when I could squeeze one in. My weekends and vacation time were focused on this blossoming effort, but God was getting ready to put my personal dreams on hold for another seasonal "calling." It was a great season of life for our family. We had just celebrated our 10th anniversary, Jacob had just accepted the Lord, and we had just helped raise $200,000 for our church building campaign. We were living full, happy lives. However, we were both definitely burning the candle at both ends.

God soon had other plans for our small "margin" of spare time. It was May 14, 2003, and our friends, Scott and Karin and the Hag crew moved forward with the unofficial launch of Cornerstone Christian Academy[227] (CCA). Two couples, none of them educators. No facility. No teachers. No money. But we were armed with PowerPoint, Excel, a brochure, a mascot (Warrior), and a school name (CCA). We were four ordinary, unschooled peeps embarking on a mission never to be forgotten.

If we knew of the blessings, stories, and testimonies
for hundreds of families, we would have started **sooner***!*

If we knew the details of the hurdles, roadblocks, and heavy spiritual battles that
would be fought, we **never** *would have started!*

The "Call"

Other than my passion for PowerPoint and Excel and Scott's affinity for small-town mascots, we were a woefully under-qualified team for this effort. Thankfully, Scott and I had two smart, incredible wives with a passion for our kids' education and a knowledge of the UMS model and all of the intricate details that would go along with it. Before I personally committed to signing on for this endeavor, I needed more confirmation from God than just the desire to fill a need for our family. We had seen this model blossom across the nation, had seen the blessings, and had heard the success stories. We had also been warned at a NAUMS seminar that other founding families had lost everything they owned. We heard stories of others involved in launching a school during which time schools and churches split and we heard of shipwrecked relationships and families. And this was motivation and training for starting a school?

Yes, we heard the blessings-and-successes stories too, but second and third thoughts crept in and tested my faith walk. The questions and wrestling began. This is not just about me. Is this a call? Is it a need? Is it neither? How badly do I want to make a generational impact? I knew this decision was no longer just about our three kids and their academics and discipleship. It was weighty because it could influence hundreds of families for generations to come. I began to seek God desperately to hear His voice. I asked Him to reveal His will beyond a shadow of a doubt. This decision moment was one of the milestones that is etched in my mind. One night in intercessory prayer, I had a carpet slobbering experience of tears and confirmation. It was at this moment that I truly considered the cost, gave our house and all of our earthly belongings back to God, if that was a consequence He required. It was not exactly a burning bush moment, and I still heard no audible voice or saw dew on the fleece (other than the wet carpet), but I had a peace beyond explanation that I knew God would walk through this with us and that He was giving us the green light—or at least that we did not have a red light. He did not assure "smooth sailing" or "overnight success," but He did provide an "inaudible" assurance that this was indeed His will. That is all we needed. The door was opened.

Deep inside us was a desire to help rebuild our communities and our nation through strong families with a biblical foundation. I became burdened for American families, about how the government had taken God and prayer out of the schools. I shuddered as I read of schools like Yale and Harvard that were founded on the gospel of Jesus Christ but now mocked Christians openly. As we studied, read, and researched, we realized that this would have to be a "God-thing." Were my wife and I educators? No. Had we started a major business/ministry on this scale before? No. Were we totally clueless? Yes. We knew nothing of test standards, accreditation, articles, and bylaws, and very little about curriculum, budgets, and rental agreements. Nevertheless, God knew that we could be trusted and that we were humble, teachable, and available for Him to use. We were naïve about the spiritual battles that would take place. Satan does not like anyone to take a stand for Christ or to make a generational impact. Anything worthwhile will require some battles.

Crossing the Faith Threshold

We began to hold informational meetings at night and on weekends in our living rooms through the summer of 2003. We quickly gained a list of interested families and developed a "foundational dialogue" questionnaire that we used to interview five candidate founding families to ensure that we had a like-minded vision for a school. This continued through the fall of 2003. We had more questions than answers to sort out. Discipleship? Evangelistic? Protestant? Academy or school? Spiritual or academic emphasis? Business or ministry? Classical or traditional? Athletics? Arts? Staff? Location? Policies? Banks? Tuition? Curriculum? Calendars? Schedules? Dress code? Immunizations? Insurance? Legal? Handbooks? Applications? Interviews? Incorporation? Yikes! Just a few I's to be dotted and T's to be crossed.

We ended up with only three founding families total, quite short of the four to five that were recommended, but we are ever so grateful to all of those families for their role in the process of getting God's school launched. Each of those families played a key role in the birth of CCA. Some of them are no longer with CCA, which saddens me greatly, but I know that God sent them ultimately to get His will and the mission of the school accomplished. Although any separation is difficult, I am grateful for the years we had together and grateful for their contributions and role in the process. Our mission was to "partner with parents to build a firm foundation in academic excellence and Christian discipleship."

An e-mail on February 22, 2004, officially announced the start of CCA: "It is with great excitement and expectation that we announce the launch of Cornerstone Christian Academy for August 2004." We crossed numerous "faith thresholds" as we held the first informational meeting, hired the first teacher, and signed the first lease. There was no turning back now! Six months later, a humble birth followed: forty-six students, representing thirty-seven families from ten cities. It is truly amazing what God accomplished through a humble group of people during that year before the launch. The founding families secured a facility, developed a website, attended three seminars, read multitudes of resumes, conducted dozens of interviews, held twelve informational meetings, hired ten teachers and had many all-nighters that resulted in more than two hundred documents, spreadsheets, presentations, and marketing materials. We had an incredible couple of years! It was the busiest of times, but it was the best of times. It was beyond the Porterhouse steak experience.

A flood of wonderful ministry partners and incredible relationships were built, and many families were being influenced positively. We had an opening night celebration beyond our wildest dreams, a Fall Festival bonfire, an incredible chapel and character program, hot lunches, a yearbook, teacher recognition, and a robust curriculum. And we were unified in mission—one body, one spirit. I saw the incredible gifts of my wife in full expression. Dana took the ball and ran with it. She was a humble, loving, dignified, and gifted administrator, although she had never done anything like this before. She cared for each student, parent, and teacher individually and loved them in words and action. Only God knows the sacrifice of time she put in to ensure a successful launch of CCA. Karin was a one-woman marketing and word-of-mouth promotion machine, and she started an incredible chapel and character program. Likewise, the founding families and many other families gave sacrificially of their time and finances beyond public knowledge. God was so good!

He blessed us so incredibly time after time. God sent the right teachers, the right buildings, the right leaders, and the right families as only He could have accomplished. We had story after story of His faithfulness and provision, often at the last minute but always right on His schedule. Through God's providence, our hard work, and with the help of many volunteers, we actually ran a financial surplus for several years! Many families had laid down their own lives, denied themselves, and sacrificed their time for God and CCA. God only knows to what level. Families were investing their time and money in something that went beyond their generation.

*"Children are the living messages we send to a time
and place we will not see."*
—Neil Postman

As parents, it is *our* responsibility to write these messages, first in our children's hearts and then in their minds. If only it were an easy task! In hindsight, I am utterly amazed at the blessings that have resulted from making our kids a priority. The spiritual emphasis in our home, coupled with this model of education, was mind-blowing to me. I cannot adequately address all of the fruit we have seen over the years: the first CCA graduating class, the school's continued growth in numbers and spiritual maturity, an incredible like-minded board, a strong administrative leadership team and an incredible staff with hearts for the Lord and for families. I am so grateful and know that God sees and recognizes this and one day the warm embrace of a loving Father's words will be whispered to them, "Well done, good and faithful servant." Each of them has his and her own story, blessings, and battles.

As I peer in the rear-view mirror of launching this multigenerational ministry, I am absolutely overwhelmed by the immensity of time and effort it took to launch a school, and I thank God that He did not give us more than a glimpse of the future before we started. It was a humbling and exhausting experience, yet so rewarding. As I prayed about what and how much to share about this experience, I felt like I should spend the majority of the content of these two chapters focused on the battles and challenges associated with starting something "big." That is where many of you are in your lives.

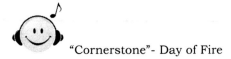

"Cornerstone"- Day of Fire

Legacy Lesson: Leaving a legacy requires big decisions, weighty choices, and divine intersections at the crossroads of life. Any generational impact "second half" project will require sacrifice and investment of your time and money. Make sure you have sought God for direction.

CHAPTER 34

RAISING THE FUTURE: THE BATTLE

I can safely say that we never would have had the strength to make it on our own. The spiritual battles that were waged we shared with very few. The nights we cried ourselves to sleep or paced the bedroom or office floors during the wee hours of the morning were all too familiar scenes in 2006. I could relate to David's Psalm 6:6–8. We never questioned God's hand on us and the school but often wondered if it was still worth it. The wear and tear on our family. The feelings of betrayal by those closest to you that still haunt us at times. The spiritual and emotional gashes and cuts that took years to scab over, yet to be peeled back off again unexpectedly when bumping into a once-friendly face in the store that is now the stony face of a stranger. Friends that you shared some of your most treasured times in life with, now but a distant memory, clashing memories—good and bad, sweet and bitter. Care for a side of sauerkraut or Brussels sprouts with that Porterhouse?

It is during times of battle that one can most relate to some of David's honest yet heart-breaking psalms. During times of loneliness or seasons of attack, during those long nights of fear and doubt, God was still ever so close, ever so faithful. Authenticity is healthy. A humble and broken spirit is what God works best with. That is why David had God's favor. How could David, a man who loved God and was a man after God's own heart, still doubt Him at times? Why didn't God always act on his behalf when those closest to him opposed him?

Battle Scars

We loved God, we were obedient, and we acted out of a pure heart and pure motives, and yet we seemed to be attacked on every side—some were public attacks, but most were stealth ambushes. The merry-go-round of e-mails, gossip, back-biting and even the formation of a "parent-led board" intent on hijacking control of the school's leadership and direction were all hard pills to swallow. The weapon of choice was the tongue. It was brandished fiercely and boldly. Most of the people involved might have had pure motives to start, just doing what was best for their children. Some of them were gentle and kind and engaged in dignified dialogue. Others engaged in public lynching's and tongue whippings. A few were fighting a battle for *their* vision for the school, and it was taking a toll on us. No judge. No jury. No defense. But this was a battle worth fighting. We had fear, but we had faith. We needed God more than ever. He began to give us spiritual backbone and helped us rise above personal battles and not defend ourselves with words. He was our defense. (See Psalm 16:8; 18:1–3; and 62:1, 6.)

He was our protector. He was our guardian. We knew this battle was not personal. Some of the people involved were good-intentioned people who just wanted what was best for their children. Others pursued control at all costs with a frightening vengeance. It was not only a battle for our family but a battle for generations to come. Even those who attacked us the most were not the enemy, but they were being used by the enemy. Although we were wounded deeply, we knew that even men in the Bible disagreed and parted ways (Gal 2:11–21 and Acts 15).

"A perverse man stirs up dissension,
and a gossip separates close friends."
—Proverbs 16:28

Be reminded of the power of the tongue. It is a weapon of great warfare. Read Proverbs 11:13; 15:2; 20:19; 26:22; Eph 4:29; Titus 1:10; James 1:19, 26; and 3:2–10.

Storm Clouds

It was during these times of warfare that the honest questions and feelings come out. *Do you want me to quit, God? Am I the problem? Maybe the naysayers, finger pointers, and control grabbers are right after all.*

I recall one blindside "woodshed" lunch invitation vividly. I was invited to lunch and bluntly told that *I* was the problem, and that *I* was limiting God's blessing. I listened with an open heart and set out to seek God and ensure that I was teachable and correctable. We also wanted the school to be the very best it could be so we often solicited input and feedback via survey, town-hall meeting, or in person. It was a healthy time of searching my heart. I often went back to Question 29 on the Founding Family document: "Am I willing to put my personal interests and desires aside for unity and benefit of the whole more than my family?" We certainly made mistakes along the way, but God knew our hearts, our motives, and the truth and that we were always willing to lay down our personal desires, our family needs, and selfish interests for the sake of the whole. God had tasked us with protecting the vision He had given us for the school. The knowledge that He was for us and the Holy Spirit was with us gave us peace through the battle.

There were several dark and stormy months where I felt as though I were in the thick of a Frank Peretti novel. I had read about spiritual warfare. I had heard missionaries who had encountered spiritual warfare. I have heard the stories of angels, demons, deliverances, and miracles, but I have never been a character in those stories. It was all second-hand information. Some dimensions of spiritual warfare can be theological hot buttons and fruit-less denominational debate gasoline. I am not going there. I can share that I was in this battle and experiencing it firsthand. It seemed I was living out my own biblical "greatest hits" parody but with real characters. Thankfully, during this season I had a Paul and I was Timothy. I had a mentor, a teacher, a counselor. We had our Mordecais, our rescuers, when we were Esther and the Jews. Just as Moses needed his hands held up, I am so grateful that we had our Aarons and Hurs.[228] We also had Thomas- and Judas-like doubters and felt the sting of betrayal more than once. We often felt like Job with his "friends," yet we were blessed by those who stood in the gap on our behalf.[229] Although we had a few people stirring up trouble, gossip, slander, and lies, we had many others who helped us build and encouraged us greatly as we built. We also had those who inspected the "building" at every step and opposed us.[230]

Be a Maximus!

Each of us sometimes feels and lives in that "Roman coliseum." Some people will be for you, and some people will be against you. Some will cheer and some will jeer. Sometimes you won't know who the cheerers are and who the jeerers are. Sometimes they will change sides. Some will cheer you publicly then jeer you privately. Although critics abound, surround yourself with authentic warriors who speak words of life, publicly and privately. Be a spiritual gladiator. God will stand with you (Psalm 54:1)!

That is easier to say now that we have survived the battle, but quite often fear and doubt crept in like a mist, and the words, accusations, and actions permeated my world like a raging thunderstorm with a permanent cloud cover. It seemed as though the devil had my number and was using a handful of people to destroy me, my family, and God's school. Most of the families and the overall school experience was wonderful. So why were others not going through what I was going through? The spiritual warfare was as thick and as present as I have ever felt it. Where was that power, love, and a sound mind when I needed it the most? This was clearly a spiritual battle, and I could literally feel it throughout my innermost being. Yet God continually made clear that we were on the right path and gave us an inner peace of the knowledge that our hearts were pure and a continued confirmation that we were to lead the school and protect it with our very lives. He gave us strength in the battle. We weren't fighting for just our kids but also for those of other families. We fought on our knees.

"He alone is my rock and my salvation;
He is my fortress. I will not be shaken."
- Psalm 62: 2,6

"For you have been my refuge. . . .a strong tower."
- Psalm 61:3

"God is our refuge and strength, an ever present help in trouble."
- Psalm 46:1

"The Lord is my strength and my defense."
- Psalm 118:14

"He is My Defense," Marty Goetz

Who Will Be Used?

I am thankful for my wife. She knew the truth. She believed. She loved. She encouraged. She challenged. I am thankful for those who believed with us, those who stood by us, those who encouraged, those who intervened and rescued us, and those who helped us stand in the gap. You know who you are. I am thankful for those who prayed in spirit and in truth. I am grateful for those who kept their commitments and were faithful. Only God truly knows a man's motives and a man's heart, so we can judge no individual.

We have had a saying since the kids were little: "Hagedorns aren't quitters." There have been many times they wanted to quit something when the going got tough, or when they didn't get their way, or things didn't go as planned. It is so easy to quit. Quitting is much easier than working things out, compromising, sticking to something that is hard work. We wanted to quit many a night, but we refused. Through it all, God was teaching us, growing us. My wife was Christianity in action. She metaphorically laid down her life for her kids, for other families, for the sake of the school.

God was teaching me to humble myself, to turn the other cheek, to not lean on my understanding, to trust Him, to bear others' burdens, and to stay faithful. These verses I had heard for years, but they were all just ink and paper until we lived them. When you live through a trial, a test, or a tribulation the words come to life. Now they are written on our hearts. It is funny how *God chooses to use people*. I am still humbled and amused by how He chose to use us to start a school. It is not so funny, and some people struggle to believe that *Satan can indeed use people* as well. Even good people, the people closest to you. God might allow it for a purpose or a season like He did with Job and his sorry "friends." It might be a very quick statement by someone that has a profound negative impact on you emotionally, mentally, or spiritually. Peter was the disciple that was probably closest to Jesus, and without knowing it, he was being used by Satan. Jesus had just revealed His plan. It was a very critical time when doubt could have crept in or a temporal perspective could have become front and center instead of a focus on the big picture. Jesus had to rebuke him, "Get behind me, Satan."[231] Peter had a focus on himself. He had a temporal, here-and-now life focus. It is so easy to get focused on "our needs," "our will," "our desires." It is easy to have a selfish or a temporal perspective rather than God's perspective. Jesus then goes on to talk about self-denial, unselfishness, and an eternal perspective.

Never underestimate the power of a spoken word.
Out of our mouths come blessing and cursing.

That one hug, that one note of encouragement, that one prayer you pray, or that one thank you might be all someone needs to get them through a battle. That one critical word, that one back-biting juicy bit of gossip or slander might be a stronghold or ammunition for Satan to win a critical battle.

"The tongue has the power of life and death."
—Proverbs 18:21

Satan used Judas. Satan tried to use Peter. God allowed Satan to test Job and was asked by Satan to sift Peter like wheat. A "sifting" is a "shaking." A vigorous shaking is required to separate wheat kernels from debris. The enemy wanted to shake Peter's faith. Prayer is what prevented Peter's falling away. Although he denied Christ, he did not fall away. Before you breathe a word of gossip or approach someone with an issue, complaint, or accusation, know that Satan would love to use you, Christ-follower or atheist. If you are being "sifted," know that God has a greater plan. Know that the shaking is for a season only and do not lose heart. Use the time for a spiritual housecleaning in your own life. This testing will ensure that your motives are pure, and you will be brought out stronger for the experience. A testing process can cause you to be bitter or it can lead you to a purified walk with God, refined "through fire" sifting and purging.[232] Keep battling!

Ultimate Victory!

Although authenticity and honest feelings were important, I knew better than to question God. He is God. I am not. If only His purpose was plastered on a billboard or blared from a loudspeaker while we are going through tough times. If only. That is why it is called faith. Trust. "Be still and know that I am God." As we survived the battle, we realized that as we were faithful and obedient and humble, God would pour out His favor and blessing on the school. Sometimes that is not always visibly evident as we desire. Most of the time it does not happen in our fast-food, instant society timeline. Sometimes it takes generations. As I am writing this final edit of this book, nearly ten years after my carpet-drenching CCA moment, an anonymous couple whose family has been blessed by CCA delivered a large six figure check and CCA now has its very own building! A godly, humble couple, investing their time and money into things that go beyond their generation! God is good!

If only big callings and making a generational impact were easy. Know that you are in good company, my friend, if you are going through a battle or a trial. Our trials and tribulations are simply a walk in the park in contrast to Jesus' road to the cross, to His persecution, to His sacrifice. What about His disciples who were martyred, crucified upside down, or imprisoned for their faith? If you want to make a generational impact, you will have a battle. A little blood, a lot of sweat, and maybe even some knife wounds in the back as you turn your back and others retreat. Pull yourself up by the bootstraps and remind yourself who the battle is really against. Remind yourself who is ultimately defeated. Remind yourself and Satan that Jesus is interceding on your behalf at the throne of your heavenly Father. Although spiritual battles are being fought against the enemy, you also have angels battling with you. Stay strong.

Your Spiritual Battle

You might have a battle of your own.

- A battle with your teen's rebellion. Stay strong. Be consistent. Love them, but discipline them.

233

- A battle with temptation and sin. Fight. Don't give in. Get others to join your team to help you and hold you accountable.
- A battle with your spouse. Deny yourself. Show understanding. Honor. Respect. Submit. Listen.
- A battle in a relationship. Be quick to listen. Slow to speak. Slow to anger.
- A battle with Satan. Put on the full armor of God. Pray. Fast. Transform your mind.
- A battle inside you to be complacent. A battle to keep you restrained and ineffective in finishing strong in your second half.

Know that your battle is not your own to fight. Although we do battle with our human nature, with the sin nature, with the flesh, with others, and with the world and its desires. However, there are times, places, and seasons where you will encounter spiritual warfare. There is power in prayer and power from the very God who created you. Put on God's battle armor. Read Ephesians 6:10-20.

Spiritual warfare is real. Read about the power of prayer and fasting, and better understand spiritual warfare.

- Peter had the church praying for him constantly (Acts 12:5).
- Submission to God will help you resist the devil (James 4:7–8).
- Be aware of Satan, your adversary. God will give you strength (1 Peter 5:8–11).
- Don't be ignorant of Satan (2 Corinthians 2:11).
- Don't let Satan use you (1 Chronicles 21:1).
- Use prayer and fasting to influence the war in the heavenlies (Daniel 10:1–21).
- There is power in the blood of Jesus and in your testimony to overcome the accuser (Revelation 12:7–12).
- Let God make you alive; don't walk according to Satan's plan (Ephesians 2:1–3).
- Use God's weapons to help with your thoughts, don't let Satan corrupt your mind (2 Corinthians 10:3–5; 11:3).
- Use worship to help calm the spiritual storms (1 Samuel 16:13–23).

Rise up, God is for you! He will not leave you or forsake you. Be courageous!

"The Sound"- Daniel Bashta

Legacy Lesson: Making a generational impact may not be easy. Lean on God when you feel betrayed, lonely or battle-worn. Let God defend you. Stay faithful to your mission, to your calling and to God's plan for your life. Battles will come and go. Jesus will be your rock and a faithful friend. Let the battles be the Lord's!

CHAPTER 35

RAISING THE FUTURE— YOUR GREATER PURPOSE: A BATTLE PLAN

I remember playing the board game "Risk" as a teenager. My sister and I had some competitive and emotional battles. Some of the games ended with one of us in tears (and it wasn't me). Some of the games ended with one of us grabbing the game board, folding it up, and scattering all the soldiers (and it wasn't her). These games would last for hours some nights and other nights they would be over very quickly. Each territory was taken little by little. Often, a small battle would turn into a large war, and it would bleed over and affect other territories.

That game parallels our families, our homes' and our country's battles. The enemy is working on one home at a time and has a greater strategy. God is working on one individual and one home at a time as well. The battle rages. Some battles in our souls and in our homes are brief and won quickly. Other battles rage for years with no apparent victory in sight. A relationship battle or a sin battle can easily bleed over into other areas and relationships of our life. We must let God be part of the equation.

If God purposes something, then He is faithful to complete it. It will succeed. It will stand. I remember reading Isaiah 14:24-27 during this time of battle. Who can stand against God's ultimate purpose? This was a prophecy concerning Judah's threat from the enemy. I knew that God purposed the school. It was His school! He had ultimate control. It was encouraging to know that we were not in the battle alone. He will crush any enemies that are standing in His way. Who can thwart God? Do not underestimate His power. God purposes marriage. He purposes family. He purposes you to follow Him. Know that your battle has an ultimate purpose that is greater than you and your situation. Think generationally! Get involved with someone else's battle. Be a reinforcement to your kids, grandkids or a single mom.

One day during this season, I drove down the road listening to a preacher say, *"Take your hands off. It's not your ministry; it's mine."* When the enemy throws his knockout punches or when the "good advice giver" blankets the soothing words with an intent to control or manipulate, simply stand firm in what God has called you to. Know that the battle is the Lord's. Be courageous. Trust Him. Obviously, in a business or a ministry we need to please the customer or the client, but ultimately we are to please God[233] and are account-able to Him. We must endure hardship, as a soldier, ultimately pleasing the enlister.[234]

This section might have made you uncomfortable. Know that not every battle is spiritual. It might be a battle with the flesh. There is not a demon or an angel behind every rock, but know that spiritual forces are at work. Maybe you haven't been in a battle yet. God might be challenging you to get involved with things that have an everlasting value, things that make a generational impact. If you do, you will have some battles. They might be brief conflicts, or they might be major spiritual battles, but the victories are worth every battle! If we spend our second half on the beaches and golf course, we might not have much of a battle on our hands. The devil will find a battle worth fighting. As I read the Old Testament, I see battle after battle, but I also see that God is still in control. If you are ready to get serious about future generations, your kids, grandkids, and/or the lost, get ready for battle—but also get ready to see some great victories!

How we lead and influence our children has a major impact on the battles they—and their children and grandchildren beyond them—will fight. It seems as though the church is struggling just to hold on to spiritual territory gained by previous generations in America and parts of Europe. Many people have even given up the fight or compromised with a watered-down, lukewarm battle plan. It is no longer time to be a wallflower or just play defense. We need to go on the offensive. We need to take back some of the ground the devil has stolen in our families, in our lives, and in our churches. Expect some betrayals along the way, even from some of the people closest to you. Expect to be let down by other Christians. People will quit on you. Just remember, Jesus is not letting you down, so don't give up on Him. Expect some major victories as you take back ground. What is your battle plan?

Your Purpose, Your Battle

The big picture, purpose. As I reminisce about starting a school, it all comes back to "purpose" in life. Why did we start the school? For our kids. For a firm foundation. For discipleship. No one will fight quite like you do for your own kids. You cannot delegate this battle to a teacher, pastor, or youth worker. This is *your* battle. We were not battling for just our three kids but for hundreds of families, for future generations, for future leaders, and for future parents! I am convinced that is why we were experiencing this immensity of spiritual warfare. We are battling for a generation's soul. Many days you will just battle the flesh, but for big generational endeavors—your kids, grandkids, how you spend your second half, your future, there will be some warring in the heavenlies. Do not cave in to compromise. Do not surrender. It is not too late. Pick up your sword, God's Word, muster your army, and win some battles. Start with some small battles, such as daily prayer and Bible reading with your spouse and family or dinner with your family.

Anything worthwhile will involve battles.
Anything worthwhile will require dreaming.
Anything worthwhile will take hard work.
Anything worthwhile will take an investment of your time and money.

Think beyond that current battle, that struggle at home or work, that family argument. Think and act generationally.

We are leaving a generational footprint. Our children are the legacy that we leave to make a generational impact. Our 401(k), our careers, our successes are nothing of eternal value. Our children should be our most valued "asset." Raising our children and the pursuit of the lost should be the greatest investment in our giving "portfolio." This is our greatest opportunity to influence the next generation. We are changing a generation! *We are* making a difference!

 Read Joshua 1:1–9 and Deuteronomy 31:6.

Lessons Learned

We learned many lessons as we journeyed through the launch of a generation-influencing adventure such as starting a school. As you prepare for your second half, you must have a plan. Be courageous! Whether it is a small business, ministry, volunteer work, or a family focus, as you prepare your plan and put it on paper, you might also consider some of the lessons we learned from our case study!

- Pray! Make war on the floor. Your greatest offensive and defensive weapon is prayer.
- Put your strategy or vision on paper and make it visible—early and often.
- Lean on God more than on your own wisdom (James 1:5; Proverbs 3: 5–6).
- Seek God in all major decisions—with your spouse and your family as appropriate.
- Nothing faith-filled will be easy. If you didn't need God, it would be easy.
- Get to know your business/ministry partners fully before the "marriage."
- Ask for and trust your spouse's wisdom.
- Be quick to listen, slow to speak, and slow to get angry.
- Practice servant leadership. Listen. Lay down yourself.
- Seek God's will and favor.
- Be sensitive to what might be going on spiritually. Nothing is coincidence.
- The Holy Spirit is the Comforter and Helper. Seek out His comfort and help.
- Do not underestimate the power of the spoken word—positive and negative.
- Do not blindly accept things. Strive to understand agendas and motives and those who seek control.
- Avoid gossip at all costs. Take a problem, concern, or issue directly to the person involved.
- Encourage. Be positive. Be optimistic. Be faith-filled.
- Deal with the doubt, discouragement, problems, or your lack of faith privately, not publicly—with God and with a close circle of those you trust for prayer support.
- Do not run from problems or delay action in dealing with them. Make decisions; don't punt.
- Surround yourself with honest, humble people.
- Watch for multiple "red flags," and address them promptly.
- You cannot separate personal behavior from business behavior. If people are deceptive personally, they will be deceptive in business. If they gossip personally, they will

gossip in business. If they lack staying power and run at the first sign of trouble personally, expect that same behavior in business or ministry.

- Delegate—at the right time, to the right people, and when they have earned your trust.
- Know when to pass the torch. Don't listen to the wrong voices.
- Protect your family time and your spiritual quiet time with God. Keep them first!
- Don't take credit. Give God the glory, and recognize others.
- Don't blame God. Don't blame others publicly. The buck stops with you. Move on.
- Don't be overly concerned with titles or hierarchy.
- Get faith and trust. Know that if God ordained it and birthed it, then it is His. Relax in that fact.
- Do what you are good at! Know your role as leader, protector, etc.
- Don't be too eager to take too many leaps of faith. Be sure that you know when to leap. It might be by small steps. It might be by a series of steps. Be patient. Be faithful in the little things. Be ready to leap when called upon.
- Remember that God is your defense.
- Leadership is lonely. Be sure you have God, your spouse, and a true friend who sticks with you to lean upon.
- Stir up the gifts in others. Don't try to do it all yourself.
- Consider the costs—financial and familial.
- Pray. Our motto was "Take two a day for CCA." Start with two minutes a day praying for your venture.

My friend Clay Wallace taught me another important lesson: everything should begin and end in prayer. We begin and end meetings with prayer. We start a family decision process with prayer, and we thank Him after the decision is made. Pray continually. You are a soldier.[235] Battle on your knees.

Legacy Lesson: Leaving a strong heritage for your kids and grandkids, or impacting your circle of influence will involve battles. Get involved with something/ someone worth fighting for. Anything worthwhile will require some spiritual battles. Use the weapons available to you.

CHAPTER 36

YOUR CHILD'S EDUCATION: THE PURPOSE

"Education is the soul of a society
as it passes from one generation to another."
—G.K. Chesterton

The burning question that agitates and divides educators, teachers, politicians, religious leaders, and parents alike is this: "What is the purpose of education?" This is a question that parents must wrestle with and answer. Your children will spend fifteen to twenty years being "educated" in some formal model, so you should do some soul searching about your goals first. Before you dig into educational models, worldviews, styles, approaches, and statistics, you must answer the question "What is the purpose in educating my child? We too quickly jump to the second question: "Which model is best for my child?"

Is the purpose primarily of "teaching the three R's"—reading, 'riting, and 'rithmetic"? Is it about developing strong leaders? Is it about preparing your child for life? Is it about developing the child's character? Is it about spiritual discipleship?

Following is a little survey that will help you and your spouse assess your intentions for educating your child.

STOP Score each "educational goal" on a scale from 1 to 10, with 10 being an absolute must, a non-negotiable, most important, and 1 being not important at all.

	Husband		Wife
Acquire knowledge			
Think critically			
Develop the whole person			
Equip for life			
Moral values			
Mental development			
Social development			
Leadership development			
Productive citizen			
Character development			
Biblical foundation			
Christian discipleship			
Job/vocational			
God's calling preparation			
Family preparation			
Salary/financial Income			

What are the three most important priorities or goals for educating your child(ren)?

Husband: 1._____ 2. _____ 3. _____
Wife: 1._____ 2. _____ 3. _____

Seeds for the Soil

Most people believe that the purpose of education is more than the "3 R's." We are truly equipping our children to assume leadership roles and be productive participants in their communities and nations. We often lose sight of the fact that education is equally critical in preparing our children for life—establishing a foundation for their families and building a spiritual foundation. It is a passing the baton of the soul, as Chesterson says. Teaching and instruction are seeds that settle in the soil of our children's minds, our children's emotions, and our children's wills.

Education is often pigeon-holed with an acquisition of intelligence only when in reality it is discipleship as well. Someone is discipling your child. It is a process of training the whole person, not just the mind. Your child is being discipled in a worldview when in your home and when away from your home—at school or at church. Ensure that your values align with these institutions and that you understand the risks and can correct any incorrect discipling. In 1947, Dr. Martin Luther King Jr. wrote an article for the Morehouse College student paper about "The Purpose of Education." He said,

"We must remember that intelligence is not enough. Intelligence plus character—that is the true goal of education."

Our top five educational priorities or goals as a family were

- Biblical foundation
- Christian discipleship
- Preserve and strengthen the family
- Acquire academic excellence
- Prepare the child for life

Settle on a top five list of educational priorities or goals for you as a couple. You will use the data in a later chapter to help you determine which model will be best for you and your child.

There are obviously variations on how your child will be educated based on the institution's and the teacher's worldviews. A public or private or home school will obviously also have different life values and academic success. The National Educational Longitudinal Study[236] by the U.S. Department of Education surveyed high school seniors. It compared a number of levels of public versus private schools, including various life values, and mastery of math concepts.

1) Life values characterized as "very important"

	Public	Private
Find the right spouse and have happy family life	81%	89%
Have children	49%	55%
Give my children better opportunities than I had	83%	70%

2) Mastery of math knowledge and skills

	Public	Private
Level 1—Simple arithmetic whole numbers	96%	99%
Level 2—Simple decimals, fractions, powers	78%	93%
Level 3—Simple problem solving	62%	84%
Level 4—Intermediate level math concepts	35%	60%

Education: A Brief Look in the Rear-View Mirror

In discussing the purpose of education, it is important to reflect on the history of education and the responsibility for that child's education. It is a similar history in Europe and America. In early America, no colony centralized control of education. In the 1600's and 1700's, the responsibility lay with the parents. In fact *"it is important to note that the responsibility for providing education was placed on parents rather than borne by the gov-*

ernment."[237] "Ninety-five percent of children attended private schools and the first school law, in 1642, required parents to provide three areas of teaching in their educational programs: reading and writing, the laws of the land, and religion.

Biblical values and a God-centered philosophy were the norm."[238] "*The General Court of Massachusetts enacted into law a condemnation of parents who did not take steps to guarantee that their children could 'read and understand the principles of religion and the capital laws of this country.*"[239] One of America's first education acts was the Old Deluder Satan Act of 1647. Teachers were required to teach reading, writing, and the Bible. Satan was the "Deluder." The Puritans believed strongly that teaching the Bible would help the children resist evil temptations.

The Northwest Ordinances of 1787 led to a major effort for the federal government to provide education. The purpose, according to the Continental Congress, was because religion and knowledge were necessary to run a good government and to mankind in general. Congress stated, "*Religion, morality and knowledge being necessary to good government and the happiness of mankind, schools and the means of education shall forever be encouraged.*"[240] Notice that religion and morality were part of the purpose of education and were taught in public schools.

My favorite book on the history of education is a very quick read: *Four Centuries of American Education* by David Barton. As public institutions and universities became more prevalent, the integrated purpose of educating a child continued. The Bible and Christianity were fully taught. "Harvard was established as a school to train ministers of the gospel. It's two mottoes were "*For Christ and the Church*" and "*For the Glory of Christ.*" Yale provided an education based on knowing Christ and studying biblical principles. Yale admonished its students, "*Above all, have an eye to the great end of all your studies, which is to obtain the clearest conceptions of Divine things and to lead you to a saving knowledge of God in his Son Jesus Christ.*"[241]

"At the university level in 1860, 262 out of 288 college presidents were ministers of the Gospel—as were more than a third of all university faculty members. Ninety percent of the state universities conducted chapel services; at half, chapel attendance was mandatory; and a quarter required regular church attendance as well. Inclusion of religious and moral lessons was the accepted norm for 400 years in America." In our early days, public education was unabashedly Christian. The *New England Primer* taught the alphabet but also provided children a Christian foundation for life. Students also learned biblical doctrine and recited the Lord's Prayer.

In 1867, the U.S. Congress established a department of education for the purpose of collecting statistics and facts to show the condition and progress of education. The department was headed by a commissioner and three clerks for a total budget of $9,400. By 1900, only 10 percent of children were enrolled in private schools, but the Bible was still on the desk of most teachers and the principals. The Bible still dominated the curriculum. The control and ownership of the education process passed from the hands of families to the government. A secular, values-neutral philosophy began to creep in.

Marlin Maddoux talks of the agendas of public education and the impact of its leaders in *Public Education Against America.*[242] John Dewey had a profound influence on education. He was an atheist and a socialist. He praised Vladimir Lenin in Russia and believed that socialism was the ideal organization for our society. He wanted to emphasize a focus on beliefs and values instead of traditional education. He wrote, "*I believe that the true center of correlation on the school subjects is not science, not literature, nor history, nor geography, but the child's social activities.*" He also wrote, "*There is no God and there is no soul. There is no room for fixed, natural laws or moral absolutes.*" The American public school system still bears his humanist, socialist imprint.

Beginning in 1962, the courts ordered a completely secular approach to public education.
- Voluntary prayer was forbidden.
- The inclusion of Scripture was terminated.
- The Bible was ordered out of school libraries.
- Displays of the Ten Commandments were ordered removed.
- Invocations were excluded from graduation and athletic events.
- Traditional Christmas programs were halted.
- The names of holidays—Christmas, Easter, etc., were changed to winter break, spring break, etc.

We covered some of the results of that fateful event earlier. However, the most important changes came about in parental thinking. The most important change in education in the last generation has not occurred in a school building; rather it has occurred in the minds of parents, who no longer take primary responsibility for their children's educations." Harry and Rosemary Wong, long-time educators, noted that

- the average child receives twelve minutes of attention each day from his or her parents.
- the average parent watches five to six hours of television each day.
- the number one problem reported by high school students is loneliness.

The Carnegie Foundation surveyed 22,000 teachers and discovered that

- 90 percent said that a lack of parental support was a problem at their schools, and
- 100 percent described their students as "emotionally needy and starved for attention and affection."

Dr. John William Turner Jr., author of *Character Driven College Preparation*[243] and advocate of the University Model School approach, which offers an educational alternative that provides greater opportunities for parents to be involved with their children's education, states that even the U.S. Department of Education validates that parental involvement greatly affects a child. "*One study states that controllable home factors account for almost all the differences in average student achievement across states.*"

State of Our Schools and Society

Education has had a great influence in bringing about changes in attitudes, behaviors, beliefs, and values. Political correctness—tolerance in the extreme—has taken over. Kids are taught not to express a judgment about someone else's ideas, values, or beliefs. Thus, there is no absolute truth. They must value and accept others' viewpoints—unless, of course, those ideas are based on Judeo-Christian values. Moral relativism became prevalent in the 1960s. God was no longer honored as the absolute authority, so absolute truth began to get watered down and a moral fog set in. "That may be okay for you, but it is wrong for me." The Bible is no longer the standard.

Legacy Lesson: Weighing the "purpose of education" for your children and grandchildren is one of the most important things you will do. The decision will have a multi-generational impact.

CHAPTER 37

EDUCATION AND WORLDVIEW: THE BEST MODEL FOR YOUR CHILD

The great task of the school is to counteract and transform the beliefs and values that the child brings from the home and the church."
—Professor John Dewey

"The philosophy of the school room in one generation will be the philosophy of government in the next.
—Abraham Lincoln

*I*n a George Barna survey,[244] he asked "What do we want most for our children?" The number one response from parents was "that their children would get a good education." This was true for both Christians and non-Christians. It is understandable why most parents answer that way. Education has a domino effect. Seventeen years of a child's life is with us as parents. Thirteen of those years are spent in formal education of some sort. We want those thirteen years to be well spent—a "good education." The thought process goes something like this: This domino of a "good education" will lead to other dominos—a successful job, then a successful career, then a successful family, and a successful life.

But reflect a little longer and go a little deeper on that survey question. Shouldn't our primary goal be that our children follow God, glorify Him, and live their lives sold out for Him and His will? If they were a successful nurse and not a Christ-follower, I would consider that a failure. If they were a successful athlete or artist and not a Christ-follower, I would consider that a failure. If they married a successful person who was not a Christ-follower, I would consider that a failure. We might be participating in a cultural mindset that might not align with our worldview, or maybe our worldview needs a tune-up. We might need to rewind the tape farther and even beyond "What is the purpose of education?" Take a few minutes and reflect.

"What do you want most for your children in life?" Have a discussion with your spouse and God about this question.

Your Shades

I buy my sunglasses at the dollar store—mostly because I am cheap, but also because I lose or break them once a month. Some people swear by a certain brand, certain shade or tint, or particular lens style. I swear by a buck—$1. That is my favorite lens style, regardless of the style points I might lose out on. Undoubtedly, the lens tint does impact your vision, but my trade-off is price.

What is "a worldview"? Some people like to come up with grandiose definitions and lengthy essays on the subject. I will make it simple. I see worldview as the pair of sunglasses you wear in looking at the world. The lens is your framework of our world, and the tint is your basic assumptions about God, man, and nature. Your glasses affect your vision, how you see the world around you.

I remember putting together our trampoline and assembling the first half of it with the aid of an instruction booklet. Then I got a tad proud and felt that I didn't need the booklet for the second half of the assembly process. I was cruising along on autopilot. We put it together and after one day of the kids' jumping, I heard the kids scream. I rushed out the back door to see the kids crumpled up in a caved-in trampoline. One of the braces had caved in. It was a mess. After taking a quick look back through the instructional booklet, I realized that I had missed one small step and forgot to install just one small, two-inch connecting piece that gave it more stability.

Our family has a biblical worldview. I see the world through that lens. If we say that we have a biblical worldview but don't use God's instructional manual, we can mess things up in a hurry by taking a shortcut or missing one little thing that can affect our children and our families. The Bible is the source of our direction. It is the best spousal help book and parenting book you will ever read. You would think that most Christians would have a biblical worldview, but according to Voddie Baucham Jr., quoting George Barna [245] *less than 10% of "born-again Christians" in America have a biblical worldview.* What's worse, he found that only 51 percent of *pastors* have a biblical worldview!

As discussed earlier, whoever spends the most time with our children shapes their worldview. Education is the greatest shaper of worldview.

Josh McDowell sounds an alarm in his book *The Last Christian Generation.*[246] He warns that young people are redefining what it means to be Christian. Their attitudes and behaviors are virtually no different than those of non-Christians. Could that be due to the fact that 90 percent of Christian youth are schooled under the same roof as non-Christians? Could it be they are being taught a worldview that is no longer Christian?

Nehemiah Institute[247] looked at these questions and has studied over 20,000 students from 1000 schools with PEERS testing to identify a young person's views on politics, economics, education, religion, and social issues. Students were tested in world-view Christian schools, other Christian schools, and those who come from Christian homes but were educated in public schools. The good news is that many students are seeking God and haven't rejected Him. The bad news is that their version of Christianity is often not biblical.

- 85 percent of youth from Christian homes who attend public schools do not embrace a biblical worldview.
- 74 percent still haven't figured out the purpose or meaning of their lives.

- 65 percent want a close relationship with God.
- 63 percent don't believe Jesus is the Son of the one true God.
- 58 percent believe that all faiths teach equally valid truths.
- 51 percent don't believe that Jesus rose from the dead.
- 65 percent don't believe that Satan is a real entity.
- 68 percent don't believe that the Holy Spirit is a real entity.
- 70 percent of churched young people believe that there is no absolute moral truth.

Christian students who are in public schools, and to some extent those in private schools, have been influenced greatly over the past few generations. The findings are clear that Christian youth are adopting secular humanist and socialist worldviews without even knowing it. The generational impact is alarming and so drastic that it could signal the end of Christianity in this country as we know it. The student from the typical evangelical family who is in a public school scores about 30 to 40 percent lower on biblical world-view testing than students in Christian schools. The trend is becoming worse and worse. In the past sixteen years, that trend has continued on a massive slide in public schools, decreasing by 80 percent. Traditional Christian schools have also tumbled by 54 percent. Only Christian worldview schools have shown an improvement.

The challenge for us as parents is to choose an educational model that aligns with both our worldview and our purpose for education. The moral of these statistics is that we as parents should *not* assume that the couple of hours they spend with a youth pastor or children's leader in church is sufficient. They are not the main influencer in their lives. We as parents are and those educating our children are. (If you want to do a deeper study on Worldview types, I refer you to Probe Ministries[248] with Kerby Anderson and team.)

"A teacher impacts eternity; one never knows when his influence will end."
—unknown

The Solution: What Is the Best Model for My Child?

The question that most families struggle with is "What is the best education model that aligns with: (1) our worldview and (2) our purpose for education?" Which model best cultivates the soil of your worldview for your family? How can you best raise successful, well-educated, grounded, confident children? What are your child's needs?

We must protect the values we hold most dearly. The educational system chosen will either dry up those seeds you have planted or fertilize them. This choice is one of the most pivotal decisions you will make as a parent. I do not usually read *Robb's Report Worth* magazine because its focus is on the ultra-affluent consumer with a heavy emphasis on wealth and prosperity and with a secular slant. However, this particular issue jumped out at me *"Lessons in Legacy—the role of academics."*[249] Although the article did not focus on spiritual or moral values, a statement leapt off the page: "Today, we enjoy an unprecedented variety of educational options. There are 27,000 private schools in the United States and many excellent public schools. **Deciding which one is right for our child requires us to carefully weigh our family's goals and values, and only then seek out the school that can best help us achieve them.**"

Let's be honest. Many times we choose a school specifically based on financial concerns and don't even take the time to wrestle and analyze with our life priorities and our family's goals and values and how those are aligned with the model we choose. Since we as a family have experienced all models of school—private/university model school, public school and homeschool, I believe that there is not one school that will satisfy everyone. This should *not* be a one-time, one-size-fits-all decision. We pray and fast each year to ensure that we are still on the right track. The thirteen years of pre-college education and the four plus collegiate years should be an annual wrestling match. Is this school meeting the needs and values of my family and child? Is it nurturing our worldview or destroying it? The answer might be different for each child.

The educational choice for a child is a monumental milestone that will greatly affect generations to come. We often spend more time researching or making a decision on a hobby purchase or automobile than this vital decision. Your child might need a more nurturing, smaller environment. An extraordinarily social and extroverted child might need access to greater activities in a larger school setting. A child might have a learning disability that requires additional attention. Your child's bent and the school's offerings are just two of many considerations. Here are some other things to consider in addition to the "purpose-of-education" exercise we discussed earlier:

- Academic excellence
- Christian discipleship
- Church denominational distinctive/linkages
- Athletics programs
- Art and music programs
- Teacher/instructor qualifications and degrees
- Extracurricular activities and options
- Facilities
- Class size/student-to-teacher ratios
- Test scores
- Alumni success
- Philanthropy, community service, school involvement, and volunteer approaches
- Cultural considerations
- Economic and social considerations
- Financial/budgetary
- Alignment with Family values/worldview
- Alignment with purpose of education

For college, the list gets longer and more complex:

- Instructors have degrees in the chosen field
- Size of student body
- Campus size
- Courses/degree-plan alignment
- Job-placement record
- Academic reputation
- Financial aid/scholarships

- Campus crime risk
- Credit transfers
- Social life on campus
- Location geographically
- Admissions

You might need to create a massive Excel spreadsheet for each of your children to help assess and weigh the best alternative for your child, and be sure to go back to the "educational-purpose" exercise. For us, the private university model school (NAUMS) was the best fit for our value system and our budget challenges for the majority of our children's education, although I am not a stockholder!

STOP Go back to the exercise in which you and your spouse listed your top educational goals/priorities, then score from 1 to 10 how each institution stacks up with this list. An <u>example</u> is provided in the following table.

Educational goal	**Public**	**Private**	**Homeschool**	**NAUMS**
Biblical foundation	2	8	10	9
Christian disciple	2	8	10	9
Family preparation	4	7	8	7
Academic excellence	6	7	5	7
Life preparation	7	8	7	8

This obviously doesn't include a priority-weighted average, but it can provide the basis for a good discussion. A blank version in the appendices can be printed for use. For us, using this example and much prayer, the best choice was homeschool for the early years, then transition to NAUMS through middle school, then transition to public or private school in high school. We heavily weighed our worldview and purpose of education. Although it has been a financial sacrifice, it was the right decision for our family.

Do your research—both internally with your spouse and your child's bent and externally with the educational offerings that you are considering. Do a pros-and-cons spreadsheet with these "educational-purpose" items considered. But most importantly, do some serious seeking of God with your spouse and children. Ultimately, Glen Schultz, author of *Kingdom Education,* said it best: *"Education, no matter how good it is, can never transform a life. It can never produce a moral person or a moral society. Only the redemptive work of Christ can perform such a miracle."*[250]

Final Words

Our child's educational decisions are some of the most important we make as parents. We are not only shaping our child for life but also shaping the next several generations.

"A child is a person who is going to carry on what you have started. . . . He will assume control of your cities, states, and nations. He is going to move in and take over your churches, schools, universities, and corporations. . . . The fate of humanity is in his hands."
—Abraham Lincoln

All education teaches morality and shapes a worldview, so we cannot take the decision lightly or overweight the financial determination. Luke 6:40 makes clear that a child will become like his teacher(s). To choose an alternative to government education will require a sacrifice of time and money, yet might be the best alternative for most families with a biblical worldview.

"Our country spends more on education per student than all other industrialized nations, yet we rank near the bottom in math and science aptitude when compared to these same nations."[251] Secular humanism and politically correct approaches such as "personal preference, tolerance, and being non-judgmental" are the norm instead of right, wrong, and moral absolutes. The new absolute seems to be that there are no moral absolutes. Know your children's teachers and textbook content and how they are influencing your child, regardless of the institution. Also remember that, ultimately, we as parents are responsible for their training and instruction. It cannot be outsourced.

"Children are God's homework assignment to parents."
—Glen Schultz

Legacy Lesson: How do you want an educational system to impact your child? Does the institute(s) you have chosen align with your life and value goals for your family? This choice will impact your children and grandchildren's legacy more than any other.

CHAPTER 38

CHOOSING A COLLEGE

"Teach us to make the most of our time, so that we may grow in wisdom."
—Psalm 90:12

My wife, boys and I walked slowly out of the dorm complex with a heavy heart. It had been an exciting weekend as our daughter was chalking up one of her first milestone markers. We had moved the furniture, décorated the dorm room, enjoyed movie and a lunch and found a local "on-fire" church with her that morning that seemed to fit her like a glove. We really never dreamed this day would come. Now here we were saying our good-byes. We all had a good laugh when she asked us for a group hug. Something we had forced on her for years and often participated in with a groan or an eye-roll or two. Yet we were at peace with this college choice and her path forward because of much prayer and the lengthy and involved process we went through together to choose her college.

Just a year or two earlier we were discussing a number of "challenges" we were having during a teenage season of parenting: the hustle and bustle, teenage independence, and an overall frustration with our ineffectiveness as parents. We discussed the need to keep our eyes on the big-picture progress—the marathon approach to parenting. We are proud of our kids, but we all have our days and seasons when we struggle. I don't ever recall reading Erma Bombeck, but I stumbled upon the following letter published in Erma's newspaper column on January 29, 1969. Although some of the references are dated, and despite the fact that I was only three years old when this was written, I know my parents went through similar times of struggle. Reading it was a timely reminder that as we approach empty-nest life, time indeed flies, so don't wish it away so quickly. A young mother wrote to Erma:

"I know you've written before about the empty-nest syndrome, that lonely period after the children are grown and gone. Right now I'm up to my eyeballs in laundry and muddy boots. The baby is teething; the boys are fighting. My husband just called and said to eat without him, and I fell off my diet. Lay it on me again, will you, Erma?"

Here was Erma's reply:

> OK. One of these days, you'll shout, "Why don't you kids grow up and act your age!" And they will. Or, "You guys get outside and find yourselves something to do. . . and don't slam the door!" And they won't.

You'll straighten up the boys' bedroom neat and tidy: bumper stickers discarded, bedspread tucked and smooth, toys displayed on the shelves. Hangers in the closet. Animals caged. And you'll say out loud, "Now I want it to stay this way." And it will.

You'll prepare a perfect dinner with a salad that hasn't been picked to death and a cake with no finger traces in the icing, and you'll say, "Now, there's a meal for company." And you'll eat it alone.

You'll say, "I want complete privacy on the phone. No dancing around. No demolition crews. Silence! Do you hear?" And you'll have it.

No more plastic tablecloths stained with spaghetti. No more bedspreads to protect the sofa from damp bottoms. No more gates to stumble over at the top of the basement steps. No more clothespins under the sofa. No more playpens to arrange a room around.

No more anxious nights under a vaporizer tent. No more sand on the sheets or Popeye movies in the bathroom. No more iron-on patches, rubber bands for ponytails, tight boots or wet knotted shoestrings.

Imagine: A lipstick with a point on it. No baby-sitter for New Year's Eve. Washing clothes only once a week. Seeing a steak that isn't ground. Having your teeth cleaned without a baby on your lap. No PTA meetings. No car pools. No blaring radios. No one washing her hair at 11 o'clock at night. Having your own roll of Scotch tape.

Think about it: No more Christmas presents out of toothpicks and library paste. No more sloppy oatmeal kisses. No more tooth fairy. No giggles in the dark. No knees to heal, no responsibility.

Only a voice crying, "Why don't you grow up?" and the silence echoing, "I did."

 "Watercolor Ponies"—Wayne Watson

Where has the time gone? We never thought this time would come. The years went by as a blur as they appeared in the rear-view mirror. Time to say goodbye. A mixture of pride, celebration, and joy coupled with grief, sadness, and an emptiness, but still an overriding emotion of love. We know she will be back, but more as a beloved guest passing through. Daddy's girl, for practical purposes, is gone for good. An empty room awaits. Gulp. Leaving not just our home but childhood. Leaving not just our neighborhood, but our full-time care. Moving from dependence to independence.

Letting go is tough. You are never fully ready. Get ready! Time flies!

For some people who are reading this, the transition years leading up to this "sending-them-off" day might be brutal. There are days *they* are ready, and days *you* are ready. At times, they seem to step over the invisible line of adulthood only to return to a childhood attitude days later. However, cherish these days because you don't get them back again.

Milestones—Again!

This first day of college is one of the milestones of a parent's life, and the first real "adult" milestone of a child. Yes, those first days at kindergarten and high school were big. Yes, that driver's license was a major event. Sure, the first time they went on a youth or missions trip and spent some time away from home were fear-filled and faith-filled. Certainly the first date is a milestone not soon to be forgotten. But this milestone is different. It has a sense of permanency and is a roller coaster ride filled with dips and turns of emotions and pride.

You want so badly for this college choice to be the right choice. It is a weighty decision. Think of the habits that you formed or cemented during college years. Think of the social aspects, the relationships that were established or broken—good and bad. Think back to the impact this choice had on your future—your job, where you live, your relationships, your lifestyle base, and your life period. It is significant. It was life changing and life directing. If you did not attend college, that too was significant.

Do an autopsy on *your* childhood events and relationship with *your* parents. Did your parents have an impact on you? You bet! Does their influence still have an impact on you decades later? Of course. Be encouraged right now as a parent that you *did* have an impact. You think that your kids might not hear your voice now or won't as they continue to grow and mature. They do. Those disciplines and scriptures you have taught will come back. When they are alone in their apartment, or on a plane far away, or struggling with an issue of their own, your voice will come back. The years you spent instilling habits will not have been wasted. Know that this college milestone is one of many future milestones. Celebrate it and enjoy it! You can mourn later.

Kids' Seasons/Dreams

In *Letting Them Go,*[252] Dave Veerman explains the need for parents to adjust their mindset in the years, that precede the college road trips and decisions. "Children seldom live up to our idealistic dreams for them when they were very young. Each child is special, a unique creation of our loving God and packed with his or her own blend of talents, gifts, abilities, and potential. Parents' dream adjustments come in stages throughout the parenting process. You might have to make a series of mid-course corrections—releases—in the next few years."

Purpose—Again!

We just concluded a section on purpose, but now it is time to have a similar discussion with your college-bound high schooler. Maybe use the prior exercises on purpose and goals of education. Take them to dinner and interview them.

1) What do you want to accomplish in the next five years of your life? Consider personal, financial, spiritual, academic, and relational?

2) Why do you want to go to college, and what do you want to get out of it?

3) What is the purpose of college?

4) Do you believe in our "family vision?"

5) What is your worldview? (This might be a little deep for the youngster.)

6) What colleges align with your "family vision," "college vision," and "worldview"?

7) What colleges don't?

Here are the top reasons high schoolers selected their first college.[253]

	Four- year school	Two-year school
Location	70%	74%
Program of study	63%	42%
Reputation	59%	29%
Cost	47%	62%
Personal/family reasons	30%	22%

1) What do you want to accomplish in the next five years of your life?

    a. Personal   _____

    b. Financial   _____

    c. Spiritual   _____

    d. Academic   _____

    e. Relational   _____

2) Why College and what do you want to get out of it?

    a. Job preparation   _____

    b. Life preparation   _____

    c. _____

    d. _____

3) What is your life vision?

4) What is your worldview?

5) What are you good at?/In what areas are you gifted?

6) What do you *love* doing?/What are your passions?

The College Choice—A Partnership

So whose decision is it? Many parents say that if they are footing the bill, then it is solely their call. Many kids think that they are independent enough to make the decision on their own. We parents have been involved greatly with the decision-making process, the

254

prayer, and the college visits. We determined that it would be a "joint partnership" during the process, and that we would lead and guide, but our daughter would make the ultimate decision. We leaned heavily on God to lead and guide as well. This process might vary by child and their decision-making wisdom and maturity.

Our Family vision is to "know God, love God, and serve others." We all decided together upon a Christian college because it was best suited and aligned best with our family's goals. That helped narrow the field of choices greatly. Remember, however, that the child might not fully adopt your family vision, or their goals and purpose for college might differ from yours. This is where regular dialogue is necessary. We had been talking about her college choices for five years before "the day". More on that later.

Remember, this is not solely a parent's decision or ultimatum, or rebellion might seep in later. The shepherd approach vs. the dictator approach will serve you well. Marketing your alumni clothing gear to the child when they are but an infant has its time and place (Go Sparty). Steering or manipulating a decision to a particular location close to (or far from) home might not be the right thing. We wrestled with our flesh and some of these things but always yielded to the fact that this is about what *God* wants for your child. It might be that he or she chooses your alma mater or picks a school close to home, but this is really about teaching your kids to hear from God. We have had seasons of prayer and seasons of fasting for this milestone, and we believe God will open doors and close doors, and that the Holy Spirit will speak ever so gently to our children. Our challenge is not to drown out God's voice or limit His plans. Obviously, there might be financial and admission constraints that need to be considered, but God can do some miracles along the way (scholarships, finances).

Choosing a college is about deciding which values are your top priority. Most students will learn more about life and shape their future life outside the classroom than inside the classroom. For those of you who went to college, you know what I mean! What type of socialization will they be getting?

I would highly recommend the book *Summit Ministries Guide to Choosing a College* to help you think through this major decision. "A recent study indicated that about one-third of college freshmen who profess to be Christians deny their Christianity after graduating from a secular university.[254]" Start your preparation and discussions early! This is not a last-minute decision.

Preparation

Deciding where to go to college is not an easy decision and should not be made overnight. It is imperative to start the discussions and prayer in your freshman year. "Thirty-seven percent of college-bound students plan to start before their junior year." This is *too late*! It is a time-consuming process if done correctly and can be stressful if you wait until the last minute. It can also be very rewarding as the young student begins to discover themselves in the process. It is in essence a journey of self-discovery, and for the first time they will be asking some tough questions of themselves: What do I want to do? What are my life goals? What is the purpose of going to college? Where do I want to live? How can I afford this? What should I study?

Be involved. Do not assume that your student counselor or student will take care of everything themselves. "Seventy-nine percent of college-bound juniors and seniors say their parents are involved just the right amount, when it comes to applying to colleges and deciding which school to attend."[255] There are more than four thousand colleges and universities so where in the world should you begin and when should you begin? Some questions that the teen will want to start to answer together with you the parents are as follows:

- Which subjects and/or majors are you passionate about?
- Which states do I *not* want to be in?
- Do I want to stay close to home? (This answer can change often, depending upon the parents' and the student's relationship!)
- Do I want to be in a large city or a small town?
- Do I want to attend a private or a public school?
- Do I want a large school or a small school?
- What about my special interests, such as sports, arts, and academic specialties?

In our challenging economy choosing a degree is a very important decision. Many graduates are unable to find work because this choice was not a priority. The more you read and research different colleges and degrees, the more questions you can add to your key careabout list.

Another very important decision for the student is choosing a church. I challenge parents to *help* the child research local churches, bible studies, and on-campus young adult events. This will eventually be their choice, but one of my last "helicopter papa" acts was to research all 100+ local churches and simply hand her a list of 7 "potentials". We talked about what mattered to her—on campus fellowship, proximity to campus, size of church, contemporary worship, passionate/thriving atmosphere, and good Bible teaching. I then created a spreadsheet of options and let her do the choosing (truth in reporting.....we actually visited a church while on campus for welcome week that was NOT on my list. It was recommended by many students and was her decision, so I bit my lip. It was a GREAT church and was blessed for biting my lip).

Legacy Lesson: Prepare and pray early for this major life milestone. Your child will be shaped and molded in the college environment. A Life Foundation will be built and a Life Legacy will be built on this campus. Don't weigh the decision lightly.

CHAPTER 39

COLLEGE PREPARATION AND ADMISSIONS: CHECKLISTS AND TOOLS

*T*here are many excellent websites and books on how to choose a college. There are three "choose tools" that I developed to start you in the correct direction.

1) Preliminary/overview research
2) Site visits
3) Current and former student comments feedback

1) Choosing a College: Preliminary/Overview Research

The absolute best place to start is www.collegeboard.com. You will be there often throughout the next four years. The next logical place to spend time is on the specific university websites as you begin your research. You can begin to collect data, such as tuition, admissions requirements, etc., and build a comparison spreadsheet. You can also double check some of the collegeboard.com data, such as tuition, school size, awards, etc.

The best place to start is with a blank spreadsheet to be populated with things that you really care about. Begin a spreadsheet similar to the one in the following table, and update this frequently over the years. As a disclaimer, this is included as an example only, as the data is outdated and is not accurate. This spreadsheet will help you stay focused, plan visits, and eventually narrow the list, although initially it might be very large. (A blank version is also provided in the appendices.)

Visit Priority	School Name	State	EMILY RATING	% app admit	under grads	in st	grads top 10%	top 25%	in Cost	Out Cost	Room Board	1 year TOTAL	4 year Cost
done	Texas A & M	TX	High	70	36430	97	54	86	7844		8010	$15,854	$ 63,416
done	Dallas Baptist University	TX	High	46	3533	93	19	39	18690		5868	$24,558	$ 98,232
done	Abilene Christian	TX	High	47	3906	86	23	58	18855		7236	$26,091	$104,364
done	Texas Tech	TX	Low	72	23000	96	21	52	6783		7310	$14,093	$ 56,372
done	UT- Arlington	TX	Low	76	18985	97	19	59	7780	-	5900	$13,680	$ 54,720
done	Lubbock Christian	TX	No	66	1541	82	17	45	16180		5146	$21,326	$ 85,304
done	Baylor	TX	High	51	12162	82	41	72	27910	-	7971	$35,881	$143,524
3	University of Texas- Austin	TX	TBD	44	37300	95	75	95	8500		9246	$17,746	$ 70,984
done	University of Florida	FL	Med	39	34000	97	76	92		20640	7150	$27,790	$111,160
done	Florida State	FL	Med	47	29800	91	31	71		16243	8100	$26,343	$105,372
done	Southeastern University- Florida	FL	Med	78	2867	56	-	-		14470	7000	$21,470	$ 85,880
done	Palm Beach Atlantic University	FL	No	69	2434	60	25	54		23400	8400	$31,800	$127,200
done	Pensacola Christian College	FL	No								4800	3300	$ 8,100	$ 32,400
3	Oklahoma Baptist University	OK	TBD	63	1595	62	28	59	-	17624	5570	$23,194	$ 92,776
2	Oklahoma University	OK	TBD	82	20136	-	36	72	-	17404	7376	$24,780	$ 99,120
3	Oral Roberts University	OK	TBD	73	2858	32	23	45	-	19106	7916	$27,022	$108,088
1	Arkansas State University	AK	TBD	77	10024	86	20	44	6040	14860	6544	$21,404	$ 85,616
1	University of Arkansas	AK	TBD	56	15835	64	30	60	6755	16000	8042	$24,042	$ 96,168
done	Lee University	TN	High	65	3903	47	25	46		12160	5850	$18,010	$ 72,040
1	Bryan College	TN	TBD	75	1100	49	-	-		18620	5454	$24,074	$ 96,296
1	Rhodes College	TN	TBD										$
1	University of Tennessee	TN	TBD	73	21182	90	39	70	-	22420	7800	$30,220	$120,880
4	Liberty University	VA	TBD	75	28863	40	5	23		17264	5996	$23,260	$ 93,040
4	Patrick Henry College	VA	TBD	-	404	-				21270	8010	$29,280	$117,120
4	Regent University	VA	TBD	64	1918	38				15100	5900	$21,000	$ 84,000
4	Pepperdine	CA	TBD	34	3404	46	40	75	-	37850	10900	$48,750	$195,000
4	Azusa Pacific University	CA	TBD	63	4858	74	31	62		26640	7242	$33,882	$135,528

Research what is important to you and begin to determine the site visit priority as high/medium/low (or 1-2-3). After the site visit, we had our daughter rate the school and application probability as high/medium/low. This might change over the years. Our spreadsheet also included percentage of applicants admitted, number of undergraduates, percentage of in-state attendees, graduates in the top 10 and 25 percent, and tuition and room/board (both in-state and out-of-state). Almost all of these data are available for most schools on collegeboard.com or the school's website.

We then tracked more things specific to our key concerns (see the following figure). Do they have a Fellowship of Christian Athletes? Do they have the majors that are our potential targets? How do they score in the *U.S. News & World Report* surveys? Did they win any awards, recognition, or key care abouts from *Princeton Review, Kiplingers, Forbes,* and others? Many of these magazines and institutions come out with annual scores online. Some are published in an annual magazine summary.

Visit Priority	School Name	FCA CCC	Majors	Rank/Scor US News	Awards / Recognition (Princeton Review, Kiplingers, Forbes)
done	Texas A & M	y	Education, Prevet, Nursing, Drama,	69/52	Best Value, Best BuyK, BBF, LGBT unfriendly, #1 Most Conserv, Student Pack Stadium
done	Dallas Baptist University		Education, Art	61/94	
done	Abilene Christian	y	Nursing, Prevet, Ministry, Education	19/57	Best Western Colleges
done	Texas Tech		Nutrition, Health Services	159/28	Best Western Colleges, Best Buy Forbes
done	UT- Arlington	y	Nursing		
done	Lubbock Christian		Education, Nursing, Theatre, Ministr		
done	Baylor	y	Nursing, Nutrition, Pre-Nursing	79/47	BestBuy Kiplinger, LGBT unfriendly, Intramurals all, Most Religious Students
1	University of Texas- Austin	y	Nursing, Health Services	45/59	Career ser, Best Buys KF, Lib, Newsp, Beer, Lkj, Party Scn, Study Least, Pack St
done	University of Florida	?	Nursing, Health Services	53/55	BBKF Career News Dorm Dungeons Intramur Jocks Beer Lkj Party Sturdy L Pack St
done	Florida State		RN, Pre-vet	104/41	Best Buys Kpl/Forbes, Jock Beer, Party, Study Least
done	Southeastern University- Florida	Y	Premed, Journalism, Ministry	53/39	
done	Palm Beach Atlantic University			54/42	
done	Pensacola Christian College		Nursing, Premed, Ministry, Art		
1	Oklahoma Baptist University	y	Art, Drama, Journalism, RN, Ministr	2/59	Best College Buys Forbes
2	Oklahoma University	y	Nursing, Education	111/40	Best Value Princeton, Kiplingers
3	Oral Roberts University	y	Nursing, Acting, Ministry, Education		Best Western Schools
1	Arkansas State University		Nursing, Education	58/40	
1	University of Arkansas		Nursing, Education	132/35	Best Buys Kiplingers, Forbes
done	Lee University		Education, Ministry, Journalism, The	54/42	Best Southeastern
1	Bryan College		Education, Ministry, Journalism, The	16/66	Best Value
1	Rhodes College				Best Southeastern, Most Beautiful Campus
1	University of Tennessee		Education, Ministry, Journalism, The	104/41	Best Southeastern, Least Beautiful Jock
4	Liberty University		Education, Journalism, Nursing, Theatre		
4	Patrick Henry College		Journalism, Classical Liberal Arts		
4	Regent University		Education, Ministry, Theatre		
4	Pepperdine	y	Art, Journalism, Education, Acting		
4	Azusa Pacific University	y	Nursing, Premed, Journalism, Education		

2) Choosing a College: Site Visit

Packing the Suitcases

As I was socializing and small talking at a work dinner event, I purposefully steered the discussion toward family and began my "twenty-questions" game. I always lecture the kids on how to interrupt those awkward, introverted silent social moments or how to get to know someone. My turn now. I pitch some softballs to start: "Do you have family?" "How many children?" "What ages?" Within five to ten minutes, people usually open up because they have a passion for their families and love to talk about their kids.

At the work dinner, we joked that most of us had not done ANY college touring when we were high-schoolers. A few catalogues, a counselor, and maybe a sprinkle of parental involvement. I certainly don't recall having a color-coded spreadsheet, eighteen college visits in thirty-six months, reading multiple books, or conducting an analysis of the acceptance rate or job-placement rate. I certainly don't recall the emphasis on SAT and ACT scores, the concept of superscoring, flex-dollar-dining plans, or the incredible variety of Greek life and campus social clubs.

The conversation turned from light to meaty as we discussed the speed at which our lives and parenting days had seemingly flown by. Visiting colleges didn't cross my mind much a decade-plus earlier as I cradled my daughter. It never occurred to me that the backyard ball with the boys, the picnics and kite flying would soon be gone and discussions of proms, teenage temptation, and college-prep testing would fill our agendas. We had just burned our videotapes to DVD and we were shocked at the dozens of tapes where we are simply looking amazed and full of joy as we simply held our children, rocked them, or just gazed at them for hours with love that words could not express.

Time seemed to stand still for a few minutes as I reminisced and choked up a little as I explained that my spring break would be spent with my daughter touring colleges and that this was possibly our "last hoorah." Eyes were damp across the table as they all either reminisced or were coming to grips with this knuckleball that time was indeed short. The kids would be gone before they knew it.

Two thousand one hundred eighty miles. Four states. Seven colleges. Four days. One dad. One daughter. Priceless.

Taking this roadtrip with my daughter and writing this section brought out more emotions than I had forecasted. It was so rewarding. The times talking about nothing. Sampling the hot sauces and wearing fire hats at Firehouse Subs. We laughed as we recalled together the dumbest campus-tour questions. (The top two winners were: "Do you have underground tunnels on campus?" and "Does Rihanna or Ludacris visit the campus?") We enjoyed reminiscing about earlier college trips while picnicking on one campus.

Then there were the milestones, talks that I snuck in and sandwiched around the relationship building. Talking about life choices and priorities. Talking about the weight of the decision of choosing a college. My mistakes (a couple of them) and "do-over list" in college. I shared with my daughter the life impact of my college choice—both the positive and the negative. I told her that I was proud that she was taking time to pray and research this monumental choice. My own decision criteria list when I applied to a college was not too weighty: 1) Close to home. (2) Can I get in? (3) Do they require a speech class? My list of school candidates was one. I applied to only Michigan State University. (No sarcastic e-mails from University of Michigan alumni and the "can-I-get-in" criterion, please.) My choice of a major was due primarily to the influence of a friend's choice and the near 100 percent placement rate. My decisions were not full of deep-thinking analysis when I was considering my college choices. With unemployment rates hovering around 50% for new graduates, a major must be considered carefully.

Do not take this process lightly. We have visited campuses small, large, and somewhere in between. We have covered a primary and a secondary major. We have viewed public and private schools. We have traveled near and far. Cheap and outrageous. We started with a broad list targeted to two majors and then narrowed to a region of the country, then researched and narrowed the list to a group we would visit during vacations, weekends, and summers. We visited eighteen schools before her junior year was completed. That list was then whittled to six schools she would apply to. One or two stretches (financial and/or acceptance), one or two easy-to-get-into schools, and one or two likely possibilities.

Gems and Duds

We were together "spying out the land" (Numbers 13). We experienced some hidden gems along the way that did not have large advertising budgets or national appeal. We also made some quite amazing discoveries of the condition of American values simply by picking up the student newspapers on campus. Ask how the faculty is selected. Ask how the faculty's faith or religious denomination is considered in the hiring process. You would be surprised by some Christian schools that do not even consider it. How visible was Christ on the campus? Scriptures on building walls at Lee University. *For Learning, For God, Forever* motto at Samford University. One "Christian" school had a code of conduct that affirmed and celebrated an "alternative lifestyle" and welcomed a weekly lesbian newspaper columnist (front page). None of this was discovered on their website, but it was prevalent on the tour. Another school hosted a Dalai Lama visit courtesy of our tax dollars. Some public schools hosted pro-Islamic groups and speakers and celebrated political correctness. Emily knew immediately that some schools did not align with neither our family vision nor her educational and spiritual goals. None of this would have been discovered in a catalogue or on a website. If you can visit a campus while school is in session, especially after you narrow the list down, that is critical.

Choosing a college is about the entire experience. It is educational, but it is also social, physical, emotional, and spiritual. The foundation for their future life will be built. Consider the bent of your child, closeness to home, clubs, safety, an outlet for their hobbies or passions, chapels, nearby church, spiritual emphasis on campus, and weekend activities.

A site visit will determine how the school "fits." Visiting college campuses will usually make or break the deal for the kids. We visited eighteen schools with my daughter. Some were drive-bys and that is all she needed. Some were formal, full length visits. Websites can only do so much. Only three made the final cut. I cannot overemphasize that there is nothing more important than that campus visit and tour. We looked for specific things while on campus: the spiritual feel, the campus aesthetics, her major's strength, academics, some of her extracurricular care-abouts, safety, city life, Greek life, and other activities. She then gave an overall grade based on her visit. Be sure that you bring a list and create your own spreadsheet. You might not get everything answered, and some of it might come from www.collegeboard.com or other tools. But we completed our spreadsheet after every site visit. The different shades are color codes. I had my daughter rank or score after each visit. (A blank version is included in the appendices.)

	SAMF	BAYLOR	ACU	A&M	DBU	HARDI	UARK	TTECH	RHODES	LEE
Christian / Spiritual										
Location / Distance	10	2	3	3 hrs	1	5	5	6	7	11
Campus Feel/Visit										
Nursing										
Academics % > 3.5	68%	-	65%	-	57%	60%	58%	-	72%	54%
Academics Rank (10/25)	35/64	36/71	25/55	50/87	19/37	25/53	27/56	21/52	53/81	23/49
SAT Reading (mid 50)	520-640	540-650	500-610	530-650	460-640	490-630	500-610	490-580	590-700	460-600
SAT Math (mid 50)	515-620	570-670	510-620	570-680	470-630	490-630	520-640	510-610	590-690	440-590
ACT Consol (mid 50)	23-29	24-29	22-28	25-30	19-27	22-28	23-28	22-27	28-30	20-27
Photo class / Art Minor	N / N	Y / Y	N / N	N / N	N / Y	Y / Y	Y / Y		N / Y	
FCA/Christian Greek	Y / 42%	Y / 14%	Y / 23%	Y / 12%	Y / 15%	Y / 46%	Y / 24%	Y / -	Y / -	Y / 10%
Safety										
Neighborhood/City										
Sports										
Activities										
Admission Prob										
Apply	Yes	Yes	May	Yes	Yes	Yes	Yes	May	May	No
Overall Grade	8		7	9	9	6	6	8	7	6.5
Cost	$29K	$42K	$32K	$18K	$26K	$21K	$16/$25	$17K	$44K	$19K
Undergrads	3000	12000	4000	39000	4000	4000	17000	25000	2000	4000
Accept Rate / App date	87%/3-1	48%/11-1	53%/2-15	69%/12-1	43%/1-15	73%/-	60%/11-15	72%/-	45%/12-15	84%/9-1
Positives	Chr, Nurse Campus Bell Twr Shopping WholeFds		Chr, Schol Nursing Iphone Art Gall ChicFila	Campus	Campus Christian Dorm	Christian Nursing Distance	Nursing Campus	Pretty Campus	Size Campus Acad	Christian Campus
Negatives	Alabama		Campus small	TX	Nursing	Campus	Size Dalai Lama	Drive Large	Nursing Liberal	Nursing Location
Awards/Comments / Visitation Overnite Date		Conserv Best Buy	Western	Conserv Value/Buy			Best Buy	Western Bbuy	Beauty Seastern	Seastern
Date Visited	3/11		12/10	6/09	12/10	3/11	3/11	12/10	3/11	3/11

HIGHEST / BEST
VERY GOOD
GOOD
MEDIUM
POOR / WORST

Site visit rankings

Immediately after each visit, she graded each college from 1 to 10 and jotted down the positive and negatives of the visit. We did our visits over four years, so this helped document what she liked and disliked. They all can run together if you do more than a couple of visits. This is a very helpful tool.

3) Choosing a College: Student Feedback

Another very important piece of data is what current or former students think of their college experiences. There are a number of great on-line tools to get direct feedback. We used studentsreview.com, collegeprowler.com, and unigo.com, although there are many others. Students are blunt and honest. Some are current students, and some are former students. The opinions vary widely, but it is a good perspective to have. Although scorecards are provided, the most valuable thing is to take a few hours and read through the comments. When we narrowed the list of colleges down to a manageable number, we created a spreadsheet to compare the feedback in key areas. They use many more areas than the ones I used, but we selected those we cared most about. (See the example in the figure.)

As a disclaimer, again, this is an example that was compiled from multiple websites. It is not accurate and is out of date. (See a blank version in the appendices.)

	Student Reviews[1]	Grade Overall[2]	Education	Campus Aesthetics	Friendly	Social	Extra-Curricular	City	Campus Resources	Perceived Safety	Would I Return %	APP DATE	Preview Days Family Weekend
Texas A&M	231	B+	A-	B+	A-	B+	A-	B-	B	A	76%	Aug 1- Jan 15	SEAL- Nov
Texas Tech	132	B+	A-	A-	A-	A-	A-	B-	A-	A-	71%	Nov 1- May 1	17-Oct
Univ Arkansas	26	B+	B-	B+	B+	B	B	B	B	B+	62%	Sept- Nov 15	Sept 16-18
Baylor	115	B-	B+	A-	B+	C+	B	C-	B	B+	67%	June 1- Nov 1	1-Oct
Harding	75	B-	B+	A-	A-	B-	B	C+	B	A	53%		10/7-10/8
Samford	16	B-	A-	A	A-	C-	C	B+	B-	A-	63%	Aug 1- Nov 1	9/17-10/15
Dallas Baptist	43	B-	B	A-	B+	B	B	B+	B	A	51%		10-Oct
Abilene Christian	33	C+	B	C+	B+	C+	C+	D+	C+	B	50%	Aug 1 - Nov 1	9/17-9/19

Student Feedback Website Summary

This tool and the student comments cut out all of the idealistic thoughts a student might have about campuses and gets down to the nitty-gritty.

Preparation

"Less than half (47%) of students are preparing themselves for college while still in high school by taking Advanced Placement and college preparatory classes."[256] Colleges are not just looking for the GPA or class rank. SAT and ACT test scores have become more and more important to admissions and scholarships. Taking AP classes and SAT/ACT tests will prepare them for college and also net you some better scholarships.

Although some schools are now so very driven by the raw numbers on GPA and test scores, other colleges are looking for the total-package kids—the academic risks they took, the community service, the volunteer work, athletics, awards, how they spent their summers, their extracurricular activities, their class rank, etc.

Start your college planning in the child's freshman year! Start your resume and list of extracurricular activities, awards, jobs, etc., the summer after middle school. The list will grow quite long; don't expect to remember everything. Write down anything and everything. Be socially active throughout high school and summer and spring breaks. These are great times to do volunteer work. We took a missions trip, volunteered for community and church events, entered photo and art competitions, played musical instruments, played sports, joined clubs, and became a member of the National Honor Society.

Following is a checklist that I amended from *Destination College Parent's Resource Guide* to assist you in your preparation.

Freshman year
- Have the student meet with the high-school counselor and plan his or her coursework.
- Start a list of activities, awards, community service, and extracurriculars for the resume.
- Start to discuss and research potential majors. This will plant the seeds for college "thought."
- Create the "potential college list." (See the appendices.)

Sophomore year
- Begin a list of potential college locations—states, types of schools, etc., and request information. (Update. See the appendices.)
- Begin site visits while on vacation or on weekends. (See appendices.)
- Start prep-test planning for SAT and ACT. These tests are big tuition swingers.
- Consider college credit, dual credit, and Advanced Placement testing for the future years.
- Update the list of activities into a formal resume.

Junior year
- Review courses with counselors. Plan for the senior year.
- Take PSAT and SAT/ACT late in the year.
- Research financial aid/scholarship opportunities.
- Visit top colleges while traveling or on vacation.
- Update Appendix spreadsheets.
- Request additional information from colleges; make contacts in the degrees of interest.
- Attend college fairs. Meet with college representatives. Ask a lot of questions.
- Update the resume with activities, extracurricular, etc.

Senior year
- Take ACT/SAT tests. Many colleges "superscore" and take the best of each section.
- Make your final college visits, narrow the list, and plan for parents'/student visit weekends.
- Update the Appendix spreadsheets.
- Meet with the high-school counselor.
- Complete all applications/admissions for first semester.
- Complete FAFSA, financial aid application (usually not available until January).
- Have the high-school transcripts sent to prospective colleges.
- Have letters of recommendations sent to prospective colleges.
- Open checking/debit accounts for the student, and initiate a budget plan.
- Establish a budget, agree to financial sharing arrangements with the student.
- Understand the timelines/deadlines for scholarships, admissions, and introduction sessions.

College Admissions: The College Essay and Resume

You should start applying in the fall or during the first semester of the senior year. All applications should be completed by the end of November. Some colleges will give you longer, but others give early admissions and residence housing priority for early applications. Check to see if housing deposits are refundable. You might want to put a deposit down at more than one school.

The college essay is not required for every application. The college essay[257] is a variable that is critical in college entrance for those schools that require one. Do not peanut butter your approach to these. The following tips are helpful:

1) Read and understand the questions, and be sure that your response addresses the question specifically.
2) Take your time to read, reread, write, rewrite, edit, and have others read and review the essay. Do not rush.
3) Be creative. Take some time to brainstorm all possible ideas before starting to write.
4) Create an outline. Remember your training in writing classes! Have a good beginning, middle, and end. The introduction, body, and conclusion should all be considered equally.
5) Be yourself. Don't have your parents write for you. Be personal. Be original. Be concise.
6) Edit. Proofread. Have others read it. Edit. Proofread again. Read it aloud to see how it sounds.

Your resume might also be required along with the admissions essay. As was discussed earlier, start your resume when you are a freshman, and add achievements and activities each year so that the resume is solid in the junior year. Include all interests, honors, activities, hobbies, and extracurricular activities. You will never be able to remember everything. We used our daughter's National Honor Society application to begin that process.

Legacy Lesson: Invest a good amount of time as a parent in the "choosing" process. It is more important than a car purchase decision or your 401k. This is a Legacy impacting choice! Pray hard and plan hard!

CHAPTER 40

SAVING AND PAYING FOR COLLEGE

*E*ducation is a powerful thing. There is much more to it than a good future income. However, that is a factual benefit. A good, quality education can affect a person's life and the lives of future generations significantly. "Studies have shown that for every year of schooling someone has, there is a 10 percent increase in that person's wages."[258]

A College Board report[259] showed that the median income of bachelor's degree recipients was $55,700. The median for high-school graduates with no college degree was $33,800. A study by The Georgetown University Center on Education and the Workforce[260] researched the average lifetime earnings by education level. The gaps are astounding. The lifetime income for a college graduate versus a high-school graduate is >$1.5 million more! College is, in fact, a good investment most of the time.

Students and parents might need that earning power because The College Board reports[261] "that in the last decade, published tuition and fees at public four-year colleges and universities increased at an average rate of 5.6% per year *beyond the rate of general inflation*. These diverging trends—reduced family wealth and increased tuition—are putting pressure on the majority of families; only one-third of families are able to pay the full "sticker price" of college."[262] For the first time, "student loan debt outpaced outstanding credit card debt and is likely to top a trillion dollars."[263] This might be one debt worth having.

Your financial situation might obviously play a major factor in your college decision. If your kids are young, start saving *now*. If your kids are in elementary school, start saving *now*. If they are in middle school or high school, start *now*. If you are a grandparent or family member that can help financially, by all means, start *now*. Even a little saved per month will keep you focused on the gigantic financial task at hand. Have your kids save 10 percent of their money for college. To teach the kids the value of saving, we did a five-for-one match for their college savings account, beginning at the age of 5. For every dollar they saved, we put in five. It was more of an instructional vehicle and only a drop in the college tuition bucket, but it still taught them a saving principle at a young age.

Getting Financial Help

Financial need is determined by a number of factors. Even if you are not in a low-income bracket, it might be worth your while to look at all options. Every family should complete the Free Application for Federal Student Aid (FAFSA) in January/February of the senior year. Opportunities for assistance can come in the form of grants, work-study, or loans. Factors such as the number of children in your family and the number of children you have enrolled in higher education influence your success.

Although economic and state budget challenges are affecting the amount of financial aid, do not throw up your hands. There is still plenty of aid available.

- Scholarships (independent)—These are based on academic achievements, test scores, grades, class rank, and extracurricular achievements, such as athletics, music, or the arts. They tend to be merit based and are usually available regardless of your financial need. A good resource for this information is www.fastweb.com. Apply for as many scholarships as you can, even if they seem small. Start early.
- Scholarships (school)—This will be the highest probability of achievement and will not be financial-need-based. Each school and each major has different scholarship opportunities. Most of these are published on the school's website. Again, I counsel you to start focusing early on academic success because the largest scholarships are academically driven—GPA, class rank, and SAT/ACT scores
- Grants—These are funds that don't have to be repaid. In most cases, you will have to demonstrate a financial need to be eligible for a grant. Your eligibility will be determined by the FAFSA application results. The sources of funding can be state or federal governments or the college to which you are applying.
- Loans—These funds must be repaid. Many families borrow funds through the Federal Stafford Loan program. These funds are based on financial need. Federal student loans are very competitive and usually offer the lowest interest rates around, and often payments can be deferred until after graduation. Be careful!

The options will become more limited for government assistance because of our nation's debt challenges. Students are relying more on private loans to pay for their degrees. Saving early and regularly is the best option for financing quickly rising tuition rates. Most families are unable to pay cash for the entire degree so the options are to (1) accumulate debt or (2) find as many resources as possible to help make college affordable. Another way to help put a dent in the tuition is to seek both school and private scholarships. The best thing you can do to achieve better scholarships is to score well on SAT or ACT tests. Have your child take both to see if he or she does better at one than another.

Much free money is also available that might require some scouring to locate. Ensure that you check the details on financial aid and scholarship site of the prospect school. You might be able to get some scholarships through church, through a family educator, your employer, or directly based on academics as well as extracurricular activities. A number of websites, including fastweb.com and scholarships.com, can get you steered in the right direction. Maybe offer an incentive plan to your child to spend the summer of the junior and senior years pursuing these, and offer them a "commission" for any monies gained. One source talked of having a child spend a summer working on scholarships instead of a taxable, small-paying job. Getting one or two scholarships could easily equal what was earned working a summer job. Know that "free money" is hard work, so don't underestimate the essay writing and fine-print reading necessary to succeed.

Financial Planning

I have written a book called *Ease the Squeeze* on budgeting, saving, debt, and financial freedom with an emphasis on teaching children as well. So I will only touch on a few highlights here. I will also cover some of these concepts in Section 3 of this book. Before your student moves out of the house and moves on to college, be sure to help train him or her financially. Share your personal strategies for saving, spending, debt, giving, and investing. Having time for discussion is key. You might even need a contract that discusses who is paying for college and the ground rules. Here are the key areas:

Expenses: Determine who is paying for tuition, books, housing, gas, insurance, food, and entertainment. Will your child work during college? We set up debit accounts while the kids were in high school to begin teaching them. Our daughter paid for recreation and clothes from her babysitting. We paid the auto gas and insurance. Be sure to determine if it makes sense to have your child work during high school. There will be tradeoffs with educational success and life priorities (church, friends, and family).

Health Insurance: Most full-time students are covered by their parents' policies. Some universities charge your child for health insurance, so be sure to check with both your health provider and the college your child will be attending.

Auto Insurance: Confirm that your child actually needs an automobile while away from home. Check with your insurance provider to understand any premium differences while your child is away at school. The location of the college also could affect your premiums. We also have an agreement that if our child gets a speeding ticket, they will pay for both it and the premium increase difference.

Personal Property Insurance: Most students do not have enough possessions to worry about this, but you might want to research your homeowner's policy to see what is covered and what is not. You might have to pursue renters insurance if your child lives off campus. Also, check your laptop and cellphone coverages. Laptops can be a target for thieves.

Housing, Books, and Meal Plans: These are usually forecast in the college's tuition and expenses. Be sure to plan for these expenses because they are quite hefty. Books can be a shocking expense, so ensure that you shop around for books if possible. Meal plans can be a savings but can also cost you more than you need to spend if your child does not eat regularly or follow a disciplined eating schedule.

Entertainment/Recreation: "The average college student spends close to $300 a month on everything from pizza to shampoo, which is one reason why 21 percent of undergraduates owe more than $3000 on their credit cards."[264] A part-time job might be necessary just to cover these expenses. Gas, food, recreation—it can all add up in a hurry.

Saving: We offered incentives to our children while they grew up to save for college. If your child is working during high school, determine how much is being saved for college. It might be very difficult to save during the college years.

Credit or Debit: We highly suggest a debit card to teach the children the ins and outs of finances. Encouraging debt at a high school or college age is not wise. You might be teaching unhealthful spending habits. If you are trying to build up a credit rating, be sure to teach them to pay the balance off in full every month.

Other ways to help defray some of the costs of college are the following:

- Start savings as early as you can.
- Do well on the SAT and ACT testing! Test multiple times. Significant tuition discounts are available.
- Apply for as many scholarships as possible.
- Apply early.
- Take dual-credit classes in high school to reduce your college tuition bill.
- Consider a junior college to start with basic coursework.
- Consider a 529 savings plan. These plans are state sponsored and offer a number of options, some that include some tax benefits. These plans let your savings grow tax-free, and earnings are not taxed if withdrawals are used for qualified college expenses. Currently, there is a very high limit on contributions and no income limit.
- Consider a prepaid plan. If you are fairly certain that your child will attend an in-state college, consider a prepaid tuition plan. Such a plan will allow you to lock in tuition prices at public colleges within your state. These plans also have tax benefits, but they might not be offered in every state. Understand the terms if you change your mind and attend a private school. The market will drive how much you get refunded.
- Consider a Coverdell education savings account. The money grows tax-deferred and is exempt from tax if used for qualified educational expenses.
- Consider custodial accounts, such as Uniform Gifts to Minors and Uniform Transfers to Minors. You manage the account until the child reaches a certain age. They can also be used to save taxes and give freedom in investment choices.
- Financial Aid. The formulas used for calculating financial aid change often and vary widely, so ensure that you understand them. Federal financial aid formulas differ from private schools'. How assets are counted vary. How savings and income affect financial aid eligibility vary, as do child-owned and grandparent assets. Retirement accounts and distributions are counted differently. The moral of the story is that if you hope to qualify for financial aid, do not wait until your student's senior year. Understand the formulas and approaches used by the institutions to which you are applying.[265]

When we had narrowed our list of colleges to three for our daughter, we sat down with her and showed her what we and she had saved and how much was still required. We created a spreadsheet that showed tuition, room and board, books, etc. We then subtracted scholarships and the amount saved and then discussed how that gap could be closed. How could we afford the college of her choice? What sacrifices would she have to make? How much would she have to work? How could better test scores help?

Her top choice was a school that we could not afford, so we had to do everything possible to close the gap. We determined that if she was serious enough that she would also get some "skin in the game." We would pay 70 percent and she would pay 30 percent—whether that be through scholarships or a student loan in her name. We also brainstormed a list of money-generating ideas as a family. It would require major sacrifice from each family member. Each family member ranked the idea. (See the appendices.)

"A study by the National Endowment for Financial Education found that more than 25 percent of parents surveyed took on additional debt to help their children."[266] It is good to set some boundaries before the final college decisions are made. It is hard, but these make for great teaching moments regarding financial decisions.

As we conclude the section on parenting and children, do not limit the impact your children and grandchildren will have on this world. Think generationally. Consider your life as something to be laid down for your children to walk upon with destinations of greatness that you might not be able to see. The decisions covered in these past few chapters are not easy. Wrestle with them. Consider the cost. You will quite likely have to make many financial sacrifices for the next several years.

We must have long-term vision. Consider and meditate upon Psalm 78:4–7. You are now that forefather telling the next generation. You are the teacher, the farmer, and the bill payer. You are having a generational impact!

Legacy Lesson: Start saving young or start saving now! Debt and poor money management can have a very long-lasting and negative generational impact.

CHAPTER 41

A MEMORY MUSEUM:
YOUR FAMILY LEGACY

*T*he dingy streets, broken-down cars, and dilapidated houses aren't exactly a magnet for a romantic lovers' stroll. This is blue-collar country, industrial life at its best. The Corner. Michigan Avenue and Trumbull Avenue. As they stroll through this Detroit neighborhood, the wide-eyed boy clasps the hand of his grandfather with eyes fixed not on these sights, but rather the glimpse of a white towering, aging steel-and-cement complex in the distance. He is awestruck by the rafters and girders that hold up a massive porch and deck. This place is the home of history and heroes. The aroma of hot dogs grilling fills the air and greets me as I hand over my ticket. The smell and the sight of freshly manicured and mown green grass awakens my senses. The cracking sound of a bat hitting a ball and the loud smack of a ball hitting a glove hold me captive. One vendor hawks programs, another peddles peanuts. Tiger Stadium. Was this thirty years ago or yesterday? Time flies.

Ernie Harwell's soothing voice proclaims from the ghetto box nearby, "He stood there like the house by the side of the road and watched that one go by" as the baseball approaches me at sixty miles per hour. It's actually a tennis ball. Another neighborhood game of baseball. I mimic one of my left-handed childhood Detroit Tigers heroes, and turn on the pitch, and blast it toward the home run porch in right field. It's actually not a porch at all, but rather a fifteen-foot silver monster chain link fence. Nevertheless, I round the bases as the imaginary crowd cheers and my opponent, my best friend shakes his head and vows to get me the next time. Was this thirty years ago or yesterday? Time flies.

These multisensory explosions are still fresh in my mind three decades later. The history. The tradition. The simplicity. The memories. A road trip to the 1984 World Series with friends. A return back to my childhood memories with my son for the last game at Tiger Stadium on September 27, 1999.

A Construction Site

Fast forward nearly thirty years. The sights, the sounds, and the smells haven't really changed that much, but Grandpa is gone, and my family and friends are scattered. A different city now. A different ballpark. A different team, though the memory and love of my childhood team is still permanently imprinted on my sports DNA. The sea of red, white, and blue are a sight to behold. The deafening shouts of "Let's Go Rangers!" and "Na-po-li! Na-po-li!" fill the stadium. The electricity of the crowd has the few hairs that I have left standing on end. New memories are being constructed without any knowledge or deep analysis that we are standing upon a construction site, a memory monument:

"Build them and they will come."

The baseball baton is being passed as I chat with my kids about ducks on the pond, runs batted in, and pitch counts, and reminisce about my own childhood memories. I secretly watch my children as they savor the same sights and sounds that gave me pleasure as a young boy. A visit to the memory museum. As their towels waved, the scenes were being etched on their minds and hearts. Although they give little thought to their future or my past, I was reminiscing about the past and reminiscing about the future at the same time. I hid a sports tear as only a man can do and recognized the prominence of my massive Adams apple as it tried to make way for a deep swallow as I soaked the moment in. That night the diamond-shaped field that is wedged between Ballpark Way and Nolan Ryan Expressway was just a ballfield to some. For me it was a milestone. The sounds echoed through my generations. "Take me out to the ballgame. . . . I don't care if I ever get back." The drama and emotion ran high, but the shouts were drowned out by the joy in my heart that memories were being created with my family.

An Imprint

I love the game of baseball. It relaxes me. It is my escape from everyday life. A game of backyard baseball or "pickle," coaching my sons Tigers T-ball, machine pitch, and Little League games, having a "catch" with the kids, watching batting practice, getting a Josh Hamilton autograph, taking in a minor league game with my kids. The memories of celebrating an American League Championship Series clincher in 2010 and World Series wins in 2011 were great times to be shared. But beyond the team's success on the field, was the satisfaction of knowing that baseball was one generational, timeless expression of family, friends, rest, relaxation and recreation that was being passed on.

I have always struggled to articulate why I love baseball so. I think the memories fuel that. It is one of the lines drawn between the dots of four generations. The quiet times when the game slows down, where I sat back with my kids, relaxed and had a non-baseball talk about life, about friends, about challenges. Those fond memories of visiting Tiger Stadium as a young boy with my grandfather, family, and friends. Playing high school ball with my very best friends. Listening to Ernie Harwell on the radio while playing tennis baseball with friends and neighbors. Enjoying great baseball movies with my family like *The Rookie, Field of Dreams,* and *Moneyball.*

Some moments in time are imprinted in your heart, your mind, and your eyes. You don't even realize the engraving process is going on at the time. However, these multi-sensory moments turn in to multigenerational memories and traditions. The sights, the sounds, the smells. For you it might be hunting trips, Sunday pot roast dinners, Christmas gatherings, family worship, or that quiet moment with a family member. Be sure not to minimize these moments. These moments are autographed in time.

Be sure to autograph some memories for your children. Fill your memory museum!

The Tribute

Preserving your memories will not just keep the wonderful times alive but also pass on a legacy of God's faithfulness to future generations. They also can be a protection and a reminder of what is at stake if there is a temptation to "blow it."

I celebrated Memorial Day a little different this past year. It is so fitting for the country to commemorate a day to keeping remembrance alive for the war dead. I had recently read a couple of books—*Letters to Dad* and *The Blessing*—and was challenged that I really had not shown my gratitude, appreciation, and vocal love to my parents over the years in a lasting way. I also had not really preserved memories of them as I should have. I had done better verbally with my mother, but I tended not to be as visible or vocal with my dad. I also had never written them a letter, other than little "sound bites" in Mother's Day and Father's Day. I determined to start with a "My Tribute" letter to Dad since Father's Day was just around the corner.

I did a little extra Bible study and reading and then started to brainstorm the things I was thankful for—the content for a purposeful letter that would help carry and communicate my dad's impact on me and future generations to come. It took only a couple hours and a few drafts to write the letter. I then bought a frame and some nice paper and signed it. The "My Dad, My Tribute" project was complete! Or so I thought.

Graduate-Level Tribute: Master's Degree

After I wrote the Tribute to Dad letter, I began to think of my dad's influence in my life. I thought how little my children knew of my grandparents. They had seen one set of grandparents only a few times when they were very young. In fact, a couple of years ago I realized that my children really only knew my father on a surface level, since they see each other maybe twice a year.

My kids really did not know where their grandfather or grandmother grew up, their favorite childhood memories, or their spiritual story/testimony. Or if I had told them, they didn't remember that much with all the busyness of their own lives. So I determined to set that straight and drafted seven "interview questions" that would be pertinent to carrying on my parents' legacy and communicate who they were to future generations. So a "My Dad, My Tribute" package was now in the making. I had a bunch of old pictures of me and my siblings with Dad, I would soon have a one-hour legacy interview on DVD, and I had a tribute letter I had just recently written him. I then brainstormed with my kids about how to make this Father's Day extra special for my dad. I decided to create an edited video tribute to him. He was seventy, and I wanted to ensure that I gave him his due while we both still had life and breath.

The Tribute: Doctoral Degree

As I began to plan the video content and sections for this tribute video, I knew that it would create some lasting memories of my dad, but it also could preserve some memories of me and our family for my children. I decided to include some fond "visuals" from their childhood growing up, so that this one video could preserve multiple generations of remembrance. This project was now taking on a life of its own!

I decided that I would make a list of some of my favorite "family locations and mile-stones" over the years. Where did my kids have their John 3:3 salvation experience? Where had we lived? Where had I worked? Where did I meet my wife? Where had we spent some good times together (ballpark, parks, etc.)? So I now had a list of memorable places from our local family history.

Now the question was what in the world would I do at each of these sites for the DVD? Break dance? Sing an angelic tune? Actually, I did break dance at one of the locations and preserved that for the "bloopers segment" at the end of the tribute. I did some other obnoxious things at each site as well and included some of the sayings my kids have come to chuckle at. However, I digress.

I decided instead of just break dancing with a Texas Rangers, Michigan State or Texas Instruments shirt and hat on that I needed to preserve some of my favorite generational scriptures, and instead of just mailing my "Tribute Letter" to Dad, that I would read it on video. I ended up reading a paragraph from the tribute letter at each of these milestone sites and brought along a wardrobe change with my favorite sports team or clothing souvenirs from our family vacations.

So here it was Memorial Day, and I was remembering my childhood history, my father, and future generations. I piled in the car with my youngest son (who promised to keep this a secret), fifteen baseball hats, twelve shirts, some hair goop and a hair brush, a tripod, and our video camera. My son and I had a memorable and laughable three hours of taping. He helped me with the blooper ideas and it was a great Memorial Day for both of us.

The challenge now was the editing! Some people might opt to pay someone to do that, but this project had turned into a hobby for me and had been a great way to preserve our memories. I came up with a pretty decent forty-five-minute tribute video to my dad that included segments of his Legacy interview, my reading of his "Tribute Letter" (see the appendices) from different locations with different wardrobe changes, some pictures of his grandparents and my dad and I, as well as some video footage from our childhood with Dad. As an extra touch, I asked his wife to tell me his favorite songs, so those provided the backdrop for the video.

I closed with a commentary on some memorable times we had spent together as a father and a son. This was a very rewarding time for me and helped me appreciate my father even more because I took the time to pass on a legacy. Dad was in tears and could not express enough his appreciation for this Tribute.

Warning

Whether you decide to write a tribute letter or get your PhD and create a video, this might be a painful experience at times. It might feel as though you were writing a eulogy while your parent is still living. It might be difficult because your parent is already gone. It might be that you don't have much positive to write about your parent. I still challenge you to do this because it preserves some history—both good and bad. It also might be cleansing and force some healing that needs to take place. It might also help you deal with any regret you might have had. My parents are divorced, so I had to take that into consideration when writing the letter and making the video and editing content. Did I want to address failures in my letter? You might have anger or bitterness toward one parent and have a real struggle with this. I challenge you to deal with it and not avoid it. Do not wait until they are gone.

If they are gone, it can be cleansing in some respects to proceed with a tribute anyway. Future generations need to know.

Family Treasure Chest

"What would your children hold in their hands tomorrow that would let them know they were the treasures of your life? What is on the mantel of your life?"[267] When our children graduated from high school, we wanted to send them off with a treasure chest of memories and spiritual signposts. I have been working on a Family Museum of Memories photo album for my daughter that captures her life and fun family memories in picture. This will be part of a Treasure Chest[268] for her graduation that will include

- a framed blessing
- a museum of memories photo album
- A tribute/memory DVD
- laminated Guideposts for Life (see the appendices)
- a quilted blanket with all their high school t-shirts
- a framed family picture

Your Scrapbook of Life

Ensure that you are spending more time creating memories than preserving them. Enjoy the moments and plan those times together. Quantity will give you more quality. If you participate in the Family Activities, you will be more apt to have good memories. Begin some new traditions, put family events on your calendar, and budget for vacations and times together.

Memories
ought to be planned,
ought to be chosen,
ought to be budgeted for,
ought to be given proper time,
ought to be protected,
ought to be passed down to the next generation.[269]

Memory-Making Ideas

Here are some ideas to start the memory making.

- Start some meaningful traditions.
- Take pictures.
- Journal your times.
- Have the family dinner feast.
- Go camping.
- Plan for a daily "tuck-in" time.
- Pray a blessing over your family daily.

- Play games.
- Participate in volunteer projects.
- Celebrate with Christmas lights and Advent candles.
- Participate in baptism if your kids have been saved.
- Have holiday dinners.
- Go on vacations.
- Have daily story time.
- Attend sports teams events.
- Attend kids' events.
- Attend concerts/plays/musicals.
- Attend church and church events.
- Attend worship services.
- Have daily prayer.
- Have regular devotional times.
- Conduct library trips.
- Read together.
- Family bike rides/jogs/hikes.
- Play catch.

Our Memory Museum

We have not "built out" our virtual family museum, but the pieces are in place to ensure that we preserve our family memories for our children and for generations to come. For me to recall *anything* is a minor miracle. That is one of the reasons we take pictures, burn DVDs, and write things down—from to-do lists, to annual goals, to Christmas newsletters, to books. The ink and paper help me remember. The words and ink also help hold me accountable. As a bonus, writing things down journaling, preserve memories for generations to come. Here are some of the things we are including in our family museum that might give you some additional ideas.

- Compile vacation and holiday photo albums.
- Create a year-end photo CD.
- Make vacation, birthday, and Christmas scrapbooks.
- Write a year-end DVD summary.
- Write year-end newsletters.
- Make a year-end blessing list.
- Set yearly goals.
- Memorize yearly memory verses.
- Make tribute DVDs and letters.
- Make prayer passage letters and documents.
- Keep a journal.
- Keep a file with activity memories—school, vacations, events, etc.

Legacy Lesson: Memories start with T-I-M-E. Give yourself away. Many of the memories you are creating will be passed on like a baton from one generation to the next (good and bad).

CHAPTER 42

YOUR FAMILY PLAN: SECURING YOUR FAMILIES FUTURE

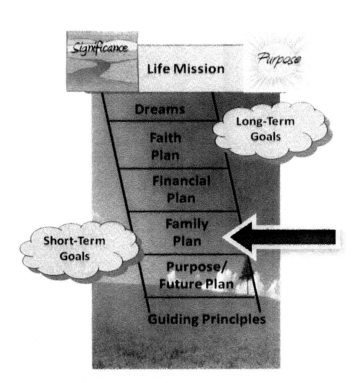

*I*f you are feeling a little overwhelmed at this point, take a deep breath and remember that this is an idea buffet. You cannot and will not do everything. Be still and know that God is for you! Supermoms, I encourage you—hang in there! You are making the greatest investment of time and money that any human being can make! You are investing in the lives of your children. It might be the messy clean-up season, or the car-pooling season, or maybe the kids are gone and you are in the praying season. Grandparents, you play a big role in your kids and grandkids' lives. What are your priorities? Take a minute and soak in the following passage:

"Let us not become weary in doing good, for at the proper time
we will reap a harvest if we do not give up. Therefore, as we have opportunity, let us do
good to all people, especially to those who belong to the family of believers."
—Galatians 6:9–10

Dads, be strong and courageous. Be encouraged! God sees your heart. Take those baby steps. Do not wait until Mother's Day to honor your wife. Honor her with a surprise bouquet of flowers, help her with the chores or dishes, stand by her with the discipline and correction, offer to taxi, or just stop and thank her. Thank her in front of the kids. Find out what is important to her. Often, we partition our lives and don't partner with our wives. Take time to listen, to understand, to honor, and to help. Dads, do not wait until next month to give your kids your *time*! Start now!

If you are in a challenging season, know that your reward for doing all these things for your kids will not be seen quite possibly in the next week, the next month, or even the next decade. The harvest time might even be after you are long gone. Try to make your reward in doing all these things for your children. The serving, the sacrificing, the laying down of your life—know that your self-denial is a long-term blessing for your children. It certainly might feel more like a crucifixion than a blessing or a reward on some days! Try to make your service your reward. It is a privilege to have the gift of your children while they are at home. Do not take that time for granted. The silence will soon be more deafening than those days of challenge!

Family Plan

We will cover five areas that will make up your family plan:

1) family vision
2) scriptures to memorize
3) code of conduct/miscellaneous contracts and incentives
4) battle plan
5) Scorecard (You can use the same template as in the appendices.)

1) Family Vision

Recently, I ran across a word I had never seen before, probably because I don't make a habit of reading much Greek. *Oikonomia*. I thought it might be someone who was afraid to eat pork, or possibly the study of pig noises. But it means "stewardship, administration, household management, or the law of the house." It sounded good, but we had always called it a "Family Code of Conduct" and a "Family Vision." Our Family Vision for 2012 is simple to write harder to execute:

To love God, to love each other, to serve others.

Writing it down is easy. Doing it is a tad harder.
How can I practically do that?

"As For Me and My House"- John Waller

Be repetitive with your vision so it soaks in. Make it visible. You can see our Vision everywhere: *To love God, to love each other, to serve others* is taped to each computer, on our kitchen chalkboard, in each of the kids' rooms on their post-it boards, in my Bible, and in my Daytimer so I can see it each day.[270] We recite it every week during our family Bible reading. We remind each other of them when we fail at these things, and we recognize one another when we are successful. We hold each other accountable to it. Guess what? They remind me sometimes as well.

The repetition, the reminders, and the visibility help to keep this vision front and center. We also have a plan and memory verses that align with each of these three goals.

2) Scriptures to Memorize

You can view our Vision and an excerpt from our Scripture list in the appendices. We work on one memory verse a week and recite that during dinner and in our devotional time. We set a very high goal of fifty-two verses a year; but, to be honest, we memorized only fifteen last year. I would rather have them get fifteen key verses in their heart than to forget fifty-two.

Come up with your own family vision and goals, and plan activities that help you meet these goals. Assess your progress. Strive for family excellence, not just being "good enough."

3) Code of Conduct

As parents, we set the tone for family priorities and behaviors. Children eventually model the behavior they witness. It is important that you have a set of family rules or a code of conduct when your children are younger. Some of these rules should also be focused on us as parents. I have heard of some parents who believe having their children try alcohol in a "safe setting" under the watchful eye of parents will instill a "responsible drinking" atmosphere and prevent them from exhibiting out-of-control behavior as they get older. *The Journal of Studies on Alcohol and Drugs* conducted a study recently in which they compared Australian teens and American teens. [271] "In 7th grade 59% of Australian students used alcohol vs. 39% of American students. In 8th grade two-thirds of Australian students were drinking vs. one-third in the U.S. and more than a third of the Australian students reporting having a drinking-related problem by the 9th grade. In both countries, the younger the students were when they started drinking, the more likely they were to have problems with alcohol, but those who drank under the watchful eye of their parents had higher rates." This probably doesn't need to be addressed in your elementary school child's code of conduct, but it is an example of a boundary that might need to be set when they are older.

Code of Conduct/Core Values

Spiritual leadership is not optional. It cannot be delegated, and it is not a part time job. Let me be honest, I am a much better spiritual leader and visionary on paper than I am within the confines of home sweet home. I try hard and have had many successes, but I also have had many failures and am still struggling. Being a great spiritual leader to your kids is admitting that you don't have it all together and that you are still learning. Humility. Vulnerability. Kids need to see it in small doses from you.

Each family is unique and will have unique goals for their family. I share with you a set of goals from Michael Farris[272] that challenged me early in my fatherhood years.

1) My children will be sure of his or her salvation.
2) My children will love and understand God's Word.
3) My child will know and willingly obey God's rules of right and wrong.
4) My child will be maturely walking with God.
5) My child will know his or her individual spiritual gift(s) and call from God.
6) My child will be able to teach spiritual truths to others.
7) My child will be an effective witness.
8) My child will spend time with God daily.
9) My child will have a servant's heart.
10) My child will be self-disciplined.
11) My child will be in fellowship and under the authority of a local church.
12) My child will understand the power of prayer.

Here is a great example of Core Values from Tim Stafford[273]

1. God first
2. Concern for others
3. Hard work
4. Truthfulness
5. Generosity
6. Submission
7. Sexual fidelity
8. Family unity and love
9. Boundaries
10. Joy and thanksgiving
11. Rest
12. Care for creation
13. Contentment
14. Grace

Consider creating a "Core Values" document for your family.

Boundaries

We have set boundaries in our home: no alcohol, no R-rated movies or pay TV channels. Our body is a temple of God, and the church we attend is a temple of God, but our home is also a miniature temple of God.[274] It is my job to fill it as much as I can with worship music, family devotions, and prayer. Having convictions and having courage to stand up for those convictions is paramount. With the onslaught of compromising cultural values, taking a narrow path is not easy. Dennis Rainey talks about building a fence or drawing the lines. Sometimes it is difficult to know where and how to draw those lines. Here is an example of a code of conduct we used when the kids were younger.

Hagedorn Family Code of Conduct:

1. I will RESPECT and HONOR
   a. God—be Holy and Reverent
   b. Mom and Dad—No talking behind back or arguing
   c. Brothers and sisters—No quarreling, no fighting, no interrupting
   d. Others—all Adults
   e. Matthew 7:12—Do to others as you would have them do to you.

2. I will OBEY
   a. God's Ten Commandments
   b. My father/mother
   c. Others—adults/teachers

3. I will SERVE
   a. Be a diligent helper and serve my father and mother
   b. Others

4. I will LOVE
   a. The Lord my God with ALL my heart, soul, mind, and strength
   b. Love my neighbor and friends and family as myself
   c. Not yell or argue

5. I will be UNSELFISH
   a. Consider others better than myself
   b. Be a cheerful giver—of my time, my stuff, my money, and my life

6. I will be HONEST and TRUTHFUL
   a. I will tell the truth at all times—"let my yes, be yes and no be no. . . ."
   b. The Lord detests lying lips.

7. I will be DISCIPLINED
   a. In my Bible reading, prayer, worship, homework, and chores
   b. I will work and not be lazy and will minimize TV

8. I will be HEALTHY
    a. In my eating and taking vitamins
    b. In my exercise
    c. With my language and my bodily appearance

You might need more discipline in certain areas. We had a media fast week annually when the kids were younger. Maybe you need a family media constitution or contract to define the amount of time and when kids are allowed to play video games, how much they can play, how much time on the internet, etc.

The Ultimate Code of Conduct

My wife and I were volunteering for Dallas Metro Ministries, a local inner-city sidewalk ministry. The leader asked the kids how many of them knew the Ten Commandments. I sheepishly raised my hand about one-third of the way up. I sure didn't want to be called on to recite them, but I thought I knew the Ten Commandments. Funny thing was that I could only rattle off seven or eight on my own. We used a silly, misspelled acronym to teach the kids to remember them. GIVS FM MASLE. We pretended to be a radio DJ and said "you are listening to GIVS FM radio, now show me your muscle." Okay, an English teacher would shudder, so *muscle* isn't spelled M-A-S-L-E, and maybe the "short-hand" Ten Commandments doesn't sit well with you, but for a simpleton like me, twenty years later it sticks, and I actually remember something.

G	no other **Gods**
I	no **Idols**
V	don't take God's name in **Vain**
S	remember the **Sabbath** to keep it holy
FM	honor your **Father and Mother**
M	no **Murder**
A	no **Adultery**
S	no **Stealing**
L	no **Lying**
E	no **Envy**

This is the ultimate memory verse and code of conduct for your kids. Obviously, the New Testament red letters that say to "Love the Lord your God and love your neighbors" is a good one, too. I recall listening to one of the most influential messages I have heard in twenty years when I was a new believer: Ray Comfort's *"Hells best kept secret"*[275] that focuses on the Ten Commandments. If you have never heard it, it is an incredible tool to help win people to Christ.

   Consider creating a code of conduct for your family.

When the kids get older, you might need to refresh these and also create more specific boundary documents.

We created a purity contract for our two older teenagers, and I also gave my daughter a purity ring. We also have a driving contract with our sixteen-year-old, and all of our children have a grade incentive plan as well. (Examples of these are in the appendices.) Dollar values and terms will obviously vary from family to family.

Birds and Bees/Purity

Teaching and talking to your kids about the "birds and the bees" might be tough and you assume that the school or church is teaching it. Do not assume that, start when they are young. A OneHope survey[276] found that 61 percent of young people would like to be virgins when they get married. Another 63 percent said that they would regain their virginity if possible. We also have a purity commitment with our middle-schooler and high-schooler. I recall doing a study on holiness, temptation, and sexuality on a tennis road trip with my boys when we did "church in the hotel room." I covered the following principles.

- Don't let your body control you. This can be true of overeating, alcohol, drugs, and lust for many things. When you feel the impulse, the cravings, or that overpowering urge, immediately turn toward God and take that thought captive. Do not let the mind yield to the body.
- Spend time with God, walk in the Spirit, be filled with the Spirit, saturate self with the Word and prayer, not with other things (Gal. 5:16–17).
- Hide the Word in your heart. It will help you during times of battle (Col. 3:16).
- Stay away from the line. Dabbling with sin this time can be the doorway for the next time. If you draw a line in the sand, then stay far away from that line. If you know movies lead you into temptation, stay away from movies. We added Safe Eyes software filters on all of our computers. It not only restricts the amount of time the kids can spend daily on the computer but also protects them. They are only allowed to use computers in a public place, not in a room with the door shut.
- Crucify the flesh, be dead to the world (Col. 3:5).
- Be aware of bodily feelings and the depraved mind. Beat your body into subjection (1 Cor. 9:27).
- Be a slave to righteousness, not to sin (Rom. 6:15-16).
- Honor marriage; wait until marriage. God will judge the adulterer and the sexually immoral (Heb. 13:4).
- Our body is God's temple (1 Cor. 6:19–20).

4) Battle Plan

You are the general(s) of your family. You need a battle plan for the upcoming campaigns. There will be campaigns. Most will come to you unannounced. Some will be spiritual wars, some will be economic wars, and others will be emotional wars. The actual wars might occur in your relationships, family, job, and church. You will have obstacles: finances, failures, fear, opposition, or lack of experience. You simply need an offensive plan and a defensive plan. Do you have a battle plan on paper? How will you wage war? Are you anticipating the enemy? Do you know the enemy? Let me give you a hint—it is not your spouse or teen! Do you have the right alliances, troops, and forces? Do you have a plan for how you will deal with them? Have you defined what success looks like? How will you measure success? Your plans should change regularly. Your strategy might not change as often. Each family's battle plan will vary. I share with you our family battle plan below and associated campaign strategies. Develop your own. Measure your success every couple of months, and discuss it regularly with your spouse.

FAMILY BATTLE PLAN HIGHLIGHTS
Ultimate Strategy: Love God, Love One Another, Change Lives

	Campaign Strategy	Offensive Tactics	Defensive Tactics
Self	Better Disciple, Father, and Husband	1. Church weekly 2. Daily Bible/prayer	1. Men's small group 2. Calendar family times
Spouse	Love, Honor, Understand and Respect Her	1. Daily listening time 2. Monthly date night	1. Discipline kids 2. Do my chores; help!
High-School Child	Why Faith? College Choice, Ministry avenues	1. Youth group 2. College visits	1. Apologetic DVD series 2. Missions/volunteer times
Middle-School Child	Respect & Honor, Good Friends, Work ethic	1. Discipline consistency 2. Chore and behavior charts	1. Monitor media/friends 2. Prayer with spouse
Elementary-School Child	Academic Focus, Good Friends, Identify Gifts	1. Discipline consistency 2. Academics/athletics	1. Hugs/love with discipline 2. Family devotions time
Spiritual	God as a Priority, Family 2nd / Ministry / Mentor others	1. Daily Bible/prayer 2. Weekly family devotions/code of conduct	1. Accountability partner 2. Write and publish a book
Financial	Get out of Debt, Give liberally Pay for College, Teach Kids	1. Budget balanced 2. Give >10% missions	1. College and 401k savings 2. Debit cards/checkbook
Physical	Be Healthy, Eat Healthy Maintain Weight	1. Work out 3–4 times/week 2. Zero fast food	1. Jog 3–4 times/week 2. Take lunch/no sodas
Job	Strong Ethical Leader Servant Leadership/Mentor	1. No gossip; be an example 2. Offer to help one-on-ones	1. Pray "without ceasing" 2. Mentor three individuals

5) Family Plan: Goal Setting

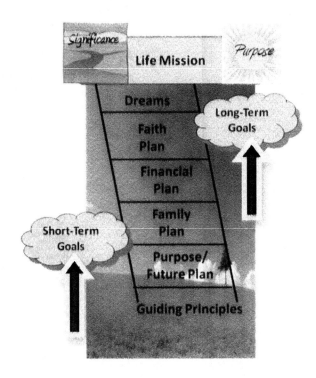

Earlier, we discussed goal setting. The most important thing you can do after reading this family section is to determine what steps you are committed to immediately (short-term) and what steps for the future (long-term), and document those on a form similar to the ones in the appendices.

STOP Review this entire Family section and complete some goal sheets for your most important family goals. Complete a short-term plan (refer to the figures and the appendices) and a long-term plan. This will be the foundation for your family plan. Don't gloss over this. It is the most important thing you can do, to ensure that you at least do *something!*

Short-term goal	1 S	2 M	3 T	4 W	5 T	6 F	7 S	8 S	9 M	10 T	11 W	12 T	13 F	14 S	15 S	16 M	17 T	18 W	19 T	20 F	21 S
Begin date nights	√		√			√					√			√	√		√		√		√
Begin daily Bible	√	√		√	√			√	√	√		√	√	√	√	√	√	√	√	√	√
Pray with wife																					
Bless kids																					

As you go back through this entire family section, document some longer-term actions in the blank spreadsheet (see the appendices). Some examples are provided below. Other examples can be found in the Battle Plan. The Campaign strategies are my personal goals that affect our family.

Your future action	Target date (self)	Target date (spouse)	Target date (together)	Quarterly grade
Education decision Kid 1				
Weekly family time				
Dinner together daily				
Volunteer monthly				
Missions trip				
Kids discussion survey				
Family vision				
Code of conduct				
Tribute to parent				
College visits Kid 2				
5:1				

STOP Final Selah Stop: As we close out the family section, read Psalm 78:1–8, and ask God to give you wisdom and strength to move to action with your family plan.

Family Resources

To get the latest and greatest family and parenting resource recommendation list: go to **www.astrongfamily.net**. A few of the greatest resources I have found for building strong families are as follow.

- *Egermeier's Bible Story Book*—a great, scripturally accurate daily Bible reading. We have used this for three years now for ages 8 to 18.
- *Heritage Builders Family Fun Night Tool Chest*—Family nights. This turned mundane family devotions to nights the kids would scream for.
- *Polite Moments*—Illustrated, concise booklets that encourage old-fashioned polite behavior. Scripture based and can be used as a devotional.
- *Your Child and Money: A Family Activity Book*—Larry Burkett
- *God's Design for Sex* Series—four booklets for ages 3–5, 5–8, 8–11, and 11–14
- *The ABC's of Handling Money God's Way*—Crown Ministries
- *The Giving Bank*—Larry Burkett
- *Let's Make a Memory*—Gloria Gather and Shirley Dobson
- *Lynda Morley's Outings & Adventures* with children ages 1–5
- Larry Burkett's *Great Smoky Mountains Storybook* Series—financially focused stories
- *Surviving the Money Jungle*—Larry Burkett
- *Money, Money, Money: The Meaning of the Art and Symbols*—Nancy Winslow Parker
- *The Summit Ministries Guide to Choosing a College*
- *College Countdown*—VanGruben
- *The All in One College Guide*—Barron's
- *How to Survive Getting into College*—Rachel Korn
- *Smart Parents Guide to College*—Earnest Boyer
- *College Match*—Steven Antonoff

- *Along the Road to Manhood*—Stu Weber
- *Shepherding a Child's Heart*—Tedd Tripp
- *I Kissed Dating Goodbye*—Joshua Harris
- *Truth & Grace* Memory Books
- *A Puritan Catechism with Proofs*—Charles Spurgeon[277]
- *Best College's* —U.S. News and World Report
- Here are some great illustrated read-alouds for ages 5–15:
    o Lamplighter Books/Materials—*Beggars Blessing, Hedge of Thorns, Teddy's Button*
    o *The True Princess*—Angela Elwell Hunt
    o *You are Mine*—Max Lucado
    o Illustrated holiday books by Liz Curtis Higgs
    o *The Giving Tree*—Shel Silverstein
    o *The Tale of Three Trees*—Angela Hunt
    o *Beautiful Feet* books—historical figures—Ingri & Edgar Parin D'Aulaire
    o *Famous Artists*—Jen Green, Antony Mason, multiple Barron's titles
    o G.A. Henty books—Vision Forum
    o *A Hive of Busy Bees: Stories that Build Character*—Don and Joyce Discover
    o Janette Okes's *Spunky* books
    o Sonlight novels and readers
    o Vision Forum materials
- *One Home at a Time*—Dennis Rainey- Its resource list (pp. 263–67 is worth the price of the book!)
- Family-oriented ministry resources:
    o Vision Forum
    o Tim Lambert
    o Family Life/Heritage Builders—Dennis Rainey
    o Focus on the Family
    o American Family Association
    o NAUMS
    o Summit Ministries
    o Lamplighter

****

Your Finances

CHAPTER 43

FUTURE TENSE:
TIMES OF ECONOMIC UNCERTAINTY

"The first generation makes it [money/wealth],
the second generation saves it, and the third generation spends it!"
—-Proverb, Lancashire, England

The future is tense. The past was tense. The present is tense. Money issues and financial security are a concern for most families and every generation. Regardless of
whether you are a boomer, a buster, a Gen-Xer, a Gen-Yer, or a Millennial, you no doubt are
concerned about your finances. The recent surveys show that people are more concerned
about their financial future than ever before. Financial fear is running high—both personally
and nationally. Will I lose my job? Will I save enough for retirement? Will the market crash?
Can I pay for the kids' college? Will our country be bankrupt? Will inflation soon run out of
control? Is another crash coming?

The good ol' days are behind us. If you are paying for major purchases with saved
cash, or if you are debt free, including your mortgage, or if you have your child's education
paid for in advance, congratulations! You are the few, the minority. The days of no debt,
10 percent savings rates, and early/full retirement seem to be far in the rear-view mirror.
How do we gain that financial security for our families and our nation? As you have come
to recognize (possibly painfully so), I like to peer into the rear-view mirror first and then
assess our current situation before we look too far into the future.

Economic Security

The word *security* conjures many positive feelings, including "safety, freedom from fear
or anxiety, confidence, freedom from risk of loss, assurance, protection." We all want a
secure future. Unfortunately, no one is fully secure. There is definitely the element of faith,
but also the element of action on our part. We have many uncertainties in our society that
could lead to "insecurity," including unemployment, illness, disability, aging, divorce, and
major expenses. Historically, one of the major roles of family was to take care of each other
during such times. As societies grew and an agrarian society gave way to an industrial
society, as urbanization occurred and life expectancy began to increase, organizations took

on some of that responsibility. "These organizations began appearing in England in the 16th century. Friendly societies and fraternal organizations were forerunners of trade unions, which led to life insurance. By the beginning of the 19th century one of every nine Englishmen belonged to one of these organizations. As colonial America grew there was some limited movement to state financing and the creation of almshouses and poorhouses."[278]

Retirement is something we have come to take for granted. Following the Civil War, in the mid-1860s, there were hundreds of thousands of widows, orphans, and disabled veterans who depended upon Civil War pensions. In fact, in 1894 military pensions accounted for 37 percent of the entire federal budget! America had transitioned from self-employed farmers to "corporate" workers supporting the Industrial Revolution. Company pensions were the next program that extended "security" to the broader populations. Then, following the crash of 1929, America fell into the Great Depression: unemployment exceeded 25 percent, about 10,000 banks failed, the Gross National Product declined by 50 percent, and poverty among the elderly grew dramatically. This economic crisis was the worst in modern history. Some economists (and I personally) believe that we are soon in for another crisis, an economic earthquake like none we have experienced before, but more on that later.

"President Roosevelt would address the permanent problem of economic security for the elderly, with 'Social Insurance,' which was already widespread in Europe. On August 14, 1935, FDR signed the Social Security Act into law. It would pay retired workers age 65 or older a continuing income after retirement."[279] President Lyndon Johnson signed the Medicare bill into law in 1965. It extended health coverage to almost all Americans aged 65 or older. Thus, nearly all elderly citizens were now dependent upon the government. This dependence had now officially replaced dependence upon family, community, and church.

The life expectancy at the time of the Social Security Act in 1935 was 61.9.[280] The average life expectancy is now ~78 years of age. At its humble beginnings, Social Security was helping a few of the most needy in 1937; there were 52,236 beneficiaries for $1.3M. We now have more than 50,000,000 beneficiaries and more than $600 billion in support. Social Security and Medicare are not affordable in their current state.

On October 3, 1913, Woodrow Wilson signed the personal income tax law. At its inception, 98 percent of American families were exempt. A "normal rate" of 1 percent was charged on incomes above $3000. Just one generation later, President Hoover passed the Revenue Act of 1932, which increased the top individual tax rate to 63 percent. Roosevelt jacked it up even higher to a peak of 79 percent. The size of the government and the size of the tax burden on citizens had exploded in just one generation. We are there again.

> *"The proper role of government is to protect equal rights,*
> *not provide equal things."*
> —The Seventh Principle of Freedom, W. Clean Skousen

Prison Cell?

I believe that the Congress of the United States is more guilty than Bernie Madoff. Not only is their bookkeeping corrupt but also they deceive the people with politics, talk, and rhetoric. In Washington, D.C., if you don't increase your budget spending, it is a "cut." The government rarely decreases or "cuts" its spending from year to year. The governments accounting practices would land you in jail in corporate America. Their approach conceals trillions of dollars of spending from the normal American. "Off-budget" accounting and trust funds are not counted in the budget deficit (Social Security, Medicare, U.S. Postal Service, federal pensions, etc.), yet the projected "unfunded liabilities" will bankrupt us very soon. In fact, the Social Security Administration Annual Report [281]states that "projected long-run program costs for Medicare and Social Security are not sustainable under currently scheduled financing." Yet our politicians sit back and do nothing, and most citizens expect more and more from a government that is near bankruptcy.

Social Security is the federal government's largest single program. As the United States population continues to age, the number of Social Security beneficiaries will rise and expenses will be more than income unless changes are made. In fact, for the first time, according to the Congressional Budget Office (CBO),[282] "Social Security's annual outlays will exceed its annual tax revenues." There is no "lock box" or "fund account" with the Social Security funds that have been paid in. That fund is raided yearly and replaced with IOUs. The "lock box" is empty, and the funds are spent elsewhere. The Heritage Foundation[283] has a good article on how the trust fund really works. Politicians know what needs to be done. CBO has a list of thirty detailed options, and many other organizations/foundations have good plans, but the gutless leaders, in aggregate, refuse to act.

> *"Figures lie, and liars figure."*
> —John Mitchell,
> Attorney General, Department of Justice, under President Nixon

A Painful Reminder

Most politicians are worried about the next election, not the next generation. The government is not the only guilty party. Greed and corner cutting led to financial collapse in 2008. Panic spread with the housing market collapse, and bank lending was crippled. Meanwhile, unemployment increased and the stock market collapsed. Two wars were being financed while the size of government went through the roof. Personal and national debt skyrocketed, personal savings was low, and balance sheets were leveraged. Cheap credit, get-rich-quick, high-yield investments, and accelerated home appreciation were now the norm.

America went from being a major creditor to the world's largest debtor nation in less than twenty years. For much of the twentieth century, the United States was a creditor nation. In the last generation, loans have flowed in from other countries. Foreign investors owned roughly half of all marketable U.S. Treasury bonds at the end of 2008, up from 15.4 percent in 1982. The America's top import from China is not a product; it is cash. China has become America's financial sugar daddy.

In a little over a decade, the U.S. debt has tripled. U.S. households gorged themselves on easy money and bought larger homes, larger cars, and virtually anything else that suited their fancy, all while depending more and more upon other countries' oil and natural resources. The debt-fueled U.S. consumption boom went hand-in-hand with ever-rising government spending levels. In hindsight, the good times were basically funded with borrowed money.

Here are just a few of the stunning reminders of the debt, greed, affluence, and financial mismanagement:"[284]

- a $700 billion bank bail-out package
- a $787 billion stimulus package (which was not a one-time event, but now a permanent annual budget increase)
- In 10 years, total U.S. debt more than tripled from $5.6 trillion to its current state with no plan to repay the debt, let alone balance the annual budget deficit. We only bring in about $2 Trillion a year in tax revenue.
- The U.S. posted its first trillion-dollar annual deficit: $1.4 trillion, an increase of nearly 500 percent from $250 billion
- The share of public debt owned by foreigners has risen from 7 percent in 1970 to 48 percent today.
- The U.S. has increased the money supply by 200 percent, from $800 billion in 2008 to more than $2.4 trillion today.
- The average Chinese household saves a quarter of its after-tax income, the average European 10 to 15 percent, while the average American saves ~5 percent.

The days of reckoning will soon be upon us unless we make tough political decisions, balance our budget, impose tough financial disciplines, and get our own financial houses in order. "The U.S. economy has never been more dependent on foreign natural resources and foreign capital. America is rapidly losing control of its own economic fate."[285]

Is America heading toward bankruptcy? Laurence Kotlikoff estimated that real liabilities were on the order of $70 trillion, which includes the help of projected tax receipts. Some people estimate $100 trillion. There is no fund for this. To come up with it, we must tax it, borrow it, or print it.

Been There, Done That

The good news is that we have arisen out of crisis before. We have been in economic crisis before in America:[286]

- The early 1930s: The Great Depression, unemployment rate of 25 percent, bread lines, stock market wariness
- The early 1940s: World at war, rationed key basic staples
- The early 1970s: Oil crisis, Vietnam War, income tax rates at all-time high, wage-and-price controls
- The early 1980s: Interest rates 20 percent, inflation in double digits, stagnant industry
- The 2000s: 9/11 terrorist attacks, two wars, technology bubble, housing collapse, banking crisis, bailouts, massive debt explosion

Twilight of a Great Civilization

British scholar C.E.M. Joad, who studied the collapses of the worlds' great empires, said that the declines all had several things in common: decadence, weariness, and irresponsibility. British historian C. Northcote Parkinson added that collapses are usually marked by an overcentralized government, heavy taxes, and bureaucracy."[287]

Consider the recipe from the downfall of Rome.[288]

1. A great civilization arises.
2. The state encroaches on freedom and demands more power.
3. People take less responsibility for themselves and want more handouts from the government.
4. Taxes go up to pay for the handouts.
5. The size of government explodes, and economic growth slows.
6. The government seeks to divert the public's attention from what is really going on
7. Collapse, economic or otherwise, ensues.

> *"When people shirk individual responsibility and expect*
> *more from government, they fall prey to tyranny."*
> —Edward Gibbon, *The History of the Decline*
> *and Fall of the Roman Empire*

We are now experiencing a major shift in global economic power in our world. The seven billion people on this earth are starting to see and feel much volatility, which is bringing along with it a global rebalancing. We have been through turmoil in the Middle East, worldwide financial crises, massive debt, natural disasters, terrorism, stock market collapses, housing collapses, and the shifting of currency values. There are more discussions than ever about the viability and confidence in the dollar as a reserve currency, and "other governments are moving towards a more diversified basket of currencies."[289] All of these things are leading to a transition of the balance of power in our world.

Although the U.S. economy is still more than double China's, it cannot grow its way back to the pre-financial collapse world power. Both the government and the consumers are living beyond their means. The drunken spending spree is coming to a close, and many people are questioning America's ability to meet its obligations for the first time. "The U.S. borrows more than $4 billion per day, much of it from China. So, China is loaning Americans the money that allows them to live beyond their means."[290] There are multiple countries who no longer accept U.S. leadership. For nearly a half of century, American consumers were the worldwide growth engine. They are now focused themselves on getting out of debt and saving. The long-term prognosis and impact is that U.S. consumers will have to pay more taxes, save more money, delay retirement, and have less generous pensions and healthcare benefits.

Foreign Policy validated this shift in the world's balance of power and global thoughts on America. Fifty-five of the world's top economists were surveyed[291] on the new rules of the global markets. Here is what they think:

- Only ten of fifty-five respondents thought that U.S. deficits were not a problem. Eighty-two percent of them ranked the problem six or greater on a scale of one to ten, with ten being a full crisis.
- Only twelve of fifty-five thought that the United States can overcome its dependence upon foreign oil by 2050. On a scale of 1 to 10, with 10 being very confident, 79 percent of them scored this a four or less.
- When asked "If you had $1 billion to invest in emerging market countries," the three countries chosen were India, Brazil, and China.

294

- Eighty-one percent thought that China's GDP would surpass that of the United States by 2050.

The global economy is in the process of transformation. An economic "cold war" could be starting. After years of amassing trillions of dollars of debt, living far beyond its means, and ignoring warning signs, "the last economic superpower went bust in September 2008. New economic powers are on the ascent, led by nations like China, India, Brazil, Korea and Turkey. Up until the early 1970s the United States had been the unchallenged leader of the free world.[292]" For much of its history, the United States has been the only indigenous economic superpower in the western hemisphere. The United States is no longer the economic superpower it once was. The G-8 has been supplanted by the G-20.

A recent report[293] from Bloomberg/*Business Week*, showed that fifteen of the top fifty innovative companies in the world were now Asian, up from just five companies a few years earlier. For the first time, the majority of corporations in the top twenty-five are based outside the United States.

"The West can no longer dominate, given its partial loss of moral authority. For the first time in centuries, the developing East has some say."
—Ronnie Chan, Chairman of Hang Lung Properties, Hong Kong

So is the debt problem and financial mismanagement a U.S. problem or a worldwide problem? More to come on this tender subject.

"The United States can be likened to Rome before the fall of the empire. Its financial condition is worse than advertised."
—David Walker, former Comptroller General of the United States.

Legacy Lesson: Looking at our past is sometimes painful. Will you learn from it? Watching your leaders and countries avoid action is no longer an option. Our children and grandchildren will pay a dear price if we don't act now. What role will you play?

CHAPTER 44

THE DEBT TIME BOMB

*"To preserve our independence, we must not let our rulers
load us with public debt."*
—Thomas Jefferson

We are Number 1! We aren't talking about your local NCAA team or the index finger you flash Momma-bear on national TV after scoring a touchdown. This is one area you *don't* proudly wear the badge of Number 1. The United States is the world leader in external debt. As opposed to growth with little debt, like India and China, the United States is growing little and spending a lot. The problem with publishing these numbers is that they are outdated as soon as the ink dries on the paper. The numbers are spiraling out of control. Our world is *debt addicted* with zero chance of ever paying it off. This is just government debt and does not include the multiple trillions of personal or corporate debt amassed internally, nor the staggering unfunded liability of future bills to come.

	External Debt*	Population	Debt per person	GDP	Debt % GDP
United States	**$14.2 trillion**	313 million	$45,000	$14.7 trillion	95%
United Kingdom	$9.0 trillion	63 million	$143,000	$2.2 trillion	409%
Germany	$4.7 trillion	81 million	$58,000	$3.3 trillion	142%
France	$4.7 trillion	65 million	$72,000	$2.6 trillion	181%
Japan	$2.4 trillion	126 million	$19,000	$5.5 trillion	44%
Ireland	$2.3 trillion	5 million	$460,000	$204 billion	1150%
Norway	$2.2 trillion	5 million	$440,000	$414 billion	550%
Italy	$2.2 trillion	61 million	$36,000	$2.1 trillion	104%
Spain	$2.2 trillion	47 million	$47,000	$1.4 trillion	157%
Switzerland	$1.2 trillion	8 million	$150,000	$524 billion	231%
Belgium	$1.2 trillion	10 million	$120,000	$466 billion	255%
Canada	$1.0 trillion	34 million	$29,000	$1.6 trillion	63%
Sweden	$850 billion	9 million	$94,000	$456 billion	186%
Austria	$800 billion	8 million	$100,000	$377 billion	212%
Hong Kong	$750 billion	7 million	$107,000	$225 billion	333%
Denmark	$560 billion	6 million	$93,000	$311 billion	180%
Greece	$533 billion	11 million	$48,500	$305 billion	174%
China	$405 billion	1.3 billion	**$300**	$5.9 trillion	**7%**
India	$237 billion	1.2 billion	**$197**	$1.5 trillion	**16%**

*External debt includes government debt and corporate and individual debt to entities outside of their country.

Table: Debt Statistics, Central Intelligence Agency, The World Factbook[294]

Deficit Delusion

Many European nations are currently facing severe economic crises. The U.S. federal debt has grown ten-fold in just three years, and the "cuts" talked about by both parties are not spending "cuts" at all, but rather just drops in the bucket of "future spending increase reductions." Both parties have been guilty of financial mismanagement. Democrats have pushed for more spending. Republicans have pushed for lower taxes. I guess you could say that Congress has accomplished their objectives, yet it has destroyed our future. Every American taxpayer now owes $1,000,000 each if we were to pay off the federal debt and cover our unfunded liabilities (Social Security, Medicare, etc.). Can the next generation afford that? That is $5,000,000 for a family of five taxpayers. Most families don't make that much in a lifetime.

Future generations will pay the price for the past couple of generations' lack of self-control, lack of discipline, and mostly lack of leadership. If only a few voices would just stand up and speak out and not worry about the next election. We need term limits and a constitutional balanced budget amendment. If politicians would only serve the people, and not their political future, we might have hope of dealing with the debt delusion head on.

"When a man assumes a public trust,
he should consider himself public property."
—Thomas Jefferson

The Debt Bubble—Overdue to Burst

According to Addison Wiggins, Forbes.com columnist, "the next financial crisis will be hellish, and it's on its way."[295] The article discusses the sobering facts that we haven't solved any of the things that caused the previous crisis. American citizens, corporations, and local and federal governments have racked up a staggering amount of debt. The following graph shows how quickly this small bubble has ballooned into a massive bubble. I used four data points for comparison, four years of data—1977, 1987, 1997, and 2011—to show the amount of debt outstanding for each year in each of six different sectors. What should strike you is the black (top) quadrant of each sector (2011). The debt we have now in every sector dwarfs that of 1977. From 1977 to 2011, home mortgage debt grew from $603 billion outstanding to almost $10 trillion, a factor of sixteen-fold growth!

As an example explanation from the following figure, the consumer's home mortgage outstanding debt was as follows:

1977: $603 billion (bottom quadrant)
1987: $1.8 trillion (grey, second quadrant of the bar chart)
1997: $3.7 trillion (striped, second quadrant from the top of the bar chart)
2011: $9.9 trillion (black, top quadrant of bar chart)

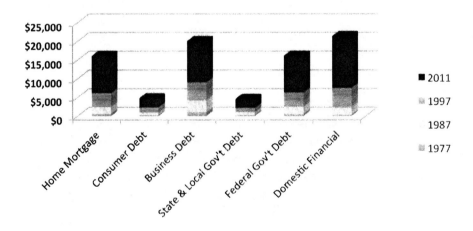

U.S. DEBT BY SECTOR

2011, Axis X = Section, Axis Y= Billion Dollars in Credit Outstanding
Source: Federal Reserve Statistical Release, Flow of Funds Accounts of the United States,
2nd Quarter

Though our GDP has grown by 7-fold since 1977[296], our debt is growing much faster. Our Federal Debt has grown by 17x, our Business Debt by 11x and our TOTAL debt in all 6 sectors by 16x. These 6 sectors had a total of $3 Trillion in debt in 1977. That is now > $50 Trillion in 2012! The cumulative view of the total debt is even more depressing. See the graph below.

Total U.S. Debt

Total U.S. DEBT

Interest on the Debt

Just as you personally understand the waste of funds you spend on interest, the other ticking time bomb is the interest expense on the federal debt. In 1977, that was $40 billion. It is now >$450 billion. We are faced with a mountain of debt personally, corporately, and governmentally. The days of easy credit are over, and this bubble will soon burst. You need to position yourself personally to get out of debt, tighten your belt, and get ready if other bubbles burst at the same time—the dollar, inflation, etc. My hope would be that the federal government would do the same, but they usually act when the bubble is bursting, and in this case that will occur when the Chinese stop lending.

"Our lives begin to end the day we become silent about things that matter."
-Martin Luther King Jr.

Legacy Lesson: Choosing to live within our means is everyone's responsibility. The past generation has chosen to live beyond their means. These decisions will greatly impact future generations unless drastic and quick changes are made.

CHAPTER 45

THE STORM IS HERE:
A CRISIS IN PICTURES
WARNING: GRAPHIC MATERIAL

∞

"Not to stand is to stand. Not to speak is to speak."
- Dietrich Bonhoeffer

ow is the time to stand and to speak. Our future is at stake. Your children and grandchildren's legacy is at stake. Our world has not been down this path before. Scott Burns[297] says "the game is up, but no one knows what to do next." Our current politicians continue the charade, but everyone knows that "the emperor, otherwise known as our government, has no clothes. The government is broke, naked, still borrowing and shivering in the dark." It is not just an isolated nation or economy. It is a debt dilemma, throughout the industrialized world. It is not just a couple of lone-voice economists crying in the wilderness anymore.

John Mauldin states, "People don't understand that we are down to difficult choices and bad choices." He references Greece, Ireland, Portugal, and Italy as having to make really bad choices. He says no nation has faced the music. Pictures tell the story better than any graph or numbers. (The following graphics are used with permission and created and credited to Oto Godfrey, www.usdebt.kleptocracy.us.)

One HUNDRED United States Dollars: $100

Ten *THOUSAND* United States Dollars: $10,000
A small stack of $100 Dollar Bills
This is more than the average / median household
yearly income around the world.

$1,000,000

***One MILLION* Dollars**—what most humans will <u>not</u> earn in their lifetimes
If you are a U.S. taxpayer, this is also your current, personal share of the America's
unfunded liabilities ($15 trillion)!

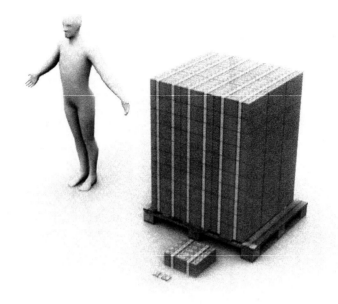

$100,000,000
One HUNDRED MILLION Dollars---
a standard pallet of stacks of $100 dollar bills
This is also approximately the amount
of U.S. debt that is being racked up every <u>hour</u>!

$1,000,000,000
One BILLION Dollars---10 standard pallets of stacks of $100 dollar bills
The United States' YEARLY interest Payments on the national debt outstanding is more
than 4500 of these pallets.

$1,700,000,000,000

One TRILLION SEVEN HUNDRED BILLION Dollars—Double stacked pallets of ONE
HUNDRED MILLION each

The United States' recent ANNUAL federal deficit

(just one year, mind you)

This pictorial also represents the amount of interest expense the U.S. will pay on our outstanding debt over a four-year period!

$15 TRILLION

What the United States owes—the U.S. national debt

—dwarfing the Statue of Liberty.

The cumulative federal budget deficit

—Can you find that tiny $100,000,000 pallet?

$115 Trillion

What the United States is projected to owe (our unfunded liabilities)—
see the super skyscraper on the right.
This works out to be more than $1,000,000 debt per U.S. taxpayer.
I guess we are all millionaires after all.
See if you can spot the $100-million pallet.
Even the $1.7 trillion football field is now dwarfed by the debt tower.
U.S. unfunded liabilities: Social Security, Medicare, military,
and civil pensions. (www.usdebtclock.org)

These are eye-opening graphics and are used with permission and created and credited to Oto Godfrey (www.usdebt.kleptocracy.us). You can also find more graphs with European and worldwide pictorials. These made me so angry that it almost brought me to tears. What an inept bunch of leaders we have! It is time the people speak up for a balanced budget and term limits with no loopholes. Yes there will be a near-term impact for balancing the budget, and there might be higher unemployment, but what are the perils of continued inaction in balancing our budget and dealing with our debt monster?

"How long can the world's biggest borrower
remain the world's biggest power?"
—Larry Summers, President Obama's Chief Economic Advisor

"If the federal government was a private corporation,
its stock would plummet and shareholders would bring in new management and directors."
—David Walker, former U.S. Comptroller General

Legacy Lesson: Our nation is sleepwalking through a financial disaster. We ignore the burning building in front of us as we stagger like a drunken man ignoring the catastrophe in front of us. What is your role in the wake up call?

CHAPTER 46

THE TIPPING POINT: BUBBLES READY TO BURST

"What has been will be again, what has been done will be done again; there is nothing new under the sun."
—King Solomon, Ecclesiastes 1:9

*A*merica's economy is a bubble economy. The fine book *Aftershock*[298] by David and Robert Wiedemer and Cindy Spitzer, shines a bright light on this. There are multiple bubbles waiting to burst. The real estate bubble, the stock market bubble, the government-debt bubble, the private-debt bubble, discretionary-spending bubble, and the dollar bubble. The government and the Federal Reserve have taken radical actions to keep the bubbles from popping, including massive borrowing and massive money printing (increasing the money supply), which only delays the inevitable and often shifts bubbles. We shifted a banking bubble to a debt bubble. We bailed out our largest banks and financial institutions and auto companies and induced home buyers with money we don't have. Forty percent of everything the government spends is with borrowed money.

Don't forget the "feel good" emotions from the mid-2000s. The Dow was at an all-time high, gold prices were skyrocketing, and U.S. home prices were appreciating in double digits and were at an all-time high, often with no money down or wildly low interest rates. Nearly anyone could get a loan as credit flowed freely. Then—pop—America's bubble economy burst. "Why did so many fail to see the financial crisis coming? As to the standard indicators of financial crises, many red lights were blinking well in advance. Above all, the huge run-up in housing prices—over 10% nationally over 5 years—should have been an alarm, especially fueled as it was by rising leverage."[299]

This Time Is Different

"Those who cannot remember the past are condemned to repeat it."
—George Santayana

We have been here before. Financial crises are nothing new. The book *This Time Is Different* investigates crashes and crises throughout world history. We have been through rhythms of booms and busts throughout the years. Only a relatively small number of countries—Australia, New Zealand, Canada, Denmark, Thailand, and the United States—have avoided defaults on government debt to foreign creditors.

During each boom cycle, a society convinces itself that the current boom "is different," that financial crises are things that happen to other people in other countries at other times. Crises do not happen to us, here and now. There is a lack of transparency and realism. The difference this time around is that bubbles are far more dangerous when fueled by debt.

For the past ten years, there has been a "false boom." The apparent continued economic growth is simply people, businesses, and government borrowing money they don't have and quite possibly cannot afford to ever repay. "Worldwide debts, public and private, have more than doubled since 2002, from $84 trillion to $195 trillion. Ireland had amassed debts of more than twenty-five times its annual tax revenues. With Greece, Ireland, and Japan, it wouldn't take much of a rise in interest rates for budgets to be consumed entirely by interest payments on debt."[300] GDP has grown at an annual rate of 4 percent while debt has grown at an annual rate of 11 percent. There is no other alternative but defaults and a global restructuring. An atonement time bomb is coming. The fuses have been lit, and no printing of money, bailouts, or political banter will prevent the pending explosions. The question is only a matter of when. In fact, the problems continue to get masked because governments continue to move all sorts of expenses (e.g., pensions, retirement, and health programs) off the books.

The bull markets of late have been fueled by massive money printing by the Federal Reserve. The Fed has created more than $2 trillion out of thin air in the last couple of years. In the mid-1980s, this was only ~ $200B. This fuels inflation's fires. You will hear this referred to as Quantitative Easing (QE). This bubble will pop once the "Feds Medicine (printed money) becomes poison (high inflation)."[301] The European Central Bank (ECB) is no better because they have done the same.

Leadership Corruption?

As a taxpayer, you are subject to audit from the IRS. Corporations are also subject to audit by the government. The Federal Reserve, the central bank of the United States, however, has unchecked power. They can print endless billions of dollars out of thin air, and have done so recently to the tune of more than $2 trillion. The Quantitative Easing "electronic printings" as a result of the recent financial crisis increases greatly the risk of runaway inflation and continued freefall of the value of the dollar.

The Fed was created in 1913 as a result of financial and banking panics plaguing the United States. The bill transferred Congress's constitutional duty to issue America's currency into the hands of a private corporation. "Since that time the dollar has lost more than 96% of its value, and has recklessly inflated the money supply."[302] A dollar today would buy less than a nickel's worth of goods and services in Woodrow Wilson's time. The United States was on a gold standard from 1792–1933. The following graph might lead one to believe that the experiment of a Federal Reserve System, with no explicit link to gold and no effective external check on its activities, has failed the public's interest."[303]

The Purchasing Power of the Dollar

January 1913 = $1.00

August 1971 = 24 cents

June 2009 = 4.6 cents

Congressman Ron Paul has worked unsuccessfully to uncover and reveal the secretive practices of the Fed. They are currently not subject to an audit like you or I. They have little or no accountability to the people. "Its decisions do not have to be ratified by the President or anyone else in the executive branch of the government. Its monetary policy is exempt from audit by the Government Accountability Office. Certain functions, such as transactions with foreign central banks and open market operations are excluded from audit as well. The Federal Reserve System was founded to provide the nation with a safer, more flexible, and more stable monetary and financial system. Over the years, its role in banking and the economy has expanded."[304] Why all the secrecy? Why all the power?

A Sign of Things to Come?

We can only hope that the city of San Jose, California, is not an example of what might be on the horizon. In *Boomerang*, Michael Lewis covers the details of this sad example. A city of 250,000 that has a triple-A rating from Moody's and Standard and Poors, is not far from bankruptcy. As a result of caving in to unions and living beyond their means, public employee-projected pension and health costs will bankrupt the city. It is a mathematical inevitability. The mayor says, "Our police and firefighters will earn more in retirement than they did when they were working. San Jose could cut its debt in half and still wind up broke."[305] They had to close libraries three days a week, cut back servicing parks, lay off staff, and cut pay by 10 percent. Vallejo, California is yet another example. "The lobby of city hall is completely empty. In 2008, Vallejo declared bankruptcy. Eighty percent of the city's budget was wrapped up in the pay and benefits of public safety workers."[306]

The bubble dominos are waiting to spill. Interest rates can go nowhere but up as the dollar buys less and inflation rises. When interest rates rise, consumers and businesses will buy less and borrow less. Less money will be loaned, and more jobs will be lost. When interest rates rise on the federal debt, we will have a hard time paying the interest, then the next snowball and the next round of multibubbles bursting begins. Our risk of default is growing all of the time. Multiple government promises of cradle to grave security and twenty-four months of unemployment benefits can no longer be afforded. The next bubble burst will be felt around the world.

Train Wreck Coming

One very scary fiscal train wreck will hit America soon. "Retirement programs for former federal workers are growing so fast they now face a multitrillion-dollar shortfall nearly as big as Social Security's. The federal government hasn't set aside money or created a revenue source to help pay for these benefits, so these retirement costs must be paid every year through taxes and borrowing."[307]

The government seems to make laws for everyone but themselves. Corporations and private employers are legally required to put money into pension funds to match retirement promises that will come due. "Private pensions have $2.3 trillion in stocks, bonds, real estate, and other assets. State and local governments have $3 trillion in retirement funds. The federal government has nothing set aside, and now have a $5.7 trillion unfunded liability."[308] Watch for chaos soon as the federal government has to tell retired military and civilian citizens, who served their country faithfully, it cannot pay the full share of their retirement due them.

Why the Chaos and Lack of Progress?

Are we living in the twilight of a great civilization[309] as Carl F.H. Henry says? He says that the books of Daniel and Revelation seem to be stalking us. He says that we are not embracing practical Christianity but are really living out an apostate compromise with the spirit of the age. He talks of accommodating divorce and rejecting traditional marriage. He talks about America and Western Europe and the takeover by secular humanism and political atheism. He talks of the West's losing its spiritual compass. Yet he wrote those things back in 1988!

The church and our civilization is at a crossroads. It is up to the church to be revived, to intercede, to repent, to seek God wholeheartedly, and to divide the Word of God correctly. It will not start with the government or the Fed. It is up to a godly remnant. Will God relent? Who knows?

At some point, the debt will catch up with us. We are already "subject" to other countries around the world, with our paying out >$450 million in interest a year on our debt to the Chinese and others. We are "subject" to many countries with our trade deficit. This could only be the beginning—until the debts come due.

Look no further than Deuteronomy 28:12–13, 44–49. The Bible is clear that God's blessings are upon a land that obeys God's commands. It is also clear that God's curses are upon a land that lives in disobedience. I have shared with you the evidence in statistics concerning our debt. You have experienced terrorism and war on our domestic soil for the first time in our history. We are already under God's disciplining hand. He is withdrawing some of His favor. Yet, as a nation we do not fear His hand. God pleads for our obedience, and with it would come blessing, favor, and prosperity.

Read Deuteronomy 28:12–13, 43–45; Nehemiah 5:3–5;
Proverbs 22:7; and Jeremiah 17:4.

We are slaves to debt and to our debtors. Our masters will soon treat us like the slaves we are and stop lending us money. It is not too late, but we must relent and repent of our disobedience.

Our founders warned against the "welfare state" in which the government tried to take care of everyone from the cradle to the grave. That is primarily a family and individual problem.

 Read 2 Chronicles 7:14 and Joel 2:12–19.

Carl F.H. Henry wonders aloud whether the multitudes in the streets hear a stirring in the wind and sense afresh that Pentecost is blowing our way, or will we let the drift continue? Will a remnant take action? Will God withhold His judgment? My hope is that we are not like Romans 1:24–27 or Psalm 81:11–12, in which the dreadful words "God gave them over" are used three times. "God gave them over" to

- the sinful desires of their hearts
- shameful lusts
- a depraved mind

Hopefully, we have not crossed the line, but we are ever so close. Sin is paraded publicly, celebrated, and even legislated and protected. We call evil things good and good things evil.[310] Our educational institutions and government do not allow the public use of prayer or the name of God. Many pulpits do not preach sin, heaven and hell, or salvation. Will God relent? Who knows?

 "For Such a Time as This," Wayne Watson

 What is my role in turning myself, my family, and my country back to God?

Do Not Assume!

Do not leave your financial decisions in others' hands—even those of so-called experts. Many experts were wrong and assumed that we would continue to live fat, dumb, and happy with continued real estate appreciation and unhindered stock market growth. Many people have been humiliated, humbled, embarrassed, and left poorer by making financial assumptions or trusting someone else to look out for their best interests. The lessons learned and memories from the economic bubbles bursting over the recent years should by screaming at you not to make assumptions.

✓ Do not assume that market cycles are easily forecast.

✓ Do not assume that everything will bounce back to normal.

✓ Do not trust *one* financial advisor (including yourself).

✓ Do not assume that your house is a major asset for your retirement.

✓ Do not assume that inflation will stay low; it will not.

✓ Do not assume that your same level of income and benefits from Social Security and Medicare will remain the same.

✓ Do not assume that interest rates will stay low; they will not.

✓ Do not assume that the dollar bubble will not burst.

✓ Do not assume that standard retirement savings withdrawal rates are correct.

✓ Do not assume that your nest egg will grow in retirement.

✓ Do not assume that tax rates will stay low or deductions will stay as they are now.

✓ Do not assume that the real estate collapse is over.

✓ Do not assume that the government or the Fed can rescue us.

Some of these things might occur, some might not, and some might go through cyclical change.

What's Next?

The good ol' days when people could count on their home being their main retirement asset or that steady appreciation was the norm are over. I have no audible voice, only my gut and a study of cycles, but I believe that we will see inflation, much higher interest rates, and possibly a continued correction in values and depreciation. Some people have a more optimistic forecast, but many others predict much gloomier scenarios, and all have facts to substantiate their forecasts. You must simply prepare for all scenarios.

Generational Giant

Albert Einstein. Einstein was not only the father of modern physics but also one of the most prolific intellects in human history. In addition to his having great intellect and making many contributions he was exiled from Germany because he was a Jew. He noticed the faithfulness of a particular remnant in Germany. Einstein, a secular Jew, was quoted in *Time* magazine, December 23, 1940:

"Being a lover of freedom, when the revolution came in Germany, I looked to the universities
to defend it, knowing that they had always boasted of their devotion to the cause of truth;
but, no, the universities immediately were silenced. Then I looked to the great editors of the
newspapers whose flaming editorials in days gone by had proclaimed their love of freedom;
but they, like the universities, were silenced in a few short weeks."

"Only the Church *stood squarely across the path of Hitler's campaign for suppressing truth. I never had any special interest in the Church before, but now I feel a great affection and admiration because* **the Church alone** *has had the courage and persistence to stand for intellectual truth and moral freedom. I am forced thus to confess that what I once despised I now praise unreservedly."*
—Albert Einstein, *Time*, December 23, 1940 (p. 38)

Einstein's comments reveal how important it is for the remnant to respond when a government's leaders are evil or are not acting according to moral thinking and action.

"The only thing necessary for the triumph
of evil is for good men to do nothing."
—Edmund Burke

Legacy Lesson: You are that remnant. "If my people." The church will decide the fate of future of generations.

CHAPTER 47

BETTER DAYS: A SECURE FINANCIAL FUTURE

Whether you want to weather a future financial storm, prepare for retirement, pay for your child's college, or just manage your money more effectively, there are some principles that will lead you to success. Instead of being impatient, keeping up with Joneses, or falling for the slick advertisement cajoling you to shift a "want" into a "need," how can you best secure your family's financial future?

The Millionaire Next Door[311] studied self-made millionaires and "three words that describe the most affluent. Frugal, frugal, frugal. Being frugal is the cornerstone of wealth building." They also discovered the following facts about self-made millionaires:

- They live below their means.
- They drive cars older than three years old.
- They wear inexpensive suits.
- They know what they spend on household items.
- The majority of them operate on a budget.
- They avoid luxury items and don't own a home beyond their means.

Preparing for your financial future might mean making some radical changes. If you have been living with a debt mindset, living beyond your means, and saving little, you might need more than a tune-up. You need to be prepared, especially if the economy worsens or bubbles burst. Some of the preparation might need to start with some mental or attitudinal changes. You might very well need a lifestyle change. The recipe differs for every family, but there are some basics that are tried and true.

MINDSET/LIFESTYLE
1) Place your priorities in eternal things—relationships and people's lives. Do not put your hope in wealth, but put your hope in God.[312]
2) If you are reading this book, most of the world would jump at the opportunity to trade places with you. Have a grateful mindset.
3) Be content with what you have (Heb. 13:5; Phil. 4:11–12).
4) Be in unity with your spouse.

5) Live as though nothing is yours but it is all God's, as if you are just His steward.

6) Control what you can control. Do not worry or be overanxious. (Read Matthew 6:25–34 and Philippians 4:6–8. Believe these promises, and meditate on them.)

7) Live a lifestyle of giving—give generously and give cheerfully. It is the only guaranteed return you have!

INVESTING/SAVING

8) Think long term with your investments and goals. Do not make changes like the blowing of the wind or react based on emotions. Your spouse provides objectivity.

9) Don't look for insider secrets and get-rich-quick schemes. Be careful of stock tips from friends/family.

10) Diversify to spread out your risk. Understand your risk/reward trade-offs (Ecclesiastes 11:2).

11) Diversify widely: by asset class, by category, by investment style, by investment location, by geography, by manager, and over different time periods.

12) Use dollar cost averaging through your entire life.

13) Review and rebalance your portfolio annually.

14) Seek wisdom from many people, including your spouse, and pray for God's wisdom (James 1:5).

15) Continue to invest and save despite challenges, difficulties, and downturns.

16) Do not borrow to invest. Invest after your monthly bills and debts are paid.

17) Let your money grow little by little (Proverbs 13:11).

18) Start investing young or start investing now!

19) Retirement: With the many areas of risk upon us, you might need to work longer.

MONEY MANAGEMENT/SPENDING

20) Have a budget. Spend less than you earn. Separate your needs from your wants.

21) Minimize the use of debt/credit. Pay with cash or a debit card.

22) Plan for downturns. Have an emergency fund.

23) Balance your investments with giving; do not hoard. When in doubt, give!

24) Have your goals in writing, and review them regularly.

25) Pay off all of your high-interest debt first. Use the debt snowball plan.

26) Buy low-mileage used cars; do not get suckered into the depreciation hole.

27) Don't buy more home than you can comfortably afford on one income.

28) Read; educate yourself.

29) Use the Save-to-Spend Tool for unforeseen expenses.

30) Use the Big-Ticket Tool for major expenditures.

Probably the most important areas we all need a refresher course on are as follows:

STOP Read Deuteronomy 8:18; Haggai 2:8; Matthew 25:21; Luke 16:1–13; 1 Corinthians 4:1–2; and 1 Timothy 6:17–18.

God is in control. We are just stewards of his possessions. Let us each be found faithful.

Basics and Borrowed Time

We live in a society of fast and instant gratification and a lack of self-control. It is evident in the growth of the debt or even the growth in our waistlines. We are sacrificing our long-term stability and civility for short-term satisfaction, gains, and rewards. When and where did we go wrong? When did we stop buying things after saving for them? When did we get tricked into living a lifestyle of pretenders? When did we start spending as though we *were* rich instead of desiring to be rich? Where did our models of fiscal responsibility go?

It is time to get back to the basics. You can't control the federal debt, trade deficits, unfunded liabilities, the value of the dollar, interest rates, or inflation, but you can control your household budget. Let's start with a quick self-test.

 Do you need a financial shakeup?

	Yes		No
Do you spend more than you make?			
Do you buy only new cars?			
Do you have nothing saved for an emergency?			
If you were fired tomorrow, would you panic financially?			
Do you have credit card debt?			
Do you argue with your spouse/family over finances?			
Do you buy major items impulsively?			
Do you fail to live by a budget?			
Do you ever bounce checks?			
Do you receive past-due notices?			
Are you paying the minimum amount due on bills?			
Do you dip into your savings/401k to pay expenses?			
Have you had to borrow from friends?			
Are you upside down in your mortgage?			

If you answered yes to more than a couple of these, you might be in need of a tune-up. If you answered yes to > 5, you might need a shakeup.

Spending

Our spending patterns have changed drastically over the last few generations due to technological advancements, economic shifts, and our values. A recent comparison[313] showed the following shift in family consumption shares of the budget:

Expenditure area	1917–1919	1986-1987
Food	41%	19%
Housing	27%	34%
Transportation	3%	26%
Clothing	17%	5%
Health care	5%	4%
Other	7%	12%

Your two biggest lifetime expenses outside of raising children are your home and vehicles. They make up 60% of the average household budget. If you and your spouse buy a vehicle every 5 to 7 years, you will buy 20 vehicles between the 2 of you over your lifetime. If you buy a new one every time, that could range from $300,000 to $500,000. If you have just one mortgage of $200,000, you will pay at least $400,000 for that home if you have a 5 percent interest rate. So between these two purchases, you could spend nearly half of your lifetime earnings! This obviously varies from family to family; nevertheless, these two expenditures will drive your future. Be very wise in how and when you purchase these. Do not rush, do much research, get much counsel, and be in unity with your spouse.

Regardless of the spending category, it is imperative, with all of the financial and economic risk circling us like a buzzard in the sky, that we have our financial houses in order. Some very simple questions that often go unanswered are as follows:

- Do both spouses know the details of your current financial condition?
- Do you have a financial plan? A spending plan? A budget? A retirement plan?
- Are plans clearly defined and targeting different time periods? Monthly? Yearly? Long-term?
- Do you know how much you spend annually on food, clothing, shelter, transportation, interest, etc.?
- Do you spend as much time planning your financial future as you do on recreation—entertainment? sports? television?

Making some little changes could radically change your financial future. An investment portfolio change or just halting a habit such as smoking or eating lunch out can pay for a college education and a couple of years in retirement. In *Ease the Squeeze*, I detail a number of tools to get out of debt, set up a budget, reduce spending, save, and give more.

Every man ought to have money on his mind.
No man ought to have money on his heart.

Legacy Lesson: We have a great opportunity to pass on a financial heritage to our children. Basic money management, disciplines and self-control will allow you to have an impactful 2nd half and make a generational impact.

CHAPTER 48

HOW TO ACHIEVE FINANCIAL FREEDOM

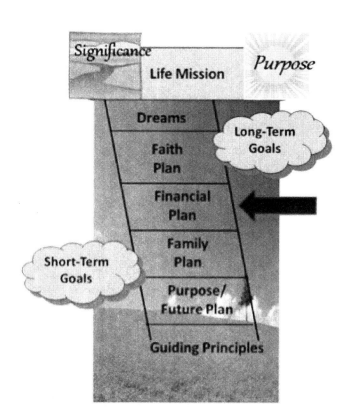

" *What* exactly is *financial freedom?*" I have read many different definitions of it. Almost all of the definitions and solutions are focused on a black-and-white financial answer. We like to package our answers into sound bites that make everything seem simple. But life is not simple, nor is pursuing financial freedom an easy, simple task. Financial freedom is not "more stuff." In fact, it is not just "getting out of debt."

I believe that one can be out of debt and still not be living in financial liberty and freedom, especially if he or she is ignoring other foundational issues. Our society has been saturated with what Wall Street and the American dreammakers have told us is financial freedom. One of the most rewarding and fulfilling moments of our family's life was when we could say that we owed no man anything. We were completely and totally debt free! *That* is real freedom! We no longer feel handcuffed. We were free to give. We were free to pursue God's dreams and leave a legacy. But there is more to it than just owing no man anything. You are free *financially* when you

1. are completely and totally debt free (owing no man);
2. can truly feel *content* with what you have;
3. truly know that *everything*—100 percent—is God's, and you live like it;
4. give cheerfully, generously, completely, and immediately;
5. have conquered the tithe "law," are not bound by 10 percent, and give freely above that amount;
6. obey when God speaks and give sacrificially (beyond what you can foresee);
7. can properly balance temporal and eternal investments;
8. and your family are united;
9. know where your money goes;
10. have a financial plan for your second half/retirement;
11. are free from excesses; and
12. live selflessly and serve others *above* yourself.

Do some of these goals seem unachievable? Join the club! Although we have not yet achieved all of these goals, with God's help and our own self-discipline, we have accomplished most of them. Some of these goals will require a continuous, daily challenge and struggle and will not be achieved once for all. However, we are living proof that you can and will achieve them in life—if you practice two simple (not really) things: *action* and *obedience.*

Here are a few tests to see how financially free you are.

Readiness Test

1. Who really owns your material things? Does the way you live reflect that?
2. How badly do you want to be financially free? Are you willing to make some radical changes to reach that goal?
3. What if the stock market crashed today? Would you still be financially free?
4. What if fire destroyed all of your property? Are you prepared?
5. What if you lost your job today? Are you prepared?
6. What if your spouse/parents/family died today? Are you prepared?
7. What if God called you to the ministry or mission field today? Could you go?
8. Do you still feel stressed or bound although you might be out of debt?
9. Does watching the stock market make you anxious?
10. If a major unexpected medical emergency arose, could you afford it?
11. What if a major energy crisis occurred and significantly affected your finances?

12. What if you had an unexpected child (or even a planned child for that matter)?

13. If you died today, would it put your family in financial turmoil? Have you left them with a plan and an inheritance? Do you have a will?

14. If you died today, what would your epitaph say? Have you left a legacy? What would your financial legacy be?

15. If you died today, would Jesus say, "Well done good and faithful servant. You took care of what I let you borrow during your short time on my earth"?

Warning Signs Test

Following are some warning signs that indicate potential troubles on the horizon. Score yourself according to the following color scale:

RED (This describes me/us perfectly.)
YELLOW (I/we struggle some.)
GREEN (You must be talking about someone else.)

Problem area	Assessment		
Considering debt consolidation	GREEN	YELLOW	RED
Not paying off credit cards at the end of month	GREEN	YELLOW	RED
Paying bills late	GREEN	YELLOW	RED
Creditor calling	GREEN	YELLOW	RED
Spending more than you make	GREEN	YELLOW	RED
Savings are minimal	GREEN	YELLOW	RED
Giving is less than 10 percent	GREEN	YELLOW	RED
Giving is not joyful	GREEN	YELLOW	RED
Anxious about the stock market	GREEN	YELLOW	RED
Overtime or second job is necessary	GREEN	YELLOW	RED
Hiding charges from your spouse	GREEN	YELLOW	RED
Domestic disputes about finances	GREEN	YELLOW	RED
Daily concern over your investments	GREEN	YELLOW	RED
Time spent thinking about money/finances	GREEN	YELLOW	RED
Not able to invest in your 401k to the maximum	GREEN	YELLOW	RED

Scoring:

10 or more Red = Time to make some radical changes—a financial overhaul is needed.

5–9 Yellow or Red = Time to make some changes—too many warning signs.

0–4 Yellow or Red = Time to make some targeted changes— tune-up in certain areas.

Read Proverbs 27:23 and Luke 14:28.

We must know the condition of our finances, consider the costs before large expenditures and investments, and then take appropriate action. Although you might not have sheep running around your backyard, you do have kids and you do have college and "your second half" to pay for, so you must know the condition of your finances (your flock). This is one of the most critical steps toward financial freedom. You may have failed up to now with money management. Now is the time to take action!

 "Consider the Cost," Steve Camp

Generational Giant

R.H. opened a small thread-and-needle store in Boston. He worked hard, but the business failed within a year. His second store failed the next year. His third attempt, a partnership, did not work out. He moved to another state for his fourth attempt, which did fairly well for a while, but then they sold out to a competitor. He had learned a lot from these four failures, so started a fifth business. It too failed. But he was not defeated. The next year he tried business number six. His advertising and low prices were clever, but he declared bankruptcy three years later. R.H. then moved to another state and worked as a stockbroker. He made some modest money and then determined that a seventh try in retail was in order. In 1858, R.H. opened a fancy dry goods store in Manhattan, and after twelve months he was grossing $80,000 a year. Nearly twenty years later, the store averaged more than $1 million in annual sales. R.H. Macy learned from all of his failures and revolutionized retail trade. Today, the company serves customers with about two hundred Macy's stores!

"No one who is financially bound is spiritually free."
—Larry Burkett

Legacy Lesson: Getting out of debt and having a financial plan frees you to live a fulfilling second half, to be content and to give more. Doing so will help you impact someone else's legacy sooner.

CHAPTER 49

YOUR FINANCIAL FUTURE: A SOUND PLAN- A BUDGET AND MORE

*S*omeone always seems to be reaching out for your hard-earned money or tempting you to give it to them. The shopping temptations are growing by the year. "Shopping center space has grown every year for the past 30 years and has more than doubled to 7.2 billion square feet since 1980. That figure has grown 4 times as fast as the population, and every American has 22 square feet of shopping center space. Sweden and the United Kingdom are next with 3 square feet of shopping center space per capita."[314] Corporate advertising budgets are at record levels due to their effectiveness in influencing consumers.

> *"Many of the desires of the individual are no longer even evident to him.*
> *They become so only as they are synthesized, elaborated, and nurtured by advertising and*
> *salesmanship. Few people at the beginning of the nineteenth century needed an adman to*
> *tell them what they wanted."*
> —John Kenneth Galbraith

The first part of a sound financial plan is getting your spending in order. I will touch on a few tools here, but they are covered in great detail in *Ease the Squeeze.*

1. A Spending Plan—The Daily Spend Sheet
2. A Save-to-Spend Plan
3. A Big-Ticket Plan
4. A Debt Hit List
5. A Cash-Only Control List
6. The Budget

Tool 1: The Daily Spend Sheet

What is the Purpose of the Daily Spend Sheet?

To pinpoint *exactly* where your money is going.
To establish accountability for your expenditures.
To instill discipline in your financial record keeping.
To set you on your way toward financial freedom!

Completing the Daily Spend Sheet for your family for two to three months is really the only way to see how much you are truly spending. We *think* that we know what we're spending, but we really do not. The tool simply documents every nickel that you spend and totals the dollars by day and category. Many other sophisticated tools and software exist, but I suggest this simple method that maximizes your participation.

It has been said that the road to financial freedom is 80 percent behavior and 20 percent knowledge.

A Wake-up Call!

After doing this simple exercise, I realized that I was frittering away *$1500 a year* at work on coffee, periodic lunches, and vending machine purchases. It is not always easy to begin a new daily habit. Collecting receipts and writing down all of my purchases at the end of the day was tough initially, but became simpler after a couple of weeks of discipline. They say it takes 3 weeks to create a new habit, and another 3 weeks to make it for a lifetime. If you make one financial change out of this book other than giving, it should be to complete this simple spreadsheet. I can almost guarantee that it will have a positive impact on your financial situation when the alarm clock goes off after 60 to 90 days.

"First you make a habit, then a habit makes you!"

Tool 2: Save-to-Spend List

Why the Save-to-Spend List?

To save money for expenses that you know will occur throughout the year.
To plan for those mini-surprises.
To help you avoid borrowing from others and to begin borrowing from yourself.
To encourage you to live within your means.

Another area of struggle for some people is non-regular expenses that seemingly pop up at the worst possible time. Money for such expenses usually is not available because most people typically do not save regularly for such expenses. We know that these "non-regular" expenses are coming. Many of them occur on the same day and time each year;

yet, we do not plan accordingly. We do not limit our spending when we are fully aware that we cannot pay cash for them. Some typical examples of such expenses include:

- insurance,
- home improvement,
- furniture,
- Christmas and other gifts,
- automobile maintenance and tags,
- vacation,
- pet,
- medical, and
- some of the "Big-Ticket" items.

Generate your "save-to-spend list" for those expenses that occur non-regularly throughout the year. This list actually will be part of your budget and should be adjusted accordingly as you become more familiar with your spending patterns and cash flow.

You might need to reduce these items or delay some of your "Big-Ticket" items until your debt is paid off or reduced significantly. Radical changes might be necessary in some cases. Even if you cannot currently afford to save for these items now, you will be able to do so within a few months as you reduce your debt.

> *"Make all you can, save all you can, give all you can."*
> —John Wesley

Tool 3: The Big-Ticket List

What is the Purpose of the Big-Ticket List?

To avoid surprises that will cause you to slip into the credit trap.
To prioritize your major expenditures.
To look toward the future so that you can save in advance.
To help you spend less than you make!

One of the major areas people avoid is preparing for their *major expenditures*. They usually avoid this for 2 reasons. First, if they analyzed it too much, they would realize that they really could not afford many "big-ticket" items. Many people are just struggling to pay their current bills, and they want to avoid cutting back on some expenses. Second, most people do not plan more than a week ahead in their finances anyway.

The entire family should generate this list annually. It should include all potential "big-ticket items" that you expect to purchase during the next 12 to 18 months. After you have completed the list, target an expenditure *month* and an estimated *cost*. After your budget is complete this list will give you an idea of what you can afford and cannot afford. This list will also help you differentiate between your *wants* and *needs!*

Think Before You Buy!

Always ask the following questions before making a major purchase:

1. Is it on our Big-Ticket List?
2. Should I discuss it with the rest of the family? (Set a minimum dollar amount that *requires* family approval before purchase. We use $50.)
3. Can we afford it?
4. Do we need it *now?*
5. Can it wait until next year? How long can we delay the purchase?
6. Can we buy it used?
7. Is it on sale?
8. Have I priced it multiple times so that I know what a *great* price is?
9. Have I waited sixty days once I get the desire to buy a Big-Ticket item?
10. Is it a *want* or a *need?*
11. Have I prayed about it?
12. Will this purchase affect my giving priorities and commitments?
13. What will I need to give up or sacrifice as a result of making this purchase?
14. Will this impact our ability to save, invest, or pay for college or retirement?

Tool 4: The Debt Hit List

What is the Purpose of the Debt Hit List?

To begin accountability to a specific plan for becoming debt free.
To set specific goals for specific debts.
To establish a timeframe/long-term plan to be totally and completely financially *free!*
To encourage you to end the addiction of debt.

Many people who begin the debt-payoff journey never totally solve the problem because they have not made a commitment to *no new debt!* If you have struggled with credit card debt, I would recommend destroying all but 1 card (for emergency only) and make a written vow not to use them again until you have regained control. We destroyed all but 1 card and did not use it for 2 years. Now we use credit cards for frequent flier miles and pay them off at the end of the month.

Read My Lips—No New Debt!

I have known some people who became radical in their new debt-free journey. They froze their credit cards! Then if they had a "spending bug" hit them, it would be very difficult to use the card. Others have cooked them at 350 degrees until they melted and then framed them as a reminder of their commitment. We just cut our credit cards in half and moved on. In parallel with completing the Daily Spend Sheet, you should take a "photograph" of how much debt you currently have. This exercise will help you determine how you want the picture to look in 3 months, 6 months, 1 year, 3 years, etc. The Debt Hit List is a simple tool that documents *all* of your current outstanding debts.

Begin by listing each of your current debts and the total balance owed. Also identify the current minimum payments for each debt so that you can identify your minimum monthly outlays and establish your monthly budget based on your debt payments. Next, prioritize the payoff of your debts. Always prioritize to eliminate the *smallest* debt *first!* This will allow you both to see immediate progress and to apply the previous monthly allocation to the next highest debt as soon as it is paid off. I always recommend paying off the cards with the small balances first so that you can gain some momentum. Set a target date for each payoff, and identify major milestones: credit card payoffs, auto payoffs, and finally the mortgage! You will see a snow-ball effect (the *freedom multiplier*) as you apply the amounts that you were previously paying towards numerous debts to the quickly pared-down list of debts.

Tool 5: The Cash-Only Control List

Why the Cash-Only Control List?

To aid you in monitoring specific budget line items.
To help you develop new spending habits and to break you of your old habits.
To make your money more difficult to part with. (Cash is harder to spend than credit!)
To focus you on specific areas that can quickly affect your debt pay-off plan.

Independent financial advisor Dave Ramsey references a recent Dun and Bradstreet study that showed that you *spend as much as 64 percent more when using credit cards versus spending cash.* "You do not emotionally register the pain that you do when you lay down cash. When you use cash it hurts and you tend to spend less. Cash is visual and emotional and a great behavioral management tool." After my wife and I completed our Daily Spend Sheet for six months, I realized that I needed an "allowance" for certain areas. When the "allowance" is gone—it is gone! This is not necessary for every expense area, but it is necessary for some areas. My vending machine weakness could have paid off 3 credit cards quickly! We discovered we needed to make some immediate changes.

Cash control does not need to be a permanent part of your freedom plan, but you should use it until you get a firm grip on your spending and budget. A one-year focus on cash and no new debt might be realistic. A little friendly debate and compromise within the family will need to occur on the specific items that might require a "cash focus," especially when you are establishing the actual dollar amounts! Be gentle! To avoid too much conflict, you might want to start conservatively and then get more aggressive as you pursue debt reduction! You will want to develop the Cash-Only Control List as a family, but typical items to be included are:

- recreation/entertainment,
- dining out,
- vending machine purchases/coffee,
- groceries,

- books/magazines/music,
- hobbies,
- clothing,
- health/beauty,
- allowances, and
- miscellaneous. (Beware of lumping too much into this category!)

After you have identified cash focus areas, and preliminary amounts for each category then create a **storage location** for your cash accounts. Storage ideas include envelopes, cookie jars, or soup cans. Label each account separately and include a detailed expenditure list nearby to monitor your spending for each item. The beauty (or frustration) of this system is that when your monthly allocation of cash is gone, *it is gone!*

THE BUDGET

This is one of the most frightening words in the English language. Someone has estimated that only 3 percent of Americans actually have a budget. Most people have attempted a budget at one time or another in their lives, but then they drop it altogether after they failed. If a budget is unrealistic, it is nothing more than a piece of paper. However, if it is used correctly it can be a rudder for your family finances. The budget is the one document that addresses your life plan (your priorities), your giving plan and your financial plan. It ties them all together.

Why?

People have asked many times, "Why do I need a budget?" I believe that a few significant reasons exist for a budget, including the following:

- to know where your money is going.
- to set specific goals and promote accountability for achieving them.
- to have a roadmap (a plan) linked directly to your goals.
- to offer a realistic assessment of where you are today and changes needed.
- to stimulate communication with your spouse and family on priorities.
- to plan for unforeseen expenses.
- to plan and save for economic uncertainty.
- to pay cash for major expenditures (vacations, autos, big-ticket items).
- to prepare for retirement, career changes, children's education or a job layoff.
- to plan and save for emergency medical needs.
- to reduce debt quickly and purposefully (financial freedom!).
- to position yourself to be able to give generously, cheerfully, and flexibly.
- to build family unity.

Start your budget conservatively and adjust some of your spending patterns as necessary. If too aggressive, you might get frustrated and quit. Unity is key to creating a budget. It will be the most important document by which the family will live (other than the Bible) and will be critical for both short- and long-term planning. It should be flexible enough to change quarterly, if necessary, based on your progress and increased understanding of your spending patterns. Above all, *your budget must be realistic!* All of these tools and blank spreadsheets, plus a thorough section on budgeting, is included in *Ease the Squeeze* if you desire further detail.

STOP Refer to the appendices as discussed in the Future section, and set some financial goals for yourself. See the following illustration as an example.

Financial Goal	Target date (self)	Target date (spouse)	Target date (together)	Quarterly grade
Develop budget				
Spend less than we make				
Save-to-Spend Tool				
Big Ticket-Item Tool				
Get-of-Debt Plan				
College Expense Plan				
Investment Plan				
Start investing—Dollar cost averaging				
Rebalance portfolio				
Giving plan				
Retirement discussion				

Measure your progress against your goals, and determine what needs to change to get back on track or if any goals need to change.

Legacy Lesson: Financial management takes discipline and planning. Avoiding action only delays your ability to leave a lasting legacy.

CHAPTER 50

INVESTMENT STRATEGIES FOR SUCCESS

"The wise man saves for the future,
but the foolish man spends whatever he gets."
—Proverbs 21:20 (Living Bible)

"Sometimes I lie awake at night and I ask, 'Where have I gone wrong?' Then a voice says to
me, 'This is going to take more than one night.'"
—Charlie Brown, *Peanuts*, Charles Schulz

*H*ow much you spend or save is very dependent upon how you were raised and how you are "built." It is good to understand that fact before embarking on major investment decisions, planning for retirement, or early in a marriage! Your spouse might throw some knuckleballs at you over the years because he or she is built differently. Following is a little checklist that helps you discern your perspective about the future.

Who Are You?[315]

You and your spouse rank the following from 1 to 5
(1 = you fit best, 5 = you fit least).

1) The Strugglers: few financial resources, pessimistic about the future, little saved for retirement, unstable employment, expect to have to work to make ends meet or rely on Social Security ____ ____

2) The Anxious: have some retirement resources but not enough to be very confident about the future; stable employment; concerned about health care; see retirement as a time of economic challenge, not leisure ____ ____

3) The Enthusiasts: have significant retirement savings, optimistic about retirement, anticipate freedom from responsibilities and look forward to enjoying leisure, don't plan to work, confident about health care and work ____ ____

4) The Self-Reliants: high likelihood of significant retirement savings, anticipate being connected to the community, anticipate doing more volunteering, plan to work part-time in retirement ____ ____

5) Today's Traditionalists: middle income, moderate retirement resources, support entitlements, expect some family support, favorable view of Social Security and Medicare, confident in having adequate health coverage, expect to work in retirement ____ ____

This survey was given to Boomers recently. At the time the survey was taken, most respondents fell into one of three categories: "Self-Reliants" (30 percent), Today's Traditionalists (25 percent), and "The Anxious" (23 percent). Obviously, this can vary greatly depending upon the state of the economy, the stock market, and overall economic uncertainty.

Investment Choices—WHERE?

Unless you want to be 75 years old and living on Ramen noodles, you need to put your savings somewhere. Choosing how to invest your hard-earned money is one of the most difficult decisions you will make. The best thing you can do is to have a mix of investments. Some will have higher risk than others. The key is to understand the risks and the rewards. Having a diversified portfolio will help you to reduce risk when a downturn occurs in one area, industry, or investment type. American Express publishes a *Common Sense Guide to Personal Money Management,*[316] that includes a table that identifies potential risk/return. The only addition I included was "Giving." I look at this as an eternal investment that is low risk, high reward!

Higher Potential Return / Higher Potential Risk

GIVING		
Options	Commodities	Futures
Foreign Market	Stocks and Bonds	Precious Metals
Speculative	US Common Stocks	and Bonds
Real Estate	Investment	Properties
Growth Mutual Funds	High Grade	Common Stock
Balanced Mutual Funds	High Grade	Preferred Stock
High-grade	Corporate/Municipal Bonds	Fixed Annuities
Investment	Certificates	Certificates of Deposit
Treasury Securities	Money Market	Accounts
FDIC-Insured	Savings Accounts	Cash

Lower Potential Return / Lower Potential Risk

Many people are terrified to invest because they have been burned before. Many people I know sold low, and got out of the market at the bottom of the collapse, and stayed out. They have missed out on major gains after the collapse. Sometimes the fear of losing outweighs the risk of any gains. Sometimes playing it safe is the right game plan. Sometimes it is the absolutely worst game plan and can cost you. I think we are in one of those seasons now, where playing it safe might make sense.

We personally are not invested heavily in the high-risk areas at this time. We do have a portion of our investments in stocks and bonds, but instead of being too heavily invested in actively managed funds that often have high-load fees (commission), trading fees, and expense ratios, we choose index funds.

Hopefully you have decided not to put all of your eggs in one basket. Where you save and invest might be just as important as how much you save and invest. Once you decide where to invest, you next need to decide how to invest.

Diversification and Risk

"Divide your portion to seven, or even to eight,
for you do not know what misfortune may occur on the earth."
—Ecclesiastes 11:2 (NASB)

Dividing up your investments reduces risk. I have known people who had too much invested in their company stock or in real estate, and when a financial collapse or housing crash occurred, they were set back twenty years. Dividing your portions helps insulate you from swings and market shocks.

Have a plan and stick to it, but reevaluate your plan and risk levels at least yearly. A portion of your money could be split into housing (own house or rental), in money markets, bonds, stocks, gold, mutual funds, foreign stocks, large companies, small companies, etc.

I think that we will not continue to run from inflation and high interest rates and I also believe that our currency, the U.S. dollar might eventually be in for a beating. The million dollar question is: When? Unfortunately, no one knows that.

Diversify. It is not safe to have all of your investments in one country, one stock, or one investment area. Other countries continue to grow faster than the United States. In fact, U.S. growth has nearly flattened while countries such as China and India grow at or near double-digit rates. More and more money is being poured into international markets. Americans have increased their foreign equity fund allocations from 13 to 27 percent over the last decade.[317]

Study and get good counsel. Again, many people fall prey to a "sure thing" because they are only getting counsel from one person. Read, study, pray, and seek advice of experts. There are many excellent books and ministries on the subject of finance, including *Sound Mind Investing* by Austin Pryor, Crown Financial Ministries, Christian Financial Planning Institute, and many others.

Investing—When and How?
Dollar-Cost Averaging

Many people foolishly try to time the market. I don't know anyone who wants to buy high and sell low, but timing the market turns into gambling of the highest adventure. Guessing when to get in and when to get out of the market is akin to playing slot machines in Vegas. Timing the market is risky business. Even trying "spiritual investing" by praying when to enter and exit is a slippery slope, although I have done pretty well with this approach. God doesn't want to pick winners and losers, although I cannot discount how He might allocate His favor and anointing.

The best approach for ensuring that you don't buy high and sell low is to have steady, regular investments. This is called "dollar-cost averaging." Instead of attempting to guess the market's directions, just keep saving and investing regular amounts at regular intervals. With this approach, you will be buying more shares when prices are low and fewer shares when prices are high. Over months and years, this approach will average the cost of your shares. The hard part about this is when the market is down or way down. This becomes very important to continue investing during these times.

Don't make this too difficult. It simply means to invest the same amount each month, through thick or thin, crash or bull market. In down times, that monthly amount buys more shares. In up times, that monthly amount buys fewer shares. Instead of risky guesses, this is a disciplined approach that will yield diversification, and help you avoid greed and also avoid fear and a daily watching of the market. Rejoice when the market goes down. You are buying at a discount! Rejoice when the market goes up. You are doing better on paper!

Swim upstream. When others are panicking and exiting, that is the time to consider buying. When others are jumping on bandwagons of extreme investment schemes, and pinnacles of performance, these might be bubbles ready to burst, and it might be a time to consider exiting.

Other Considerations

People know what they should be doing; they just delay taking action. Here are some investing priorities that will help you reach your long-term goals:

- Automate your investments. Make it a non-negotiable. Have money taken right from your paycheck.
- Maximize your 401k matches. The 401k is actually replacing Social Security in regard to money you can actually count on in your retirement.
- Stay diversified.
- Do not panic or react in the heat of the moment.
- Keep some cash.
- Consider Individual Retirement Accounts; they are subject to income levels, but withdrawals are tax free.
- Consider Roth IRAs.
- Consider Health Savings Accounts—you can stash pretax dollars into an account that grows tax free if you use the funds for medical expenses.
- Give! Give to your church, educational institutions, charities, and your kids—you might get to itemize deductions and deduct those gifts, depending upon your income level.

A Financial Advisor?

Many people choose the "do-it-yourself" approach and shun financial help. "According to recent studies, nearly 30% of young investors choose not to use a financial advisor; of those, about 40% say they can get better returns on their own. Self-directed Gen-X investors saw their assets grow 28% from 2009 to 2010, compared with just 3% for those with advisors. Also, nearly 60% of them describe themselves as conservative investors."[318] Many of these investors have been through the dot-com and real estate crashes, so they are a little suspicious. Let me say up front, truth in advertising, that I do not use a financial advisor. Although I am by no means a trained broker, I tend to do a lot of the planning myself with study, calculators, and spreadsheets. In fact, I have done better than many of the brokers or high-load funds over the past few years. You might decide to outsource this activity to a paid professional, so a financial advisor might be a perfect match for your long-term planning.

The first step in deciding on a financial advisor is to research. You might get a Certified Financial Planner to advise you and help you with the plan. Take advantage of that first free visit. Find someone you and your spouse are comfortable with both personally and professionally. Check references, history, experience, and credentials. Think about exactly what you want. Make a list of questions, and be sure that you understand how they are compensated. Is it a fee or a flat rate? Does the advisor receive any commission, reimbursement, or incentive for selling specific types of investments? Are you comfortable with the advisor on a personal level?

Charles Schwab provides a good list[319] of things to consider when choosing an advisor:
- Educational background
- Years in Business
- Number of clients
- Assets under management
- Services offered
- Preferred types of investments
- Commission or fee-based compensation
- Minimum assets required per client
- Results for similar client
- Who maintains control

Warning

Many financial counselors and advisors who are linked with investment products are salespeople who put their financial needs ahead of yours. In essence, they have a legal conflict of interest. Most of them will sell you something that puts extra money in both their pocket and their companies.

Index Funds

A stock market index fund is like a grocery basket with thousands of stocks in it that represents the entire market. You can buy index funds in many countries and also in stocks and bonds. These usually outperform these high-load funds over the long term anyway. In a recent study,[320] "96% of actively managed mutual funds underperformed the U.S. market index after fees, taxes, and survivorship bias."

*"In aggregate, people get nothing for their money
from professional money managers. . . . The best way to own common stocks is through an
index fund.[321]"*
—Warren Buffet

*"The most efficient way to diversity a stock portfolio
is with a low fee index fund."*
—Paul Samuelson, 1970 Nobel Prize in Economics

*"It's getting worse, the deterioration by professionals is getting worse.
The public would be better off in an index fund."[322]*
—Peter Lynch, one of the greatest mutual fund managers of his day

Legacy Lesson: Investing advice must be tailored to your financial and spiritual goals. It must take into account your short term and long term goals. When, where, and how much you invest greatly influences the timing your when, where and how of your 2nd half!

CHAPTER 51

FAMILY AND FINANCES

$\mathcal{I}$n a recent survey,[323] retiree couples were asked to share their best financial advice for newlyweds. The top four items were:

1. Make all financial decisions together.
2. Make a budget and stick to it.
3. Make sure you have an emergency fund to cover six months of expenses.
4. Don't hide expenditures from each other.

Spouses are rarely built the same. Before marriage, love is discussed more than money. As couples get to know each other over the years, money can take a front seat in discussions as they often find that different hobbies and different levels of risk-taking lead to money disagreements or at least affect a family budget. Men and women truly are different, and emotions can run high regarding money matters.

Although we are built differently, it is encouraging to know that we have similar fears and similar goals. In a recent love-and-money survey,[324] "the number one financial fear among men and women was not having enough money for retirement. Both men and women also ranked their biggest financial goals in exactly the same order, with paying down debt and saving for retirement as the top two spots."

Here are some additional survey results:

- 65% maintained joint bank accounts.
- 70% talked about money with their spouse weekly.
- 36% of men and 40% of women lied to their spouse about a purchase.
- The biggest cause of "money fighting" was about debt (37%), followed by spousal spending.
- 62% of men said they were more willing than their wife to take risks; only 19% of women asserted the same thing.
- Spending on children was a common source of conflict, more so than investments or saving for retirement

You might look at your spousal differences as hot and cold, oil and water, or maybe even gasoline and matches. We are built differently and we need to take advantage of and see those differences as a benefit rather than as a wedge. We need to seek each other's wisdom before making major expenditures or investing decisions.

According to a number of finance professors,[325] "men are more often than not the greater risk takers, and more likely to implode their investment accounts, chase get-rich-quick stocks, and try to second guess the economy's direction. Some people suggest that women's investment returns beat men's returns, on average, by one percentage point annually because they trade less frequently, take fewer risks, and expect lower returns."

Communicate, Communicate, Communicate

You have heard it said: Location, location, location." That is so true for real-estate, and it is also true for retirement. The unfortunate reality is that many couples avoid this topic of discussion until the months or years just before retirement, quite possibly because a previous conversation did not go smoothly. It is so important for communication and unity on the major expenditures and major decisions in life.

A spouse's assumptions about finances and retirement will vary. Your dreams will differ, and your goals might clash. You can almost count on that. Thus, the tough discussions should take place long before you enter your 50s or 60s. You are not alone if you are different than your spouse. In a recent study,[326] only 41% of couples report making investment decisions for retirement jointly. 33% of couples don't agree or don't know where they plan to live in retirement. 47% of couples approaching retirement don't agree on whether they will work in retirement. 34% of couples have different lifestyle expectations once they are no longer working. Far more women (45%) than men (27%) claimed to be "worriers."

Communication about spending and investments is necessary. Men fear losing their jobs and making bad investments significantly more than women do. Men overwhelmingly make the final spending decisions about cars and investments; women have the last word on major appliances and buying things for the kids. Different is not bad; consider it complementary. Ensure that you and your spouse understand each other and have agreed on a plan. One of the worst things that happened during the recent financial collapses is that many spouses and families were surprised when a collapse occurred and they had not had a discussion about the risk levels of the spouse who made the decision. Finances and investments are not enjoyable to talk about in most families, but it must be done.

STOP Schedule some time with your spouse to talk money. Talk about your budget, college expenses, and investments. What are your retirement goals/plans?

Document, Document, Document

We discussed documenting your spending plan (budget) and your financial plan. Without these things written down, you will make assumptions that are usually wrong. There is no need to guess at these numbers. They are factually known for each family. These "disconnects" could lead to vastly differing plans for savings, investments, and spending decisions. Keep all financial records available for both spouses. This will help if an emergency or disaster occurs. It also ensures transparency. Do not assume each spouse understands the family financial situation. Usually, one spouse has a bent toward handling the family money. Sit down and review your finances regularly and retool as necessary. You might need to rebalance your investments if the market has swayed significantly.

Work!

With our financial downturn, the topic of employment might be a difficult one to address for some families. One spouse might be out of work for an extended time. As providers, men have a responsibility to work. We must be diligent in ensuring that we do this for our families. There might be seasons of temporary unemployment, but eventually some work can be found. Some key scriptures on the topic are as follows.

- Work with your own hands. Do not be dependent upon anyone (1 Thess. 4:11-12).
- Provide for your immediate family and relatives (1 Tim. 5:8).
- Fight against laziness; be diligent about working (Prov. 10:4–5; 12:24; 13:4).
- If a man doesn't work, he shouldn't eat (2 Thess. 3:10).
- Deny self, and lay down your life for your family (John 10:15).
- Sacrifice, do good, and be rich in good works (1 Tim. 6:17–19, James 2:17-26).
- Find models, and look up to those who work hard (1 Thess. 5:12).
- Do not be out of balance with empty pursuits (James 1:10-11, James 4:13-15)

The Two-Income Decision

A tough decision for a couple might be whether the wife works. I recall our decision as we awaited the birth of our first daughter. God was challenging us to take a step of faith and have my wife manage our home and raise our children. It was a major decision and a financial challenge. We have been blessed for nearly twenty years with that decision. My wife is now contemplating work again (college expenses!). Some people might not be able to do this for that length of time. I encourage you to pray, fast, and seek God and, above all else, be united.

On the strictly financial end, having a spouse work often does not net as much cash for the family as one expects. Be sure to tally up all potential expenses. Here is one example of a $30,000 income or staying at home:

	Scenario 1	Scenario 2
Income: (after taxes)	$30,000	$0
Expenses:		
Childcare	$ 7,000	$0
Gas/transportation	$ 2,000	$0
Lunch/snacks/coffee	$ 2,000	$0
Wardrobe/clothes upper	$ 1,500	$0

Business items/miscellaneous	$ 1,000	$0
Cell phone/technology	$ 500	$0
Office social/miscellaneous	$ 1,000	$0
Stress/exhaustion	priceless	
Time with kids		priceless
Total expenses:	$15,000	
NET SECOND INCOME	$15,000	

This might be an extreme example, but be sure to consider all of the costs associated with entering the market. What is your family vision? What are you priorities? Obviously, the $15,000 full-time job is less attractive than the $30,000 full-time job. Be sure to do the math! We look back over the last 18 years, and my wife's not working was one of the best "major milestone" decisions we made. God blessed us with additional unplanned income and blessings we did not foresee.

Having Children

Children are not a light investment. The U.S. Department of Agriculture, Center for Nutrition Policy, compiled a report on the expenditures on children[327] that estimated child-rearing expenses at $10,000 (lowest income group) to $25,000 per year (highest income group). This includes housing, food, transportation, child care, clothing, health care, and other miscellaneous expenses. It does *not* include college education. So, to raise a child through college can cost $200,000–$400,000. If you tack on the college education, your budget quickly becomes a real challenge. Raising a child in the United Kingdom at approximately £201,000[328] (> $300,000), which included education. Various China sources showed ranges of 300,000 to 1,000,000 Yuan to raise a child ($50,000–$150,000).

If I had seen this before having kids, I might have choked. Having children is a step of faith. When we looked at the budget it never did add up. This is a step of faith that God will honor. Children are a blessing. We always found a way to make ends meet.

"Like arrows in the hand of a warrior, so are the children's of one's youth. How blessed is the man whose quiver is full of them."
—Psalm 127:4–5

Teaching Kids Money Management

"A recent *Schwab Teens* and *Money* survey of teens aged 16 to 18 reinforced the fact that frank discussions about money are essential in helping teenagers develop responsible financial habits. Nine of ten teens say that their family has been impacted by the recession, and the majority of these kids express a greater feeling of gratitude for what they have and a greater appreciation for how hard their parents work."[329]

Teaching them about the value of money and putting its role into proper life perspective is our job as parents. Seeing our values visibly acted out sends a powerful message. I recall involving our kids in a financial decision on our recent mission trip to Belize. We had one day allocated for vacation—and the cost of a boat trip and snorkeling. We were confronted with a need that one of the missionaries had for their child to attend a semester at college. It was nearly the exact amount that we had budgeted for our vacation day. We had a quick family meeting and let the kids make the decision as to whether we should give those funds to this family or to proceed with our vacation plans. It was a good time of having them grapple and wrestle with the decision and enact what we had taught them over the years in word about giving. We knew as parents that we wanted to help the family but what a great chance to involve the kids with the decision. We were surprised that there was no debate or discussion but that they wanted to give. It was very rewarding for us as parents, but more importantly, a great teaching moment. You will have daily opportunities to teach your kids about money management. Take advantage of those opportunities.

We also teach them the value of earning their money, so we do not allocate an "allowance." Rather, we give them "commission" based on how successful they are with their chores and jobs. If they do a poor job or spend less time than normal, they are compensated less. It is a powerful message. If possible, teach your kids or grandkids budgeting concepts at a young age. We used a Larry Burkett "My Giving" bank when the kids were younger that taught them to save 10% and give 10%. We also matched dollars they saved for a car/college. My wife teaches the kids the value of comparison shopping and coupons.

Following are some age-appropriate teachings you might consider.

Ages 4 to 6: Teach them the value of the currency and coins, use a piggy bank or giving bank; let them spend money and take them on shopping trips; have them give in the offering at church.

Ages 6 to 10: Start a weekly chore chart with compensation; open a savings account and match deposits; let them give money to different charities.

Ages 10 to 15: Get them a debit card; have them track their expenses; modify the chore chart with incentives or penalties for nonperformance; provide more emphasis and matching dollars for car and college; incentivize grades and consider rewards for A's; allow jobs outside of the home, such as babysitting, lawn work, taking care of pets, etc.

Ages 15 to 19: Focus on college savings, and incentivize extra savings; consider additional work outside the home or support a home business; let teens see you pay bills; put additional emphasis on debit/credit card teachings; take the kids on a missions trip and have them raise money; draft a budget/contract for college expenses (car, gas, etc).

"If you are not teaching your kids money management, someone is. . . ."

Legacy Lesson: Being on the same page as your spouse is critical. Take the time to understand each other and make decisions and generate a plan together. Involving and teaching your kids and grandkids money management and stewardship principles is leaving a great legacy.

CHAPTER 52

PROTECTING YOUR INVESTMENTS: PREPARING FOR HARD TIMES

"If we command our wealth, we shall be rich and free;
if our wealth commands us, we are poor indeed."
—Edmund Burke

I am not a doomsayer, and in this chapter you will not find me recommending that you convert all of your retirement funds to gold, dig a well, or buy a two-year supply of food. However, I do believe that another financial meltdown is coming and that the debt bubble and others will soon burst. This does not call for panic but rather for prudent planning.

How should one manage his or her money and invest in the event chaos occurs? Follow the thirty steps I outlined in Chapter 47. A book titled *Aftershock* looks at some high-risk investment options as well, notably in the chapters "Covering Your Assets" and "Cashing in on the Chaos." However, guessing at the timing of bursting bubbles is risky business. We have partially adopted a few of these strategies but will not fully adopt many of them. We are following the thirty steps I've outlined previously. We are researching and praying about downsizing our house; have paid off all debt, except the mortgage; and cut our expenses by 10–15 percent over the past year. We have done this partially because we expect another financial storm, but primarily because of the costs of college!

The Ultimate Survival Guide

This is not about living in a cave, moving to the country, or preparing for Y2K again. Rather, it is about prudent, logical preparation and readiness in the event of an emergency or another bursting bubble. You might choose to ignore this section, or to go to the extreme and plan for a massive financial collapse. I cannot counsel you. However, the odds are increasing that you will experience some crisis or disaster in the not-too-distant future. Just look back at the natural disasters, economic crashes, terrorism, power-grid blackouts, water shortages, blizzards, earthquakes, oil crisis, swine flu pandemics, etc. Some of them are real and local; others are distant and not a risk for you personally. What can you do that is practical? I would recommend doing at least five simple things:

1. reduce and pay-off your debt.
2. live within your means.
3. store some food and water.
4. buy some emergency gear.
5. develop plans for an emergency.

We are living in the wealthiest, richest of all times. Now is the time to get ready, not during a collapse.

Plan, Don't Panic

Yogi Berra once said, "It's difficult to make predictions, especially about the future." What will the tax rate be when you retire? Will there be any benefits left when you retire? Will your pension survive? Will the economy tank? What is the best investment? Where is the best place to give? What impact would a natural or financial calamity have on me?

We have all witnessed our share of financial chaos, earthquakes, tornados, and hurricanes, not to mention the calamity of war or a death in the family. Although we cannot control these things, we *can* control how prepared we are for a natural disaster. These events seem to be occurring more and more frequently, so you won't be viewed as the neighborhood Y2K loony anymore if you stock up on a few key things. Some very practical things you can do are:

1) Prepare a personal and family emergency supply kit—food and water (enough for three to five days), candles, matches, medical supplies, batteries, flashlights, prescription medicine, cash, fire extinguisher, first aid supplies, tools, etc.
2) Compile an emergency resource contact list—police, fire, ambulance, poison control center, doctors, utilities, family/friends/neighbors' phone numbers, etc.
3) Compile important paperwork and copies of documents—insurance, banking, passports, birth certificate, driver's license, will, etc.
4) Consider buying flood insurance if that is not covered by your homeowner's insurance. Consider buying earthquake insurance if you are not covered.
5) Buy some gold bullion. Have some cash on hand in the event of ATM outages.

Your Finances: Plan for the Holes in Your Pockets

- Plan for inflation.
- Plan for high interest rates, and lock in the rates as low as possible.
- Consider investing less aggressively (age dependent).
- Re-examine all of your insurance coverages.
- Understand your pension and Social Security income levels and risks.
- Contemplate a future without you—will, estate planning, legacy, etc.

Many websites have great checklists of things to include in your emergency kits. The Federal Emergency Management Agency is a good place to start. We have a small kit in the attic, a waterproof/fireproof small safe where we keep key documents and also a thumb drive and some CDs with our favorite pictures and videos. We also have a larger emergency kit in the pantry. You might also want to keep a small kit in one of your vehicles in case you are stranded.

Protecting Your Investments

"I'm not afraid of dying, I just don't want to be there when it happens"
—Woody Allen

Many horror stories exist of people whose dreams have been annihilated by a catastrophe. It could be a death, a fire, a flood, an illness, or even a lawsuit. Any of these events can lead to a financial nightmare. Part of your planning involves protecting your greatest asset—you and your family—against such a catastrophe. There is nothing more important than faith in God, but insurance also provides an extra level of security if you are able to afford it. Consider including the following as part of your long-term protection plan:

- Disability income insurance
- Life insurance
- Health insurance
- Liability insurance
- Car insurance
- Home insurance

A Will

Draft a will! It is surprising how many families do not have a will. In a 2009 survey, just 39 percent of adults reported having a will. Even fewer had a power of attorney, and fewer still had set up a trust."[330] This can lead to generational hurt and dissension, not to mention confusion and financial disarray. In fact, complete strangers might decide how to split up your estate and raise your children. Unless you appoint a guardian for your minor kids, their future will be determined by the court. You might want to leave a separate list of "bequests" that is also referenced in your will. Leaving a spouse and children to sort out who gets what could get messy. Some people also like to personalize their "send-off" and depict whether they want a traditional burial or a cremation. Although estate planning seems like something to do "down the road" and usually falls to the bottom of the priority list, it is absolutely necessary to be ready for the future. At least start preparing by making a will and executing power of attorney documents!

 Read Isaiah 38:1 and 2 Corinthians 12:14.

It is biblical to leave an inheritance for your children. It is also biblical to set your house in order. Since none of us knows the day or the hour we will breathe our last breath, now is the time to begin planning for that day.

Once the game is over, the king and the pawn go back in the same box.
—Italian Proverb

Worry

Refer to the scriptures I mentioned on worry in Chapters 15-16. Worry helps no one. Just plan and then react accordingly. If you are checking the stock market daily and watching your 401k balances daily or weekly, you might be worrying too much or at least focusing too much on monetary things.

"The more things you obtain the more you have to track them, plan for them, store them, analyze them, insure them, pay tax on them, dust them, fix them, discuss them with others, store them, and bequeath them."
—Larry Burkett and Ron Blue

"Money never made a man happy yet, nor will it. There is nothing in its nature to produce happiness. The more a man has, the more he wants. Instead of its filling a vacuum, it makes one. If it satisfies one want, it doubles and triples the creation of others. That was a true proverb of the wise man, rely upon it; "Better is little with the fear of the Lord, than great treasure, and trouble with it"
—Benjamin Franklin

Legacy Lesson: Passing on a financial inheritance is not as important as a spiritual inheritance, but you must prepare for the worst and have faith for the best. Don't let someone else declare your legacy.

CHAPTER 53

PREPARE FOR YOUR SECOND HALF / RETIREMENT: RETIRE EARLY!

When one gets to retirement, the tendency is to convince yourself that you have earned a break and now is the time for "me." Although on the one hand it is a new season of life and one to enjoy a shift in priorities, the challenge is to ensure a strong finish, to think generationally, and to leave a lasting legacy. Most often that will occur not by a self-indulgent lifestyle but rather by a laying down of your life, a sacrificing of your time, and a shifting of priorities to serving and giving.

Until the end of the nineteenth century, retirement planning was not as complicated as it is today. You worked until you were buried, or you became too old to work the farm or labor in the factory, and then your family took care of you. Retirement is actually a twentieth-century American phenomenon, and is not a Biblical concept. Emily Yoffe explains about the evolution of retirement: "In the 1880s, about 75 percent of men 65 and older were still in the labor force."[331] In the early 1900s, pensions became a more regular fixture and mandatory retirement took hold. The introduction of Social Security in the 1930s led to more workers leaving the workforce early. "In 1948, just under 50 percent of men 65 and older were still in the workforce. By 1968, it was just under 30 percent, and by 1988 just under 20 percent."[332] However, the era of earlier and earlier retirement seems to be over. In 2010, 22 percent of men over 65 were employed, and the number of women age 65 and older in the workforce increased almost 150 percent in the last thirty years.

It seems as though the closer we get to retirement, the more distant our goals seem. We feel the shortage of time and the urgency to save more. Many older adults are having to provide some financial support that they did not foresee. According to Gail Sheehy, "almost 70 percent of Baby Boomers are providing some financial support to their adult children and grandchildren."[333] The cost of health care for an aging population can take a major toll on not only our pocketbooks but also our emotions. Most people groups are living longer and longer, so the need to plan and save becomes even more critical. "According to the United States Life Tables, 83 percent of Americans will still be alive at age 65. Sixty-seven percent will live to be 75, and 38 percent will survive until 85.[334]

Are You Ready?

Yet more than half of Americans underestimate their life expectancy and are woefully unprepared financially for life's latter days. "The American Society of Pension Actuaries found that more than 50 percent of preretirees underestimate their life expectancy, and 46 percent have saved less than $50,000 toward retirement."[335]

The retirement landscape will change dramatically over the next generation. No longer will governments be able to afford the funding of an aging society. Current levels of state and company pensions, Social Security, and other benefits must change for countries to stay solvent. Many people are not saving enough, and have too much debt, too little job and career security, greater health care and education costs, more taxes, and greater risk to investments and stocks because of the global financial crisis that we continue to encounter. Be sure that you are communicating with your spouse about retirement. According to *Money* magazine, "Eighty-two percent of couples say they disagree about key basics, including the age at which they'll quit working and the lifestyle they'd like to maintain."[336] Brainstorm your individual wish lists, dreams, and needs, and then plan for a getaway to discuss and come up with a joint plan. Many of us procrastinate these tough discussions when they need to take place decades in advance.

The Aging Population

Our world is aging. This will affect some societies more than others over the next generation. China will have the most massive shift of those over the age of 65, but this is a worldwide issue, and governments worldwide will not be able to foot the bill. It is incumbent upon you individually to prepare for your own latter years. Consider the findings of HSBC's *The Future of Retirement* report, which interviewed 17,000 respondents in seventeen countries.[337]

	US	UK	France	China	India
% age 65—**2010**	13.0	16.6	17.0	8.0	5.0
% age 65—**2050**	21.6	22.9	27.0	23.0	14.0

A Happy Retirement

Retirement will be an opportunity for a new chapter in life, a time for rest and relaxation, family, fitness, and possibly new levels of service/volunteer, to put one's faith to action, or the pursuit of a new career, starting a business or other ambitions. How does the definition of a happy retirement vary from country to country? When asked what constitutes a happy retirement,"[338] the respondents' replies were surprisingly varied with different emphasis on faith, fitness, family, and the level of work.

	US	UK	France	China	India
No worries of money	73%	70%	67%	60%	50%
Loving family and friends	71%	65%	61%	66%	64%
Keeping fit	62%	64%	67%	84%	60%
Avoiding stress	56%	51%	32%	38%	53%
Ambitions and dreams	44%	37%	39%	17%	36%
Work you enjoy	42%	29%	14%	20%	48%
Having a strong religious faith	42%	12%	5%	10%	32%

The Chinese and Indian populations tend to plan more and save more, so they have fewer worries about money. The Chinese also tend to emphasize health and fitness more as they age. Americans and Indians plan to work more in retirement and also have more of a faith emphasis. Americans tend to desire pursuit of ambitions and dreams more.

Expectations About Retirement[339]

Another question asked regarding both one's financial condition versus that of parents in retirement and how worried one was about coping financially in retirement:

	US	UK	France	China	India
Better or worse than parents in retirement	-37%	-22%	-56%	62%	69%
Worried about coping financially in retirement	66%	62%	68%	67%	51%
Do not intend to retire	4%	1%	2%	0%	3%

Again, the Chinese and Indians believe that they will be better off than their parents, yet they are still worried about coping financially in retirement. In a recent Harvard study,[340] 84 percent of Boomers thought that their generation will need more money to live comfortably in retirement than did their parents. Much of this is due to the government debt situation and the fragile state of our economy. Different generations will deal differently with how they approach spending, saving, and retirement and what their expectations are of this future season of life.

Are You a Planner?

The next question focused on how much planning was done and the advice sought regarding finances.

The Types of Consumers:[341]

	US	UK	France	China	India
Nonplanners: disengaged	49%	36%	53%	20%	17%
Nonplanners: advice seekers	15%	25%	17%	3%	7%
Planners: active self-guided	14%	13%	17%	28%	26%
Planners: advice seekers	22%	26%	13%	49%	50%

The Americans and Europeans tended not to plan nearly as much as the Chinese and Indians. It is very clear in the data and evidence presented in the HSBC report that those who were planners tended to have retirement savings and investments that were five to ten times greater than those who were "non-planners."

"Those who have a financial plan in place and seek professional advice are the best off financially. They have the largest retirement assets out of all consumer types." Although many people are optimistic about retirement, "there is not much evidence that ordinary Americans have taken the steps to ensure their hopes and expectations for retirement are met. Although 67 percent are worried they haven't saved enough, 60 percent still have no plan in place! Those who have a plan in place are far more confident." [342]

HSBC recommends the following:
1) Set some clear goals, both short and long term.
2) Benchmark yourself.
3) Establish a comprehensive financial plan.
4) Implement the plan.
5) Review your plan regularly.

How Do You See Your Second Half / Retirement?

We discussed this topic in the Future section of the book, but it is very important that you begin to discuss how you see your latter years as it will impact your finances greatly. Put dreams and goals squarely on the table so that you do not make the hard decisions in haste. Discuss how you resolve these differences and determine what is most important to your spouse. This will require compromise and much prayer. Here are some questions you might want to tee up:

- What is your vision of retirement?
- How much do you want to travel?
- What are the top five things you want to do in retirement?
- How close do you want to be to family and friends?
- If living out of state from family/friends, how often will you visit them, and how much will it cost?
- Do you want to volunteer?
- How do you see your lifestyle changing?
- What age do you envision retiring?
- Is this a full retirement or do you plan to work in retirement?
- Do you see yourself living in a house, condo, RV, or apartment?

- Where would you want to live (beach, mountains, city, country, or overseas)?
- Do you foresee family members (parents or children) living with you?

STOP Discuss these issues with your spouse. Consider the fact that the Bible does not speak much of retirement. Do we need more leisure or more significance and influence?

Also, discuss what your biggest concerns are. In a recent survey the top-cited concerns were health-care expenses, inflation, pension/Social Security reductions, and death of a spouse. You might get to the root of some real spousal concerns about retirement or why some of the preceding questions were answered the way they were by discussing each other's concerns. According to the HSBC report, women tend to be less optimistic about retirement than men.

Retire Early!

According to a CNNMoney.com[343] poll, 45 percent of respondents intend to fully retire early, before age 65, whereas 26 percent intend to partially cut back on work before age 65. Most people want to start their "second half" as soon as possible but have no plan for doing so. Some people have no desire to quit their jobs and will work well into their 70s and 80s. Then there are the majority who would love to escape their "first-half" careers or life. A recent study[344] showed the "success factors" of these "early retirees." These focused individuals are more likely than the average person to

- Save for retirement outside of just their workforce plan (69 percent).
- Defer a high percentage of their salary into a retirement plan (a median of 10 percent)
- Start saving at a younger age (The median age early retirees begin saving is 25.)
- Have a thought-out retirement savings strategy. (Seventy-one percent of early retirees have either a written or a nonwritten plan.)
- Be very involved in managing and monitoring their retirement accounts. (Seventy-one percent of early retirees are very involved.)
- Save the same amount or more despite economic recessions. (Seventy-one percent of early retirees are doing this.)

Are you on track to retire early or on time?
How well are you doing at these success factors?

	Yes	No
Are you saving for retirement outside of your work plan?		
Are you saving 10 percent or more annually for retirement?		
Did you start saving for retirement at age 25?		
Do you have a written plan for retirement?		
Are you involved in managing your retirement accounts?		
Are you saving consistently despite economic ups/downs?		

If you could not answer yes to most of these questions, then you might not be able to retire early. But if you want to retire before you turn 90, you had better get going now! This might mean some radical financial changes, including a budget, getting out of debt, reducing expenses, and gaining additional income.

Retiring early sounds nice, but these six success factors are not easy, especially if you are not 25 anymore! You might have to sacrifice some things to bump up your savings and get a new plan on paper. Start now!

Money management is not about finding get-rich-quick schemes, getting into high-yield investments, or timing the market or finding magical formulas. For most of us who are not in the financial investment business, it is more about the basics, such as spending less than you make, effective financial planning, setting achievable goals, and following through on plans to achieve your goals. It is about information and action, not about short-cuts and short-term miracles.

Legacy Lesson: Having some of the tough discussions about your future now will actually allow you to make a 2nd half impact sooner. After having these discussions, taking some tough actions will be your ticket to an influential life. Make sure to involve God and your spouse.

CHAPTER 54

YOUR SECOND HALF / RETIREMENT MONEY: SAVING FOR IT AND SPENDING IT

Face the Music

*I*t seems difficult enough to keep up with paying bills on time, planning for your children's college expenses, and trying to save for retirement. One of the biggest failings with individuals and families regarding their finances is a lack of planning. Whether that be budgeting, paying off debt, saving for college, or planning for a retirement. Most of the time, this is because we just don't want to face the facts.

We know we don't have enough saved for our kids' college costs, or our nest egg is much smaller than it should be. Running from the issue will not solve it. It might be that you need to delay your retirement by three to five years because of the recent stock market roller coasters. It might be that you need to downsize your house when your kids are gone because you can't afford the taxes, upkeep, and insurance on a smaller income.

Save Early and Often

Almost everyone starts too late in saving for retirement or college expenses. "According to a Harris Interactive Survey, 1 in 5 adults over the age of 65 had not saved for retirement. Among all adults, 1 in 3 had not saved for retirement."[345] For a college graduate in his or her early 20's, saving $200 a month will lead to a hefty $1.2 million at retirement (age 67). For one who starts 10 years later in their early 30's, you'll have just $494,000 at age 67. Waiting that one decade costs ~ $700,000! Start early, or start now!

Your Home

As you approach and enter retirement, you might need to make an emotional and traumatic decision to sell your house since you will have less money for repairs, yard work, insurance, and taxes. Planning in advance is key to this determination so that you don't make a decision on a whim. Many people punt on this decision because of the drop in the housing market and depressed values. On the flip side, buying a smaller home might also be cheaper than it was several years ago. Because of the economy's fluctuations, many retirees are not moving out of state to warmer climates as did previous generations. "The trend among Boomers is not to move at all. The Boomers are staying put more than anyone though. People of that generation tend to own their own home and stay there."[346]

The children and grandchildren may play a key role in your decision. Costs and affordability will also play a role. The tradeoff and tradition/nostalgia of having the opportunity for your kids to come back to the house they grew up in versus the real need for the extra square footage, and higher property taxes and utility bills associated with this larger house is a financial analysis worth conducting. Each family's priorities will differ.

Selling a long-time home with memories can be an emotional event, so do not make the decision lightly. Years, not weeks, of planning and talking about the pros and cons are necessary. Leaving an area with a network of family, friends, church, or school connections is not easy. Also, the costs associated with selling and buying a house, and the risks and timing of the housing market, all play a part. However, moving the anchor can be an adventure, lead to a more rewarding life with a clean-slate start, be a big cost savings, and be part of embarking on your "second half."

Many books, websites, and financial calculators are available to assist you with both the "soft side" and the "money side" of the decision. Narrow your search by taking vacations over the years in your targeted spots. Some things to research:

- Talk to the locals and read the local papers
- Understand recreation and cultural attractions
- Consider the distance to outdoor, natural areas (parks, mountains, beaches)
- Understand political leanings
- Visit churches
- Research the year-round climate/weather
- Research/compare the tax rates (property, state, and city)
- Compare the cost of living
- Determine airport and medical locations
- Determine distances from family, friends
- Research crime rates
- Research weather risks (tornados, earthquakes, hurricanes, etc.)

Create a spreadsheet with things you care about, and rate each city. Conduct site visits, and develop a spreadsheet similar to the one you used in choosing a college.

Empty Nesters

Many empty nesters think that their big spending days are over! No more college bills, no more sports or music lessons, no more clothing splurges, no more unforecast expenses. Don't get too excited. The grandchildren are on the way. The aging parents might need help. The boomerang kid might be back. Many empty nesters splurge and impulse buy during their new-found freedom phase. Whether it be that costly hobby or spending therapy from those long frugal years, or the empty nester might simply be trying to fill a void, but the numbers are shocking. Many empty nesters and grandparents struggle with prioritizing their spending and instead spoil their children or grandchildren! Many of them know that they can't afford it, but the love outweighs the budget. Planning is essential.

A study released by the Center for Retirement Research at Boston College found that "when kids jump ship, parents *increase* their per capita consumption of nondurable goods by a rather startling proportion: an average of 51 percent!"[347]

The Jif Generation

"Nearly half of Americans 55 and older say they expect to provide support for aging relatives and adult children."[348] Empty nesters and early retirees are often subject to the "Jif" syndrome. They are the peanut butter that holds three generations together. The "sandwich" phenomenon can often lead to the nest getting refilled with either an aging parent or a recent college graduate who is unable to find work, or just continued expenses from parents' lending a helping hand. "Roughly 40 percent of Gen-X and Gen-Y have received financial support from their parents after college, while 25 percent of Gen-Y report parents are paying for discretionary items like phone bills, insurance and care expenses."[349]

Your parents might be unable to afford medical expenses or have been hurt by shrinking home values. You might get requests from kids for funds. Be wary of the new cash attacks and discretionary doldrums upon you. The mortgage down payment for a child. More gift and spending opportunities for grandchildren. More weekend jaunts. Children hit by financial challenges may need help with monthly expenses. It is hard to say no—to your kids, parents, and your splurging urge. The temptation to convert or renovate empty rooms. Graduation or continuing education expenses for you or children. Health-care coverage for parents. The list goes on. Plan for future expenses. More importantly, have those difficult discussions now! You might have to make an immediate decision to work longer, spend less, save more, or adjust your retirement expectations.

One of the most fruitful things you can do is to have a discussion *before* the event or *before* the requests start coming. Sit down with your child before they graduate to discuss some ground rules. Sit down with your parents before the tough decisions come. What is going on with their retirement funds, their estate, their health? Where can they cut some costs? What are their preferences regarding long-term care, selling their house, etc.? Create an action plan with your parents or with your child.

Having a rushed discussion with your parents about their desires when emotion takes over is the wrong time. Investigate long-term-care insurance, adult day care, or a home health aide. Costs vary wildly. Are you willing to have your parent live with you? Have you discussed it with your spouse? Have you prayed about it?

The best thing you can do is to anticipate expenses—whether they be for empty-nest or retirement. Some of these surprises can jeopardize your financial future if you don't plan for them. Some areas to consider in your financial planning are unexpected medical costs, inflation, replacement costs of high-ticket items (car, appliances, house, maintenance), relatives in need, and required distributions of funds from tax-deferred accounts. Sometimes these distributions push you into a higher tax-bracket, and that can also translate into higher Medicare premiums. All of these should be planned for before determining your retirement age or your "magic number" retirement amount.

Retirees

Many households operating in a retirement season cannot afford the transportation costs each year—gas, insurance, etc. "Households with 65- to 74-year-olds spend an average of $7033 on transportation each year!"[350] According to the Center for Retirement Research at Boston College, many of them are still paying on a mortgage. "Forty-one percent of U.S. households aged 60 to 69 maintained a mortgage."[351] This might motivate you to move to a community where shopping, pharmacy, and restaurants are within walking distance. This might mean fewer vacations or at least planning for those vacations.

All of the preceding items affect how much you need to save for retirement. It is important to plan for them all in your financial planning.

Have you incorporated aging parents, a boomerang kid, and any of these unforeseen costs in your financial planning?

How Much Money Do I Need to Retire?

Talk to a number of advisors about how much you should save for retirement, and you will get multiple answers. Just as you would get competitive bids for a major purchase, be sure to pursue varied counsel for this answer. Retirement calculators and financial advisors are plentiful. Get some simple answers, but also take the time to dive deep into the long-term planning aspects of how much you will spend each year and scenarios calculating how long you might live. The best calculators use dozens of variables and ask for frequent updates. Think of the "magic number" as a rule of thumb not as an absolute.

Normal retirement planning suggests that a couple's expenditures will increase a certain amount annually throughout retirement. However, data from the U.S. Bureau of Labor's Consumer Expenditure Survey[352] show that a couple's expenses actually decline as retirees age. So, some people are actually oversaving for retirement. A more realistic approach is to increase spending projections for inflation but to decrease expenses incrementally over the retirement years. This tug of war will balance out the risk. Inflation might increase your spending, and a conservative-spending retiree will not spend as much.

A Consumer Expenditure Survey showed a 27 percent reduction in average annual expenditures between the 55–64 age group and the 65–74 age group. Harry Dent[353] defines Consumer Expenditure Survey data into two-year groupings and summarized as follows:

Age	Average Expenditures	Annual Spending Decrease
55–59	$45,862	-
60–64	$38,218	16.7%
65–69	$32,103	16.0%
70–74	$27,517	14.3%
75+	$21,402	22.2%

Either approach yields a reduction in spending as an individual ages (on average). To analyze whether spending decreases voluntarily or out of necessity, one should view the net worth of these individuals. According to the U.S. Census Bureau, net worth is increasing at all income levels as individuals age. Ty Bernicke, CFP, does a nice job of connecting the dots in his analysis,[354] which provides very strong evidence that people spend less, by choice, as their age increases. There are exceptions, however. For example, a nursing home situation or long-term care issue might arise that blows these averages out of the water.

So should you plan for 80% of your income, 100% or 120%? The answer varies wildly based on your goals, location, and financial objectives. You hear generalizations aplenty. "Plan for 80% of your preretirement household annual income," "withdraw 4% annually." Do not accept a generalization. Get multiple inputs before developing your strategy.

It is true that you will have no more commutes, no more business attire, no more kids to feed, but you will quite possibly have more spending on entertainment, a desire to give/donate with little income, and quite likely more travel, etc. Have you assumed any expenses for taking care of aging parents or helping your kids if they can't find a job? How conservative are you in your estimates? Health-care costs will only continue to rise, and your health-care expenses will increase as you age. Factor in these facts as well.

A wise recommendation is to live for a full year on your projected retirement income, and see how the test-drive goes before you lock in your assumptions. Many people "go broke" because they assumed a standard retirement number or they lived too long or quit working too early.

Many online tools are available to help you generate different scenarios for how much money you need at retirement. You can include your assumptions on a pension or Social Security, when to claim your Social Security benefits, etc. The AARP also has a Social Security Benefits Calculator and other free planning tools available online.

Is Your Pension in Peril?

Many younger employees might scratch their heads and look at you quizzically if you mention a pension. A pension is a rarity in today's world where a (401)k has now replaced a defined-benefit pension plan. A defined-benefit plan promises a specified monthly benefit at the time of your retirement, such as $200 per month, or it might calculate a benefit through a plan formula that looks at service years and salary. The employer contributes all of the money and makes the investments. Most middle-aged and younger workers have a defined contribution plan, not a benefit plan. In these plans, the employee or the employer (or both) contribute to the employee's individual account. These contributions are then invested on the employee's behalf. Examples of this plan are a 401(k), 403(b), employee stock-ownership plans, and profit-sharing plans.

Millions of people are relying on company pensions to fund their retirements. Some have experienced the pain from a merger or corporate failure that wiped out thousands of these plans. During the economic collapse, pension troubles became more visible since many of them were banking on double-digit returns from their investments. Some bankrupt companies shut down their plans, and others have reduced their benefits. Many corporate pension plans have insufficient assets to cover benefits, but most employees have no visibility into these risks. A 401(k) simply has the investment risk that most employees have some level of control over, but the defined-benefit pension is controlled by the corporation, so you must research how well it is funded and what its risks are.

Check the pension footnotes in your company's annual report. A rule of thumb is that if assets are less than 80 percent of funds needed to cover current and future liabilities, then the plan is at risk. You also might find the interest-rate assumptions, which can help you assess the risks. If you work for a private company, you can request a Form 5500, the plan's annual report, prepared for the U.S. Department of Labor.

Holes in Your Bucket?

A recent movie called *The Bucket List* focused on two men living out their life-long fantasy to-do list before they "kicked the bucket." The idea is exciting. However, the reality is that most people will not be able to afford most of the things on this bucket list. The gap between our "savings and cravings" often is just too great. I encourage you to make such a list, hopefully to also include influential trips. If you make the list when you are young enough, maybe you can save for these items, or at least prioritize the list and scale it back as the years go by. Most people, however, live paycheck to paycheck and have not set aside enough money for college costs, retirement, or an emergency. The prophet Haggai wrote that it is like having holes in your pocket.

STOP Read Deuteronomy 8:17–18; 28:1–2; and Haggai 1:2–14.

Do you have holes in your pockets now that will affect your retirement and bucket list? What changes do you need to make in your money management and possible giving?

 Legacy Lesson: Where, when and if you retire are weighty decisions. Consider these decisions carefully and prayerfully. Much planning and prayer should go into these plans. These decisions will impact your influence, your kids and grandkids.

CHAPTER 55

YOUR MONEY:
A GENERATIONAL MINDSET

"But what do we mean by the American Revolution?
Do we mean the American War? The Revolution was affected before
the War commenced. The Revolution was in the minds
and hearts of the people."
—John Adams, 1818

*Y*ou might need a revolution in your mind and in your heart. We have a difficult challenge to discern God's ways versus man's ways. A conflicting tug of war is at hand.[355]

God's perspective	World's perspective
- Diversify your investments	- Timing strategies
- Generational horizon	- Short-term horizon
- Slow, steady growth	- Get rich quick
- Save, invest before spending	- Spend/consume as you get it
- Consider costs/long term	- Don't budget/short term
- Give cheerfully and liberally	- Greed, stinginess, hoarding

In *Ease the Squeeze*, I included an entire section on biblical finance and stewardship with a detailed scriptural study, so I will not repeat that here.

"We Can Change the World," Hawk Nelson

Our Part and God's Part—A Partnership

- God is owner (Lev. 25:23; 1 Chron. 29:11; Psa. 24:1; Psa. 50:10; Haggai 2:8).
- We are stewards; He is Lord (Matthew 6:24; Luke 16:10–11; 1 Cor. 4:2).

- He is in control (Psa. 135:6; Rom. 8:28).
- He is provider (Psa. 139:1–16; Matt. 6:26–33; Phil 4:19).

Giving

One of the most important things to consider in your "investment portfolio" is your giving. Not your estate planning or your will, but your giving *now*. When you think of the short time we are on this earth—seventy to eighty years at most—it really is a short time in contrast to eternity. We often focus much time and strategic thought on our "earthly portfolio."[356] What about our "eternity portfolio"? The Bible talks of laying up treasure in heaven. The rate of return on our giving to life-changing causes pays far greater dividends than the low rate of return we might receive on a CD or a stock market investment.

You might have a diversified portfolio that includes local church, Christian school, mission field, poor international, poor local, and widows local. Pray about how and where you should give. You can also receive financial benefit and give cash to children tax-free while you are still alive. Understand gift taxation laws because they change often.

> *"The great use of life is to spend it for something that will outlast it."*
> —William James

A Global Glance

We tend to be "internally focused" both as individuals and as a country. Although America and other countries are very benevolent when a world-wide disaster strikes, we also tend to think poverty is someone else's problem. The Barna Research Group conducted a survey[357] that found the following:

- Americans spend nearly fifty times as much money on fast food as they do helping children in poverty.
- A typical household spends only $5 a year on assistance to poor children.
- Nearly 60 percent aren't sure that addressing poverty is really their responsibility.
- Half of households had donated nothing to causes or organizations that assist the poor in the preceding year.

Dr. Wesley Stafford says that times have changed as have attitudes toward charity. "After World War II, we basically turned that over to the government. We said, 'Government, you take care of the poor among us and take it out of my taxes.'"[358] Automatically, the word *missions* triggers a switch in many people's minds. Usually it is an "off" switch. People are struggling with finances; they don't want to deal with guilt, or they are so consumed with a *me, my family, my community* focus and with our day-to-day living, that they don't stop to understand how blessed they are and what the needs are elsewhere.

The "not-so-good news" regarding the lack versus the plenty is this.

- If you are reading this book, you are among the world's "haves," not the "have nots."
- If you earn > $34,000 annually you are in the richest 1% in the world[359].
- Twenty percent of the people in the world live on $1 per day.
- Another 20 percent live on $2 per day.
- Americans make up 5 percent of the world's population but consume 50 percent of the world's resources.
- More than two billion children live in our world, half of them in poverty.
- One of every four children in the world has to work instead of going to school.
- Eight percent of the people in the world own a car.
- Thirty thousand people will die today from preventable diseases.
- A child dies of hunger every 16 seconds.
- Americans use about a hundred gallons of water at home each day, whereas 46 percent of the world does not even have water piped into their homes.
- More than a billion people have unsafe drinking water.
- One in 3,700 American women die in childbirth; 1 in 16 women in sub-Saharan Africa die in childbirth.

> These statistics bring perspective. We are so blessed in America. I remember when I was a young husband trying to get my financial house in order. I had attended a Larry Burkett seminar and was shocked at the statistics being rattled off. Although we Americans were only 5 percent of the world's population we had 90 percent of all of the Christian resources. I looked around over the next week and validated this statistic. How many Bibles, Christian books, and churches we have. We have more ordained pastors, more Bible colleges, more full-time Christian workers, more Christian radio and television stations, and more publishing houses, than the rest of the world combined. We need to redirect how we are spending our time, talents, and money and where we are giving, and give more thought to a world-wide lasting legacy.

The "**good news**"[360] is:

- Approximately one-third of earth's people call themselves Christians.
- Daily, 178,000 people convert to Christianity.
- Approximately 40 percent have heard the gospel or been evangelized but are still non-Christian.
- In 1974, approximately 50 percent of the world's population was beyond the reach of the Church, living in unreached people groups; today, less than one-third are unreached peoples.
- Overall, the world population is growing by 1.6 percent per year, but the number of Christian believers is growing at a rate of 2.6 percent per year.
- In 1430, only 1 percent of the world's people were Christians; now that is more than 30 percent.
- Two billion people claim to be Christians, larger than any other religion.

Christians	2.0 billion
Muslims	1.1 billion
Roman Catholics	1.0 billion
Hindus	0.8 billion
Non-religious/ atheists	0.8 billion
Evangelicals	0.7 billion
Buddhists	0.3 billion
Other	0.5 billion

- The growth of Christianity around the world is astounding. Christianity is the fastest growing religion in the world.[361] The growth rates are:
  o Christianity 6.9%
  o Muslims 2.7%
  o Hindus 2.2%
  o Buddhists 1.7%

The "not-so-good news" regarding evangelism and the Christian church:[362]

- Over the last 20 centuries, in 238 countries, 70 million Christians have been martyred (killed, executed, murdered) for Christ.
- Sixty-seven percent of all humans from AD 30 to the present have never even heard of Jesus' name, despite Christ's command to evangelize.
- All persons born in the last 2000 years: about 37 billion; Christians in the last 2000 years: about 8 billion.
- Estimates show that more than 1.6 to 2 billion people still have not heard the gospel of Jesus Christ.[363]
- Of the 16,713 people groups by country, 6,926 are still considered unreached. Of those unreached people groups, 3,400 groups are Muslim, 2,600 groups are Hindu, and 600 groups are Buddhist.
- More than one-third of the unreached people are in India.
- Other large unreached groups are in China, Bangladesh, Afghanistan, Algeria, Iraq, Saudi Arabia, Syria, Morocco, Pakistan, Iran, Indonesia, Myanmar (Burma), Nigeria, Azerbaijan, Tunisia, Cambodia, Kazakhstan, North Korea, Turkey, Malaysia, Sri Lanka, Somalia, Thailand, Uzbekistan, and Yemen. Pray for the people of these countries.

Tortured for Christ

Tortured for Christ[364] was written by the founder of Voice of the Martyrs, Richard Wurmbrand. It has been translated into sixty-five languages and millions of copies have been distributed throughout the world. We don't witness martyrdom in the West. A martyr dies for his faith, but it is not *just* dying for one's faith. Eleven of the twelve disciples were murdered for their faith. St. Augustine stated, "The cause, not the suffering, makes a genuine martyr." T.S. Eliot says that a martyr is one "who has become an instrument of God, who has lost his will in the will of God, he has found freedom in submission to God. The martyr no longer desires anything for himself."

I simply state martyrs' experiences below to put Western Christianity in context and to illustrate how blessed we are. People around the world are suffering and dying for their witness to the life and power of Jesus Christ. I read a few pages of the following visually disturbing incidents, the worst of which were not told in the book, to my children while we were on our first mission trip, to help set the tone of the minimal suffering we were getting ready to endure.

- tortured with red-hot iron pokers and knives
- forced to stand for two weeks, day and night
- whipped a 14-year boy in front of his father
- handcuffed with sharp nails into the wrists
- hung upside down on ropes while being beaten
- placed in ice-box "refrigerator cells" with ice with little clothing, then just before death warmed up and repeated the cycle, over and over again
- forced to stand in wooden boxes slightly larger than the body with no room to move; nails were then pierced into the box, when the person moved, he was pierced
- tied to crosses where prisoners were forced to relieve themselves over the faces and bodies of the crucified ones
- forced to eat human excrement and drink urine as though they were the elements for Holy Communion
- carved their bodies in a dozen places
- burned and cut eighteen holes in the body
- girls raped by guards
- forced to eat grass
- starved
- years in prison with no Bible or any other book
- fingernails torn out
- electrically shocked and put in straitjackets

Approximately 200,000 Christians per year are martyred. Stories are told of thirty villagers cutting up a Bible to share it with each other. There was the story of a Russian begging for just one page of the Bible to feed his soul. I read of another man trading his wedding ring for a New Testament.

In the West, we are ignorant of not only the suffering but also the flames of passion and zeal they have for their God. The passion and courage to lead someone to Christ is convicting. There are no cathedrals or padded pews. They have secret meetings in basements or fields. Some meet in caves or tunnels or rotate the meetings from house to house to avoid suspicion. Some Christians hide in underground, sealed basements for months at a time to print Bibles. I read of one story of a printing press that had to be dragged piece by piece through a long, hand-carved tunnel and assembled in a room chipped out of stone. Many believers who are discovered were executed or spent years in prison for sharing their faith. These martyrs "to be" are not being entertained. We in the West sometimes spend more time trying to convert someone from one denomination to another or waste endless time with theological debates about nonessentials.

"Home Christianity" Focus

Although the Christian world is about 2 billion strong, about 33 percent of the world's population, there is a very "internal" or "domestic" home Christianity focus, instead of an "international" or "world" focus, especially with our finances.

Christians:[365]

- ☐ Are 33 percent of the global population
- ☐ Have 53 percent of the global income
- ☐ Have 61 percent of all telephones
- ☐ Have 47 percent of all televisions
- ☐ Have 74 percent of all computers
- ☐ Spend 99.9 percent of their income domestically/on themselves/on the evangelized, Christian world
- ☐ Spend 0.1 percent of their income on the unevangelized world
- ☐ Present cost of home Christianity: $163 billion/year
- ☐ Foreign missions to other Christian lands: $13 billion/year

Think Globally!

According to David Livermore, PhD, Michigan State University, and executive director of the Global Learning Center, the largest Christian communities today are not in the U.S. Bible Belt but in Africa and Latin America. His book *Serving with Eyes Wide Open* gives some compelling evidence that the face of Christianity is radically changing. The Western church is no longer the center of Christianity. We have such an internal focus, but it is time to see what is going on world-wide.

Of the world's seven billion people:
- 20 percent live in China
- 20 percent in India
- 5 percent in the US
- 55 percent in other nations

The growth of Christianity outside of the Western world has been staggering:

In 1800, only *1 percent* of Christians lived outside of North America and Western Europe
In 1900, increased to *10 percent* of Christians lived outside North America and Western Europe
In 2000, *more than 67 percent* of Christians live outside North America and Western Europe

Here are some mind-blowing reasons to get excited. Revival might not be occurring in the West, but check this out:

361

- There were 50,000 believers in Latin America in 1900; now there are more than 480 million!
- There are 28,000 conversions daily in China, mostly through the underground church.
- There were one million Christians in China in 1950; today there are about 100 million!
- In Indonesia, the largest Islamic country, more than one million people convert to Christianity each year.
- India has more than 85 million believers.
- In 1900, Korea was impenetrable; today, South Korea is more than 40 percent Christian.
- In Iran, more people have come to know the Lord in the past ten years than the last thousand years.
- There are 20,000 conversions daily in Africa; 40 percent of Africa is Christian now.
- From 1900 to the present, Pentecostals, Charismatics, and Neo-Charismatics have grown from 1 million to more than 600 million.
- None of the fifty largest churches in the world are in North America.
  - ☐ Seoul, Korea—253,000 in Yoido Full Gospel Church
  - ☐ Abidjan, Ivory Coast—150,000 members
  - ☐ Santiago, Chile—150,000 in Yotabeche Methodist Church
  - ☐ Lagos, Nigeria—120,000 in Deeper Life Bible Church

We need a global mindset, in our giving and in our prayers

Reality Check—Open the Window[366]

Ninety-seven percent of the world's unreached people live in the 10/40 Window, a rectangular-shaped area on our globe extending from West Africa to East Asia, from 10 degrees north to 40 degrees north of the equator. In this part of the world, millions live with little or no chance of ever hearing the gospel. The Window also encompasses the majority of the world's Muslims, Hindus, and Buddhists. Although 97 percent of the world's unreached people live in the 10/40 Window, less than 0.05 percent of the Church's total resources in the West are being sent to help share the Good News.

Within the 10/40 Window:

- The darkest of all areas within the 10/40 Window is Asia.
- More than 80,000 people a day die in Asian countries without knowing about the love of Jesus Christ.
- In India alone, 500,000 villages have never heard the gospel.

This is not meant to be a guilt trip but to give perspective. While most of the world spends the day barely clothed, without running water, we sit on our porch with a cold drink watering and fertilizing a green lawn. We must guard against falling in love with our comfort, pleasure, and the lusts of the flesh. We must strive after God's will.

Read 1 John 2:15–17.

A Missions Trip

One of the most rewarding things we have ever done as a family was to go on a short-term missions trip for ten days. We had been putting it off for years and had all of the pat answers memorized: couldn't afford it, didn't have the time, needed to make a difference in our hometown, etc.

Since our youngest child was only eleven, we wanted to have our first trip be English speaking and not a Third World poverty experience. After much research, we decided upon Belize, a British colony until 1981, half way between Guatemala and Mexico. It is about the size of Massachusetts with a population of about 300,000. Sixty percent of the population is under 25, and some people call it a "fatherless nation." The median per capita income is $4,062 versus $47,280 in the United States.

Yes, there was plenty of lack and poverty, and it was an adjustment not having air conditioning, or being able to flush toilet paper, or drinking or touching the water. The mosquitoes and beans and rice were also an adjustment. We had prayed for weeks before that we not only be affected but also affect others and that we would love, serve, and meet the needs of the people of Belize. I think they blessed us as much as we blessed them.

It did stretch us, but it transformed us. The kids and I were able to share our testimony in front of two Belize churches; we did two days in an orphanage, three days of park ministry, and three days painting. I was proud of our kids as they shared publicly, and they even wanted to adopt one of the kids in the orphanage. They led skits and worship in the park and in a church and grew closer to the Lord. We did a prayer walk, had great worship and were able to be used by God. One of the most exciting things was seeing multiple denominations come together in unity to minister. We had Wesleyan, Liberty Evangelical Free, Episcopalian, Charismatic, Assembly of God, Baptist, nondenominational, and Catholic working together with one spirit, one body, one mission.

 Read Romans 15:5–7, 1 Corinthians 12, and Ephesians 4:3–6.

We need to focus on our common ground and common goals as a "body" more than the differences, walking together in unity as "one body."

Wrestling

It has now been almost two weeks since our family mission trip to Belize. As I cruise the interstates of Massachusetts, Illinois, and Indiana, it is really my first time to meditate quietly alone about all that God did in us during the trip. The opportunity to focus 100 percent on one goal or one project is rare in our family in the world we live in. Solitude seems to be a rare commodity. I am on a media fast to help me search and find God, to keep the flame burning that was sparked by people I had never met in a country I had never visited.

We found in our visit that the same Holy Spirit we have encountered and the same Word of God that we read and try to live by is alive and well in believers thousands of miles away.

I am relishing this time to reflect, and I know deep down that our "Mission" was accomplished. As a family, we have strived toward a vision this year: "Know Him, love Him, love one another." With nine days of honed-in focus, we were able to have a new-found intimacy with our Maker, to know Him more and to pursue Him in a greater way. The environment created for us really helped to cultivate that. We had worship and teaching every morning and evening, and we set aside quiet time daily and had believers gatherings/church services three times a day. We journaled what God was doing in and through us. It was a constant, consistent focus on Jesus that resulted in our tanks being filled to overflowing so we could love and serve without a care or concern for our usual comforts.

Now the rat race is back in full force. The multi-tasking, the taxiing, the to-do lists. Life was so simple for those nine days. So focused. It is past midnight as I drive through the countryside of Indiana on a different mission. My mission is my family, my community. Right now, my mission field is here. Serving. Writing. Leading. Providing for my family.

Six hours in the car alone, just me and my thoughts. I am processing. I am an external processor. My wife is an internal processor. This writing is a result of that processing. It is therapeutic. I have been on this "media fast" for four days because I want to continue this intimacy with God and live in that refreshing, rejuvenated spiritual atmosphere. I don't want to settle for lukewarmness or "good enough." The images of the mission sites, the mission workers and the faces from our brief stay are still fresh in my mind. I think I am more burdened for those who have surrendered all for God's mission work than for some of the actual children and families in poverty we encountered. One day stands out, however.

The bus pulls up to a house the size of our master bedroom. It is the mother of one of the mission workers. Our ministry today is to paint the inside. We discover that the mom and dad are raising eleven children in that small area. As I begin to dust the walls and a small shelf, my eyes dampen as I see a few isolated hangars with a couple of tattered dresses hanging from the ceiling. The lump in my throat grows as a smiling young girl begins to help me move the pile of clothes in the corner (her dresser apparently) so we can begin painting. I don't think she even recognizes her "lack" or "need." All I see is joy. Two young boys, about three and four years old, pick up a paint brush and begin painting with me with smiles a mile wide. I notice eight brand new "D" batteries on the shelf I am dusting. These are the only new things in this house. My heart grows heavy as I discover these batteries are their "electricity." They are used for the flashlight that lights their "house." No electricity. No stove. No television. Yet smiles that soothe my aching heart. A family following Christ with joy. I tell the two young boys, who are dripping with paint, to run outside and "hose off" since we are done now. I walk outside fifteen minutes later and see the older brother riding his bike with a bucket of water on his shoulder. The hose is the "river" fifteen minutes away, and the bucket of water is for us. The boys bounce over to a handcrafted wooden basketball hoop and climb a tree as I notice the hole out back for the toilet. The images and visuals come fast and furiously and my heart races as fast as my cardio workout. The tape rewinds and continues to play in my mind.

The crippled orphan curled up in the corner. All I know is to pray and sing softly. My kids play with the orphans. A product of someone's neglect or abuse. Alone. Mario painting my son's name. Children's faces full of joy from a bracelet or a hug given. Although they have nothing that this world values, we are connecting, a bond is being created, as I hear a child's laughter, as we throw or kick a ball, paint a face, or color a picture. Simple deeds of service. Love. I recall the flooding rush of gratitude as we washed feet and gave sandals that bring smiles or a thankful nod. You can sense the hurt that many of them have been through, but they are enjoying this moment in time. Sharing and receiving the love of Jesus. The true, gut-level joy of giving and serving. Images and feelings that will wash over our families minds for years to come.

The lasting relationships and the bond we established with those who are "on mission" 24/7/365 remains front and center. Those are the relationships and the lack that seem to be foremost in my thoughts, memories and prayers. That college education that only 1,000 out of the 300,000 get. That ministry team's mom raising those eleven kids in that shack. The ministry leader who can barely afford a vehicle or is wondering where the next pay-check is coming from. The front-liners. That bond cannot be described in words. They are not just friends, but now I feel like Paul did writing to other churches, our care runs deeply for them, their ministry and their future. They are brothers and sisters in Christ and that bond now runs deep. The unity described in Ephesians 4, Romans 15, and 1 Corinthians 12 comes to life. These relationships were cemented during our nine days in Belize—Bill and Kathy, Mark and Sharon, Jamie and his family, Kevin, and others. It is personal now.

One Body. One Spirit. One Mission—souls for the Kingdom.

So in this solitude, this alone time, I wrestle. It is not a spiritual wrestling like Jacob did. It's not with God or an angel. It is not a wrestling in spiritual warfare against Satan. Rather, it is a wrestling match with myself. Hard questions. God knows my heart. I love Him. I love to give. This issue, these questions have to do with the level of sacrifice. The level of blessing. The level of need. The level of equality. It is not socialism equality or gov-ernment redistribution but 2 Corinthians 8:1–15 equality. I have written about it before. Now I am face to face with it, living it. These questions loom like a sumo wrestler in my rented vehicle. Why am I so blessed but these people struggle to pay for a high-school education for their kids? Or use a flashlight for light? Why can I flush my toilet paper and enjoy air conditioning, a shower, a restaurant, a dry cleaner, a refrigerator, a television, a microwave, and even a car? This list could go on for pages.

Why should we not adopt an orphan or two? God calls us to reach the widows and the orphans. He speaks more on the topic of "giving to the poor" than any other financial topic other than warnings about riches. Am I a rich young ruler? Am I willing? What am I doing about the equality issue? Why should we not sell our house and give to the poor? What if God does judge America through a financial collapse? What if the savings and investments are worthless? This house and stuff are God's, not mine. We are simply stewards. How can I not involve God in this decision of giving versus hoarding? My own words to my son a few days earlier haunt me: "That is not your ball. Share it. Technically, it is God's. You are just taking care of it."

 "Kingdom of Comfort"- Delirious

I live in a kingdom of comfort. I am my own affliction.

Save me from the kingdom of comfort where I am king
From my unhealthy lust of material things
I built myself a happy home
In my palace on my own
My castle falling in the sand
Pull me out, please grab my hand
I just forgot where I came from
—Delirious

A Head on Collision

We had confronted a need head on. A blessed American family driving down the divided highway of life. careening over the solid yellow line and colliding head-on with ministering brothers and sisters in Christ, in need, and in a world far away. A collision for eternity. Not just memories; now an obligation. A Christian duty. Not just a Christian duty; a human duty. Or is it a hit and run? Really? Back to life. Back to comfort.

This is a divine intersection.[367] A crossroads. A junction. Call it what you will. What will we do with this?

Is it right? My eyes dampen as I open the phone bill, the electricity bill, and the cable bill. How can I plan the next international excursion with brothers and sisters in need? I am not wrestling with God. I am wrestling with myself. Can I really write "return to sender' on this "blessed Belize package" and just return it to God? Now that I have new-found knowledge of this need, how can I turn and run? I can't just flip this channel and avoid the images. Or maybe I can. This rat race and multitasking affords me that ability fairly easily.

So, am I wrestling with my selfishness or wrestling with the Spirit of God? Or both? Most people don't have the benefit (or the burden, not sure which it is) of confronting this type of need head on. Yes, I now am convinced that I have an obligation. I don't need a voice from God. His Word has already spoken. It now becomes the level-of-sacrifice decisions. No arm-twisting; I know God better than that. He knows our heart, our giving, this tug-of war going on. But can I continue to build my kingdom of comfort? Is that what living is all about? My prayer at the beginning of this missions trip and this recent media fast was, "Lord, change my heart. Make my heart Your heart. Soften my heart. Rebuild me. Renew me. Use me. Mold me. Shape me. I want Your perfect will. Help me pursue You with an undivided heart."

As we prayed about our giving, we determined that instead of going back to Belize this year, we would simply give that money to those who are ministering there. As we aim for a generational and global perspective, we will dedicate all net profits from *A Lasting Legacy* to world missions and ministries like Voice of the Martyrs, Gospel For Asia, and a couple of other influential ministries. We deserve no pat on the back for that. It is simply obedience. It is shared with you, the reader, to ask you to seek God about your generational role in our world's eternal future.

We need to think generationally, but we also need to think globally.
We need to have a Kingdom mindset, not a domestic
or a denominational mindset.

STOP Read Proverbs 11:24–26; Isaiah 61:1–4;
1 Corinthians 12:25–26; 2 Corinthians 8 and 9

Missions Trip: A Warning

"As many as four million American's now take short-term missions trips out of the country annually, and American churches spend as much on short-term missions trips as on long-term missionaries."[368] Our comfort mentality travels with us on short-term missions trips. If you do go on a missions trip, and I hope you do, I would read David Livermore's book *Serving with Eyes Wide Open* first. It does a nice job of preparing you, maximizing effectiveness and cultural awareness but also ensures that you are not just focused on "transformation of the missionary" but rather have a mindset of "long-term sacrifice for the sake of others." Although this is a generalization, the following comparison rings true:

> Through the eyes of Americans: "This trip isn't a rough-roach-in-your-bed kind of experience. We'll be housed in nice clean hotel rooms, eat lots of salsa, and have plenty of time to shop."

> Through the eyes of nationals: "Thousands of young men and women in China will go as missionaries who are not afraid to die for Jesus. They are not only willing to die for the gospel, they are expecting it."

God might call you to the mission field, but He also might use you to start a business to raise funds for missions or to give to missions to help the poor and the widows, to heal the brokenhearted, to rebuild some old ruins and to repair ruined cities. "Eighty percent of the world's Christian wealth is presumed to exist in the 150,000 churches in the United States. Yet only one in thirty congregations in the United States sends and supports even one of its members in full-time missionary activity elsewhere in the world."[369] You may give or you may go!

How can you help? Pray. Give. Give them the tools (Bible, literature, radio, etc.) to win the lost.

Your Role/Your Call

We each have different gifts, talents, and assignments from God. Some people think that they must sell everything and move to the mission field. You had better seek God before you do that. He might call some people to do that, but He also needs people to support those who are called to the fields. God doesn't call the equipped, but He equips those whom He calls. There are many examples of God's using people without demanding a change in their careers:

- ☐ Aquila and Priscilla (Acts 18:1–3; 18:25–26; Romans 16:3–4; 1 Corinthians 16:19)
- ☐ Cornelius (Acts 10:1–8)
- ☐ Gaius (Romans 16:23)
- ☐ Lydia (Acts 16:13–15, 40)
- ☐ Paul, tentmaker (1 Thess. 2:9)
- ☐ Publius (Acts 28:7–10)
- ☐ Simon (Acts 9:43)
- ☐ Zenas (Titus 3:13)

Use your gifts!

The Mold[370]

I remember after years of God's tugging at my heart, I finally decided to surrender all. I believed in Him as Savior, but now He was Lord. I was on fire for Him, wanting to make a difference and searching out His call for my life. I was ready to jump in head first, go to seminary, and become a pastor or get into the "full-time" ministry. I had no idea what "full-time ministry" would look like or how my calling would be fulfilled. The only thing I knew was what everyone else seemed to be doing: get a seminary degree and become a youth pastor, children's pastor, or teacher. Yet I struggled with that approach because I couldn't find it biblically, and none of those "callings" quite fit me. God gave me perspective over the next several years that as we went through life and our family changed, God wanted to use me right where I was. I began to get plugged in to different ministries as needs arose. I taught a Sunday school class, volunteered for homeless ministry, helped out with inner city ministry, taught financial seminars, taught at a university, wrote a few articles and papers, and served where I could. God began to open doors to use my skills and talents part time. "The calling" of a pastor never seemed to fit me, and I began to realize that "the calling" is not a specific task or job but rather "in all I do." I was trying to fit into a mold of what the world or Western church was teaching me about what ministry should look like. He wants to use you where you are, with your unique talents, gifts, and abilities. Don't fit into someone else's mold. You were created uniquely with a God-given purpose.

Whatever you do, do it *all* for the glory of God.[371]

Fear and Risks

I recall being fearful of public speaking. It literally paralyzed me. I can remember staying home from high school "sick" on the day of one of our group presentations just because I had a small speaking part. I would shake, stutter, and nearly pass out. When researching local Michigan colleges, I wanted to make sure that a speech class was not a requirement before I applied.

Overcoming that fear was a process: presentations at work, teaching a small college-and-career class, and teaching a Sunday school class. I couldn't keep ducking and running. I didn't even realize public speaking, communications, and teaching was something I would grow to love, nor would I have if I hadn't taken some risks and taught as a guest speaker at a Sunday school class. Now, teaching and public speaking are among my greatest joys. I have been on the radio before millions, in front of large crowds with hundreds, on video camera both live and taped. The journey has been amazing. I look back and realize the risks that I took, and overcoming of my fears (with God's help!) opened up a whole new world of joy and of influence.

Fear never seems to be a one-time conquering. I recall being asked to teach a financial class at our church, and the fear of that "small group" intimacy came roaring back. I recall knowing that I needed to be part of a small group but was fearful about rejection and taking a risk to start one. I was encouraged as I thought of God's using ordinary unschooled men, and I read in 1 Corinthians 2:1–5 how Paul, the great author, was weak, fearful, and trembling, yet he relied upon the power of God to work through Him. He was not bringing his own wisdom or wise words. Even Moses was not an eloquent speaker and possibly even had a speech impediment.[372] These men overcame their fear and realized that fear was not from God. God will give you power, love, and a sound mind as you move out in faith. Discover your gifts!

  What things excite you? What causes your heart to jump or brings you joy? What areas are you nervous or fearful about? God might want to use that area or gift in your life. He wants to use each of us, and when we are forced to rely fully on Him, the best results usually follow. God wants to use you. Pray about how!

STOP Read Acts 14:27, Colossians 4:2-3, 2 Corinthians 2:12, and Revelation 3:7-8.

Make it a regular prayer to pray for open doors and closed doors in your second half. See how God will use you. Know that time is short, so start seeking His will now. Redeem the time.

Generational Giant

Truett Cathy owned a single local restaurant called the Dwarf House in Georgia for more than twenty years. He was nearing fifty and easily could have contemplated slowing down or selling out. Instead, he opened the first Chick-fil-A in 1967, and now there are more than a thousand of them. The company's purpose statement is "to glorify God by being a faithful steward of all that is entrusted to us and to have a positive influence on all who come in contact with Chick-fil-A." He will turn 90 this year. He has taught Sunday school for more than fifty years. He has testified that the Bible is his guide-book for life.

369

All of the company's locations are closed on Sundays—a rare policy within the food-service industry—to allow its employees to attend church and spend time with their families. In 1984, Cathy established the WinShape Foundation, named for its mission to shape winners. He has fostered children for years, and has since taken in nearly two hundred foster children through WinShape Homes. His estimated net worth tops $1 billion.

"If we want to transform our culture, we need transformed Christians."
- James Robison and Jay W. Richards

 "We Could Change the World," Matt Redman

Legacy Lesson: Getting a generational global mindset will stretch and challenge you. Doing so will extend your legacy to a world that needs Jesus Christ. The Western church can be a partner in that mission of "going to all the world to preach the good news."

CHAPTER 56

GET A GLOBAL PERSPECTIVE

"I have made many millions, but they have brought me no happiness."
—John D. Rockefeller

*M*oney issues entangle us all. One area of difficulty for some people is the balancing of or the tug-of-war between eternal and temporal investing. A fine line exists between hoarding and saving. To *hoard* means to "lay up," to "store up," to "keep." Many individuals and families struggle even to consider having some money available to invest. Some people are struggling just to make it from payday to payday. But part of the journey toward financial freedom is the balance of giving and saving or giving and investing.

Is It Biblical to Save and Invest?

Solomon commended the ant for its initiative in saving and storing: "Go to the ant, you sluggard; consider its ways and be wise! It stores its provisions in summer and gathers its food at harvest." The Bible says that "a foolish man devours all he has." The parable of the talents says, "[Y]ou should have put my money on deposit with the bankers, so that when I returned I would have received it back with interest." It also is biblical to leave an inheritance for our children: "A good man leaves an inheritance for his children's children." If we are "working for the Lord, not for men," and if it is the Lord Christ whom we are serving, then we need not focus on building our own kingdoms with the income with which He has blessed us. *He* is, in fact, our "employer/boss," and the entire earth and everything in it is the *Lord's*. We are just "house sitting." He is giving us our *eternal* inheritance. Our final payday is coming! We need a global perspective with our giving.

When Have We Crossed the Line?

So when does investing become hoarding? It's too bad that we don't have a black-and-white checklist that tells us when we have crossed the line between investing and hoarding. This issue is a matter of prayer and reflection. It is a heart issue. Following are some warning signs that you might have crossed over that fine line:

1. you thirst for more, and your thirst for more never seems to be quenched;
2. you watch the stock market/investments more than you read the Word or pray;
3. you spend more time considering your temporal investments than you do planning and strategizing your giving; or
4. you worry or are afraid. (Read Matthew 6:24–27: "[T]he birds. . . do not. . . store away in barns, and yet your heavenly Father feeds them."

It is so easy for us to hoard. We have so much financial protection in our society. If we are not careful, we can push away our dependence upon God and not truly live one day at a time, without worry about tomorrow. We have insurance. We have 401k's. We have retirement accounts. We have pensions. We have Social Security. We have IRAs. We have unemployment benefits. We have Medicare. We have government aid and assistance. We have private and corporate financial aid and grants. If we are not careful, we can come to think that our security and solace are in ourselves and our bank accounts.

 Read the following two Scripture passages:
Job 31:24–28 and Luke 12:13–21.

If we put our faith in things, money, or bank accounts, we have said of them, "You are my security." It is easy to get caught in the trap of rejoicing over our wealth. If we do either of these things, we have sinned. To consider these acts sin is difficult because they are not overt. But the Bible calls such attitudes *sin*. We are walking a tightrope of idolatry and comfort similar to the rich man mentioned in Luke. His intention was to lay up good things so he could take life easy. Cushy Christianity is not biblical. God called him a fool! We must beware! We must be on our guard against all kinds of greed. No matter how much we get, it never seems to be enough! We "need" more for every want, desire, and contingency. Fear awaits us at every turn. College tuition, retirement, stock market crash, inflation, recession, layoffs, war, a call to the ministry or the mission field—*Fear! Fear!* But God has not given us a spirit of fear!

> One man *gives freely*, yet gains even more; another *with- holds* unduly, but comes to poverty. *A generous man will prosper,* he who refreshes others will himself be refreshed. *People curse the man who hoards* grain, but blessing crowns him who is willing to sell. *Whoever trusts in his riches will fall,* but the righteous will thrive like a green leaf (Prov. 11:24–26, emphasis added).

Based on this passage alone, I would choose giving over hoarding. I would rather err on the side of giving too much instead of hoarding or investing too much. No, I will not leave my children broke. I will leave them a spiritual inheritance and hopefully a financial inheritance. But I will focus on storing eternal treasures with my giving!

Warning!

We are *all* rich here in America. James issues a warning to rich people. He talks of hoarding wealth in the last days. He talks of financial injustices, but I think that the most incriminating verse could possibly describe America as a land of rich young rulers: "You have lived on earth in luxury and self-indulgence. You have fattened yourselves in the day of slaughter." We can use our wealth either on ourselves or to advance the gospel and to help those in need. It is a choice that each of us makes *daily*. A "soft life," a "life of luxury," is a challenge for even the most saintly and superspiritual. Will we hoard? Will we spend on ourselves? Or will we give? Will we have a global perspective in our giving?

We are blessed with so much. God honors your desire to give and your acts of giving. I think that the most appropriate scripture that obligates the American church to care for our brothers and sisters laboring in other countries is as follows:

> Our desire is not that others might be relieved while you are hard pressed, but that there might be *equality*. At the present time your *plenty* will supply what they *need*, so that in turn their plenty will supply what you need. Then there will be *equality*, as it is written: "*He who gathered much did not have too much, and he who gathered little did not have too little*" (2 Corinthians 8:13–15, emphasis added).

When 85 percent of the world's population lives in the Third World, and the Bible is for everyone, *the Scriptures about hoarding do not apply to very many countries or people.* Are we doing our personal part? Should we feel guilty? No. Should we be convicted and make a change in our lifestyles and in our giving and missions support? I will leave that decision up to you and God. I am accountable for *me,* and the answer for *me* is *yes* on all counts.

Three Cures for Hoarding

The Scriptures offer at least three cures for hoarding.

1. Freely give: "Freely you have received, freely *give*."
2. Give with a glad heart: "[D]o not be hardhearted or *tightfisted* toward your poor brother. Rather be *openhanded*. *Give generously* to him and do so *without a grudging heart;* then because of this the Lord your *God will bless you* in all your work and in everything you put your hand to."
3. Share: the man with two tunics should *share* with him who has none, and the one who has food should do the same.

These three cures actually boil down to one cure—*give*. The balance between hoarding and investing/saving is difficult. God will guide you in your endeavors, but we must shift our thinking radically from an emphasis on how much we should give to *how much we should keep.*

Read James 4:13–15—We are a mist. Neither our time nor our life is our own.
Read Ecclesiastes 2:1–11—Consider Solomon's thesis on his life.

I think that Ecclesiastes ought to be mandatory reading once a year. "Whoever loves money never has money enough; whoever loves wealth is never satisfied with his income.

This too is *meaningless*. I have seen a grievous evil under the sun: wealth hoarded to the harm of its owner, or wealth lost through some misfortune, so that when he has a son there is nothing left for him. Naked a man comes from his mother's womb, and as he comes, so he departs." Solomon says that hoarding wealth is a "grievous evil" and "harmful" to its owner.. How can *we* really take hold of the life that is truly life if Solomon and James took so long to figure it out? I think that Paul has the answer: "Command those who are rich in this present world not to be arrogant nor to put their hope in wealth, which is so uncertain, but to *put their hope in God*, who richly provides us with everything for our enjoyment. Command them to do good, to be rich in *good deeds*, and to be *generous* and *willing to share*. In this way, they will lay up treasure for themselves as a firm foundation for the coming age, so that they may *take hold of the life that is truly life*." Here is what we should and should not do:

DO	DON'T
—put our hope in God	—put our hope in wealth or self
—get our enjoyment from Him	—get our enjoyment from stuff
—do good deeds	—hoard or be selfish
—be generous and willing to share	

Result: *Take hold of the life that is truly life!*
Sounds like a guaranteed return!

It really comes down to our choices. Sometimes we despise black-and-white issues or certain scriptures because they force us to deal with both ourselves and God. The parable of the rich fool says that we can have either an eternal perspective or a temporal perspective: "*store up things for yourself or be rich toward God.*" Not too many "guaranteed investments" or "sure stocks" exist in our temporal walk here on planet Earth. The Bible, however, is clear about a guaranteed bank, where the insurance cap does not stop at $250,000 like that of the FDIC. "Provide purses for yourselves that will not wear out, a treasure in heaven that will not be exhausted, where no thief comes near and no moth destroys. For where you treasure is, there your heart will be also."

Our *glances* should be toward our stuff, our money, and our investments. Our *gazes* should be more on eternal things. "Cast but a *glance* at riches, and they are gone, for they will surely sprout wings and fly off to the sky like an eagle." Two men challenged me:

R.G. LeTourneau, a Christian businessman and teacher, started a moving equipment company and now has a Christian university in Longview, Texas. He was known for living on 10% of his income and giving away 90%! His legacy lives on through his university and a foundation to support Christian work.

Robert Laidlaw, a New Zealand billionaire, determined to tithe at the age of eighteen. He continually and incrementally increased his giving until he was giving 50 percent by the time he was twenty-five!

Many people think that they will get an eternal giving perspective when they "hit it big," when the kids move out, or when the next promotion comes. No! We get an eternal perspective when we live selflessly *now* and store up for ourselves eternal treasures. The only way to do that is to have our hearts and minds set on things above rather than on earthly things. We must live in accordance with the Spirit and have our minds set on what the Spirit desires. Our minds must be controlled by the Spirit to please God. Our citizenship is in heaven, so we must live as such! God has been so, so good to us!

"So Good to Me," Cory Asbury

Abandonment/Radical

We are so blessed! We need to have some "giving attacks" like we have "spending attacks!" How about some "impulse giving" instead of "impulse spending"? Paul said that the Corinthian Christians "were ready to give; and your *enthusiasm* has stirred most of them to *action*"(emphasis added). We need more of a radical "abandonment" philosophy.

STOP Pray that God will help you to be sensitive to the needs around you. Get some cheer back in your giving! It is more blessed to give than to receive.

"Success is defined by bigger crowds, bigger budgets, and bigger buildings. An American middle class Jesus. A Jesus who brings comfort, and prosperity as we live out our Christian spin on the American dream."[373]

"The first call every Christian experiences is the call to abandon the attachments of this world."
—Dietrich Bonhoeffer

Legacy Lesson: Giving versus hoarding is a heart issue. Your giving makes an impact and leaves a legacy NOW! Consider and pray about your giving. Don't be constrained by the "tithe" teaching.

Information about finances, budget, money management and stewardship are available at **www.easethesqueeze.net**

Your Faith

CHAPTER 57

ALARMS SOUNDING: SHIFTING GENERATIONAL SANDS

"Restless," Switchfoot

*I*t is after midnight, Easter Sunday. I have just finished watching *The Passion of the Christ* and am still a bit numb by the provocative, gory visuals. I walk out to the front porch to the blowing 60-miles-per-hour winds. The trees are bending, the cracks of thunder shake the house, and the lightning makes for quite a sky show. I am in awe. Oddly, these moments when nature rumbles bring me closer to God. I feel in awe of a God in heaven who created our world in six days. I sometimes tremble at the thought of His power and might and in the same breath am grateful that He is slow to anger. A siren wails loudly and constantly, and the echo's reverberate through the neighborhood. The news anchor interrupts his discourse with a Doppler radar TV screen full of red and orange. The warnings are all around. The siren's constant sounding, coupled with the sighting of a tornado nearby, turned the feeling of awe to one of fear.

We heed the warnings, grab a few belongings, and head for the pantry with pillows and bicycle helmets. Sometimes you get numb to the warnings in Texas, just as those in California are probably numb to the tremors and those in Florida and on the coasts are numb to hurricane warnings. Our world is hearing varied alarms and tremors all around us. Isaiah mentions "blowing the trumpet." Friend, we are now hearing the sirens around. The terrorism sirens of war and economic crisis have already sounded. We must heed the warning signs.[374] For one reason or another, we often choose to ignore the warning signs around us. We feel that we are in control and that we don't need God's safety net or His roadmap.

Often, it is during such times of fear that we reflect on our lives. With the sirens and warnings sounding I briefly reflect on my life, the past and the future. It dawns on me that it really doesn't take much faith to believe in God. In fact, even the demons believe. I believe that if we are sensitive, we can see God in nature, in people around us, and in circumstances all the time. What is harder to do than believing is to surrender control. We like to feel that we are in control, whether it be the stock market, the weather, our families future security, etc.

During this particular moment of the storm, it quiets peacefully. We are in the eye of the storm. God is that way sometimes. He is there while storms rage around us. It turns out that He is there with a whisper if we reach out. An overwhelming amazement came over me at how deep and how wide and how long his love was for me. Regardless of the storm, or regardless of the pace of our lives. May God soften our hearts and open our eyes and ears. Can you slow down enough to feel His love? He died for us while we were sinners. This almighty God became man and gave His life for us so that we can escape hell and call heaven our eternal, generational home! That is an amazing love. In your restlessness let Him whisper His love to you!

I loved the words penned by Frederick M. Lehman nearly 100 years ago:

> *The love of God is greater far*
> *Than tongue or pen can ever tell*
> *When years of time shall pass away*
> *And earthly thrones and kingdoms fall*
> *God's love so sure, shall still endure*
> *All measureless and strong.*

It is the love of God that draws us to Him, despite our sins and past failures. He created you to love Him. No matter where you are in life. No matter what age or what season. The Westminster Catechism says that "the chief end of man is to glorify God and to enjoy Him forever." God's love draws us to Him. God's love wins in the end, but it wins out eternally, after we make a choice to follow Him entirely. Acts 4:12 says "and there is salvation in no one else, for there is no other name, but that of Jesus Christ, under heaven, given among men, by which we must be saved."

STOP Stop amid the sirens, and let God love you. Make it your prayer that you can encounter God, encounter Jesus, and encounter the Holy Spirit. Pray and ask God to teach you, to fill you, to cleanse you and to empower you. Pray, "Revive me and refresh me, oh Lord!"

Urgency

We are living in interesting times. I feel an urgency on two levels. One is a personal, familial level. As we've discussed, I believe that we each need to be positioned financially as our country is experiencing the tremors of a financial earthquake. Each of us needs to be prepared for anything that might come our way—loss of job, continued housing collapse, inflation, etc.

Time is short. Just as we have all felt the pressure or urgency of a deadline, or an appointment time, or been in preparation for a final exam, I don't think we are ready. The real challenge is, "Are you ready"? Are you ready for your kids to face the onslaught of a secular society? Are you ready for that next season in your life? Have your prepared your family as we turn the pages of the next generational chapter?

A Generational Mindset

On a more important level, the urgency is related to a spiritual level. I am not just talking about being ready for your future or with your finances, but I am also talking about being ready for the return of Jesus Christ.

My spirit is crying out with an urgency for *me* and for *my family*, but as I pen these words I feel the weight, the criticality, and the still small voice of the Holy Spirit, urging *you* to act now!

God has a generational mindset. Just read all of those genealogies in the Bible, or consider the hundreds of times the word *generation* is used in God's Word. (See the appendices for a few of the examples of how God thinks and acts generationally.) You can read often about God's generational blessings—through Abraham, Isaac, and Jacob, through Joseph and Moses. God's truths have endured for these many generations. The generational impact that Jesus Christ has had and will have is mind blowing. Our spiritual decisions will have an eternal impact for each one of us. With the Lord, *one day is like a thousand years, and a thousand years is like one day.*[375] Having a divine perspective on our daily living, with the use of our time, and the use of our gifts and callings, is something that is not for the weak of heart or those who are seeking earthly rewards and riches. In fact, it is rare to find an individual who has a generational mindset.

We read and hear often about the generational impact of man's failure—whether it be Adam and Eve's sin, the Israelites trudging through the wilderness wasting a generation, or poor choices of kings, judges, and other leaders who led people away from Almighty God. Closer to home, a moral-failure story, a "killing off" of a generation by abortion, or a crushing debt load that will affect our country for generations to come. Our choices lead to a generational impact—for good or bad.

Legacy Lesson: What warning signs are showing up in your life? Are there cracks in your spiritual foundation? Know that God's love is a mystery we cannot even comprehend. Let Him love you and help you!

CHAPTER 58

DECLINE OF A NATION: A LOST GENERATION

"The one thing we have learned from history
is that we don't learn from history."
—Winston Churchill

any doom-and-gloomers have been forecasting the end of America and of the world for decades. We recently witnessed yet another false alarm from Harold Camping's failed Judgment Day prediction for May 21, 2011. However, there is this matter of truth that nations do, in fact, rise and fall. They are born, age, and then die, just like individuals. Kerby Anderson of Probe Ministries wrote a great article called "The Decline of a Nation" in which he cited that "history has shown that the average age of the great civilizations is around two hundred years. Countries like Great Britain exceed the average whereas other countries, such as the United States, are just beyond the average age. Each of the great civilizations pass through a series of stages from their birth to their decline to their death." Anderson references the following stages that many historians use:[376]

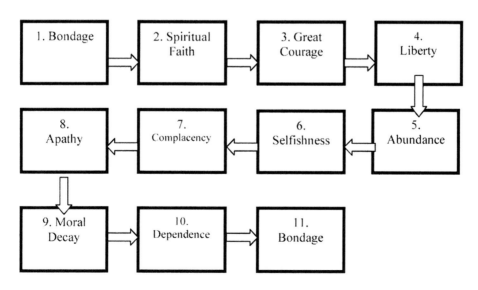

What stage(s) do you think the United States is in? Anderson points out that "nations most often fall from within, and this fall is usually due to a decline in the moral and spiritual values in the family. As families go, so goes a nation."[377] Many people look at America's problems as being economic, political, or social when the real problems are spiritual. Our world is at a crossroads in many respects. America has been a world leader economically and in some respects spiritually. However, a recent poll[378] showed that 69 percent of Americans now believe the USA is in "decline," and 83 percent indicate that they are worried about America's future. America was built on a strong biblical foundation by the blood and sacrifice of hard-working individuals. Traditions have eroded, the family structure has collapsed, our world economies are careening toward a cliff, and the nation has become divided. It is no different in other Western countries.

Peter Oborne, the chief political commentator for the *Daily Telegraph* in Britain, commenting on the recent riots and civil disturbances in London and throughout England, said, "Something has gone horribly wrong in Britain. . . it is not just the corporate boardrooms and the Cabinet. It is not just its damaged youth, but Britain itself needs a moral reformation."[379] Moral decay has crept into our societies, and the generational differences are astounding. Those growing up now lack strong faith mentors who model a healthful Christian life. We live in a culture where evil is called good and good evil. What might be legal might not be moral (e.g., abortion, pornography, divorce, and homosexuality).

Shifting Generational Sands

In a recent "State of the Church Series,"[380] George Barna explored some patterns in American religious behaviors over the last twenty years.

- Forty percent of adults read their Bible weekly outside of church (down from 45 percent).
- Nineteen percent of adults donate some of their time weekly in serving at a church (down from 27 percent).
- Fifteen percent of adults can be expected to show up in a Sunday school class (down from 23 percent).
- Forty percent of adults can be expected to attend church (down from 49 percent).
- Thirty-seven percent of adults are "unchurched in the last six months" (up from 24 percent).

The good news is that 40 percent of adults classify themselves as "born again," up from 35 percent. These adults believe that they will experience eternal salvation based only on their commitment to Jesus Christ, personal confession of their sins, and acceptance of Christ as their Savior.

The Billy Graham Association conducted a survey[381] about those who professed to have a personal relationship with Jesus Christ.

- Builder/Greatest Generation: 65%
- Baby Boomers: 35%
- Generation X: 15%
- Generation Y: 4%

"Another generation grew up who knew
neither the Lord or what He had done."
—Judges 2:10

The results are sobering. The Greatest Generation grew up during the Depression, went through World War II, and had children who became the Baby Boom. Overall, the younger generations tend to be more skeptical, more independent, and less likely to follow in their parents' footsteps, which means not as embracing of their parents faith, and are interested in exploring their own spiritual paths. Boomers, as a group, "tended to vote less and be less apt to join churches or civic organizations. They spent less time with their families and were called a "do-your-own-thing" generation."[382] Spiritual priorities are becoming less and less important with the younger generations. According to a recent *Roper Report* survey,[383]

Important component of leisure time	Builders	Boomers
Family time	62%	68%
Time to oneself	40%	47%
Relaxation	57%	61%
Outdoor activities	32%	41%
Amusement	18%	35%
Creativity	24%	34%
Enhanced spiritual involvement	**50%**	**39%**

You can see some spiritual emphasis begins to fade from the Builders generation to the Boomers generation. Likewise, three generations removed, a recent LifeWay Research study found "67% of the largest generation, the Millennials, rarely or never read the Bible."[384]

A Lost Generation

I do not cover this next topic to state a political position but rather to provide perspective that the media often do not cover. The majority is opposed to abortion, and even the most liberal politician wants to make abortions "rare." The problem is that they are not rare. The Centers for Disease Control and Prevention, Morbidity, and Mortality Report[385] reveals that a total of 827,609 abortions were reported in the United States in 2007, 84 percent of them to unmarried mothers. The total number of abortions since *Roe v. Wade* is now more than 50,000,000 (in less than forty years). The total number of American war and conflict casualties is ~ 40,000,000 (in 235 years). This is an entire generation of casualties accounting for about 20 percent of our entire population. These losses seldom are mourned or even acknowledged nationally, yet they are significant in the light of our history.

Abortion Casualties Reported (1973–2010):   **50,000,000**

Total U.S. Conflicts Casualties (1775–2010):   **40,432,544**

Revolutionary War	4,435
War of 1812	286,730
Mexican War	78,718
Civil War	2,213,363
Spanish American War	306,760
World War I	4,734,991
World War II	16,112,566
Korean War	5,720,000
Vietnam Conflict	8,744,000
Persian Gulf War	2,225,000
Operation Iraqi Freedom	4,421
Operation Enduring Freedom	1,560
Total War/Conflict Casualties	40,432,544

Sources[386]: Congressional Research Service Report for Congress, American War and Military Operations Casualties, Centers for Disease Control abortion report summaries[387]

Although these statistics are sobering, the ones that grieve me most are the leading causes of death in America. The National Vital Statistics Reports[388] show an annual mortality summary and the associated cause of these deaths. Since abortion, as a cause of death, is not included in these statistics, I have added it to provide context.

Cause of Death	Number of deaths
Abortion	827,609
Heart disease	616,067
Malignancies/tumors/growths	562,875
Brain blood vessel disease	135,952
Respiratory diseases	127,924
Accidents	123,706
Alzheimer's disease	74,632
Diabetes	71,382
Homicide/murder	18,361

Reasons for Abortions[389]

Often, the media try to make a big deal about protecting women. Rape, incest, and the risks to the mother's health are often cited as major reasons for abortion. However, a recent study shows that cases of rape or incest accounted for only 1 percent of abortions. Another study shed some light on the reasons given for choosing an abortion:

- 25.5 percent want to postpone childbearing.
- 21.3 percent cannot afford a baby.
- 14.1 percent have a relationship problem or the partner does not want the pregnancy.
- 12.2 percent are too young or their parent(s) or other(s) object to the pregnancy.
- 10.8 percent think having a child will disrupt their education or job.
- 7.9 percent want no (more) children.
- 3.3 percent cite a risk to fetal health.
- 2.8 percent cite a risk to the mother's health.
- 2.1 percent give other reasons.

It is sad that most of these reasons should have been considered long before the decision to engage in sexual activity; it is even sadder that a life was ended while families are waiting to adopt. If you line up five pregnant mothers, statistics show that one of those five will eliminate the fetus via curettage and early medical abortion. There are more than four million births a year, but more than 800,000 abortions are reported.[390]

Retreat

We discussed adultery, divorce, and other sexual sins earlier. Homosexuality is also gaining acceptance as a normal lifestyle. In fact, it is celebrated now from the highest offices of our land. "In June, 2009 President Obama signed a proclamation that declared that month as 'Lesbian, Gay, Bisexual, and Transgender Pride Month'.[391] He also became the first U.S. President to declare support for same sex marriage. "Apples iTunes App store removed a program for the Manhattan Declaration after critics decried the declaration of "anti-gay" and "anti-woman." The "Call of Christian Conscience" declaration document had more than 400,000 signers, yet Apple determined it to be politically incorrect and removed it.[392] We have become so politically correct. I think many people are all for letting people make their own choices and not legislating every behavior. However, when special rights are given or equal rights are not given for those disagreeing with certain lifestyles, then it becomes slanted in the wrong direction. Just as divorce, pride, and lying are sin. Sodomy is also a sin. Very few sins are celebrated and supported publicly. God destroyed Sodom and Gomorrah due primarily to sodomy. However other sins such as pride, fullness of food, abundance of idleness and not taking care of the poor also are cited (Ezekiel 16:49-50, Jude 7, Genesis 18-19). Thankfully, organizations such as Liberty Institute with Kelly Shackelford and American Center for Law and Justice with Jay Sekulow are helping to battle for true equal rights.

I have reflected much on a Christian's response to the double standards in the media (intolerance, bigotry, etc). My emotions have churned inside me as the media and liberal government continue embracing and celebrating 2% of the population's sinful lifestyle (homosexuals from recent census). We are a nation divided and at war within. It saddens me to see the embracing of sin and saddens me to see the anger and hate on both sides. We talk much of tolerance and rights instead of love and sin. We no longer call sin a sin, yet we also have a shortage of love. We are to be a light. To stand up for truth when most of the media and lukewarm leaders do not. Yet we are also to love. That is hard. It requires balance. Rising above the anger and name calling, I have been drawn to Romans 12:9-21.

It is a good guide for how a Christian should behave. These words jumped out at me: Love. Abhor evil. Kindness. Fervency serving the Lord. Steadfast in prayer. Blessing those who persecute us. Vengeance is God's. Overcome evil with good. Tough words for me!

God's grace is great, and He is slow to anger, but He also will judge. Psalms 78 is a great reminder of His grace for us stubborn sinful folk (me included). God has already laid out in the Bible what is right and wrong. We don't have to guess at it—-or be condemned that we are "judging". The law brings people to Christ—the Bible documents right and wrong. These are moral absolute truths. God has already weighed in with the 10 commandments and other scriptures. I won't quote them all chapter and verse but Romans 1, Matthew 24, and Ephesians 5 are a nice sample. God's word should be our roadmap and yardstick for sin and holiness. I am convicted of my sin daily. Homosexuality is not the only sin that the Bible discusses, though we in the Christian community tend to focus on that one. God also discusses divorce, anger, gossip, adultery, gluttony and lying to name a few. May we show our love to all sinners!! I am glad He had grace for me while I was yet a sinner and bound for hell!

Our country and our world seem to be on a downward spiral of immorality like never seen before. Donald Wildmon with the American Family Association cites Christians as partially at fault for the downfall. Yes, we have "special rights for homosexuals, pornography filling our televisions and internet, killing of the unborn continuing unabated, drugs ravaging our society, promiscuous sexual activity, the endangerment of religious freedom and a culture of political correctness,"[393] but we "collective Christians, have retreated into our houses of worship and turned them into houses of comfort." He cites our desire to see Christianity as comfortable, popular, and mainstream. That doesn't seem to fit Jesus' life and lifestyle very well. Before we point too many fingers, let's remove our own splinters and halt the retreat.

Church and State?

We cannot separate our faith from how we live. In many countries, we still have the freedom to worship. David Barton, Wallbuilders ministry founder, cites the correct intent of the statement "separation between church and state." This phrase "was introduced in the 1500s by leading clergy in England who objected to the government taking control over religious activities and expressions. In America, many famous early ministers also used the phrase. Thomas Jefferson wrote a letter to the Baptists in response to a letter they had sent him. His use of the terminology was simply a reassurance to the Baptists that the government would definitely not prohibit, limit or regulate religious expressions."[394]

Many religious foes today use Jefferson's statement incorrectly to imply that government or politicians should be "free from God" or have no reference to God. Jefferson did not mean that at all. In fact, "on multiple occasions, Jefferson called his state to Christian prayer and worship. In 1774, he called for a day of fasting and prayer, which included that all the legislators proceed to the Church to hear prayers and a sermon. In 1779, Jefferson again called his state to prayer and asked Virginians to pray that "he would. . . pour out His Holy Spirit. . . and spread the light of Christian knowledge to the remotest corners of earth."[395] Hmmmm. Not really politically correct today.

Legacy Lesson: Though a society decays around us, we must act. Your acting will save your kids and grandkids. We need a Reformation. It starts in your home with your spiritual priorities and pursuit of God and Biblical principles.

CHAPTER 59

REVIVAL OR JUDGMENT?
A WORLDWIDE PERSPECTIVE

Revival or Judgment?

*Y*ou read repeatedly throughout the Bible about "if/then" statements. If a nation is obedient, then it was blessed and shown favor. If it was disobedient, then it was discipline or punished. When pride takes over and God is forgotten and not glorified, He humbles and tests us. See the following scriptures for God's prescription for blessing or curses.

STOP   Read: Deuteronomy 8:14–18; 11:13–14, 27–28; 28:1-48; 1 Chronicles 21:7; 28:6–9; Psalm 5:12; 33:10–12; Isaiah 3:9; Jeremiah 1:16; Zephaniah 1:12; and Jude 6–7.

Sometimes He even uses evil nations to punish the nations that are not following Him (Amos 6:14 and Habakkuk 1:6). We must not forget God as a nation; once again we must blush at our sins (Psalm 106, Jeremiah 8:12, and Hosea 13:6).

God is looking for a change of heart, for obedience. A call to repentance is clear in Joel 2:12–15: "Turn to Me with all your heart. . . fasting, mourning, weeping. . . ." He is looking for humbled hearts, not proud hearts. There is hope. He is slow to anger (Psa. 145:8). According to Buddy Smith, American Family Association Vice President,[396] there is a history of hope when God's people pray. "The moral impact of the First Great Awakening (1734–1760) is often credited with laying the foundation for our system of government after the American Revolution. As power fell from heaven in the Second Great Awakening (1790–1840), believers lay prostrate before God in repentance."

Sometimes it is in days of hopelessness, struggle, and apathy that revival comes to a nation. A great prayer revival came out of a spiritual, political, and economic low point in America. There was much political unrest, and a financial panic hit in 1857. "Banks failed, railroads were bankrupt, factories closed and unemployment increased. Financial panic triggered a religious awakening. Prayer meetings began to spread across the country and were organized by lay people and were interdenominational. The *New York Herald* and

New York Tribune gave extensive coverage to the prayer meeting revival. This was the first revival that began in America and had a world-wide impact. Even ships coming into British ports told of the revival in America. Ireland soon began to experience a similar revival and in 1859 the revival spread to Wales, England, and beyond.

Leaders such as D.L. Moody, William Booth, and Charles Spurgeon were greatly affected by the revival. James Buchanan of the Church of Scotland summarized it as a time when "new spiritual life was imparted to the dead, and new spiritual health imparted to the living."[397] Revival started with one person in New York City when one businessman, Jeremiah Lamphier, decided to pray. "Within six months over 10,000 business men were meeting in similar meetings across America; confessing sins, being converted and praying for a revival. Across the Atlantic another million were[398] won to Christ in Britain by 1865."

Charles Spurgeon commented on the great move of the Spirit: "In the City of New York at this present moment, there is not, I believe, one single hour of the day where Christians are not gathered together for prayer."[399] In Samuel Prime's book *The Power of Prayer*, he explains the motivation behind this great move of prayer. See if it sounds familiar: "As a nation, we were becoming rapidly demoralized by our worldliness, our ambition, our vanity, and our vices. The very foundations were moving. We needed this 'great awakening' to bring us to our senses, to rouse up the national conscience, to arrest the national decay and bring us back to a high tone of moral health."[400]

The Prescription for Avoiding Judgment

Read Psalm 32:5; 51; 78:34; Jeremiah 18:7–10; 24:7; 26:3, 13, 19; Hosea 14:1–2; 5:15; Joel 2:12–15; Malachi 3:7.

God can do it again. However, he is waiting on us. Prayer can change our world, and it starts with one home at a time (2 Chron. 7:14). "If *my people*, who are called by my name, will humble *themselves* and pray, and seek my face, and turn from *their* wicked ways, *then* will I hear from heaven, will forgive *their* sins, and heal *their* land" (emphasis added). It starts with you and with me.

"Let the Church Arise"—Michael W. Smith

Gathering Storm Clouds—Hope in the Midst

God promised that in the last days He would protect His people. Jesus also talked at length about the end times in Luke 21:7–33. Whether the next calamity is another bubble bursting, a war, or something else, instead of being dominated by fear, be encouraged.

- He will be your "wall of fire" (Zechariah 2:5)
- He will be your "refuge from the storm" (Isaiah 25:4)
- He will be your "shelter from the storm" (Isaiah 4:6)

My son and I were recently out of town for a tennis tournament. He had matches on Sunday morning, so we attended "church" in a coffee bar. It was a unique experience, but you could easily sense God's presence and that He is not limited to a particular structure, timetable, or padded pew. Some of my most rewarding "church times" were when the kids were sick and we had family church, or when God surprised us and met us on a park bench, or we just worshipped in the car.

What is today's religious landscape like? People tend to be less doctrinally focused and more relationally focused. Many people are not interested in dry doctrine or "orthodoxy." Many people tend to claim that they are "spiritual, but not religious." Younger adults are not as interested in a denominational label or institutional loyalty, but rather seek to know God, worship, serve, and become part of a community that cares for each other. Many churches are trying to be more flexible without compromising the key doctrinal or theological points. Some are offering more contemporary worship, varied worship locations and times, and women in leadership.

Many churches are less hierarchical and have lay leaders as part of the ministry teams. Some of this is due to economics. Other churches follow the belief there were no professional clergy in the early church. Most young people are not interested in intermediaries but rather want to experience God for themselves. Christianity, in some respects, is going back to some of its historic roots—lay/disciple led, spirit-filled, and more democratic in orientation. Some of that change has been refreshing with much more focus on a personal relationship with God and an intimate worship. Some of that change might be risky, if orthodoxy is thrown out and a watered-down gospel is preached. Some of the troubling statistics shared in earlier sections show a true lack of knowledge of the Bible. This responsibility, however, starts with the home and should be reinforced by the church.

The balance and challenge is to have the right mix of heart and head with a strong biblical foundation. In seeing and ministering within many denominations over the years, I've noted far too much exclusivity which leads to walls. A healthy "national church body" is one that promotes unity, does not tear down, and works together to promote an eternal kingdom. As a "Christian family," we can actually learn some things from each other: from the Baptists—fervor for personal evangelism, sound doctrine; from the Charismatics and Pentecostals—a heartfelt, uninhibited worship, spiritual passion, and relationship with God's Holy Spirit; from the Methodists—service and good works; Presbyterians—study/ education in Scriptures. And we can also learn a thing or two from those outside the Christian faith: the Mormons—a zeal for evangelism and an unashamed faith; the Muslims— commitment level and spiritual disciplines.

Are We Seeing Revival or Judgment?

Atheists and agnostics have quadrupled in America over the last twenty years. Fifteen percent of Americans claim no religion at all, up from 8 percent in 1990. Mainline Protestant denominations have seen a sharp decline. Methodists dropped from 8 percent to 5 percent. Baptists dropped from 19.3 percent to 15.8 percent.[401] Revival or judgment?

David Barrett's *World Christian Encyclopedia* documents 76,000 conversions a day in the rest of the world, the largest number in Christian history."[402] Revival or judgment?

Although the influence in the mainstream media would seem to indicate that Islam is populous, only 1 percent in America identify themselves as such. Seventy-five percent of

Americans identify themselves as Christians. Worldwide, Christianity remains the most popular religion at 34 percent, although Islam is expanding rapidly.[403] Revival or judgment?

Great growth is seen in some denominations. In the late 1990s and early 2000s, the largest growth occurred in the Assembly of God denomination (68 percent), Churches of Christ (47 percent) and Pentecostal/Charismatic denominations (38 percent).[404] Revival or judgment?

According to the *World Christian Encyclopedia*, more than 2.1 billion people claim to be Christians. The *Christian Science Monitor* puts the number at 1.9 billion. Islam's adherents are 1 to 1.1 billion. Hindus and Buddhist adherents range from 300 million to 1.4 billion, according to these sources. Revival or judgment?

Pentecostals/Charismatics now claim 500 million adherents worldwide. According to a recent George Barna[405] survey, 36 percent of Americans (80 million) and 49 percent of evangelical adults accept the designation of charismatic or Pentecostal. The Assemblies of God, a relatively new denomination, less than a hundred years old, now claims 50 million worldwide adherents and is the fifth largest religious body.[406] Revival or judgment?

Conservative numbers show that one out of eight people worldwide are active, practicing Christians. According to Joshuaproject.com, the global growth of Christianity is rapid. In 1900, only 2.5 percent of the world's population were practicing Christians. By 2010, that had grown to 12 percent. These are very conservative numbers. Revival or judgment?

Some countries are experiencing genuine revival in this generation. In fifty years, Chinese Christians grew from 1 million to more than 80 million![407] A stunning prayer revival has taken hold in South Korea. One church, Yoido Full Gospel Church, now has 780,000 members. This church, started in 1958 is now the largest single Christian congregation in the world.[408] Revival or judgment?

Church attendance and spiritual influence in England has continued to wane. In 1980, 11.1 percent attended a church in Britain. By 2005, that had slipped by nearly half to 6.3 percent. The only denominational growth shown during that time for the larger denominations was the Pentecostal denominations, which showed growth of 30 percent.[409] Revival or judgment?

I believe we are indeed seeing revival around the world. Christianity and conversions are growing at rates not seen before. However, we are also seeing compromise, lukewarmness, watered-down doctrine, and targeted judgment. (I refer you to the World Missions section.) I believe that we are seeing both revival and judgment. It all depends on what part of the world you are peering in on.

Who Is a Christian?

According to George Barna,[410] "most Americans believe they, themselves will go to heaven." Forty-three percent agreed that "it doesn't matter what religious faith you follow because they all teach the same lessons," and forty percent agreed that all people will experience the same outcome after death, regardless of their religious beliefs. Forty percent also agree that "all people are eventually saved or accepted by God, no matter what they do, because He loves all people He has created." Forty-eight percent agreed that if a person is generally good or does enough good things for others, he or she will earn a place in heaven.

Barna[411] also cited that fifty-nine percent of adults believe that "Christians and Muslims worship the same God, even though they have different names and beliefs regarding God." And forty-three percent agreed that "the Bible, the Koran and the Book of Mormon are all different expressions of the same truth."

Even more alarming are the results from the group of people who call themselves "born-again Christians." Twenty-five percent said that all people are eventually saved or accepted by God, and forty percent indicated that they believe Christians and Muslims worship the same God."[412]

Do all Path's Lead to God?[413]

In the name of tolerance and acceptance, many people now claim that there are many paths to God. Universalism is growing, and many prominent leaders have now accepted this fact. Oprah proclaims it. So does Bishop Carlton Pearson's gospel of inclusion and Pastor Rob Bell's broadened view of salvation. The list of those who believe in a broader path to heaven is growing. Let's look quickly at a few of the world's major faiths and their beliefs.

Hinduism—back to 1500 BC in India; based on Vedas (Hindu scriptures); becoming one with Brahman brings liberation. The soul may be reborn in human or animal form. The Hindu path of completion is based on self-effort, from humanity to oneness.

Buddhism—fifth century BC in India; worship of Buddha (enlightened one). The world operates by natural power and law without divine command. Don't accept the existence of a personal God or the deity of Jesus. There is no such thing as sin against a supreme being. Salvation is based on human effort. "Heaven" means to enter nirvana.

Islam—AD 70 in Saudi Arabia. Muhammad received visions and revelations from an angel, Gabriel, and those became the Quran. *Islam* means "submission." *Muslim* means "one who submits to Allah," the only supreme being. Jesus is a major prophet but not the Son of God. For salvation, good deeds must outweigh the bad, although Allah determines one's eternal fate. Entrance into Paradise is guaranteed if a Muslim dies in jihad, fighting the enemies of Islam.

Mormonism—The Church of Jesus Christ of Latter-day Saints. The *Book of Mormon* goes back to New York in the 1820s. Mormons believe that Joseph Smith was a prophet. It mirrors Christian ideals. Jesus is the firstborn of God's "spirit children" but not the unique Son of God. Mormons are usually good, moral people. After death, every person goes to one of three levels of glory, depending on how he or she has lived.

Judaism—2000 BC; covenant between God and Abraham. Four primary movements: Orthodox, Reform, Conservative, and Reconstructionist. Talmud and the Torah. Judaism believes in a single God who created the universe. Jesus isn't the Messiah. They are still waiting on the Messiah. Atonement for sin is not through Jesus but by good deeds and God's grace.

Christianity—rooted in biblical Judaism. About 2000 years ago, Jesus of Nazareth, God's Son, was sent to live the life of a man but to die upon a cross out of love for all people. His death was to be the atonement for humanity's sin against God. Eternal life comes by repentance of sin and following Christ and is not achieved through works. Rather, it comes by faith as a gift from God through Jesus. Christians believe that no one will go to heaven except through Jesus (Acts 4:12).

The Rise of Islam

I address Islam more specifically due to its rise and the media's constant portrayal of Islam as a religion of peace and as being similar to Christianity. Islam began in the early seventh century and is the second largest religion in the world. Some people say that Islam is more cultural than theological. As Christianity is based on the Bible, Islam is based upon the Qur'an. Muslims believe that book was sent by God (Allah) via vision to the prophet Muhammad through the angel Gabriel during the month of Ramadan. Muhammad claimed to have a night journey with Gabriel and traveled to both heaven and hell and spoke with prophets of old.

The five pillars of Islam are confession, prayer, almsgiving, fasting, and a pilgrimage to Mecca. A faithful Muslim both believes and acts according to the Qur'an as the ultimate submission to Allah. Muslims have six basic beliefs, according to Kerby Anderson's fine book *A Biblical Point of View on Islam.*[414]

- There is no God but Allah.
- Belief in angels and ginn (spirits of good and evil).
- Belief in God's holy books. There are 104 holy books mentioned in the Qur'an.
- Believe in a number of God's prophets. Muhammad was God's final and supreme prophet.
- Predestination, or "if Allah wills," as the supreme ruler of the universe.
- Belief in a final judgment.

Many Muslims believe Islam's sixth pillar is jihad. There are more than one hundred verses in the Qur'an that call upon Muslims to engage in jihad. These verses apply against all non-Muslims at all times. Islam is not a religion of peace. Although some Muslims interpret jihad as only intellectual, the usual translation involves holy war. (See also John 16:2.)

"When you meet the unbelievers in the battlefield, strike off their heads and, when you have laid them low, bind your captives firmly."
—Sura 47:4

"Fight the unbelievers who gird you about, and let them find firmness in you; and know that Allah is with those who fear him."
—Sura 9:123

Anderson outlines some clear contradictions between the Bible and the Qur'an:

- The Qur'an teaches that Christians worship three gods: the Father, the Mother, and the Son.
- The Qur'an says that Abraham was told to sacrifice Ishmael. The Bible says it was Isaac.
- The Qur'an teaches that Jesus was not crucified.
- Allah does not love sinners.
- Allah does not love unbelievers.
- The Qur'an teaches that Jesus promoted the coming of Muhammad.

Many people say that Christianity and Islam are much alike and that they both worship the same God. Most Christians, however, would beg to differ. The biggest points of disagreement are that

- Muslims deny that Jesus was crucified on the cross.
- Muslims deny Christ's deity. They respect Him as a prophet but reject that Jesus was God. They reject the doctrine of the Trinity.
- The Qur'an teaches that Christians who call Christ the Son of God shall face judgment because "Allah's curse" will be upon them.
- Muslims reject the idea of original sin and human sinfulness and that anyone should have to pay for those sins other than themselves.
- Muslims are saved by their own efforts and following the five pillars.

Christians and Muslims do not worship the same God. Allah is distant, and the only relationship is one of submission. The relationship is not one of love, friendship, or father, or savior. In *A Biblical Point of View of Islam*[415], a survey is referenced of six hundred former Muslims who had become Christians. One of the most significant factors involved in their conversions was the realization that they could know God personally as heavenly Father and that God loved them immensely. These are important facts when sharing the good news with a Muslim.

Generational Giant

William Seymour[416] might be the least recognized of the Generational Giants. *Christian History* identified him as one of the top ten most influential Christians of the twentieth century. He was an unsung black pastor of Azusa Street Mission in Los Angeles. He was born to former slaves Simon and Phyllis Seymour. He was a porter and waited tables in his mid-20s and was blinded by smallpox in one eye. Seymour, a Baptist, joined Charles Parham's Bible school in his 30s. They were both instrumental in the Azusa Street Revival, which sparked a world-wide movement but also led to much racial reconciliation. Despite the fact that Seymour was black, many of his followers were white. Pentecostals now number more than 500 million worldwide. According to a recent George Barna survey,[417] 36 percent of Americans (80 million) and 49 percent of evangelical adults accept the designation of charismatic or Pentecostal, and it all started at a humble mission on Asuza Street with its black pastor.

"Break Open Heaven"—Christ for the Nations

 Legacy Lesson: Some nations are seeing blessing. Some are seeing revival. The Western World can once again experience both if we repent, humble ourselves, and seek God wholeheartedly. Compromise and lukewarmness must be addressed one home a time in order to avoid judgment. We are all leaving a legacy.

CHAPTER 60

TREMORS ALL AROUND:
ARE WE LIVING IN THE END TIMES?

hese are exciting but tumultuous times. Sixty-one percent of Americans believe that Jesus Christ is physically coming back to this earth in the future.[418] Many Christians believe that Jesus Christ will soon return. Others who are on the edge have predicted dates incorrectly.

The Bible talks at length about Jesus' second coming. The Bible contains more than three hundred prophecies detailing His second coming, but only one hundred prophecies detailed His first coming! Based on the signs of the times and their alignment with these prophecies, we can be more certain than any other generation that He may, in fact, return during our generation. If not, we know for sure that we are closer! That brings fear to some people but joy to others. God keeps His promises. He just never promised a date! Jesus also left us with a promise. (See John 14:1–3.)

I will not attempt to teach you Bible prophecy because its study requires much time and effort. I will, however, whet your appetite to do your own study. Most people want to know when and what the signs are. I will deal briefly with these two questions. Most Christians believe that the following timeline of events will occur soon.

When?

There is not much study required to answer the "when" question; it is quite simple.

 Read Matthew 24:36 and Acts 1:7.

What?

1. The Rapture—which ends the Church Age. All living and dead Christians will be snatched up to be with Christ in the air. It ushers in the judgments in Revelation. (See 1 Thessalonians 4:13–18, 1 Corinthians 15:51–54, and Titus 2:13.)

2. The Tribulation—which starts by the signing of the covenant between the Antichrist and Israel. Judgment will be visited on those who reject Jesus, Antichrist will reign, and chaotic worldwide conditions will exist. It will be "hell on earth." (See Daniel 9:27 and Joel 2:28–32.)

3. The glorious appearing and return of Christ to the earth for all of the people of the world. Millions of people will come to Christ, but those who have rejected Christ are judged. Christ sets up His kingdom on earth. Satan will be bound for a thousand years. (See Matthew 24:29–33 and Revelation 19:11–21.)

4. The Great White Throne—All will stand before God and be judged. Those whose names are not written in the Book of Life will be cast into the lake of fire. (See 1 Corinthians 3:9–15 and Revelation 20:11–15.)

5. The Millennium—Christ's reign for a thousand years. (See Revelation 20:1–10.)

End Times: The Red Letters

There is no better place to go than to the words of Jesus.

Read Matthew 24 and Matthew 25:31–46 and the shorter versions of these accounts in Mark 13 and Luke 21.

1. We have seen a rise in cults and false teachings (Jim Jones, David Koresh, Marshall Applewhite, Credonia Mwerinde, Warren Jeffs, etc.).
2. Far more people have died in wars during the past hundred years than in all of the centuries before.
3. The world seems constantly to be focused on a little country of 6.5 million people in the Middle East: Israel. It has less than one-one thousandth of the world's population; yet, some people call it "God's timepiece." A regathering of Jews to the Holy Land and its establishment as a sovereign state occurred in 1948. In 1917, only 25,000 Jews lived in Israel! Ezekiel 37:7–11; 21–23 predicted it thousands of years ago. We must continue supporting Israel if we want to be blessed (Gen. 12:3).
4. Earthquakes are increasing in number and in power. I quickly reviewed worldwide earthquakes in the 1990s and 2000s at the United States Geological Survey website. I combined the quakes into four charts, and just picked random five-year increments for the past twenty-one years. The graphs would be much more detailed if you graphed every year and every quake threshold. Here is what I discovered:
   o Large quakes: 6.0–9.9
   o Medium quakes: 4.0–5.9
   o Small quakes: 0.1–3.9
   o Total quakes: All

There was a big dropoff in total quakes in 2011, but as you can see, they were mostly smaller ones. I inserted a trend line so you can assess the trend upward in the larger quakes. Data collected before the 1990s would automatically be smaller because of less accurate reporting capabilities, so I thought that was misleading and did not include it.

Worldwide 0.1-3.9 Quakes

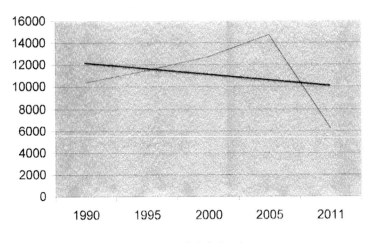

Worldwide 4.0-5.9 Quakes

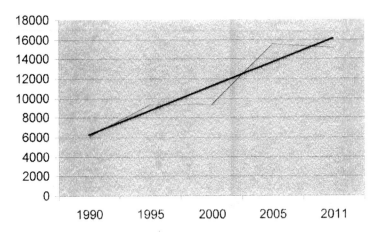

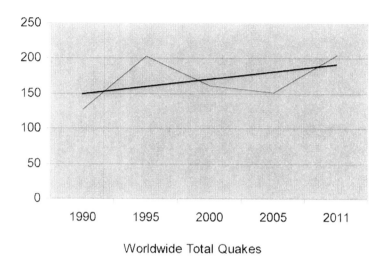

Worldwide 6.0-9.9 Quakes

Worldwide Total Quakes

Could earthquakes be a sign of God's judgment? You can read the following scriptures about the end times and determine whether you believe that the "end times" are at hand and also get a glimpse into your future. We are behaving similarly to countries of old that faced God's judgment.

- Amos 4:6–11
- Hosea 4:1–10
- Isaiah 1:4–7
- Jeremiah 5:14–19
- Jeremiah 12:17
- Luke 17:26–35
- Acts 1:11
- Romans 1:18–32
- 2 Corinthians 5:10
- 1 Thessalonians 5:2

- 2 Thessalonians 2:1–5
- 1 Timothy 4:1–2
- 2 Timothy 3:1–7
- 2 Timothy 4:3–4
- Hebrews 9:27
- 2 Peter 3:10
- 1 John 2:18
- Revelation 1:7
- Revelation 3:15–18
- Yet, we have heaven to look forward to (John 14:1–4; Hebrews 1:10; Revelation 21–22)!

 "Revelation Song"- Kari Jobe

For further study, the book, *Are We Living in the End Time?* by Tim LaHaye and Jerry Jenkins is a great resource. It also details dozens of other passages and includes pictorials (see especially pages 121 and 127). Other pending prophecies and signs interpreted by Bible prophets include the rebuilding of the Jewish temple in Israel, the Antichrist's signing a seven-year covenant with Israel, world government under Antichrist (the UN was formed in 1945), and a central domination of the money supply (in the last generation, a cashless society and a global economy have made this possible). Watch for these events. Also, if you enjoy some good fiction about the end times, you might try the *Left Behind* series of books.

Are You Ready?

If all of this brings you joy, then you are ready for Jesus' return. If you are feeling angst or worry, then maybe you are not ready. Preaching and teaching on the end times is what drew me to a decision point twenty years ago. I knew that I was at a crossroads and needed to secure my eternal destiny.

 Be ready: Read Luke 21:34–36 and Romans 13:11.

"I have been studying prophecy for over fifty years, and while I do not believe it is possible to set dates for the Lord's return, I do sense in the world today an unprecedented time of world crises that can be interpreted as being preparatory for the coming of the Lord. If there ever was at time when Christians should live every day as though Christ could come at any time, it is today."
—John Walvoord

On April 7, 2009, the U.S. Department of Homeland Security, Extremism and Radicalization Branch, issued an intelligence assessment report on "right-wing extremism" that labeled those who are opposed to abortion, same-sex marriage, and even those who simply show interest in "end-time prophecies" as "extremists."[419] It should come as no surprise. The haunting lyrics of Misty Edwards bring it home:

Time, time, is ticking by

As in the days of Noah
There will be drinking, marrying, laughing,
What a fool, they say, To build a boat on sand
What a fool, they say, It's never rained before,

So it will be in the coming of the Son of Man

And what a fool, they say, To fast and pray
And what a fool, they say
C'mon it's been two thousand years
Do you really think He's coming?
C'mon and just get real.

And remember this verse
"And many, many scoffers will come"...
And when the rain starts falling
It's too late, It's too late
And time, time is ticking by
People get ready
Jesus is coming[420]

Legacy Lesson: The greatest hope for a Christian is that this life is just a "dress rehearsal" for eternity. Eternal life in heaven is when life truly begins. The greatest legacy we can leave is to share that good news with others so they can have the same hope.

Wake Me Up- Corey Russell (with Dana Russell)

CHAPTER 61

A SCREW-UP STORY:
MY TOTAL MAKEOVER

*H*ave you ever been on a plane and had a panic attack, thinking, *What if I am on the wrong plane, heading to the wrong destination?* I was on the wrong plane of life with the wrong group of people headed to the wrong destination, and I knew it. My life was wasting away. Procrastination was an old friend; she was cozy as a blanket over me on a blustery wintery day, and I didn't want to get out from under her covers. Things were complicated. I couldn't give up my friends, my Sundays, my hobbies. Bad company continued to corrupt good character.[421] To be honest, I was enjoying my independence and freedom and having the time of my life. Plus, I still believed that I could have it all. I could keep my lifestyle, my friends, and my compromising ways and still surrender to God. Everything is negotiable. I just couldn't pray that prayer, "Give me an undivided heart." I liked my life partitioned into neat segments, compartmentalized Christianity, and God got His dues on most Sundays and even a few Wednesdays. He was getting His fair share of my time and even some bonus time once in a while with some hurried, desperate, lonely prayers thrown His way on occasion.

My sarcasm and cynicism about organized religion peaked in these years as I shuddered at the teleprompting evangelists asking for money. I remember strolling up to one Halloween party dressed as Jim *and* Tammy Faye Bakker. The costume was a hit. One side of my body was Jim, the other side was Tammy Faye. The financial and sexual scandal left a bad taste in my mouth as I progressed through my internal debates about God's role in my life and whether I should "surrender all," as the old hymn beckoned. I remember walking out of a church one Sunday when a "man of God" who preached had us hold up our wallets and declare prosperity and blessing in our lives because Jesus was the richest man who ever lived. I was sarcastic and cynical, yet searching.

I was not anti-preacher or anti-TV message. These messengers, though flawed, were talking to me. God was personally trying to get my attention. In fact, God used two TV preachers, Charles Stanley and Dwight Thompson, to open me up to the truth. However, self was still king, and my personal pursuits were attempting to fill a void with love, power, and success. But they brought only temporal satisfaction.

The cartoon showing an angel on one shoulder and the devil on the other shoulder seemed to be real, a daily charade for me. It seemed as though they had taken up permanent residence, whispering in my ears and jawing at me and each other. The whispers from the angel seemed to be drowning out the devil. God had been so patient with me. Growing up in a God-loving home and in church every week. Dad as a pastor, and Mom had a heart that was so big and full of love and mercy. I knew the truth. I had just rejected it. I would never call it full rejection but rather a partial acceptance. I had opted for the broader path, an easier road, a good compromise position.

I dabbled in Jesus, church, and religion. I hated religion, actually, but I started to open up my heart to God some in my late 20s. I even did some late-night, post-partying televangelist gazing with some Christian radio mixed in. Wayne Watson and Michael W. Smith's messages on the Christian FM airwaves began to take root. I was in better shape than the other Dilbert twenty-somethings. I even told them about church and God once in a while. Yet, why was I still so empty? Heaven would still be my home, right? It is appointed to man once to die, then the judgment.[422] I believed this, not Shirley McClain's message of reincarnation or Oprah's broad path to heaven scenario. I felt as though I would sneak in. I was good enough.

Desert Storm and My Storm

Panic began to partner with emptiness as the Desert Storm campaign launched. Operations Desert Shield and Desert Storm raged from August 2, 1990, until February 28, 1991—the Persian Gulf War. The aerial bombardment and visuals on news channels were a first. My very own Paveway bombs and HARM missiles lit up the sky on January 16, 1991. They were a wake-up call to me and only heightened the spiritual battle that was raging for my soul. Messages from the pastor at the pulpit seemed to be pointed directly toward me. The pilot was calling. I was still co-pilot. Actually God was in first class on Sundays and back in row 32F on Friday and Saturday nights. I was the portioned pilot.

The angel—really God's Spirit (my theology wasn't very correct in those days)—kept beckoning and calling. God's grace and slowness to get angry with my sin and lifestyle still amaze me in hindsight. The aerial campaign was on as the enemy kept launching lies, temptations, and fear. These Scud missiles were at times offensive but seemingly more defensive in my life now.

I was not ready to part with my past quite yet, but my best friend, Andy, and I knew that if we ever did make that gutsy decision, it would be together. Procrastination loves company. Shortly after the Desert Storm aerial attacks, Andy and I began to realize that no one is promised tomorrow, and that if we died today or the world ended and Jesus really did ride in on a white horse, or a trumpet sounded signaling the rapture of the church, we would be left in our cesspool of sin to spend an eternity in the flames of hell. Yikes. That was a bit troubling. I knew that we were living in the last days, and a healthy fear of my spiritual condition brought me face to face with a decision.

My coalition forces were gathering—Lee and Sharon Lebsack, David and Pam Fink, Mom and Dad in prayer from the control center in Michigan, and Ken Callahan, Andy Postema, Dan White, Steve Diemer, Charles Stanley, David Wilkerson, Larry Burkett, Dwight Thompson, Wayne Watson, Michael W. Smith, among many others. They were my spiritual squadron. God was using them as they sacrificed their time and gifts to speak words of challenge and life that I so desperately needed to hear. I also had plenty of voices in the darkness, still beckoning, tempting, and debating.

My brother-in-law, Sergeant Dennis Wilke, fought in Iraq during this time. He served voluntarily. Were the personal benefits great? Slim to none. He was willing to lay down his life for me, you, and anyone else living in the United States. He doesn't even know you, yet he was willing to give all. He was paying a price for us, fighting a battle we didn't have to fight. The parallels were striking. It wasn't the rainbow wig guy with the loud, obnoxious verse, just the still small voice of my Creator, calling me: *"I loved you so much that I sent my only Son that if you believe in Him, you will not perish but have eternal life."*[423]

God sent His only son to a battle, to a cross—for my sin. I believed that. Now He was asking me for my life. The battle still raged in my mind and heart. Will you make Me Lord of all? Will you make Me your everything? Your all in all? Your first love? What about my future? My job? My career? My friends? What about the sumo-wife I would get as a parting gift if I surrendered all? Surely You would send me to Africa, God, and I don't want to go. Will You make me give it all up? The answer, yet again, although not audible, was like a peaceful, still, small voice. "Be still and know that I am God.[424] Trust Me. Surrender all of your heart. I am just looking for an undivided heart."

Huh?

Wait a minute, I argued. I was already a "Christian," or so I thought. At least that is what I told people. I believed in God. Check. I believed in Jesus. Check. He was a good man. Check. I even believed He died and rose again, that He loved me, and that I loved Him. Check. Check. I believed that Jesus was the only way to heaven. I believed that He was the way, the truth, and the life. Check. What more did I need to do? I went to church almost every week! I volunteered. I even talked about Him. A sure ticket to heaven and to a pretty decent religious life. I knew I stacked up pretty well with my friends, and surely God would let me slide on the Halloween get-up. They were, in fact, hypocrites and fakes I determined. At least I was real. Authentic. I am surely not a theologian, but it was all starting to become real to me. God really did love me so much that He gave His one and only son (ouch), that if I believed I would have eternal life[425] and that heaven would be my home. Piece of cake. Done. Check. I believed. Why was God's spirit still pestering me? He evidently wanted more. My Heidelberg Catechism classes taught by "faith alone" and "grace alone." I had already stood in front of a congregation and "professed my faith." However, it was in word only. I had grown up in a Christian household not only with my brothers and sisters, but also with a rotating door of other believers who sought a Christ-like community. My debates continued to be one-sided with no answer from on high.

I was one of those church attenders who was a Christian in name only. Voddie Baucham Jr., a fine pastor, teacher and leader, wrote *Family Driven Faith*[426] and shares some research done among Southern Baptists that indicated that *"nearly one-half of all church members may not be Christians."* Good decent people, many not fully surrendered, or many who had recited the "repeat-after-me" prayers or altar calls without the Spirit's John 3:3 regenerating power.

Charles and Dwight kept peppering me with a challenge that I didn't fully comprehend. The Southern drawl from the Baptist. The fire and brimstone from the Pentecostal. These guys loved me enough to tell me the truth. Lordship was a continued theme. Hmmm, what is that? I thought and researched for weeks. I even started to have some dialogue and negotiation with God. It seemed that the conversation was one way and mostly about my justifying that I was a pretty good person. If I died tonight, would I go to heaven? That was a question I kept asking myself. Maybe. I thought so, but I wasn't absolutely sure. I had no peace with my answer. "Maybe" wasn't very settling.

Deep in my gut, I knew that I had not surrendered "all." I was a fake disciple. I told others that I was a Christian, but you sure couldn't have guessed it by my lifestyle. This haunting passage about gates, wolves, and fruit[427] troubled me. Not everyone who called Him Lord would be in heaven. He didn't even "know" some of these people. I guess my relationship with Him was more of a "help, God" or a "gimme, sugar Daddy." I was probably more like Bob in *What About Bob. Gimme, gimme, gimme. I need, I need, I need.* The relationship was not give and take, it was mostly take. It was not a real candid, open, confessing atmosphere, and surely not a close enough relationship where I would give up everything and follow Him. It was interesting; I felt that way about Dana. I would do anything for her. I would give up anything for her. That was true love. Something was amiss, as I thought that through. I would do it for a human being, surrender all, but not for God.

Reject Reel

I reflect on how many hundreds and thousands of mistakes, missteps, and wrong choices dot the landscape of my life. Whether it be the temptations succumbed to as a teenager, the poor college social choices, the early career peer and friendship decisions, or the middle-aged procrastination. Many of those mistakes were purposeful sin. Ouch! That ugly sin word! I knew right from wrong and yet chose wrong. Quite often, I backed it up with pretty good rationale, a robust "gray area" internal legal opinion rendered, or at least a good excuse. Everyone else is doing it. I'm not as bad as Bernie Madoff or Wilt Chamberlain or Lindsey Lohan, or even some other fallen religious leaders.

I knew I was a sinner. My scorecard against the Ten Commandments was pretty dismal. I had idols. I took God's name in vain. I didn't honor the Sabbath. I lied and stole. I lusted. I was batting.500 at best. I knew that I was a wreck. I knew time was short and that "it is appointed for men to die, and then the judgment." I knew this "appointment time" could come at "any time" and that I wasn't ready. Although it isn't preached much about anymore—it doesn't increase the offering coffers too much—I knew hell (Luke 16:23-24, 2 Thess 1:7-10) was a real place, and that was my current destination. I knew that heaven and hell were real, as were judgment and grace. But God left the choice to me. He wasn't arm-twisting.

Time-and-a-Half

The amazing revelation that hit me upside the head while I wrote this section and replayed my "Reject Reel" highlight film over in my mind was that God really must have had to pay the angels time-and-a-half on my behalf during my younger years. The angels were dispatched early and often—and in droves—on my behalf.

If this were a confession book, the length of it would triple. As I thought of other schmuck screwups, I remembered David. God Himself gave David the most coveted title of all. It wasn't MBA, Vice President, or PhD. It was "a man after God's own heart." I think David got it right in many of the psalms he penned. He was real. He was candid. His response to his failures (sins) gives us a peek into his heart and why God recognized him with this special "title" and so much favor. Check out Psalms 51 and notice the following:

- an admission of wrong doing,
- a humble heart and spirit,
- a pursuit of God, and
- a request for purging.

I am grateful to know that after my failures—small or large—God forgives and forgets. He removes that sin and casts it away as far as the east is from the west.[428] How does 12,000 miles sound? About half the earth's circumference. *If* we confess our sins, He is faithful and just to forgive us and cleanse us from all unrighteousness.[429]His mercies and patience were and are unbelievable for a sinner like me. He is gracious and compassionate, slow to anger, and rich in love![430]

The rich young ruler parable was me. I wasn't willing to give up all, *if* he had asked. However, I began to have more open, honest dialogue with God. What if He really did want me to move to Africa? I remember the story of St. Francis of Assisi, turning his back on worldly things and becoming a beggar. I didn't quite like the idea of a convent. I didn't want to become a sissy needing a crutch. If all of that was lordship, I was not interested. Lordship is power and authority over others. It is service and obedience to the Master, the Leader, the Head. Was He my Leader? My Head? Was I really following, serving, and obeying Him or just punching the church clock? Did I look to him as my authority? Yes, he was Savior, but was He Lord? I knew the answer was no. Now what?

Peace

This peace just kept coming. Trust Me. Surrender. Trust Me. Judson W. DeVenter struggled to give *total* control of his life to Jesus Christ. He was a successful artist and painter and grappled with the personal recognition and career aspirations and God's whispering to him via the Holy Spirit to surrender all. He penned the words that were gripping me:

All to Jesus I surrender
Humbly at His feet I bow
World pleasures all forsaken
Take me Jesus, Take me now

Make me wholly yours
Let me feel the Holy Spirit
Fill me with your love and power
Oh the Joy of full salvation

Love the Lord your God with all your heart, with **all** your soul, with **all** your mind, and with **all** your strength.[431]

I knew I needed to take that step of faith. A real commitment. I knew that I needed to change but that I didn't have the strength or will power to do it myself. This mysterious Holy Spirit and His voice kept beckoning me. He would lead. I would follow. Don't try and clean yourself up. You are a mess. Just come to me as you, and I will do the cleaning. I will do the changing. Grace alone, faith alone, Christ alone. Not my works. A free gift. He would save me from myself!

The words in Matthew 7, *narrow* and *few find it* does not imply that it is easy. Believe and check the box. Check. Say the prayer. Check. Our modern American salvation doctrine and teachings have been compromised. You don't hear much about sin, repentance, faith, obedience, and judgment. We have defaulted to 'believe." Even the devil believes. God is looking for a change of heart. A taking out of the heart of stone and replacing it with a heart of flesh. Once true repentance and surrender occurs, change will happen. Obedience some-times happens gradually. The disciples didn't just believe in Jesus; they took action. They followed him. They changed their lifestyle. The people whom Jesus touched and changed were visibly changed, not just a quick belief or decision then back to sin or bondage.

A Generational Mile Marker

It was in the middle of January that Andy and I decided it was time. Although the devil continued to fly sorties and fire missiles of doubt and temptation, we were resolute in our decision on that day. The real news on February 10, 1991, my spiritual birthday, [432] was not that the East beat the West in the forty-first NBA All-Star Game; it was that Doug Hage-dorn and Andy Postema made a heart, mind, soul, and strength decision to surrender all to Jesus Christ during praise and worship that Sunday morning in Dallas, Texas. As Andy and I worshipped, we both sensed an overwhelming peace come over us. Tears flooded down our cheeks as we worshipped, and we knew that we had been transformed by God's immense love. Our lives had changed forever. As Andy says, "It was like a warm tide coming in over my soul and then a complete release of the burdens accrued by a life apart from Him." My most important Generational Mile Marker, 2/10/91. Thank you, Father. It was an I/He day indeed! It was the same decision my wife had made in 1972. Here was the simple good news:

I	He	Explanation
Sinned	Loved, forgave, and saved me	Gal. 2:20; 1 John 3:4–5; Rom. 3:23–26; 1 Tim. 1:15; Titus 3:4–8
Was a slave to sin	Died and freed me from sin	Rom. 6:6, 23
Received free gift of grace	Saved me, let me in	Eph. 2:8–9, John 10:9
Lived now for Him	Made me a new person	2 Cor. 5:14–17
Was dead in my sin	Set me free	Rom. 6:16–18
Surrendered	Gave me eternal life	John 12:25
Confessed and believed	Saved me	Rom. 10:9–13, 1 John 1:9
Submitted to Him	Drew near to me	James 4:7–10

Believed	Loved and gave His Son	John 3:15–17, Rom. 8:38–39
Made Him Lord	Died on a cross	Phil. 2:5–11, Rom. 5:8
Received	Gave a gift of eternal life	Rom. 5:15–21
Believed, received	Sealed	2 Cor. 1:22; Eph 1:13

"Heaven" Daniel Bashta / Mac Powell

A Major Thrill

That day in 1991 and the weeks and months to follow were truly like a new beginning. The birds chirped louder, the beauty of the nature was like a communion with God Himself. The Bible's words jumped off the pages and meant something deeper to me. My life had an incredible sense of purpose and significance. I was now living my life for something bigger than me—God's purpose and plan. I was truly now leaving a "lasting legacy." It was thrilling! I now had some new addictions! I was A-2-J—addicted to Jesus.

Rick Warren says that "nothing's more thrilling than knowing God is using me to make a difference for eternity. Once you've had that thrill, you get addicted to changed lives, and you don't have time to watch somebody else have a thrill."[433] (See James 2:14–26.) I now had an appetite for God. I wanted to know Him and serve Him. It truly was a new beginning. Like a new birth. (See John 3:3.) My second life/second half!

"It is Finished," Bluetree

"Above All," Michael W. Smith

Have you surrendered all? Are you ready to do that now? If you aren't ready, maybe have an open, honest talk with God and ask Him to help you. Read Psalm 51 out loud to God. If you are ready to surrender, feel free to pray this prayer or one from your heart. Don't just check the box! Mean it with all of your heart, soul, mind, and strength!

"God, I am a sinner. You already knew that, but I needed to say it. I have sinned against others, myself and against you. I am sorry. I ask that you forgive me for all of my sins. Forgive me mostly for the sin of living my life on my own, apart from you. I need you. I now give you all of my heart. Take out the heart of stone and give me a new heart, a new life. I surrender all. I accept your son Jesus Christ as my Savior and my Lord. I invite the Holy Spirit to take residence in this temple. I ask that you wash me, cleanse me, and purify me by the power of the blood of Jesus Christ. I proclaim a new beginning right now. I declare

that I am a new creature in Jesus Christ. I will live for you my entire life.
Thank you Lord. I love you. Amen."

If you prayed this prayer, please tell someone immediately. Pick up the phone and call someone who is a believer. Send me an e-mail. Get plugged in to a Bible-believing, on-fire-for-Jesus church. Start reading your Bible every day, and get to know your Savior, Lord, Father, and best friend!

All!

I am always struck by the word *all*. That means 100 percent, everything within you. That is a daily challenge that we fail often. Being a visual learner, I automatically thought of pie charts and how the pie would look for several areas of my life. Please don't burn the book here, but go through the quick exercise that I forced myself to do. Put a percentage after each of these areas, indicating how much of your heart, soul, mind, and strength each topic is surrendered to God. If your future is 80 percent surrendered to God, but you are hanging on to 20 percent due to worry, excessive retirement funds, etc., give yourself 80 percent of the pie. Congrats, you get the picture.

Your future	
Your time	
Your finances	
Your family	
Your thought life	
Your emotions	
Your body/temple	
Your life	
Your will/your desires	

The purpose was not an exercise in guilt, and I am not advocating that you quit your job, move to the Alps, or launch into that nun or monk lifestyle. Rather, ask God to search your heart and mind and do some pruning and surgery. This should help focus your attention on where you might need some work in surrendering *all*.

Generational Giant

C.S. Lewis. At age 50, the great atheist philosopher-turned-Christian, lost a debate to British scholar Elizabeth Anscombe. Lewis felt like a failure. He was "deeply disturbed" and in low spirits, and although he never wrote pure apologetics books again, he then determined to communicate his faith through fiction and other literary forms to include radio. The result: *Mere Christianity* was Lewis's second best-selling work written at the age of 54. Lewis wrote the blockbuster series *The Chronicles of Narnia* when he was 52 through 58, and the box office version of the first three films has now grossed $1.5 Billion worldwide and has influenced millions of lives who wouldn't have read the series otherwise. John Stott said, "His stature a generation after his death seems greater than anyone ever thought while he was alive, and whose Christian writings are now seen as having classic status. I doubt whether the full measure of him has been taken by anyone."

Lewis said "Christianity, if false, is of no importance, and if true, of infinite importance. The one thing it cannot be is moderately important."

Legacy Lesson: The most important decision you can make is to make Jesus Christ Lord of your life. If you don't know what that means simply ask Him. Read the Bible verses included in this chapter. He will show you and you truly will leave a Lasting Legacy.

CHAPTER 62

FAITH: A MULTISENSORY EXPERIENCE

What are you hungry for? How is your appetite? I love red licorice and any hard sugar-coated candy. The thought of a juicy, grilled T-bone steak gets my mouth watering. I pursue a day at the ballpark with a passion. My wife is attractive to my eyes (she will edit this if she catches it).

We all have different appetites. Some are good. Some are good with balance. Some are neutral. And some, if pursued too hotly, could lead to destruction. Having an appetite is normal. Having a desire for things or people that satisfy our desires and our senses is not wrong. The challenge in most of our lives is having a healthy balance in those appetites. Too much dessert will lead to tooth decay. Too much red meat can lead to high cholesterol. Too much time pursuing entertainment or career mobility can lead to a suffering marriage or lost time with the kids.

Often, we don't stop to analyze our appetites, passions, and pursuits. Often, we just go with the flow of how we were reared, what the menu item of the day is, what our friends are pursuing, or just what feels best. Typically, we put our time and money into what we are "hungry" for. We satisfy the appetite with the cash or the time. Peruse your checkbook or credit-card statements and that might enlighten you with what you are hungry for. A "hunger" is multisensory. It is not just the taste of that favorite food. It is the visual appeal and the smell of that T-bone. It is the sights and sounds of the ballpark. It is the touch of my wife's hand. We take for granted all of our senses.

Multisensory

I recently determined that the fogginess at night and at distances finally required a pair of glasses. When I was putting on my new glasses, I was shocked at how bad my eyesight was. I have taken my health for granted. I have taken all of my senses for granted. Read Proverbs 4:20–27. This text enlightened me as to how multisensory our spiritual lives are.

- We use our ears to listen to God's sayings.
- We use our eyes to stay focused on His ways.
- We use our heart to keep His ways in our heart.
- We are to protect our heart; the wellsprings of life flow from it.

- We are to use our mouth to bless God and others, not to curse, deceive, and say perverse things.
- We use our feet; where we go and what we do matter.

Are we using all of our senses to follow the Lord and have an appetite for Him? This next exercise will help you do a little soul searching, meditating, praying, and discussing with your spouse or kids. Some of your passions and pursuits might be out of whack, out of balance. Maybe you are consuming too much time in another area. Are any of these risk areas? Are any of them idols? Have any of them taken time from your family or from your time pursuing God? I recall a period in my life when I needed a chiropractic adjustment on how I was spending my time. Leisure consumed my time and my money. Sports center, media, and reading were what I was most hungry for. There's nothing evil in those things if they are kept in balance, but I was far from balanced.

STOP This quick exercise will help you come to grips with your appetite. What am I most hungry for? What I am I passionate for? I developed "buckets" based on our senses. If something doesn't fit somewhere, just jot it down anyway. These appetites can be good, neutral, or bad. Recognize them all. Some might be risk areas that you want to make yourself more aware of. Some might be things that you want to reinforce.

SIGHT—entertainment, leisure, where and how you spend your time, what you look at (Examples: Sports on TV, sitcoms and soap operas, reading, Facebook, watching child events, nature, Internet surfing, fast cars, muscular blondes, tan brunettes) These could be good, neutral, or bad.

_____

TASTE—food, drink, anything that goes into your mouth or body. These could be good, neutral, or bad.
(Examples: Meat and potatoes, sodas, beer, smoking, drugs)

_____

DO/TOUCH—things, stuff, relationships, activities
(Examples: Gardening, exercise, hiking, texting, basketball, travel planning, dinner dates)

_____

SOUND—what you listen to, music, speakers, teaching
(Examples: Listening to iPOD, listening to pastor, leading meetings at work)

_____

MIND—what do you spend most of your time thinking about?
(Examples: Financial markets, relationship problems, kid's issue, God, worry, opposite sex)

_____

Have you ever overeaten? Every time we eat "Tex-Mex" out, I go home too full. Sometimes, we are hungry for the wrong things, or we just eat too much dessert and not enough fruits and vegetables. Sometimes, we are so "stuffed" with the good things, the pleasure, the television, the sitcoms, the movies, sports, the entertainment, the eye and ear candy, that we have no appetite for God. A lukewarmness best describes that state. Go back and put a star next to the items that might be out of whack, and pray about what to do next.

Microwave Ovens

I was listening to a Tony Evans program on the radio[434] and he shared the analogy of food being cooked in a microwave oven that comes out hot and steamy but is cold on the inside. It reminded me of the Pharisees in the New Testament. It also reminded me of some of my backslidden days, when I talked a good game, but my spiritual time clock was not being punched as much as ESPN was. Our society and our churches often replicate those in Revelation 3.

I know your deeds, that you are neither cold nor hot. I wish you were either one or the other! So, because you are lukewarm—neither hot nor cold—I am about to spit you out of my mouth.
—Revelation 3:15–16

How would you define *backslidden* or *lukewarm*? After giving it some thought, I could easily go back to some of my lukewarm seasons and identify some traits.

- You are not hungering after God. You have a greater appetite for other things or your passion.
- You are not seeking Jesus as you once did.
- You are not passionately reading the Word.
- You are not taking part in fellowship with other Christians.

 Take a few minutes to see what your lukewarm thermometer looks like.[435]

- The most passionate relationship in your life is Jesus	Cold	Lukewarm	Hot
- Spend more than five minutes in prayer a day	Cold	Lukewarm	Hot
- Spend more than five minutes in worship a day	Cold	Lukewarm	Hot
- Spend quality time reading and studying His Word	Cold	Lukewarm	Hot
- A relationship with God driven by love, not legalism	Cold	Lukewarm	Hot
- I go to Him first when times are tough.	Cold	Lukewarm	Hot
- I spend more time with Him than with "potential idols."	Cold	Lukewarm	Hot

- I want to know Christ—His power and His sufferings.	Cold	Lukewarm	Hot
- I look forward to fellowshipping with God's people.	Cold	Lukewarm	Hot
- Focused on selfless, unselfish, self-denial living.	Cold	Lukewarm	Hot
- Hiding God's Word in my heart—memorization	Cold	Lukewarm	Hot
- God's Word comes to life daily when I am with Him.	Cold	Lukewarm	Hot
- I am in love with Jesus; my soul thirsts for God.	Cold	Lukewarm	Hot
- My relationship with the Holy Spirit is intimate.	Cold	Lukewarm	Hot

A Sold-out Remnant?

You might feel as though you have a long way to go to get "hot" for God and His priorities. You are in the majority. Seek Him and ask Him to help you.

In his book *Maximum Faith*, George Barna cites some encouraging statistics, including the following.[436]

- Eighteen percent of Americans say that they're totally committed to spiritual development.
- Fourteen percent of American Christians say that their faith in and relationship with God is their top priority.
- Twenty percent of American Christians say that their most important life decision was salvation.
- Twenty-two percent of American Christians say that they live a life completely dependent upon God.

Beware of Doug

I was captivated by a slender, beautiful brunette with take-your-breath-away eyes. My "fish bowl" Texas Instruments (TI) cubicle mimicked every Dilbert cartoon with amazing accuracy. The beauty of my cubicle location was that it faced the main TI hallway, which connected to the cafeteria and all of the production and engineering areas. Ahhh, the main thoroughfare. A productive day of work for us new hires was faithfully sitting in my Dilbert Procurement station at just the right time for a RED ALERT. If my beeper (pager) went off (yes this was in the 80s) or my other twenty-something cubical mates in our purchasing ghetto fish-bowls shouted, "RED ALERT!" That absolutely meant a pause from the conference call or shelving of the paperwork for a few brief moments of heaven on earth!

Dana was approaching—RED ALERT! A dream beyond my grasp. A Southern-belle Texan. Dream on, Yankee Boy. Maybe the yellow tie, white shirt or flowing golden locks will win her over. Was that yellow tie a sign of pending success or a sign of geekdom? The white shirt and tie were a phony front. I was playing a shell game with not much under the shell. A pretender. A surface life. Searching for fulfillment. Twenty-five years old and quite frankly getting a little nervy about growing old alone, and actually a lot panicky about my hair count and their early exits.

A past heartbreaking relationship had left me reeling and searching for answers. I had an emptiness inside that I was desperately trying to fill with a social life of a square peg trying to fit into a round hole. I did not belong, although I awkwardly tried to fit in. On many social occasions, I felt like a leper in the city square giving hugs. The career, the good money, the friendships, the relationships—nothing seemed to bring true peace, true satisfaction, a real fulfillment. I wanted to go deeper with God, but I was hot and cold. He was mostly an afterthought but got my attention when I felt lonely. He was always there. Our relationship kind of reminds me of that story of one of my favorite childhood books, "*The Giving Tree*" by Shel Silverstein. He was that tree, but He never gave up on me. He never left me. He was rock solid. A fortress that I could run to.

I kept grasping at the wind and coming up empty. Different groups of friends, different churches, more hobbies and sports. Work was a good distraction from my personal changes. I could get lost in the work and succeed. I received great raises and quick promotions. I achieved my master's degree in less than two years. Still empty. Each weekend, I pursued everything with a vengeance. I was even trying to get closer to God. He waited and His still small voice kept speaking. I sat in the church pew, worshiped, and visited different singles groups. I was trying to find both God and true love at the same time. In some respects, it was a tug of war internally and a debate with God about which was more important to me. Never a heavy hand from Him, just good conversations about it.

I remember a New Year's Eve late-night discussion with my friend Andy. We stared at the television feeling the growing emptiness and lack of a roadmap or purpose and debated whether this would or should be the night when we make a decision to give up our lifestyles and surrender all. Nah, too scary. I might be chained for life to a 400-pound bearded woman because God thought it would be good for me and because I was too selfish to be St. Francis of Assisi. Ah, the mind of a twenty-five-year-old.

In Love

I recall (barely) those early days of courtship (such a 50s word) with my girlfriend Dana more than twenty years ago. My heart and my wallet so easily connected as I showered her with flowers, long talks, longer walks and random acts of romance. I remember it as though it were yesterday (a miracle). Love in Lewisville, Texas. The innocence and spring season of new romance. Every word out of her mouth captivated me. I hung on every word. She had my undivided attention. My eyes, my heart, my mind, and every waking moment were fixed on her. My every action and thought were focused on knowing her more, learning her thoughts, her dreams, her passions. My life really was not about me at this point. I was fixated. I was passionately in love. Those times were the absolute pinnacle of my life. I had TWO loves at the same time.

February 2, 1991: My first date with Dana.
February 10, 1991: My salvation day.

Those red-alert days turned into a love relationship with my future wife. I pursued her. I changed plans for her. I cancelled events for her. I turned off the television for her. I gave of my time and my money cheerfully and with no thought. I was in love! I was thirsty for "all things Dana."

Amos 8:11–13 talks about a famine. Not a physical famine, but a spiritual famine. Oftentimes we hunger after the wrong things. Find a church environment that fuels that fire. Fuel your own fire.

Read Psalm 34:8; 42:1–4; Matthew 22:37-39; and Philippians 3:10.

David had that thirst for God. As the deer pants after water, may my soul long for you, God. Paul had that thirst to know God. *"I want to know Christ and the power of His resurrection and the fellowship of sharing in His sufferings, becoming like Him in his death."*[37] These are not words you hear on the lips of most people at the work water cooler, on the subway, or even in the church hallway. Actually, the first nine words sound pretty good. It is the rest of the verse that is a little more difficult to pray. How badly do we want to know Him and understand what He went through?

I can recall after February 2, 1991, my born-again experience, I was radically on fire for God, and I wanted the world to know it. I was hot, without an ice cube in sight. I was completely sold out and had real purpose and real life. We handed out tracts. We taught classes when we didn't have a clue how to teach. I wrote a letter to all of my family and friends telling "my story" and inviting them to participate in this "tasting and seeing that the Lord is good" buffet. I received a couple of "no thank you" letters back from old friends asking what had happened to me and wanting the old Doug back. Years later, I was talking to one of my best high-school friends about witnessing and how we needed more of that zeal that we had when we were young believers. He shared with me that he had read that letter I had written years before while he was driving along the freeway. He listened to the tape I had sent of Charles Stanley and Hal Lindsey and had been so convicted in his heart that he needed to pull the car over and surrender his life to the Lord.

You never know the impact you might have. When you are "hot," God will figure out how to use you. You will have seasons of planting, sowing, and reaping. Be sensitive to the Holy Spirit's wooing.

Lasting Legacy: We need spiritual food. Taste and see that the Lord is good. Nothing is more fulfilling than the presence of the Holy Spirit. The comforter, teacher, and guide will not only give you peace and hope beyond your wildest dreams, but will also lead you into the most joyful, fulfilling life. Life with Christ is a full life. Sit with Him and let Him love you for awhile.

"If I Could Just Sit with You Awhile"—Dennis Jernigan

CHAPTER 63

AT WAR/ AT PEACE: A BATTLE FOR YOUR SOUL

*"In any battle between the imagination
and the will, the will loses out every time."*
—Billy Graham

Is there such a thing as "sin addiction"? I see some of the problems besetting families, and some things seem to be harder than others to battle. Generational familial sins seem to be a challenge to overcome for some people. Others overcome one sin easily but struggle with others. It could be alcohol, abuse, anger, lust, or even overeating. Others struggle with "addictions" to gambling or shopping. You look at the statistics on overeating and pornography, for example, and they have taken an incredibly startling turn for the worse. A survey by the British Broadcasting Corporation revealed that almost 80 percent of relationship therapists in the U.K. said sex addiction was not only a real phenomenon but a growing problem. If you are having trouble with a habitual activity or struggling to stop a behavior, there might be a level of addiction. Some clinical psychologists claim that people can get addicted to the adrenaline flow that comes from a particular behavior. For those who are caught up in an addiction cycle, this might resonate with you. There might be a spiritual component to all of this as well. "A desire to live for the gratification of the senses. When a person lives to serve a desire that begins to take over his or her life, we call it an addiction, when in reality it is a god."[438]

I love my daily coffee. Is it an addiction? Probably so; but it is not an addiction that can destroy lives—unless I indulge in excess. However, you know yourself better than anyone, second only to God. Most of us know which of our appetites can be destructive and when those appetites are beginning to control us. Control can lead to destruction, whether it be alcohol, anger, drugs, eating, sex, smoking, or even shopping. The cure to breaking this addiction is exercising your will, mixed with the power of the gospel of Jesus Christ. If you are addicted to something, you should take steps to change your behavior. It might be an accountability group, it might be a Bible-based addiction program, or it might be a trusted friend or pastor. Ensure that you mix a supernatural God, a risen Christ, and a powerful, living Holy Spirit in helping to deliver you from any addiction that might be destructive.

We are waging a "multidimensional sin war"[439] on all fronts. We are battling
- internal evil, the flesh (see Galatians 5:16–21),
- social evil, the world (see 1 John 2:15–17), and
- supernatural evil, the spirit world (see Ephesians 6:10–20).

If you read Ephesians 2:1–3, you can see this battle spelled out: the world, the flesh, and the devil. Sin begins in the mind before it is acted out. (See 2 Corinthians 10:3–5; 11:3; and Philippians 4:8.) It is often premeditated, although we might not give it much thought in those respects. I love Dr. Ed Murphy's depiction of the Continuum of Sin:[440]

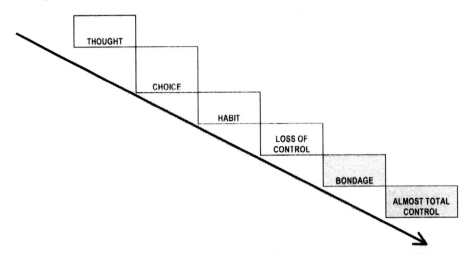

Some of our sin is not repetitive or recurring. It is not a "habit." With other sins we might feel that we have lost control and have some level of bondage to that sin. James 4:1–8 is the road to personal victory in warfare against sin. First Timothy 6:11 and 2 Timothy 2:22 give instruction to flee! Murphy argues that certain addictions or bondages that might have a dangerous, destructive gripping control might require a supernatural spiritual freedom to break that sin addiction. Alcoholism, drug abuse, sexual abuse or addiction, occult activity, pornography, and anger are a few examples. Find a prayer-share-healing partner (James 5:16) who will pray with you, encourage you, and hold you accountable. You might need someone to check in on you, someone to whom you can go when temptations attempt to take control. Your bondage will only increase if you do not stop and get help now. "The Son of Man will set you free and you will be free indeed."

Here in Texas, we have watched the incredible story of Josh Hamilton play out in his freedom from drugs and alcohol and an MVP season with the Texas Rangers. We have also seen him struggle to stay free. He is always an addict struggling to maintain that freedom. Many people who have not faced an addiction with "bondage" or "control" do not understand this challenge. Josh continually relies upon Christ but also needs the help of an accountability partner and prayer. I would highly recommend Hamilton's book, *Beyond Belief*. It is an incredible story!

It is often difficult to discern whether certain sins are generational struggles that might be a "part of your DNA." Some spiritual warfare seems to take on a generational battle along family lines, although the Bible is not clear on this. Decisions made by a father or grandfather certainly have generational implications.

The Bible does speak of situations in which the sins of the fathers affect future generations. I shared earlier how we had a prayer time with my dad, me, and my sons—three generations to pray over my children and confess any areas of "generational struggle" and ask for God's protection over my children. We must guard our hearts.

STOP Are there any "sin danger areas" in your life? Could any of these sins possibly lead to destruction of your family, your future, your faith, or your finances? List one for each area below. Read Proverbs 4:23. "Above all else" [441] sounds like a top priority. *Guard* means to "take great care." A sports analogy I picture is an aggressive defender in basketball or an offensive lineman in football. Are you doing everything possible to protect the quarterback (your heart)? The heart is your very source of life. The blood is pumped into all areas of your life. Now read James 1:22 and Matthew 7:24–27.

What will you do practically to guard your heart? You might believe that defenses are in place, that you could never fail. What action do you need to take to get out of "danger"?

	Family	Future	Faith	Finances
Sin danger area				
Action(s)				
Action(s)				

Know that if you are feeling challenged and convicted, that is a good thing! Conviction is healthy. That means the Holy Spirit is working on you. If we have low self-esteem, we sometimes feel so unworthy, and the conviction can pile up so much into perpetual condemnation. Condemnation is not healthy. There is a distinct difference between "condemnation/guilt" and "conviction." Sometimes, those lines seem to blur in our own minds. The enemy will use condemnation and guilt to whisper thoughts of unworthiness and of not measuring up. Guess what? None of us measures up! God's grace is such a gift. If Paul realized his faults, failings, and sin, yet pressed on, remember that "there is no condemnation for those who are in Christ Jesus." (See Romans 7 and 8 for a man's honest assessment of himself.) The challenge is to move from conviction to action!

Do not keep your sin in isolation. The obvious first option is to call upon a trusted friend, someone who won't betray, someone who will always be there, who will never leave you, never give up on you, one who knows you better than anyone. That might be hard, especially if your "burned percentage" is high. Start with God. His arm is not too short to reach you. Nothing is too difficult for Him. Call upon Him, and He will answer you. Ask Him for wisdom in your next steps.

Sow a thought, reap an action.
Sow an action, reap a habit.
Sow a habit, reap a character.
Sow a character, reap a destiny. [442]

419

"Slow Fade"—Casting Crowns

Legacy Lesson: The battle always begins in the mind. The enemy would like nothing more than to imprison you by a particular sin. Protecting your heart and mind and being aggressive in the sin war will protect your marriage, your children, and your future. Protect your legacy!

CHAPTER 64

MEN OF VALOR, WHERE ARE YOU?

I was recently joking that my favorite sports team was out of contention for the playoffs, so I now could direct my time into things more useful. It is amazing how we spend our time. An interesting thing will happen if you clock how you spend every hour for the next month. You would be surprised how much time you spend watching television, being entertained, or in just plain being lazy. An interesting article I recently read in the *American Family Association Journal* talked about the "impact of sport." Does sports have a greater impact than religion? I think in America that has become more crystal clear in the last generation. How much time do we spend following sports? I don't want to lay on a guilt trip and have us each count the minutes we spend with God versus watching ESPN. This is more about a heart issue. What are we pursuing with a vengeance? If I held up the mirror, I would say that I don't pursue God enough and that I very often pursue other things harder than Him. Times of "media fasting" helped bring that into perspective for me.

My son recently made a statement about a friend's house he visited that was covered with sports memorabilia and college logos of someone's alma mater. He asked why our house was so boring. I didn't have a good answer and know that I am certainly not judging another house's décor. An article[443] I had been reading referenced a conversation in which an individual feared that his children might not want to attend Ole Miss. His friend said not to worry. "You drink from Ole Miss cups, give money to Ole Miss, never miss an Ole Miss ballgame, wear Ole Miss clothes, have scrapbooks full of Ole Miss in your home, talk/joke/dream Ole Miss. Of course your kids are going to go to Ole Miss." The author then went on to address the eerie parallels with Deuteronomy 6:4–9 and said it seemed that the friend had replaced the law of God with a school. I wonder how often we have done the same? Whether it be a sports team, music, shopping, current events, TV, movies, or anything else that replaces our talk of God with our children.

A Daily Failure

I am a screwup.

There, I said it. That was painful. The truth is that it is easier to write it than to say it audibly. Try it tonight with someone and see how easily it rolls off your tongue. I guess it is easier to write than to have to proclaim it from a national bully pulpit or at an MLB steroids news conference. Thankfully, it makes it a little easier knowing that I am in good and numerous company. I surmise that my wife probably wishes I would 'fess up a little more often; but rather than just professing the obvious, she might better like to see a little more "change" now and then. Maybe I can refer her to this page of the book the next time I leave my cereal bowl positioned squarely where it doesn't belong.

It is not just okay to open up about your challenges, your mistakes, and your sins. The Bible actually encourages it. It is healthful to talk to God since He already knows about your messups, but it is also healthful to confess your faults to another person,[444] in fact, it *will* lead to your healing. We often focus on physical healing but rarely the need for healing of the soul, the mind, and the emotions. The challenge in this is to whom one should confess.

The Man Gap

I love sports. I love recreation. I love my career. I love my "me-time." I am all for men loving sports, watching television, and hanging out, but we are seeing a "man gap." We have gone through a transition during the last couple of generations—we have seen equal rights, feminism, and many strong women in the workplace and in churches. I thank God for Christian women. Most churches or classrooms couldn't operate without the leadership and service of wives and mothers. Many businesses would be in disarray without the insightful wisdom and gifts of women. In the home, however, wives have stepped up to fill a gap. A man gap.

Women are the backbone of spiritual life in America, and many of them lead their families spiritually. According to Stephen Arterburn, women are[445]

- 100 percent more likely to be involved in a discipleship program at church
- 54 percent more likely to be in a small group
- 46 percent more likely to spiritually mentor someone else
- 39 percent more likely to spend time alone reading the Bible or praying
- 29 percent more likely to share their faith with someone.

Those are powerful statistics and should make us all very grateful for the women in our lives! Men often have an emphasis on career and breadwinning—totally necessary to being the provider but maybe with an overemphasis. It is quite possible that the disciples and other men of the Bible had hobbies. We know that they were hard workers, holding down a job (tentmaking, carpentry) while ministering and leading in their communities. You just don't read much about their careers, their jobs, or their hobbies. They had a priority of spiritual leadership, leaving a legacy, leading in the community, and building strong families.

The importance of a father's being actively engaged in his children's lives is critical. A recent study[446] found that fathers "contribute to their children's cognitive abilities and behavioral functioning. Compared with other children with absentee dads, kids whose fathers were active parents in early and middle childhood had fewer behavior problems and higher intellectual abilities as they grew older, even among socio-economically at-risk families."

I know that as a newly married husband and a new father I had absolutely no clue how to lead spiritually. I took it upon myself to read, read, read. I found role models and hung around them and began to pick their brains. If you are as clueless as I was, start attending a Bible study or start a small group yourself. Our families' clocks are ticking, and our days of influence are numbered. At some point, we realize that we aren't kids anymore. I am reminded of that every day when I get out of bed, or slide into home plate, or watch the peachfuzz kids on television that are young enough to be our kids! Women- pray for your spouse! You can't guilt-trip them or change them, but God can. Be specific in your prayers—a godly friend, a small group opportunity, etc. Step up the praying and fasting. Start a women's group dedicated to this need.

Steps to Success

Here are some very practical steps for the man who wants to get started at being a loving, family leader.

- Start by admitting that you are clueless. Start with God, and be honest in prayer, asking for His help (James 1:5).
- Read from the New Testament daily/nightly, and ask for God's insight as you read.
- Talk to your spouse or someone else you trust, telling them of your desire to step up to the plate as a man.
- Get help. Begin reading books on fathering and marriage. (Focus on the Family, Heritage Builders, and Family Life are great resources.)
- Join or start a small men's group.
- Begin praying with your wife.
- Start reading a devotional together with your wife.
- Show your kids that you are serious. Prioritize your time with them. Earn their respect. Spend time with them.
- Read a Bible story with your kids. Start a family devotional time—Family Fun Nights/ Heritage Builders, *Egermeier's Bible Study Book*.
- Just start! Quit overanalyzing or operating in fear! I was clueless, but my family was forgiving of my ineptness.

Step up! Wake up! Man up!

Men's Challenge

During one of my media fasts, I felt led to start a small men's group. I knew that I needed it, my family needed it, and the church needed it. I had been reading about John Wesley's Holy Club and recalled an accountability group that I had been a part of when I was a new Christian. It helped and challenged me. It seemed that many of the relationships at church were surface and first name (if I could remember) at best. Everyone was busy, and we had no time to build relationships or "live life together." It took me nearly six months to obey God on starting a small men's group. A fear of failure and the voices of doubt and rejection crept in. "What if I am the only loser who wants to hang out with a group of guys?" "What if no one wants to participate? You know some of these guys, and that will be real embarrassing, or they will do it simply out of guilt and then quit two months later." "What if people think I am having an affair or my marriage is at high risk and that is why I am starting this group?

I was burdened for other marriages because we had three divorces in a matter of a year in our small Sunday school class. We knew of a suicide. I also knew that Dana and I were coming up on twenty years of marriage and that my parents' marriage had crumbled about that time. We didn't have a perfect marriage, but I was optimistic that I would never do anything stupid to jeopardize it. Was this optimism enough, or was it simply pride? Pride crept in, and I realized that I had thought that I could do this marriage and family thing all on my own. I recalled our early marriage when I was clueless how to be a dad. I embarked on a reading blitz to learn from godly experts. It was time to go on the offensive and build some walls around my marriage.

Men need men at all stages of marriage. Even single men need each other to stave off the world's missiles and temptations. Lord, why me? I am not capable of starting a small men's group! All the doubts and fears kept coming, but so did God's simple, gentle voice. Just obey. So I sent a proposal in to our Sunday school class leaders with no mention of an interest to lead it. We had three men say that they were interested in leading it, and in the first week more than half of the men in class had signed up! A year later, nearly twenty men are going strong to finish strong! Nearly a year later, these men are some of my closest friends and confidants. We have gone beyond surface. My doubts, my hesitations, my procrastination. Sorry, Lord, for my delay and my pride. Obey that still small voice. Be faithful in doing your part. Whew. Thanks God!

Light

The most dangerous thing for a human being is isolation. Plants and trees grow in the light. The enemy loves to work in the dark, and that is where sin can grow. (Read Ephesians 5:13–14.) Get out of the dark and into the light! Starting or joining a small couple's or men's group might be tough. "I don't know these guys at all. What will they think, that I am weak and need some sort of support group as a crutch?

In addition to prayer and having men stand shoulder to shoulder with them, some people choose to have a one-on-one time and go deeper yet and have someone hold them accountable for the important things in their lives. How are you treating your spouse? Are you hugging your kids? After you are comfortable, you can have them assist with a "secret challenge or sin" or "unfinished business," whether that be physical exercise, eating binges, hidden debt, a forgiveness, letting go of a grudge, or even shame. You need someone to trust who will encourage you and challenge you. You also need men to share a laugh with. There might be deeper issues you need to bring to a pastor/clergyman or a therapist, people who are sworn to codes of confidentiality but can pray with you and sort things out and help with a healing process.

Marriage Reflection

In our men's group, a few scriptures leapt off the pages as I was challenged to work on my marriage. I challenge you to take a few minutes to meditate on the following few passages, and see how you can practically apply them to your marriage:

Read Proverbs 31:10, 12; 1 Corinthians 11:3;
Ephesians 5:21–33; and 1 Peter 3:7.

How can you better treat your wife? Better understand her? Better give her honor? How is the relationship like that of Christ and the church?

A Vow

I recall a sermon our pastor was preaching on prayer. This was a sermon that had me riveted and locked in. At times, God speaks in "themes" to you over a period of time. There was a theme that kept popping up in this sermon—separation. He was gently poking me to "listen up." He has never spoken audibly to me, but I know when I hear something several different ways through several different media that He is trying to get my attention. What was a Nazarite? What vow was taken?

The preacher referred to a Nazarite vow. As I did a biblical study and read a few books on the topic, I discovered that the Hebrew root word meant "set apart for God, sanctified, consecrated to reflect God's glory." Some people would take a vow of separation as an act of discipline to draw closer to God. It was a choice they made. Wow. Humbling. Numbers 6:2 implies that if you desire, you can pursue such a relationship with God.

Read: Numbers 6:1–8; Judges 13:5; Lamentations 4:7;
Amos 2:11–12; and 2 Corinthians 6:17.

One thing they had in common: these Nazirites hotly pursued a heart completely abandoned to God. Samuel, Samson, and John the Baptist were divinely set apart and were mightily used to shift the course of nations. As I read Numbers 6, I determined to wrestle with "why" I needed to have a time of separation. I would deal with the "how" later.

v. 1—to hear from the Lord
v. 2—to separate myself to the Lord
v. 3–4—the how
v. 5, 8—holiness, purity

I remember the vows that I used to take when I was an older teenager. "Lord if the Tigers win this championship, I will go to church for the rest of my life." I remember the vow from our wedding, "until death do us part." As our pastor recounted the story of Samson that we all had heard so many times growing up, it was with jealousy this time that I heard of the long flowing locks of the Nazirite. I wished that I had the long flowing hair of my high-school experience. A day when I used to play with the curls of my golden locks and have my hair flowing freely from my baseball cap. Now the few hairs that I have flow freely to the shower drain or somehow get transplanted to my back. Sad days, but I digress.

425

It had been nearly twenty years since I had that pivotal moment when I made a decision to make Jesus the Lord of my life and surrender all. The twentieth anniversary of my John 3:3 birthday was just around the corner, and yet I knew that the fire was not burning as brightly as it used to. I still prayed, still went to church regularly, still was the spiritual leader of my family, but I just knew that there was something more I needed in my walk with the Lord. My spiritual life had become dry and mundane, and the prayer times I did have were times of habit and "checking the box" as opposed to real relationship. I was reading the Word as a discipline but was not soaking it up like a sponge. I knew that I was at a crossroads and needed my own "vow of separation."

The Why

I drafted my own "vow of separation" and did some reflecting on why I was doing it. It turned out that I needed this for quite a laundry list of reasons. That was probably why the Holy Spirit was prodding me. If you need a breakthrough with God, or if you are facing a big decision, I would suggest your own "vow of separation." This sounded easy, but it was a wake-up call because we are so saturated with the voices around us that you almost have to escape to a cabin in the wilderness to get truly separated!

My "separation vow" was to accomplish the following:
- to separate myself to the Lord—to have an undivided heart, wholly devoted to God (Luke 10:27)
- to stir up my gifts that had been on the shelf during this season of rest (2 Timothy 1:6)
- to revive myself—to be "on fire" once again for Him (Isaiah 57:15)
- to help me be a better husband and father
- to gain wisdom and anointing for writing this book
- to find godly friends, not lukewarm friends, for our kids
- to achieve holiness and purity (1 Peter 1:14–16)
- to express my gratefulness to God
- to prepare for the next year's priorities for me and my family
- to equip myself and the development of a long-term plan and obtain God's favor for the school we started
- to make a generational impact for our kids and ministry

Okay, so now the "why" had been determined: I wanted to pursue God, know Him better, be abandoned to Him, and be set apart for Him.

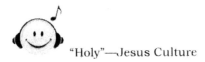

"Holy"—Jesus Culture

The How

No, I did not shave my head or find a priest to give two pigeons to. I knew that I couldn't take a convent cruise or quit my job for a month and rent a cabin, so I needed a practical way to make this "separation" thing work. Since I am not able to miss meals because of an illness, I decided that I would do an "all media" fast with a partial food fast. No beef, no pork, no fast food, no fries, no candy.

I determined not to pick up a newspaper, visit Facebook or Twitter, watch TV, listen to the radio, or spend nonministry time on the internet and to replace those times with worship, seeking God, reading the Bible, serving my family, or writing. This was a major wake-up call and in many ways more difficult than the food fast. After two days without ESPN, my hour with the newspaper, and idle chatting on the internet, I truly was empty. *That* was eye-opening! If I was empty without those things and full with them, then what place did God occupy in my life? No wonder I was dry. No wonder I had little joy or purpose. I did not realize the chasm between me and God.

We really don't realize our lukewarmness until we get hot again. I was lukewarm or cold at best, but the "frog in the boiling kettle" story really applied to me. I survived the withdrawal from my precious media and replaced those voids with worship CDs in the car, His Word, Bible reading, and serving my wife. I realized that God still loved me; He hadn't given up on me. Rather, He was gently wooing me back to Himself. The next few weeks were the sweetest times of intimacy with my Friend, my King since the early days of my salvation. One night, I spent an hour of prayer over my son while he slept, and it seemed like minutes. I still am amazed at how Jesus spent entire evenings in prayer, but I can relate to His inner circle, who always seemed to fall asleep on Him. However, when the distractions are removed, the chasm closes, and His Spirit willingly accepts our approaches. If we draw near to Him, He promises to draw near to us.

After one week, I felt so fulfilled, so complete—and so full of regret for the days of intimacy with my Father that I had missed. I regretted the bed that I hadn't help make, the prayers I hadn't prayed for my family, and the worship I used to love so dearly. My priorities were quickly back in order. I couldn't wait for the second week and was full of anticipation. This was the closest I had been to God since my salvation nearly a half of a lifetime ago, when "undivided heart" really meant something to me.

These media fasts have been so rewarding that I now make them a regular discipline in my spiritual life. I try to do one twenty-one-day period in November/December, and then do periodically shorter ones throughout the year. I am currently doing a Monday/Tuesday media fast for a season while finishing this book.

There are some great books on fasting by Bill Bright, Arthur Wallis, and Jentezen Franklin. Here are just a few of the biblical examples that might help you:

- A husband and wife's fasting (1 Cor. 7:5)
- Daniel's mourning and fasting 3 weeks, a fruit-and-vegetable fast (Daniel 10:1–3)
- Jesus' fasting (Matthew 4:1–11, Luke 4:1–2)
- The church's ministering to the Lord in fasting (Acts 13:2)
- Fasting in secret (Matthew 6:16–18)
- Ezra's proclaiming a fast that Israel might humble themselves (Ezra 8:21–23)
- David's mourning and weeping and fasting for Jonathan, the people, and Israel (2 Samuel 1:12)
- Nehemiah's fasting, weeping, praying (Nehemiah 1:4)
- Fasting, weeping, and a chastening of the soul (Psa. 69:10)
- Anna's serving God with fasting and prayers (Luke 2:37)

Holiness/Purity

One key element of living a righteous life and "staying in the light" is holiness. How can you stay holy and pure? With your eyes, ears, mind, and entire being.

1) Walk in the Spirit (Galatians 5:16–26)
2) Be filled with the Spirit (Ephesians 5:18–21)
3) Set your mind on things above; do it in the name of Jesus (Colossians 3:1–10)
4) Think and meditate on things that are pure, true, and lovely (Philippians 4:8)
5) Hide the Word in your heart so that you do not sin (Psa. 119:9–11)
6) Guard your heart (Prov. 4:23)
7) Draw the line; stay away from the line.
8) Don't act like pagans, giving in to lustful passions, overpowering urges, or cravings.
9) Crucify the flesh (Gal. 5:24)
10) Be dead to the world (Col. 2:20; 3:3)
11) Let God take the vengeance; leave it to Him. Be still and know that He is God. (Rom. 12:19; Heb. 10:30)
12) Glorify and thank God (Rom. 1:21)
13) Don't be proud (Rom. 1:22)
14) Do not be a slave to sin, but a slave to God; seek His freedom. (John 8:34–36)
15) Abstain from sexual immorality; do not reject God. (1 Thess. 4:3–8)

Your Mind and Body

The mind is where the battle takes place. The mind is a powerful weapon. How can you tame it?

1) Set your mind on things above, not on things on the earth (Col. 3:2)
2) Your entire body is the Lord's; be a slave of obedience to God. (1 Cor. 6:15)
3) Realize that the spiritual battle rages, and go to war in prayer. (Eph. 6:10–18)
4) Discipline your body (1 Cor. 9:24–27)
5) Flee! Treat your body like it is the temple of the Holy Spirit (1 Cor. 6:18–20; 3:16)
6) Be a slave of obedience to God (Rom. 6:16)
7) Take the escape path when it is given to you (1 Cor 10:13–14)
8) Use the power of God's Word (Matt. 4:1–11; Heb. 4:12–16)
9) Use the power of prayer when the flesh is weak (Matt. 26:36–41)
10) Don't let the desire give birth to sin (James 1:12–16)

 Read Galatians 6:7–8. There are consequences to disobedience and not following God. We will reap what we sow.

A Hard Heart?

I recall reading Joel 2 during a recent fast and being convicted about my hard heart and the lack of the depth of repentance for my lukewarmness. I had been reading about leaders crying before the Lord, weeping before Him, fasting and mourning. Had my heart gotten that hard? Had I taught my kids that hardness? God was gently asking me: "When is the last time you wept before me?" Not just a cry for the sake of crying. A cry because I was so grateful, or a cry because I was so awed at His awesomeness and holiness, or a cry because I was so deeply saddened and humbled over my sin and my lack of seeking Him, or a cry about the sins of our nation. It is a question I now ask myself often: Is my heart soft enough?

Our Eyes

Reading Job 31:1, I was struck that Job "made a covenant with his eyes." Our eyes and our thoughts can endanger us. Gazing, letting our eyes wander, leads to letting our minds wander. We can covet others' beauty, waistline, or hairline, or we can covet their possessions. Any of that can be unhealthful. The things we set our eyes upon can have a polluting effect. If you don't look, you are less likely to bite. The fruit was pleasant to Eve's *eyes*.[447]

Temptations abound. You don't have to go looking for sin anymore; sin looks for you, and temptation finds you at every turn. Media are a distraction, and technological advances bring an abundance of eye candy. The noise of constant media can be not only a temptation but also drown out God. It is *hard* to avoid—the billboards, the magazines telling you to drop forty pounds, TV, movies, scantily clad women popups on internet news sites, social network sites, etc. A cesspool is coming out of Los Angeles. Pornography brings in more revenue annually than the NBA, NFL, and MLB combined. It is destroying lives and marriages.

Many of these things are just plain worthless in the long run. They are not only time wasters but also temptation feeders. LOOK AWAY!

Psalm 101:3—"I will set nothing wicked before my eyes."
Psalm 119:37—"I will turn away my eyes from looking at worthless things."
Matthew 6:22-23, Luke 11:34—"If your eyes are good, the whole body is good."

STOP Read the following scriptures to help you with any temptations. Prov. 7:24-27; 25:28; Romans 6:12; 13:13–14; Gal. 5:16–17, 24; 6:7–8; Eph. 4:23; Heb. 2:18; 4:15; 12:14; and 1 Peter 2:11.

I can remember walking through the mall with my two boys and seeing soaring, in-your-face wall photos outside Victoria's Secret and Abercrombie and Fitch. The kids always knew to "look away." We held each other accountable. When the scantily clad cheerleaders or a Victoria Secret ad come on TV, they knew to look away. You might say, well, can't we just appreciate the beauty? How much are you appreciating it? Is it depreciating the beauty of our spouse? Is it leading to an impure thought life? Are you teaching your children that a glance is okay? Should we allow a thirty- or sixty-minute show into our homes with an R-rated dress code and language? Such things can become a doorway to greater lusts and greater temptations. Kids watch our actions more than they listen to our words.

A challenge to men exists in Proverbs 6:25–28 and Matthew 5:27–30. Don't play with fire. I remember reading about circumcision and thinking how utterly painful that sounded. This holiness process is circumcision of the heart, so it will be difficult and painful.

 Pray: Lord, give me an undivided heart! Help me to lead a blameless life. Help me to be a person of integrity both publically and privately. Protect my ears, my eyes, and my mind. I offer up my body as a living sacrifice. Transform my mind, Lord (Romans 12:2).

Hunger for Holiness—Carman

Legacy Lesson: We are facing a man gap. It is time for men to step up to the plate and lead spiritually. We have been sitting in the stands too long. We need some Nazarite voices. Some radical John the Baptists. Ask for help. Read. Talk to your wife. Read the scriptures in this book. Start or join a men's group. Time is short. Your family is too important.

CHAPTER 65

REAL FAITH TOOLKIT:
PRAY EFFECTIVELY-
CLOSET SECRETS OF POWER

I would rather teach a man to pray than one to preach.
—DL Moody

Come Sail Away

*S*ometimes we don't even know our hardness of heart until we "come sail away," and separate to God. I realized my backslidden and lukewarm state only after a Nazarite fast. Sometimes God is just looking for us to do the little things. I am mindful of David Wilkerson and the impact of his ministry. He passed away on April 27, 2011. He was the author of "The Cross and the Switchblade." He moved to New York's inner city, started a powerful ministry to addicts (Teen Challenge and Life Challenge), and led a church of more than 8000. A multigenerational impact all started with one act of obedience.

"Fifty years of ministry began with one act of obedience. As a young pastor David Wilkerson made the decision to turn off his television and give his time and attention completely to God. It was a decision that would have immeasurable impact on his life and ministry."448

What can you give less time to so you can have more time in prayer and more time focused on legacy lifestyle things? Start with five minutes a morning and five minutes an evening in prayer. It will change things, most importantly your heart.

PPP—Prayer Precedes Pillow. I will not sleep until prayer (Psa. 132:4-5)
BBB—Bible Before Breakfast (Mark 1:35)

We underestimate the value and power of pray. I recall hearing the story of a widow in a retirement home who had nothing to do but pray. She wrote letters to prisoners and spent her waking hours praying for them. Her wall was plastered with letters of transformed lives. Many prisoners came to visit her upon their release to thank her for her prayers.

Life is precious. Time is precious. Don't delay. Start now. Make every day count. Forget the day you wasted or when you failed; start afresh. You can achieve nothing more important from this book than growing closer to your God. His mercies are new every morning. Don't be a casualty. I have heard it said, "A casual approach to prayer brings casualties." Sometimes it is difficult to know how to pray. Here are some examples and suggestions.

1) WHO/WHAT

- Your family/circle of influence (John 17:6–19)—This was Jesus' prayer
- Jesus' prayer for all believers (John 17: 20–26)
- Anyone and everyone- to know the love of Christ (Ephesians 3:14-21)
- For your nation/people (Daniel 9:1–19)
- For spiritual eyes to be opened to the warfare around (2 Kings 6:17–18)
- For deliverance in a battle (1 Chronicles 5:20)—cried out to God in the battle
- For your heavenly Father's presence (Romans 8:15)—cry out, "Abba, Father."
- With thanksgiving (1 Thess. 2:13; 3:10)—thank God without ceasing, night-and-day
- Pray for laborers (Luke 10:2)
- Pray not to enter into temptation (Luke 22:40, 46)
- An act of worship—ministering to the Lord in fasting and prayer (Acts 13:1–4)
- Pray the Psalms in your own words as you read them

2) HOW

- The most honest prayer you can pray is, "Lord, teach me to pray." (Luke 11:1)
- Fervent, passionate (James 5:16–18)
- Give God time (Psa. 109:4)—give yourself to prayer, not dead lists
- Humbly, repenting, seeking God (2 Chron. 7:1)—"If my people. . . ."
- Don't give up (Luke 18:1)—Jesus encouraged them to pray and not to lose heart
- Boldly, expecting God to hear (Heb. 4:12–16)—come boldly to the throne of grace
- Praying for Knowledge (Col. 1:3, 9)—praying for others and praying of knowledge
- Persistent prayer (Matt. 26:36–42)—persistent prayer and prayer in solitude
- Humble, contrite heart (Ezra 10:1)—prayer, humble, weeping bitterly over sin
- Prayer time alone (Luke 9:18)
- Praying with others (Luke 9:28) - praying with Peter, James, John
- Mix prayer and giving (Acts 10:4)
- With weeping and groaning (John 11:33–38)
- God's spirit is interceding for us! (Rom. 8:26)

3) WHERE

- In a regular spot (Luke 11:1)—Jesus prayed in a regular place
- Everywhere and anywhere (1 Thess. 5:17)—pray without ceasing
- In Solitude (Luke 5:16)—Jesus withdrew in the wilderness to pray
- In Secret (Matt. 6:5–15)—pray in secret, not vain repetitions
- To a Deserted place (Mark 6:31–32, 46)

4) WHEN

- Early in the morning (Mark 1:35)—Jesus prayed early in the morning
- Continually (Acts 6:4)—give ourselves continually to prayer
- Jesus prayed all night (Luke 6:12)
- Night and day (1 Thess. 3:10)—thank God without ceasing, night and day prayer
- Constantly (Acts 12:5)—power of constant prayer

 "I Want to Be Found Faithful"—Justin Rizzo

Your Calendar

Have you ever talked to someone about getting together and said, "Hey, I look forward to getting together with you. See you tomorrow for lunch?" No, you set up a time and place to meet. My prayer life was inconsistent until I found a consistent, *daily time* and *place* for prayer. Yes, we need to pray without ceasing and pray as the Lord directs throughout the day, but we also need that regular time.

Some of my best times of prayer are in the darkness of my closet, hidden away from sights and sounds, surrounded by dirty clothes. Other times, God's sweet presence can be found as I walk about in nature. Find the place where you can get away to commune with God. Sometimes we can get too rigid, routine, or religious in our prayers. Reverence, yes. Reality and authenticity, yes. Abba, Father. Be a son or a daughter who is loved by a dad. Get away from the rigidity of the list and locale and just talk to your Heavenly Father!

Pray until You Pray

This is a bit of Puritan advice I heard recently. I have also heard the phrase "praying through." What that means to me is getting beyond the list and beyond the formality or the feelings of "I have to pray." It is praying long enough and honestly enough at a single session to get past those feelings of formalism, and past the rush to be done with the duty of praying. Stick to it for a while. At some point, you will come to sense the Holy Spirit's presence, to a spiritual depth. Many of us in the Western world pray like little children who ring front door bells and run away before we give time for an answer.[449]

I sometimes start off prayer with either worship or a psalm and then move to my Prayer Card (see the appendices) to help guide my praying for my family.

Model Praying

In James 5:14–18, James talks about prayers of faith; anointing with oil; and effective, fervent, passionate, persistent prayer. He then mentions praying like Elijah. No wonder James talks of Elijah. In 1 Kings 18:41–45, Elijah had faith and many other characteristics that we should model in prayer.

1) He had faith: "For there is the sound of abundance of rain," yet there was not a cloud in the sky!

2) He took time and was purposeful: Elijah then made a special trip to the top of Mt. Carmel to pray. Surely that wasn't a two-minute stroll.

3) He prayed passionately: "He bowed down on the ground and put his face between his knees."

4) He was persistent. He told his servant to go look for rain seven times.

5) He had faith: "There is a cloud, as small a man's hand," yet he said, "Go down before the rain stops you."

6) It rained!

Nudges

Yes, we are to pray continuously. Yes, we are to have a regular set place of prayer. These are powerful disciplines and are key to a healthy relationship with God. I had been praying and asking the Lord to give me more of an appetite for Him in my 2nd Half. He has been answering in an expected way. Nudges.

Have you ever had the craving for cookies, chips, or fast food? How does it all begin? With a quick thought in your brain that quickly races to your stomach, which usually results in quickly sprinting to the kitchen or drive-thru. That "nudge" starts with a quick thought and then results in an action. Often if we wait the urge goes away. Sometimes it is a longer wrestling match, especially if on a diet.

Prayer is the same way. The nudge for candy or a soda is NOT the Holy Spirit. The nudge to pray is the Holy Spirit. He is gently reminding us to pray and open His word. The Spirit within us is jealous and yearns for our fellowship (see James 4:5). A day rarely goes by when I don't "hear the nudge". The challenge is answering the nudge immediately, before the urge goes away. The nudge may come in the car or at bedtime. It may be when engaged in an activity. If the "nudge" occurs it is probably not your flesh! It is God knocking. Will we answer and open the door and let Him in, or will the nudge be ignored? When I do ignore the nudges, I am ignoring my best friend, and an Almighty God. If you are getting multiple nudges, know that there could be an urgency in the spiritual realm and God wants to use you in prayer.

Power!

I recall one season where my wife and I were being challenged to pray for one of our teenage children during a time of battle and rebellion. After using the normal parental weapons of grounding, taking stuff, and a bit of yelling mixed in, we realized that the normal things weren't working. We realized that this spiritual battle would take a little more spiritual firepower (Matthew 17:21). I felt like God wanted me to pray daily with my wife—just briefly—even if just for 30 seconds. "No problem God, how hard can that be", I thought. The nudge came daily. Sometimes multiple times. Yet the battle for a quick bed-time prayer was sometimes unthinkable. I spent more time battling the nudge than the prayer would take. Know that the greater battle, sometimes the louder the nudge. This particular battle was a spiritual battle so the nudge was regular.

Our small group was studying the power of prayer and the battles and obstacles to pray (*Prayer Quest* by Dee Duke). The author challenged us to pray for one hour interrupted just one time during the week. Most of us had not done that in a while, if ever. It had been a daily battle of procrastination for me. Yet 2 hours went by so easily as I watched a baseball game. We choose in life our priorities. When I finally obeyed that nudge and grabbed my Bible, and prayed out loud as I read, mixed with some worship, that hour seemed like much less (except for the first 5 minutes), as I left the outer courts and entered the inner courts to fellowship with my friend and Father.

Spiritual warfare is real. The devil isn't causing fumbles on the football field, hiding behind every rock, or making you run out of gas, but demons and the devil are real. These battles might not be about just that daily challenge; they might be about generational issues or your attempt to make a generational impact.

"Most of us as American Christians say we believe in the existence of demons and spiritual forces, but it rarely moves beyond theory for us. This is a key difference compared with our brothers and sisters in the majority of the world. They pray with a sense of urgency and dependency. We are so influenced by the comforts of life in the West that the miracles of Jesus often seem like a first-century phenomenon rather than reality for today."[450] Spiritual warfare is prevalent throughout the Bible. Consider just a few examples.

STOP Read 1 Chronicles 21:1; Daniel 9:20-21; 10:1–13; Zechariah 3:1–5; Mark 1:23–27; 5:1–13; 9:25–29; 16:9; Luke 4:8–14; 7:21; 8:12, 27–39; 10:19–20; 13:11–13; John 10:10; Acts 26:18; 2 Corinthians 10:3–6; Eph. 6:10–18; 1 Tim. 4:1; Jude 9; Hebrews 1:14; 13:2.

Know that your prayers are making an impact in the heavenlies. A battle is going on, and prayer is your ammo!

Potty Break

There are two reasons this is the last item in the chapter. First, my wife would not approve of it. Second, I am not sure that *I* approve of it. However, this is an idea buffet! Let me make this clear that this next concept might be sacrilege to some of you. My apologies, but I will blame my boys. We were talking about prayer and how hard it is to find time. After some joking about how much time they spent in the bathroom every day, I did some quick math and said, "If you guys spent as much time praying as you did in your bathroom trips, you could spend *1 year* of your life praying! To be painfully literal, if we spent our bathroom time praying each day, we would each spend a year of our life praying. This idea could be a new resolution waiting to happen for someone reading this book!

Influential Prayer Movements:
- International House of Prayer (24/7 streaming prayer with a worship room)
- The Church at Brook Hills (secret church, discussed by David Platt in *Radical*)
- Yoido Full Gospel Church (Prayer Mountain)

"When I Pray," Darrell Evans

The man—God's man—is made in the closet. His life and his most profound convictions are born in his secret communion with God.
—EM Bounds

The one concern of the devil is to keep the saints from prayer.
He fears nothing from prayerless studies, prayerless work, and prayerless religion. He laughs at our toil, mocks at our wisdom, but he trembles when we pray."
—Jonathan Edwards

"A culture of prayer is what is needed, not a prayer meeting."
—Lou Engle

"One who knew him well wrote, 'He thought prayer to be more his business than anything else, and I have seen him come out of the closet with a serenity of face next to shining."
—E.M. Bounds writing of John Wesley

"If I fail to spend 2 hours in prayer each morning,
the devil gets the victory. I have so much business I cannot get on without spending 3 hours daily in prayer."
—Martin Luther

"A spirit of intercession had so possessed me that I prayed almost day and night. My life was literally swallowed up in prayers. . . prayer literally consumed me."[451]
—Frank Bartleman

"The world has yet to see what God will do
with a man fully consecrated to Him."
—J. C. Pollock

"Make my Life a Prayer to You," Keith Green

Legacy Lesson: Prayer is powerful, but more importantly prayer is relationship. Relationship with a heavenly Father and faithful friend who is in control of all. God can influence your legacy like none other. Seek to know Him!

CHAPTER 66

REAL FAITH TOOLKIT: WORSHIP AND THE WORD- GET AN APPETITE

"A man's heart reflects the man."
—Proverbs 27:19 (Hebrews Names Version)

*L*ife's noises are plentiful and often painful. One way to drown them out, or at least deal with them in the best way, is to praise. I am not talking about singing. I am not talking about listening to a CD, a choir, or a band leader. I am talking about entering into a time of intimate worship with your Creator, your heavenly Father. Sometimes we sing as if He were not in the room, singing *about* Him and not *to* Him. Worship is a heart-and-mind exercise. It is a fixation on God. It is giving Him enough attention that makes it obvious that there is nothing we want more than Him. It is like someone who is thirsty in a desert and will do anything to be in the presence of a drink of water. To just look at the water and observe the water or watch other people drinking the water sounds ridiculous. However, we often go through the motions of singing.

As I sat in ICU this week, a desperation came over me. An insatiable appetite for God. I have devoured His Word and worshipped Him freely and regularly these past few months. I was not hungry for TV or entertainment. They were only empty. The only fullness came through the Bible and worship. *Worship* means "to assign worth" or value to. We have many reasons to worship the King of Kings and Lord of Lords.

The Westminster Shorter Catechism,[452] written in the 1640s by Englishmen and Scots, was used to educate laymen in matters of doctrine and belief. The catechism is considered by many Protestants to be the greatest doctrinal statement that resulted from the English Reformation. The first question is about our purpose, back to the "what-is-my-purpose" and "how-to-act-upon-that" questions:

Q1:   What is the chief end of man?
A: Man's chief end is to glorify God and to enjoy Him forever.

Get alone and plan for 15 minutes of worship.

1) Listen to the song "As the Deer" by Matt Gilman, or watch and worship on You Tube.

"As the Deer"—Matt Gilman

2) Read and meditate upon Psalm 42:1–4; John 4:23–24; Psalm 27:4; Psalm 84:2.

3) Listen to the song again. This time, don't just sing it; set your heart on a pilgrimage. Get hungry. Worship your Savior. Make it your prayer. Close your eyes if you need to, and shut out the distractions.

David was a man after God's own heart. His was a lifestyle of worship. He wrote hundreds of magnificent psalms. I can picture him worshiping God as he hung out with the sheep all day. God desires your worship. If you can't sing it from the very depths of your being and mean the words, then sing it and make it the cry of your heart, longing for it to be true, make it your prayer to God to help you want this passion to seek Him with all of your heart, soul, mind, and strength. He will not let you down. He will meet you right where you are. If you ask Him for bread, will He give you a serpent? The Holy Spirit is a person, and He desires to know you intimately.

Our natural inclination is to know God in our head. To know about Him instead of knowing Him or worshiping Him. We tend to read the Word for knowledge—to engage our minds rather than our hearts or souls. I have been successful at taking a weekend sabbatical retreat or a lengthy fast nearly annually to rejuvenate spiritually, seek God, and to know Him more fully. I have turned a business trip once in a while into evenings of a full media fast when it is just me, my Bible, worship music, and a notebook.

Paul and Silas sang when they were arrested and beaten for preaching the gospel. Saul was comforted, and distressing spirits left him when David played the harp. I have tried to turn my car into a sanctuary, especially during media fasts. I have Hillsong, Matt Redman, Bluetree, CFNI, Michael W.Smith, and Jesus Culture CDs in the car and on my iPOD. Find your own musical taste that brings you into the presence of the King.

Praise also unleashes God's power.

Read 2 Chronicles 5:12–14; 2 Chronicles 20:20–23; 1 Samuel 16:23; Acts 16:25–26. Go ahead and drown out life's noise with the praises of His name.

"Pursuit"- Daniel Bashta, Kim Walker Smith

"Life's Noise"—Bluetree

The Word

> *"The Bible was not given for our information,*
> *but rather our transformation."*
> —D.L. Moody

The Westminster Shorter Catechism's[453] second question deals with how to glorify God and enjoy Him forever. Obviously, worship as we just discussed, is a primary way.

Q2:   What rule has God given to direct us *how* we may glorify and enjoy Him?
A: The Word of God, which is contained in the Scriptures of the Old and New Testaments, is the only rule to direct us how we may glorify and enjoy Him.

It is incredible to me that God used forty different men over a period of 1500 years (1400 BC to AD 90) to write the Bible. These were ordinary men. David was a shepherd. Matthew was a tax collector, John and Peter were fishermen, and Luke was a doctor. God did not use the leading intellectual of the day to speak through, but rather common people. The Bible is sixty-six books, thirty-nine Old Testament and twenty-seven New Testament books. John Wycliffe was key in getting the Bible translated in 1382 and William Tyndale did likewise in 1525–1535. The King James Version we now read was published in 1611.

The Bible was given by inspiration of God, and is profitable for doctrine, for reproof, for correction, for instruction in righteousness, that the man of God may be complete, thoroughly equipped for every good work (2 Timothy 3:16–17). All scripture is of divine inspiration. Paul talked of receiving his words from the Spirit of God (1 Corinthians 2:10-13). Even Jesus quoted and thereby validated the Old Testament books (Matthew 4:4, 7, 10; 5:17–18; 10:15; 12:40–41; 22:29; Luke 24:44).

Its prophecies have been fulfilled and will continue to be fulfilled.
- The birthplace of Jesus was predicted 700 years before His birth (Micah 5:2, fulfilled in Luke 4–7).
- Christ would be born of a virgin (Isaiah 7:14, fulfilled in Matthew 1:18–25).
- Jesus' triumphal entry into Jerusalem was predicted 700 years before its occurrence (Zechariah 9:9, fulfilled in John 12:12-15).
- Christ's crucifixion and suffering were predicted 700 years earlier (Psalm 22:14–18, fulfilled in John 19:23–37).

God reveals Himself in many ways. He is creative. But His primary way is through His Word. It is God's Word, His mouthpiece. It is authoritative. It teaches, it convicts, and it leads us down paths of right living. It is a light in a dark world and lights our paths forward. It is powerful. It is life changing, and it has influenced more people than any other book. It has stood strong for thousands of years. It defeats spiritual forces. I have found that worship and reading and studying His Word is the best way to get to know Him—when mixed with prayer.

You will also get to know God through sufferings and trials. He will speak to you in your sufferings as much as He does in your blessings. God *does* bless and *will* bless. I do a detailed study on blessing in *Ease the Squeeze*, but I sure don't think that the fol-

439

lowing verses would sell too well today in our Western World. Jesus commented on Paul's conversion and upcoming Christian life: "I will show him how much he will suffer for my name."[454] Paul wrote to Timothy "that he must endure hardship and suffering, even with chains."[455] Some people have titles bestowed upon themselves and advertise them prominently—bishop, cardinal, reverend, MBA, doctor. But when you read 2 Timothy 2, Paul was bestowing upon himself the title of "prisoner of Jesus Christ." Paul, Peter and others call themselves "bondservant of Jesus Christ." Wow, you don't see that on too many business cards these days. Get to know Him!

John F. MacArthur[456] recommends five ways to know and eight reasons to read the Bible.

Ways to Know It

- Hear the Bible (Romans 10:17)
- Read the Bible (Revelation 1:3)
- Study the Bible (Acts 17:11)
- Memorize the Bible (Psalm 119:9–11)
- Meditate on the Bible (Psalm 1:2–3)

Reasons to Read It

- To be approved by God (2 Timothy 2:15)
- To grow in the Lord and taste and see the Lord's grace (1 Peter 2:2)
- To not sin against God (Psalm 119:11)
- To fear and revere God (Psalm 119:38)
- To have a light to our feet and path, and to guide, to show, to lead, and to direct us (Psalm 119:105)
- To be blessed (Luke 11:28)
- To gain faith (Romans 10:17)
- To be taught, to be corrected, to be trained (2 Timothy 3:16)

A watered down, easy gospel is getting easier and easier to find. Find a church that preaches the Word in its entirety. We must hear the good news, the self-help, the power of God, but we must hear of salvation, death, sin, suffering, repentance, and God's judgment. Be sure that the whole gospel is being taught.

> *"The Moral Law tells us the tune we have to play;*
> *our instincts are merely the keys."*
> —C.S. Lewis

> *"If there is a universal moral law,*
> *then there must be a universal law giver."*
> —C.S. Lewis

"Deep in Love with You," Michael W. Smith

Legacy Lesson: To have you better know God as a result of this book is my prayer for you. God's Holy Spirit can transform your mind and soul and set you free. Jesus Christ is interceding for you now and desires that the rest of your life roadmap is surrendered to Him. No legacy is eternally fulfilling without God's direction and favor.

Resources that will help you:

- IamSecond.com
- Need Him.com
- SearchforJesus.net
- PeacewithGod.net

Christian resources and other information
is available at **www.achristianlife.net**

CHAPTER 67

YOUR LASTING LEGACY: A LEGACY LIFESTYLE

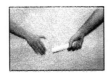

"We will tell the next generation the praiseworthy deeds of the Lord,
His power, and the wonders He has done."
—Psalm 78:4

God Moments

*A*s I covered earlier in the book, I believe it is important to document your Milestone Markers in Life. In addition to some major events, you might also have some major "spiritual" stories/"God stories" that need to be passed down and told to your children. The following list is my own personal effort to do this.

"Great is the Lord and most worth of praise; His greatness no one can fathom.
One generation will commend Your works to another, they will tell of your
mighty acts."
—Psalm 145:3–4

❖ Christ's Community: the first time "experiencing God" and His power	Age 12
❖ Internship, Texas Instruments; move from Michigan to Texas	Age 22
❖ Late-night God encounters: Charles Stanley, Dwight Thompson	Age 24
❖ Umbrella incident with Dana; thank God for timely rain!	Age 25
❖ Totaled car/seat-belt-angel incident, Lewisville, Texas	Age 25
❖ Salvation experience	Age 25
❖ Strong conviction to give up personal aspirations/idols and make Him Lord	Age 25
❖ First teaching experience in Sunday school	Age 26

❖ Fully furnished house blessing, 5088 Thompson, The Colony, Texas	Age 26
❖ Prayer counselor encounter in Dallas, Texas, with Steve Diemer	Age 27
❖ Tough meeting with dad about family priorities	Age 32
❖ Diagnosed with Bradbury Eggleston Syndrome/flat on my back	Age 32
❖ Clint Bratcher/Wylie Baptist/First Financial seminar	Age 32
❖ Children's ministry trip with Tracy Jantz/his challenge to write *Ease*	Age 35
❖ Emily's salvation (w/Dad): swingset, 5229 Boxwood Ln, McKinney, TX	Age 36
❖ Carpet moment, 4300 Meadow Hill; Be willing to give all to start CCA	Age 37
❖ Jacob's salvation (w/Dad), bedroom, 5229 Boxwood Ln, McKinney, TX	Age 37
❖ Call from Mary Maddoux/loved $ bill on cover of *Ease the Squeeze*	Age 38
❖ Call from Steve Moore (first radio guest after Larry Burkett's death)	Age 38
❖ Grand Canyon desert/timing belt incident	Age 41
❖ Justin's salvation (with Mom): 4300 Meadow Hill, McKinney, Texas	Age 42
❖ Rushed to ER/Dr. Divine Appointment/Pacemaker/*Lasting Legacy*	Age 46

"Tell it to your children, and let your children tell it to their children,
And their children to the next generation"
—Joel 1:3

Final Action

This book's purpose was to help you discern and act to live a purposeful second half and leave a lasting legacy. You are leaving a legacy—a spiritual legacy, a financial legacy, a character-and-reputation legacy, a family legacy, and a memory legacy. This legacy will last for generations. The following excerpt from *The Greatest Salesman in the World*[457] is my final bit of pulpit pounding to challenge you to move out in *action*.

My dreams are worthless, my plans are dust, my goals are impossible. All are of no value unless they are followed by action.

I will act now.

Never has there been a map, however carefully executed to detail and scale, which carried its owner even an inch of ground. Action alone is the tinder which ignited the map. Action is the food and drink that will nourish my success.

I will act now.

My procrastination which has held me back was born of fear and now I recognize this secret mined from the depths of all courageous hearts. Now I know that action reduces the lion of terror to an ant of equanimity.

443

I will act now.

I will not avoid the tasks of today and charge them to tomorrow for I know that tomorrow never comes. For it is better to act and fail than not to act and flounder. Without action all fruit will die on the vine.

I will act now.

I will repeat these words again and again, each day, every day, until the words become as much a habit as my breathing and the actions which follow become as instinctive as the blinking of my eyelids. When I am tempted to quit I will say them again.

I will leap from my cot and let failure sleep yet another hour.
I will let failure wait outside with fear and trepidation.
I will walk where failure fears to walk.
I will work when the failure seeks rest.
I will talk when the failure remains silent.
I will say it is done before the failure says it is too late.

For now is all I have.

Tomorrow is the day reserved for the labor of the lazy. I am not lazy.
Tomorrow is the day when the evil become good. I am not evil.
Tomorrow is the day the weak become strong. I am not weak.
Tomorrow is the day when the failure will succeed. I am not a failure.
I will act now.

Success will not wait. If I delay, success will become betrothed to another and lost to me forever.

This is the time.
This is the place.
I am the man.

I will act now.

"[T]he man who really counts in the world is the doer, not the mere critic-the man who actually does the work, even if roughly and imperfectly, not the man who only talks or writes about how it ought to be done."
—Theodore Roosevelt (1891)

"Do not merely listen to the Word and so deceive yourselves.
Do what it ways."
—James 1:22

A Legacy Lifestyle

It is human nature to *desire* to improve, to want to be better, to love our families, to be more like God. It is also very difficult to do, especially in our weak, human condition. Our own strength is not enough. That is why I close with the briefest, yet most important chapter in the book, the ultimate "how-to" advice.

Ezekial 36:26 says to take out the heart of stone and put in a heart of flesh. First Samuel 16:7 says that man looks at the outward appearance, but the Lord looks at the heart. Paul, who wrote much of the New Testament, knew that his "one thing" was to know Christ (Phil. 3:10). The best opinion and the best advice I can give you is not to take my advice, not to read more books, but to know Him and ask Him for His help. This really isn't a self-help book but a self-surrender book.

 Read James 1:5-8 and Philippians 4:13

Pursue Him as a deer pants for water. Ask Him to help you get thirsty for Him. You might not feel thirsty for Him, or the Spirit might be now stirring that desire up in you. Seek Him. Involve God, not as co-pilot, but as pilot. Don't be overwhelmed. He is not looking for you to have all of the answers. Neither is your family. Jesus said, "This is the one I esteem, the one that has a humble and a contrite spirit." Not the know it all.

He will help you with the priorities. Start with the little things. Make that first little thing and your ultimate dream be to love the Lord your God with all your heart, all your soul, all your mind, and all your strength. Inquire of the Lord. That is why God blessed David. The other kings did not inquire; they just made their own plans and went to war.

Never doubt that you are here to make an impact. You were not created so wonderfully and put on this earth to just bide your time. Learn from the past, live for today, prepare and plan for the future. You are here to make an impact, and God is not into wasting time. God will do His part, but He is counting on you to do your part. Always bloom where you are planted. You might not be able to choose your circumstances, but you can choose your response to those circumstances.

God has a generational mindset. Just read all of those genealogies in the Bible, or consider the hundreds of times the word *generation* is used in God's Word. You can read often about God's generational blessings—through Abraham, Isaac, and Jacob, through Joseph and Moses. God's truths have endured these many generations. The impact of Jesus Christ has had an incredible generational impact, seen by billions, and unmatched by any other man or god. With the Lord, one day is like a thousand years and a thousand years is like one day. You are here to influence generations to come, so do not take that lightly. Your choices will greatly affect how that plays out. We read and hear often about the generational impact of man's failure, whether it be Adam's sin, the Israelites wasting a generation while trudging through the wilderness, or poor choices of kings, judges, and other leaders who led others away from an Almighty God. Closer to home, you hear the stories of moral failure, or a crushing debt load that will affect you and our country for generations to come. Our choices lead to a generational impact—good or bad.

The Marathon

Living a legacy lifestyle requires a generational mindset. Life is a marathon, each choice representing a twist, turn, or choice of path. Stay on the narrow path. Do not pull a muscle or get dehydrated during this next season of your life. Drink of the Spirit, long for God, work out spiritually, be disciplined. Always be ready for the battle or the competition. Do not let others be your yardstick. Go deeper. Most of your peers throughout life are satisfied with dipping their toe in the river of God. Get wet and stay wet. Think and act generationally. Prepare now to pass the baton to your kids and grandkids.

You are great in God's eyes. He loves you and takes pleasure in you (Psalm 147:11; 149:4). Be purposeful in ensuring that you do not squander your gifts, your life, or your talents. Be faithful in the little things, and He will put you in charge of greater things. The "little things" begin *now* in this season of your life. May you set eternity in your heart (Ecclesiastes 3:11).

Leave a lasting legacy.

"I will sing of the Lords great love forever; with my mouth will I make Your faithfulness known through all generations."
—Psalm 89:1

"Your name, O Lord, endures forever, your renown,
O Lord, through all generations."
—Psalm 135:13

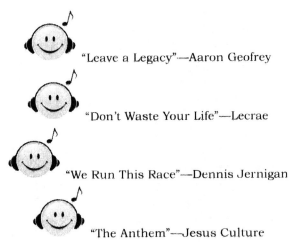

"Leave a Legacy"—Aaron Geofrey

"Don't Waste Your Life"—Lecrae

"We Run This Race"—Dennis Jernigan

"The Anthem"—Jesus Culture

APPENDIX

THE IDEA BUFFET CHECKLIST: YOUR LEGACY PLAN

*I*know it is difficult when reading a self-help book to boil 500 pages down to some actionable things to apply in your life. I have tried to assist you with that effort. Get a highlighter and your calendar, and begin to prioritize which menu items are top priority. You don't want to fill your plate too full, but know that different levels of action are needed.

A= TOP PRIORITY, NON-NEGOTIABLE,
Absolutely must do NOW, no procrastinating
B= MEDIUM PRIORITY,
I know I must do, need to start within the next month
C= LOW PRIORITY, I should do, just don't have
bandwidth now, will reconsider in 3 months
D= Broccoli / Sauerkraut, not for me, this menu item is for the dogs

FUTURE

Chapter	Priority	Legacy Action	Start Date
1		Take your "Legacy" temperature	
2		Take the Generational Gap Quiz	
3		Document your Milestone Marker Moments	
4		Take your Learned Legacy Inventory	
5		Get a multi-generational multiplication mindset	
6		Answer the 3 "rest of your life" questions	
7		Contemplate the future legacy questions	
8		Complete the Retirement Interests and Talents Assessment	
8		Complete the Retirement Location Scorecard	
10		Contemplate the Seasons of your life	

11		Complete the "Invest in You" Checklist & Priorities	
12		Identify your Fears, Failures and Regrets/Lessons Learned	
13		Complete your Life Mission	
13		Develop your Dream Plan	
13		Draft your "Second Half" Plan	
13		Draft your Purpose Plan	
13		Develop a set of Life-Guiding Principles	
14		Set Specific Short Term Goals	
14		Develop Long Term Life Ladder Scorecard	
15		Worry, Stress and Overload Anecdote (Peace/Hope)	
16		Overcoming Trials and Worry	

FAMILY

Chapter	Priority	Legacy Action	Start Date
17		Develop a Family Modeling Plan	
18		Develop Family Boundaries	
20		Determine your role in Reformation	
20		Lead Your Children Scorecard	
21		Complete Time, Touch, Talk Scorecard	
21		Develop Family Behaviors Checklist	
22		Start Your Family Feast	
23		Develop Family Spiritual Disciplines	
23		Start Date Nights	
24		Brainstorm Family Connections	
24		Family Volunteer / Outreach Activity Plan	
25		Start Family Prayer and Bible Reading	
25		Complete Teen Discussion Survey	
27		Purposeful Parenting and Discipline Plan	
28		Parenting Problems and Tough Discussions	
28		Develop Media Boundaries	
29		Conduct Rite of Passage: Child	
29		Create Memory Treasure Chest	
30		Complete Marriage Check-up Questionnaire	
31		Conduct Love, Respect and Needs Review	

31		Marriage Challenges	
32		Complete Finishing Strong Report Card	
32		Complete Husband Checklist	
34		Complete Tongue Assessment	
35		Develop Battle Plan	
36		Identify your Educational Goals/Priorities	
37		Develop Your Worldview	
37		Determine Educational Model for Your Children	
38		Choosing a College Plan	
38		Conduct Teen Goal Interview	
39		Start College Preparation Checklist	
39		Start College Site Visit Checklist	
41		Create Parent Tribute	
41		Create Family Treasure Chest	
41		Create Memory Museum	
42		Create Family Vision	
42		Create Scripture Memory List	
42		Develop Code of Conduct / Core Values	
42		Develop Family Battle Plan	
42		Develop Family Short Term Goals	
42		Develop Family Long Term Goals	

FINANCES

Chapter	Priority	Legacy Action	Start Date
46		Blessings or Curses Study	
46		Financial Debt Solution Plan	
47		Millionaire Secrets Plan	
47		Secure Financial Future Change List	
47		Financial Basics Summary	
47		Financial Shake-up Test	
48		Financial Freedom List	
48		Financial Readiness Test	
48		Financial Warning Signs Test	
49		Complete Daily Spend Sheet	
49		Complete Save to Spend List	
49		Complete Big Ticket List	

49		Complete Debt Hit List	
49		Complete Cash Only Control List	
49		Develop Budget	
49		Set Financial Goals	
50		Complete Financial Survey	
50		Develop Risk/Return Portfolio	
51		Two Income Decision	
51		Teach Kids Money Management	
52		Planning for Hard Times	
52		Execute a Will	
53		Preparing for Retirement Planning	
53		Develop Vision for Retirement	
53		Retire Early Success Factors Assessment	
54		Where to Retire Analysis	
54		Money Management Change Plan	
55		Develop a Generational Mindset	
56		Gain a Global Perspective	
56		Cures for Hoarding Self Assessment	

FAITH

Chapter	Priority	Legacy Action	Start Date
58		Revival or Judgment Study	
59		Complete End Times Study	
61		Complete Faith Multisensory Analysis	
61		Complete Lukewarm Thermometer	
62		Identify Sin Danger Areas	
63		A Mans Steps to Success	
64		Marriage Reflections	
64		Mind/Body Holiness	
65		Eyes Analysis	
66		Prayer Improvement Plan	
66		Word & Worship Plan	
67		Lasting Legacy Plans	

Appendix

Generational Scriptures
A Biblical Smorgasbord

From two years of reading through the entire Bible with a focus specifically on "generational" themes and impact

Genesis 3: 6, 16-19—Adam and Eve's sin- a generational impact- pain of childbirth, toiling for life

Gen 8:21—Noah's Obedience=Generational favor, the Lord said "I will never again curse the ground"

Gen 15:13-16—God informed Abram of his future for the next 4 generations

Gen 17:7—Covenant with Abram established for descendants and generations to come

Gen 22:16-17-—Blessings to Abraham because of obedience- descendants would multiply and generational blessings

Gen 26:3-5—Isaac, generational blessings because of obedience, generational impact to descendants

Gen 26:24—blessings to Abraham's descendants

Gen 28:13—blessing of land to Abraham's descendants

Gen 48—Jacob blessing Joseph's sons, descendant impact

Exodus 16:32-33—Manna to be preserved for generations to come

Ex 20:5—God visiting the sins of the fathers for 3 to 4 generations, of those that hate Him

Ex 31:13—Keep Sabbath a sign for future generations

Ex 32:13—remembering Abraham, Isaac, Jacob and God's promises and faithfulness

Ex 34:6-7—God's mercy and grace and forgiveness for generations to come

Lev 26—if, then statements, if obedience and keeping of His commands, then favor and blessing

Numbers 6:22-27—Blessing your children

Num 14:18—the Lord is abundant in mercy, but also visits the iniquity of the fathers- 3 to 4 generations

Num 15:38-39—reminder to remember God's commandments throughout the generations

Num 32:13—God's anger against an evil generation

Deuteronomy 1:35—a generation wasted except Caleb- vs. 36-37, why? Obedience- wholly following the Lord

Deut 4:9—teach them to children and grandchildren

Deut 4:40—keep commands and it will go well with your children

Deut 5:29—keep commands that it might be well with children

Deut 6:2—fear the Lord and keep His commandments for generations

Deut 8:2—Remember that God led you in the wilderness

Deut 8:18—God will establish His covenant

Deut 30:5—multiply more than your fathers

Deut 30:20—God's promise to Abraham, Isaac and Jacob

Deut 32:46—command your children to observe God's commands

Joshua 4:7—memorial stones for children to see

Joshua 24:15—Choose! As for me and my house we will serve the Lord!

Joshua 24:26-27—Stone as reminders

Judges 2:10—the next generation did not know the Lord

1 Chronicles 17:11—God establishing His Kingdom

2 Chr 30:7-12—Don't be like fathers, "if", singleness of heart

2 Chr 26:4-5, 16—Uzziah did was right, penalty for Uzziah pride

2 Chr 28:6—Because they had forsaken the Lord God of their fathers

2 Chr 34:25—Because and Therefore

1 Kings 3:6—God grants David and Solomon mercy because of righteousness

1 Ki 9:1-9—generational obedience and favor

1 Ki 15:1-5—because David did what was right, God granted him favor

2 Ki 10:30- 4 Generations blessed for obedience

2 Ki 17:15- Children stubborn like their Fathers

2 Ki 17:41- Children following the Father's evil

1 Chronicles 1-9- Genealogies

1 Chr 22:10- Solomon's throne over Israel

1 Chr 28:6- God chooses Solomon to build God's house

1 Chr 28:8- leave land as an inheritance for your children

Ps 90:1-2- our dwelling place in all generations

Ps 22:27,30- the next generation

Ps 30:5- His favor is for life

Ps 44:1,3- Fathers told us the deeds God did in the days of old

Ps 45:17- I will make your name to be remembered in all generations

Ps 49:10-12- That dwelling places will last generations

Psalm 78- Remembering & Telling

Ps 79:13- show forth your praise for generations

Ps 89:1- tell of his mercies and faithfulness for all generations

Ps 95:8-10- wilderness- grieved for that generation

Ps 100:5- truth endured through all generations and his mercy is everlasting

Ps 102:12,18- remember His name for generations, written for generations to come

Ps 103:17-18- God's mercy is everlasting

Ps 105:8- remembers His covenant for 1000 generations

Ps 112:2- generations of upright will be blessed

Ps 119:89- faithfulness endures to all generations

Ps 127:3-5- children are a heritage from the Lord

Ps 128- your children's children

Ps 135:13- the fame of the Lord through generations

Ps 143:5-6-remember the days of old

Ps 145:4- generations shall praise your work

Ps 145:13- everlasting kingdom, generations

Prov 17:6- children's children are a crown

Prov 27:24- riches are not forever

Is 44:3- pour my spirit on your descendants

Eccl 1:4- one generation passes away and another comes

Eccl 3:22- your works are your heritage

Is 61:4- rebuild the desolations of generations

Is 59:21- covenant with descendants

Jer 11:3- not obeying the covenant

Jer 2:9- punishment children's children

Jer 17:2- children remember the idolatry

Jer 32:18- repay iniquity of fathers

Lam 5:19- the Lord's throne from generation to generation

Ez 18:14- son following father

Hos 4:6- following God, generational

Daniel 4:3- Dominion from generation to generation

Nehemiah 1:4-9- Nehemiah's prayer of generational repentance

Zech 1:4- don't be like your fathers who didn't hear or heed

Matthew 1:1-16- Genealogy of Jesus Christ

Luke 1:50- mercy from generation to generation

Luke 2:4- lineage of David

Luke 3:23-38- Jesus genealogy

Acts 7:51- resist Holy Spirit, like Fathers did

Acts 13:18- He put up with their ways - wilderness

1 Cor 10:1-12- examples generational

Eph 3:21- glory by Christ Jesus- all generations

2 Tim 1:3, 5- Timothy's heritage

Heb 3:10- angry with generation

1 Peter 2:5-6- living stones

1 Peter 2:9- chosen generation

Appendix: Goal Sheet

Goal: _____

What do you want to accomplish?

    o _____

    o _____

Why do you want to accomplish it?

    o _____

    o _____

When do you plan to accomplish it? Short-term plan and long-term plan

    o Short term: _____

    o Short term: _____

    o Long term: _____

    o Long term: _____

Who will be involved in helping you accomplish it?

    o _____

    o _____

How will it get done? BE SPECIFIC

    o _____

    o _____

    o _____

    o _____

Appendix: Short-Term Success Goal Card

Short-term goal	1 S	2 M	3 T	4 W	5 T	6 F	7 S	8 S	9 M	10 T	11 W	12 T	13 F	14 S	15 S	16 M	17 T	18 W	19 T	20 F	21 S

Appendix: Long-Term Life Ladder Scorecard

Your Future ACTION	Target date (self)	Target date (spouse)	Target date (together)	Quarterly grade

Appendix: Choosing a College-Pre-Visit Research

Visit	School Name	State	Rating	% app admit	under grads	in st	grads 10%	top 25%	In Cost	Out Cost	Room Board	1 year Cost	4 year Cost

Appendix: Choosing a College- Site Visit

School	Student Reviews	Grade Overall	Education	Campus Aesthetics	Friendly	Social	Extra - Curricular	City	Campus Resources	Perceived Safety	Would I Return %

Appendix: Choosing a College—Student Feedback

SCHOOLS VISITED								
Christian / Spiritual								
Location / Distance								
Campus Feel/Visit								
Major								
Academics % > 3 5								
Academics Rank (10/25)								
SAT Reading (mid 50)								
SAT Math (mid 50)								
ACT Consol (mid 50)								
Extracurricular Activity								
FCA/Christian Greek								
Safety								
Neighborhood/City								
Sports								
Activities								
Admission Prob								
Apply								
Overall Grade								
Cost								
Undergrads								
Accept Rate / App date								
Positives								
Negatives								
Awards/Comments								
Date Visited								

Appendix: My Tribute, My Dad

As we run toward the final stretch in the race set before us, I want to ensure that I communicate my thoughts and feelings to you while we both still are blessed with life and breath.

We serve the same God, the one true,
living God. Thank you for introducing
Him to me and helping me to know Him.

Blessed is the man who fears the Lord,
who delights greatly in His commandments.
His descendants will be mighty on earth;
The generation of the upright will be blessed.
—Psalm 112:1–2

We are both saved through the grace of Jesus Christ and know that heaven is our home. Thank you for making Him real to me and the pursuit of Him a life-long priority evidenced by action.

We are both indwelt by the Holy Spirit and are daily taught, guided, and convicted by Him. Thank you for introducing Him to me in the fullness of His power and might and for the ministry years that had a great impact on me. As David charged Solomon,

"Be strong, therefore, and prove yourself a man.
And keep the charge of the
Lord your God: to walk in His ways,
to keep His statues, His commandments,
His judgments and His testimonies."
—1 Kings 2:2b–3a

I commit to you, to walk before God in truth,
with all my heart and with all my soul,
all the days of my life. Thank you for leaving
a lasting legacy and making
a generational impact.

"Children's children are the crown of old men,
and the glory of children is their father."
—Proverbs 17:6

Thank you for your sacrifice, your humility,
your work ethic, your discipline, your
honesty, your integrity: your heritage. Together, we have journeyed through seasons of triumph and seasons of failure. We are both sinners and miss the mark,
yet we are blessed with the favor
and forgiveness of a perfect Father. I forgive you
for your errors and ask that you do the same for me.

You are my dad. You were my provider.
You are my mentor. You are my friend.
I respect you. I admire you. I thank you.
But most importantly, I love you, Dad.

Your son,

Doug

Appendix: Our Family Plan 2012

Family Vision: Love God   Love One Another   Serve Others

Love God:

Daily Word / Prayer / Worship / Heart Change / College Choice / Fasting / Obedience

Love each other:

Honor – Respect / No Arguing / Teasing / Obey the 1st time / No Anger / Truth / Humble Heart

Serve others:

Peacemakers, Right Friends, 10:1, Discipline, Hard Work, Serving, No Procrastination, Chores, Responsibility, Selflessness, Accept Correction, Treat others better than ourselves, Listen-Don't Interrupt, Gratefulness, Give

Lasting Legacy—Think & Act Generationally—Family Focus-—URGENCY

Psalms 78:4; 145:4

Scripture Memory Verses

Love God / Know God

- You will seek me and find me when you seek me with all your heart. Jeremiah 29:13 (January)
- The word of God is alive and powerful. It is sharper than the sharpest two-edged sword, cutting between soul and spirit, between joint and marrow. It exposes our innermost thoughts and desires Hebrews 4:12-13 (Feb)
- I am not trying to win the approval of people, but of God. If pleasing people were my goal, I would not be Christ's servant. Galatians 1:10 (March)
- If we confess our sins, he is faithful and just and will forgive us our sins and purify us from all unrighteousness. 1 John 1:9 (May)
- Confess your sins to each other and pray for each other so that you may be healed. The prayer of a righteous person is powerful and effective. James 5:16 (June)
- Keep watch and pray, so that you will not give in to temptation. For the spirit is willing, but the body is weak!" Matthew 26:41 (Aug)

Love one another—Peacemakers / Responsibility / Serving / Respect

- I will give you a new heart and put a new spirit in you; I will remove from you your heart of stone and give you a heart of flesh. Ezekiel 36:26 (January)
- Keep your tongue from evil and your lips from telling lies. Turn from evil and do good; seek peace and pursue it. Ps 34:13-15 (April)

- All hard work brings a profit, but mere talk leads only to poverty. Be lazy and become a slave. Proverbs 14:23 (May)
- Make every effort to live in peace with everyone and to be holy; without holiness no one will see the Lord. Hebrews 12:14 (June)
- It is better to eat a dry crust of bread in peace than to have a feast where there is quarreling. Proverbs 17:1 (July)

Serve Others / Holiness

- The Son of Man did not come to be served, but to serve, and to give his life as a ransom for many. Matthew 20:28 (Feb)
- Therefore everyone who hears these words of Mine and acts on them, is like a man who built his house on the rock. Matthew 7:24 (Feb)
- Unless a kernel of wheat falls to the ground and dies, it remains only a single seed. But if it dies, it produces many seeds. 25 Those who love their life will lose it, while those who hate their life in this world will keep it for eternal life. John 12:24-25 (Jul)
- How can a young man keep his way pure? By living according to your word. I seek you with all my heart; do not let me stray from your commands. I have hidden your word in my heart that I might not sin against you. Psalm 119-9-11 (March)
- Do not be misled: "Bad company corrupts good character." 1 Corinthians 15:33 (May)
- Do not be yoked together with unbelievers. For what do righteousness and wickedness have in common? Or what fellowship can light have with darkness? 15 Or what does a believer have in common with an unbeliever? 2 Corinthians 6:14-15 (July)

Family and Personal Vision 2000

1. To love the Lord our God with all of our heart, soul, mind, and strength; to pursue God with an undivided heart, totally abandoned to God
2. To love Dana as Christ loved the Church; to serve her unselfishly, giving myself up for her, putting her before me, and listening to her wholeheartedly. I will provide for her physical needs and grow with her spiritually. To have a spirit of complete unity and submission between us as we follow Christ Jesus, so that with one heart and mouth we may glorify our Father. We are committed to each other as long as we live.
3. To raise our children in the fear and admonition of the Lord, training them to follow Christ wholeheartedly, to honor their Father and Mother, to be submissive and obedient,and to be imitators of Christ so that the world may know they are His disciples. To educate and train our children in the ways of the Lord, so that when they are mature they will not depart from it. To instill Biblical values and Christian principles through home education and to spend quality time together as a cohesive unit that leans upon and influences each other rather than being influenced by worldly standards and peers. To prepare our children to influence their world for Jesus Christ and help fulfill the Great Commission.
4. To love the poor and our neighbors as if they were a part of our family, giving, serving, and loving others unconditionally.

5. To be intercessors and communicate daily with God in such a way to walk in the Spirit, to listen and to follow His guidance.

6. To daily read and study the Word of God, hiding it in our hearts, living it, preaching it, teaching and being doers of the Word, not just hearers.

7. To fulfill our calling and to use our gifts as working unto the Lord, not men; to please the Lord, not men; to teach, train, encourage, serve, give, evangelize, help and administrate as the Lord leads and opens doors. Always keeping our relationship with Him first, others and family second, and then ministry to fulfill our roles in the body of Christ, both within His church and to the lost.

8. To give cheerfully and unselfishly as true stewards and caretakers of God's money, keeping an eternal focus and promoting equality amongst the body of Christ.

Appendix: Driving Contract

Driver's Responsibilities

I understand the car that I drive is my parents' property, and I may drive it only with my parents' permission and in accordance with their rules and restrictions. I agree to the terms of this contract allowing me the privilege of driving the car, which has been purchased primarily for my use. If, at any time, I violate this agreement, the driving privilege will be forfeited to the extent and degree of violation. Penalties for not having positive behaviors at home and school will lead to suspension of my driving privileges.

Privileges and Responsibilities

Driving is my top privilege linked to satisfactory behavior at home and school, including the following:

- honoring and respecting my parents
- cleaning my room and doing the dishes
- loving my brothers
- continuing with good grades (B's and above)

General Commitments

o I will obey all traffic laws and the posted speed limits and follow safe driving practices at all times.
o I will not drink and drive, or use drugs and drive and will not have any liquor, beer, drugs, or smoking in the car at any time.
o Should I get a traffic violation ticket, I agree to pay for the ticket as well as the difference in the insurance premium for as long as the premium is in effect. Also, I will be unable to drive for one month following the citation.
o I agree to pay for damages that I incur that are not covered by insurance, including all deductibles.
o I will not transport more than one passenger who is under the age of 21 and will not drive the car until all passengers have buckled up.
o Until January 26, 2013, I will not drive friends and siblings in the car unless an adult is present (exception basis approvals).
o I will keep the car that I drive clean, inside and out.
o I will inform my parents about where I am driving, when I plan to return, and if I will be late coming home.
o My curfew for night driving is 9:00 p.m. until I turn 17—then we will re-evaluate it.
o I will drive safely and defensively at all times, even if I am running late.
o I will not be a passenger in a vehicle without asking my parents first. I will not be a passenger in a car that is being driven unsafely or illegally, or where alcohol, drugs, or other things listed above are present.
o I will call—at any time of the day or night—a parent for help in getting home if—for any reason—I am not able to drive both safely and legally. The person called will come and get me immediately.
o I will not drive anyone else's vehicle, nor allow anyone to drive my vehicle, unless I have prior permission from my parents, or unless it's an emergency involving illness or injury. I will not loan my vehicle to any other person unless I have prior permission from my parents.
o I will never allow anyone who has been consuming alcoholic beverages, drugs, or inhalants to drive a vehicle in which I'm a passenger.
o I will always drive with my seat belt properly and securely fastened. All passengers will wear a seat belt, and all seat belts will be fastened properly and securely before the vehicle moves. If anyone refuses to buckle up or unbuckles while I'm driving, I will stop the vehicle.
o I recognize that driving a vehicle is a privilege, not a right, and I also recognize that each parent/guardian signing below has individual veto power over my driving privileges for the duration of my life as a minor.
o I will always drive at safe speeds for the conditions—at or below the speed limit.

o I will obey all traffic laws.

o I will not engage in thrill-seeking, stunts, or any form of racing.

o I will not conceal any tickets, warnings, or collisions from parents/guardians.

o I will provide my parents with my destination and time of return.

o I will call home if I think that I will not make curfew.

o I will not make unnecessary side trips or stops.

o I will not drive outside of agreed-upon territories or boundaries without advising my parents first.

o I will not eat, drink, or smoke in the car.

o I will pull over and park the car before using my cell phone, electronic devices, change CDs, etc.

o I will not affix stickers or decals without permission.

o I will always treat pedestrians, cyclists, and other motorists with courtesy.

Distractions

o I will not make calls or text on my cell phone while driving.

o I will not use GPS, change CDs, change radio stations, eat or drink, etc., while driving. Songs can be changed at stoplights only.

o I will keep TWO HANDS on the wheel at all times when driving.

o I will not play music loudly because it can distract from my focus on safe driving.

o I will keep my eyes on the road at all times. I will not read a map, put on makeup, or fish in my purse or glove compartment, or exhibit any other behavior that prevents me from devoting my full attention to the road.

o I will not behave rudely in my vehicle or with my vehicle—to other passengers or other drivers.

Parents Responsibilities

o We will take care of gas, oil, and maintenance requirements through high school.

o We will pay for car insurance through high school and possibly college.

o We will make monthly payment toward the car debt ($200/month).

o We will have routine maintenance checks performed through college.

o We will cover other miscellaneous expenses related to vehicle registration, inspection, and oil changes.

o We will provide and maintain a safe vehicle.

o We will pay for driver training classes/materials.

o As your passenger, we will share observations and coaching in a calm, respectful manner.

Shared Commitment

Our family pledges its support of our newest driver. We will do everything we can to promote safe driving and responsible behavior. Once every 3 months, we Parents/Guardians and Teen agree to meet to discuss driving performance and compliance with home and school behavior. These meetings are to provide helpful answers to any questions, comments, or concerns. Further, we Parents will provide feedback on our teen's driving performance at this time.

Additionally, there will be 4 random performance review dates during the year. We Parents/Guardians will ride along with our teen driver and assess his or her driving performance. Some of the key behaviors are listed but not limited to: safety-belt use, signal use, braking, stopping, mirror use, turning, speed, lane maintenance, passing, following distance, etc. A parent may determine an appropriate increase or decrease in driving privileges.

Teen: I have read the above agreement and agree to its terms. I acknowledge that I understand my legal responsibilities and commitment to my family as a driver. I agree to abide by the terms of this agreement and accept the loss of privileges if I fail to comply.

Parents/Guardians: We, as parents or guardians and owners of the family vehicles, agree to serve as good role models in our own driving. We will encourage safe driving practices by our teen by fairly and consistently enforcing the terms of this agreement.

Appendix: Purity and Patience Vow

The purpose of this contract is to remind Dad, Mom, and child of our promises to each other and, more importantly, of our commitment to God.

o God made me. Jesus died for me and saved me.
The Holy Spirit lives in me.
o I will live for God, please God, honor God, and obey God's Word.
o My life and body are not my own. I am God's child.
My body is a temple of the Holy Spirit.
My purity is a gift from God.
o I will guard my heart, my eyes (internet, pictures, TV, movies), and my body. I will take every thought captive and not provide an opportunity for lust to grow.*
o I will choose friends who help me in my vow, not tempt me to go astray, and run from those who tempt me. I will not put myself in compromising or tempting situations.
o I realize that God is teaching me obedience, patience, self-control, and how to be holy.
o True love waits. Feelings will not drive my behavior. I will keep myself pure and wait until marriage to give myself totally to the spouse whom God is preparing for me.
o I will not settle for the world's standard. I will honor the biblical standard of purity. I will not participate
in any sexual activity before marriage.

I make this promise today, _____, ___, to myself, and to my future spouse. God help me to fulfill this promise. I will renew it every year to ensure that I honor you and bring glory to Jesus Christ. May my life be a witness to others who do not know you. Amen

Dad		Child		Mom

To help me achieve this vow,

1) I will pray regularly.
2) I will read God's Word regularly, especially the following scriptures.
3) I will ask friends to help me with my vow.
4) I will share temptations with my parents.
5) We agree to the following "blessing schedule," knowing that loving God is the real reason to obey.

a. Age 14—to end of 8th grade—$50—no lip kiss or beyond*	_____		_____		_____
b. Age 15—to end of 9th grade—$100—no lip kiss or beyond*	_____		_____		_____
c. Age 16—end of 10th grade—$150—no lip kiss or beyond*	_____		_____		_____
d. Age 17—end of 11th grade—$250—no lip kiss or beyond*	_____		_____		_____
e. Age 18—to after graduation—$500—kiss only*	_____		_____		_____
f. Age 22—College graduation—$1000—kiss only*	_____		_____		_____
g. Wedding Day—down pmt. on house—$2500—kiss only*	_____		_____		_____

Appendix: Grade-Incentive Plan

1. I will keep my vow of purity and patience.
2. I will maintain a positive attitude. If Mom/Dad see a change and I don't, then they can withdraw me from high school/middle school.
3. I will LOVE. Love my siblings. Circumstances will not drive that love. I will love in words and deed (be a doer of the Word, not just a hearer).
4. I will RESPECT and HONOR my mom and dad and other adults. If this falters, they can withdraw me. (See the following scriptures.)
5. I make a commitment to schoolwork first and other school commitments (cheer-leading, piano, tumbling) second. Social things are third. (God is first plus!)
6. I will participate in a physical school sport/activity every year.
7. I will willingly have an open discussion daily about school, activities, friendships, teachers, temptations, etc.
8. I will give passwords to my computer, e-mail, Facebook, Instagram, phone, etc., to Mom/Dad. They may check on me anytime. This will hold me accountable to live to God's standards and keep me from temptation.
9. I will strive for A's in all of my classes. Whatever you do, work at it with all your heart, as working for the Lord, not for men (Col. 3:23). To help me, my bonus structure is as follows (per semester):

	Semester	Year
a. All A's	$100	$200
b. One B	$50	$100
c. Two B's	$25	$50
d. Three+ B's	$0	$0

10. I will participate in community service to the poor monthly.
11. I will eat healthfully, treat my body as the temple of the Holy Spirit (no alcohol, smoking, or drugs, take the purity pledge, etc.). I will speak healthfully (words of purity, no profanity).
12. I will complete my chores, cheerfully, daily!

Dad		Child		Mom

Appendix: Guideposts for Life

1. Know that God loves you and is with you (Jer. 29:11, Matt. 11:28–30, Ps. 9:9–10, Ps. 121, Eph. 3:17–20)
2. Pursue & Worship God / Know Christ (Ps. 34:8, Ps. 42:1–4, Phil. 3:10, Jer. 29:12–13, Mt. 22:37–39, John 4:23–24)
3. Don't Worry (1 Peter 5:6–7, Phil. 4:6–8, Mt. 6:25–34, John 16:33, Deut. 31:6, Psalm 46:1)
4. Have an Undivided, Soft Heart (Ezekiel 36:26–27, Ps. 86:11, Ps. 119:9–11, Prov. 4:23, 2 Tim. 2:22)
5. Love and Serve Others, Share God's Love (Mt. 20:26–28, John 12:24–26, Prov. 15:23, Prov. 11:30, 1 John 3:16–18)
6. Trust God no matter what (Prov. 3:5–6, Prov. 18:10, Joshua 1:9, Romans 8:28, 31, Zephaniah 3:17
7. Be a "God-Pleaser," not a "men-pleaser" (Gal. 1:10, Col. 3:23, 1 Samuel 16:7)
8. Bloom Where you are Planted—Be Faithful in the little things (Luke 16:10, Luke 19:17, Matt. 25:21)
9. Work Hard, Do Your Best (Prov. 14:23, Prov. 12:24, Col. 3:23, Prov. 6:6, Prov. 10:4)
10. Be Different, Be Holy and Separate (Phil. 4:8, 1 Cor. 15:33, Col. 3:2, 1 Peter 1:14–16, Heb. 12:14)
11. Have a Praying and Fasting Lifestyle (2 Chron. 7:14, 1 Thess. 5:17, Matt. 26:41, Matt. 6:16–18, Joel 2:12–13)
12. Be Humble, Confess your faults (James 5:16, 1 Peter 5:5, Isaiah 66:2, 1 John 1:9)
13. Be a Doer (James 1:22–25, Matt. 7:24–27, Matt. 7:12, James 2:14–26)
14. Seek God's Will and Wisdom (Prov. 3:5–6, James 1:5–7, Heb. 4:12–13, Isa. 40:31, Rom. 12:1–2)
15. Bite Your Tongue (James 1:19, 26, James 3:2–10, Prov. 17:1, Eph. 4:29, Prov. 15:1)
16. Find a spouse that loves God more than they love you—and it is obvious! (2 Cor 6:14–18)
17. Be a good steward of God's money (1 Cor. 4:1–2). Spend less than you make, live on a budget, save, avoid debt, be content, be frugal but not stingy.
18. Give liberally (2 Cor. 8, 9, Prov. 11:24–25)
19. Eagerly desire God's gifts/Seek the Holy Spirit (1 Cor. 12:28–31, 1 Cor. 14:1, Luke 11:9–13, Acts 1:8, Acts 2:17–18)
20. Think generationally—Leave a lasting legacy (Psa. 78:4–7, Psa. 145:3–7, Deut. 6:1–9, Psa. 89:1, Joel 1:3)

Love God, Love Each Other, Serve Others

Grandma Mary's Guideposts for Life: Psalm 22:30; 34:18; 46:10; 147:3; Luke 10:25–37; Phil 4:6; Romans 8:26; 9:16; 10:9–12; 15; 2 Cor. 4; 5:11–21; Gal. 3:20; Phil. 3:12–16; 1 Thess. 5:12.

Appendix: Blessing

Dear Jacob,

As your Dad, I want you to know that I love you very much and am very proud of the man you are becoming. We all have our weaknesses—you know mine pretty well, and I know yours pretty well. I am glad we can challenge each other, and I am glad that you are making a "passage to manhood" this year, 2011.

This "Prayer passage" and "Blessing passage" is significant, and I want you to look back on this day as a handing of the baton of sorts. You are transitioning from boyhood to manhood. I have asked a small group of individual who were "generational giants" or "prayer warriors" in my life to pray about your future and what God might want to impart to you. They spent time in prayer and seeking God and sent a written blessing or prayer.

God has the roadmap for your life. Let Him work out the big picture and plans while you are faithful on the street you are walking and in the season you are living. Know that we are always here for you, always loving you, always praying for you.

Love,

Dad

> These are my prayers for you — I hope you will pray them often throughout your life.

- That you would know and understand how deep, how wide, and how long God's love is for you.
- That you would know how much Mom, Emily, Justin, and I love you—always, no matter what—without condition.
- That you would remember that day of your salvation in 2003 at 5229 Boxwood Lane in your room and realize the impact that had on your life here on earth and for eternity. That you would share that testimony often.
- That you would love the Lord your God with all of your heart, soul, mind, and strength. That you would pursue God with an undivided heart, and be totally abandoned to God.
- That you would be full of joy.
- That you will find a godly wife who loves God more than she loves you, one who will make you whole as a person, and one who will partner with you in leading your own godly family one day. That you will wait on God's woman.
- That you will be a giver, unselfish, serving others above yourself, and be quick to care for and love others.
- That you would be moldable, shapeable, and buildable with a soft heart; like a piece of clay with Jesus being the potter.
- That you would seek God's will and plan for your life above your plans and trust the results.
- That you would seek to know Him—His power, His awesomeness, His gentleness, His ways.
- That you would be a doer of the Word and not just a hearer only.
- That you would live a disciplined life—in His Word, in prayer, in godly character, and in holiness and purity.

- That you would trust in the Lord with all your heart and not lean on your own understanding. That He would open doors, close doors, and direct your paths as you seek Him.
- That you would not care what people think, but be a pleaser of God.
- That you would realize and see the power of God's Word and the power of the Holy Spirit.
- That you would see the little things as important. They are what God has put in front of you for now. You will be entrusted with more as you are faithful.
- That in anything and everything that you do, you will work at it with all your heart, as working for the Lord, not for men.
- That you will be a diligent and hard worker, yet take time to slow down and enjoy life, enjoy God, enjoy your family, and enjoy God's creation. That your priorities will be in proper order.
- That you will be a leader and not a follower, unless God shows you to be a follower in certain circumstances/seasons.
- That you will live a pure, holy life, thinking on things that are true, pure, and lovely.
- That you will choose the right friends and that God will bring the right friends into your life, always remembering that "Bad company corrupts good character."
- That you will be a witness to the lost but not be yoked together with unbelievers.
- That you will flee youthful lusts and pursue righteousness, faith, love, and peace.
- That you will not waste time but redeem the time, for the days are evil.
- That you will have an eternal, generational mindset and set your minds on things above, not on earthly things.
- That you will keep your tongue from evil and your lips from telling lies. That you will have God's strength and your own strength to turn from evil and do good; to seek peace and pursue it.
- That you will blossom with the fruit of the Spirit: love, joy, peace, patience, kindness, goodness, and faithfulness.
- That you will be humble, not proud, pray and seek God's face, turn from any wicked way, so that God may bless you.
- That God's divine favor will rest upon your life, your relationships, and your future.
- That you will be blessed with many spiritual gifts and that you will eagerly desire them.
- That you will be a man of prayer—a prayer warrior—an intercessor like Rees Howells. That you will see and discern things spiritually that others do not.
- That you will win battles in the Spirit and in the flesh with God's Spirit in you and working through you.
- That you willingly confess your sins to God and to others. That you will know He forgives you immediately.
- That you watch and pray, so that you will not give in to temptation.
- That you will humble yourself under the mighty power of God, and that at the right time He will lift you up in honor.
- That you will always surrender your worries and cares to God and really know how much He cares about you.
- That you will not look at the things people look at. That you will have the eyes of the Lord and look at the heart, not outward appearances.
- That you will have a humble and contrite spirit, that you will be a man of fasting, prayer, weeping, and mourning.
- That you will be quick to listen, slow to speak, and slow to get angry.
- That you will know when to wait on the Lord and when to act. That He will give you strength.

- That God will cause all things to work together for good in your life.
- That you will deny yourself and "lose yourself," and that as you do that, your life will be one of multiplication. That as your "flesh" dies, God will produce eternal life for others.
- That both in times of trouble and during good times, you will know that the name of the Lord is a strong tower. He is a rock, and a fortress, and you can run to Him and be safe.
- That you will make good decisions and choices and not take them lightly. That you will make them regardless of whether they are lonely ones or not.
- That you will be real and authentic.
- That you will not compromise or settle.
- That you will realize you matter greatly—to God, to family, and to those around you. That you will know that you are needed. That you will make your life count and live purposefully.
- That you will worship Him regularly and freely in spirit and in truth.
- That you will ask for God's help regularly and receive an abundance of His wisdom and favor.
- That you will feel and react to God's conviction, but not to Satan's condemnation and guilt.
- That you would not doubt God but trust Him in all of your circumstances and with your feelings.
- That you will discover who you are and that you will discover and use your gifts fully for the Lord.
- That you will walk in the Spirit and not fulfill the desires of the flesh.
- That you will understand what the perfect will of God is and seek to live that out.
- That you will guard your heart, for everything you do flows from it.
- That you will remember your Creator in the days of your youth.
- That you will be a man after God's own heart.
- That you will follow the Lord all the days of your life, that you will say, "As for me and my house, we will serve the Lord," and that you will run the race, persevere, and finish strong.
- That you will tell the next generations (your children and grandchildren) of the praiseworthy deeds of the LORD, His power, and the wonders He has done.

I bless you now, Jacob, with the power of the Holy Spirit to realize, accomplish, and pursue all of these things. Although you will fail, know God's grace, repent, and turn back to Him.

I bless you now, Jacob, with the abundance of God's blessings, favor, and provision. His resources, power, strength, and love are limitless.

I bless you now, Jacob, with the power and strength of His protection—spiritually, emotionally, and physically. I ask Him to release His heavenly host—His angels—and the Holy Spirit to fully empower, protect, lead, and guide you.

I bless you, Jacob, in the name of the Father, in the name of the Son, and in the name of the Holy Spirit. In Jesus name, Amen!

Appendix: Educational Goals

Educational goal	Public	Private	Homeschool	NAUMS

Appendix: College Savings Ideas

SAVINGS IDEAS- need _____ /mo beginning _____	Savings	Dad	Mom	Child	Child	Child
Move to $_____ house, sell ours						
Move to $_____ house, sell ours						
Sell Stocks or Bonds						
Cancel 401k						
Reduce 401k to _____						
Mom part-time job- beginning _____						
Switch from private school to public school _____						
Dad part-time income						
Sell car						
Cancel fitness membership						
Cancel magazine subscriptions						
No summer vacation						
Cut spending(clothes, electricity, home etc.) 10%						
Cut eating out in half						
Sell _____						
Cancel entertainment / recreation _____						
Cancel phone						
Cut phone minutes						
Cancel hobby _____						
Cut _____						
Cancel newspaper						
Cancel cable						
Reduce cable						
Change Pet Food						
Use coupons						
Change Insurance deductibles						
TOTAL SAVINGS						

Absolutely	5
Possible	4
Maybe	3
Don't want	2
No way	1

Appendix
Example Prayer Card

Husbands, likewise, dwell with them with understanding, giving honor to the wife as to the weaker vessel, and as being heirs together of the grace of life, that your prayers may not be hindered (1 Peter 3:7).

<u>Wife</u>
- That God would be glorified in and through her
- That she will know God and love Him
- For the fruit of the Spirit—peace, compassion, etc.
- That she would be used for Him
- That we would be in unity—one heart and mind

<u>Child 1</u>
- Power, love, and a sound mind, taking thoughts captive
- Joy
- Boldness, confidence as Your child
- Comfortable in own skin, pleaser of God (Gal. 1:10)
- Godly friends

<u>Child 2</u>
- Honor, respect for family
- Softened heart
- Holy Spirit connection/conviction, draw closer to You
- Holiness/purity/integrity—Truth speaking
- Godly friends

<u>Child 3</u>
- A passion for You, to know You
- Draw closer to You
- Honor/respect for family
- Quick to Listen, Slow to Speak
- Godly friends

Blessings
- *May the God of hope fill you with all joy and peace as you trust in him, so that you may overflow with hope by the power of the Holy Spirit.*
—Romans 15:13

- *May the Lord bless them and keep them; May the Lord make His face shine upon them and be gracious to them; May the Lord be present with them and give them peace.*
—Numbers 6:24–27

Pray for Protection / Walls of Protection / Angels standing Guard

ABOUT THE AUTHOR

*I*am an ordinary man. My failures are many. I am a sinner. It is only by God's grace, favor, and blessing that He has allowed me to write this book. I am grateful. May this work be used to glorify Him and make Him only famous (Acts 4:13).

Backward Bio—In *A Lasting Legacy*, Doug Hagedorn shares his life-long "living proof" successes and failures. He is a "cusper," (one who was stuck between the Boomer Generation and Generation X). He has been a husband for nearly twenty years, is the father of three children, and is a community and career leader and manager. He has an MBA degree from the University of Dallas and a Bachelor of Arts degree from Michigan State University. He started a business and is a teacher and lecturer. He also served as a board member for a number of non-profit ministries. He and his wife founded a private school. Their family has been involved with four models of schooling. He and his wife went from massive debt to debt freedom at age 33. Doug is the author of *Ease the Squeeze*, which received a five-star rating from *Midwest Book Review* and was nominated for Christian Living Book of the Year. He was a radio guest and columnist on national shows/ministries featuring Larry Burkett, Chuck Bentley, Howard Dayton, Steve Moore, Marlin Maddoux, Kerby Anderson, and Charles Colson. He has written or spoken nationally with Moody Broadcasting, *Money Matters*, Crown Ministries, Prison Fellowship Ministries, and Point of View talk radio. Most importantly, he is a lover of God and a lover of his family, and he lives a full, purposeful life. He enjoys reading, worshiping, traveling, baseball and engaging in family/children's activities. All of the other stuff and fluff is meaningless without Christ—to Him be the honor!

www.futurefoundationbuilders.com

- **Get additional web resources**

for your future, finances, family and faith

- **Get additional copies of *A Lasting Legacy* at a discount**

- **Get copies of *Ease the Squeeze* at a discount**

- **Seminars / Speaking engagements**

Future Foundation Builders

P.O. Box 3764

McKinney, TX 75069

www.futurefoundationbuilders.com

Secure Future. Strong Family.

Real Faith. A Lasting Legacy.

ENDNOTES

"It's amazing what you can accomplish
when you don't care who gets the credit."
—Harry Truman

A special acknowledgment of credit goes to Dennis Peterson, my editor. He made me
sound more intelligent than I really am! Thanks Dennis!

A second acknowledgment to the following friends who read this tome in 10 days
and gave me valued input (good medicine):   Anna Burrow, Jonathan Dowell, Joyce
Hulkenberg, Stephen Jeffcoat, Jeff & Dawn Kregel, Jamie Michael, Brian Najapfour,
David Narramore, Brad Northcutt, and Steve Roemerman

Dedication
[1]   Proverbs 3:5–6; 18:10
[2]   Galatians 1:10; Colossians 3:23

Introduction
[3]   1 Corinthians 2:4
[4]   Mark 2:17; Matthew 9:12

Chapter 1
[5]   Neil Fiore, *The Now Habit*, New York: Putnam-Tarcher, 1989.
[6]   Og Mandino, *The Greatest Salesman in the World*, New York: Bantam Book, 1968.
[7]   Mark Muraven, *Ego-depletion: Theory and Evidence*, Albany, NY, University at Albany, April 26, 2011.
[8]   Ibid.
[9]   Deuteronomy 32:7

Chapter 2
[10]   William Strauss and Neil Howe, *Generations*, New York: Quill, 1991.
[11]   Linda Gravett and Robin Throckmorton, *Bridging the Generation Gap*, Franklin Lakes, N.J.: Career Press, 2007.
[12]   Lynne C. Lancaster and David Stillman, *When Generations Collide*, New York: Collins Business, 2002.
[13]   *Generations*,
[14]   David Kinnaman and Aly Hawkins, "The Generation of Contrast," *Relevant*, September/October 2011.

Chapter 3
[15]   John C. Maxwell, *Failing Forward*, Nashville: Thomas Nelson Publishers, 2000.

Chapter 4
[16]   Abraham Park, *The Genesis Genealogies*, North Clarendon, Vt.: Periplus Editions, 2009.
[17]   Ibid.

[18] Karen Kaplan, "Like caffeine? There's a gene for that—two of them actually," *Los Angeles Times*, April 5, 2011.
[19] Matthew Herper, "Born or Made?" *Forbes*, May 23, 2011.
[20] Matthew 10:30
[21] Psalms 139:13–15

Chapter 5
[22] Bill Wilson, inner-city minister and founder of Metro Ministries, at introduction meeting, 1991.

Chapter 6
[23] Motivated by Facebook post of Bill Scott, May 2011.
[24] Bill Craver, Dream Center International, on Belize missions trip, June 2011.
[25] John 12:24–25
[26] "How Long to Form a Habit?" September 21, 2009. Available www.spring.org.uk/2009/09/how-long-to-form-a-habit.php *European Journal of Social Psychology*, October 2010, vol. 40, no. 6, (998–1009). Phillippa Lally, Cornelia H.M. van Jaarsveld, "How are habits formed? Modeling habit formation in the real world," 16 Jul 2009.
[27] Jeremy Dean, Psyblog, How long to form a habit? September 21, 2009. Available www.spring.org.uk/2009/09/how-long-to-form-a-habit.php.
[28] Copyright Universal U Click, Ref #5.5.11PE. Used by permission for print and electronic editions, *Peanuts: A Golden Celebration*, 1999 Harper Collins hardcover.
[29] *National Vital Statistics Reports, U.S. Life Tables, 2006*, U.S. Department of Health and Human Services, CDC, June 28, 2010.
[30] Mary Beth Franklin, *Too Young to Be Old: Rethinking Retirement,* Kiplinger's Personal Finance, July 2011.
[31] *Reinventing Aging, Baby Boomers and Civic Engagement*, Harvard School of Public Health-MetLife Foundation, Initiative on Retirement and Civic Engagement, 2004.
[32] Tom White, "Taking the Bull by the Horns," *Voice of the Martyrs*, May 2011.
[33] "Ponder This," *New Man Magazine*, March/April 2003.
[34] *Reinventing Aging*, Center for Health Communication, Harvard School of Public Health.
[35] Ibid.
[36] Ibid.
[37] Ibid.
[38] Ibid.
[39] Ibid.
[40] Ibid.

Chapter 7
[41] Mitch Albom, *Tuesdays with Morrie*, New York: Broadway Books, 1997.
[42] Bob Buford, *Halftime*, Grand Rapids: Zondervan, 1994.

Chapter 8
[43] Cheryl Hall, Approaching 100, Ebby Halliday says go easy on the candles, *Dallas Morning News* Article, January 16, 2011.
[44] Missy Sullivan, "Empty nesters filling the void," *SmartMoney*, October 2011.

Chapter 9
[45] Banning Liebscher, *Jesus Culture*, Shippensburg, Pa.: Destiny Image Publishers, 2009.
[46] James Emery White, *Serious Times*, Downers Grove, Ill.: Intervarsity Press, 2004.
[47] Ann Kates Smith, "New Jobs, New Skills," *Kiplinger's Personal Finance*, November 2010.
[48] *Help Wanted: Projections of Jobs and Education Requirements through 2018*, Georgetown University, Center on Education and the Workforce, June 2010.
[49] Ibid. (Earnings data since 1983, among workers between the ages of 25 and 54)
[50] Ibid.
[51] Figure Winners, Net New $100,000-plus Jobs," *Forbes*, p 107, September, 26, 2011.
[52] "Education pays. . . Education pays in higher earnings and lower unemployment rates," U.S. Bureau of Labor Statistics. May 4, 2011, Current Population Survey.

Chapter 10
[53] Michael E. Young, Cloud coverage helps Dallas snap 100-degree streak at 18 days, *Dallas Morning News*, August 19, 2010.
[54] Inspired by K.P. Yohanon, Gospel For Asia, K.P's Corner articles, 2011, www.gfa.org.
[55] "Michelangelo's last sketch found," BBC News, 7 December 2007.

[56] "At 88 she's a millionaire—and keeps teaching," Associated Press, March 13, 2007.

[57] Bruce Frankel, *What Should I Do with the Rest of My Life?* New York: Penguin Group, 2010.

[58] Inspired by Larry Burkett and Ron Blue, *Your Money After the Big 5-0*, Nashville: B&H Publishing Group, 2007.

[59] Ecclesiastes 3:1

[60] Proverbs 3:5–6

[61] Mark Buchanan, *"Embracing the Rhythms of Spiritual Growth,"* Spiritual Rhythm, www.intouch.org, January, 2011

[62] Jeremiah 17:9–10

Chapter 11

[63] Megan Oaten and Ken Cheng, "Longitudinal gains in self-regulation from regular physical exercise," *British Journal of Health Psychology*, Macquarie University, Sydney, Australia, 2006

[64] Ibid.

[65] Jan Cullinane and Cathy Fitzgerald, *The New Retirement*, Emmaus, Pa.: Rodale, 2004.

[66] Mark Muraven, *Ego-depletion: Theory and Evidence*, Albany, NY, University at Albany, April 26, 2011.

[67] Ibid.

[68] http://www.framinghamheartstudy.org/about/history.html

[69] Judy Scharfenberg, *Secure Families in a Shaky World*, Enumclaw, Wash.: Pleasant Word, 2010.

[70] Amanda Spake, *America's supersize diet is fatter and sweeter-and deadlier*, U.S. News and World Report, August 19, 2002.

[71] Ibid.

[72] Dimity McDowell, "Reality Shows about Weight Loss Dominate Television, *Experience Life*, April 2011.

[73] http://www.cdc.gov/vitalsigns, http://www.cdc.gov/obesity/data/index.html, http://www.americanheart.org/downloadable/heart/1236358025411OVRWGHT.pdf

[74] "Health & Medicine: America's "Supersize Diet Is Fattier and Dweeter and deadlier," *U.S. News & World Report*, August 19, 2002.

[75] Monica Eng, "Obesity Debate," *Chicago Tribune, Dallas Morning News*, August 7, 2011.

[76] "Digesting the New USDA Dietary Guidelines," *Experience Life*, September 2011.

[77] "TV Time Out," *British Journal of Sports Medicine*, onWeb MD, the Magazine, October 2011.

[78] Catherine Guthrie, "Healthy Eating, Sugar Shock," *Experience Life*, May 2011.

[79] Healthy Eating, Sugar Shock, Catherine Guthrie, Experience Life, May 2011, http://www.plosone.org/article/info:doi/10.1371/journal.pone.0000698, PLOSONE Study: Intense Sweetness Surpasses Cocaine Reward, 2007

[80] Ibid.

[81] Carl Bialik, "USDA's Food Plate: Looks Great, Less Filling," *Wall Street Journal*, June 11, 2011.

[82] USDA Dietary Guidelines, January 2011.

[83] Megan Oaten and Ken Cheng, "Longitudinal gains in self-regulation from regular physical exercise," *British Journal of Health Psychology*, Macquarie University, Sydney, Australia.

[84] Janice Lloyd, "Strenuous exercise may protect brain," *USA Today*, June 9, 2011.

[85] Dimity McDowell, "Reality Shows About Weight Loss Dominate Television", Experience Life, April 2011

[86] "Your Brain Doesn't Look a Day over 30," *Experience Life,* June 2011.

[87] Inspired by Stephanie Thurrott, "Controlling Cravings," *Baylor Health*, May 2011, and Amy Paaturel, "Sneaky ways to lessen the calorie-load of your favorite foods," *Inform*, May 2011.

[88] 1 Corinthians 6:19–20

[89] 1 Samuel 16:7

[90] Laura Landro, review of Howard S. Friedman and Leslie R. Martin, *The Longevity Project*, Hudson Street Press, in Bookshelf Review, *USA Today*, March 9, 2011

[91] Jeannette Moninger, "Stop Googling your Symptoms," *Inform*, May 2011.

[92] Ibid.

Chapter 12

[93] Ted Engstrom, "Mistakes are Important", *The Pursuit of Excellence*, and Banning Liebscher, *Jesus Culture*, Shippensburg, Pa.: Destiny Image Publishers, 2009.

[94] Philippians 3:12–16

[95] Alina Tugend, "Go Ahead—allow yourself some failure," *Dallas Morning News*, April 8, 2011.

[96] Ibid.

[97] Andy Postema, "Regret," personal blog, December 18, 2010.

[98] Inspired by Billy Scott, Facebook post, December 15, 2011.

[99] K.P. Yohannan, *When We Have Failed, What's Next?* Carrollton, TX, GFA books, 2006.

Chapter 13

[100] Inspired by J. Lee Grady, *"A Promise Takes Time,"* Fire in My Bones, Charisma, December 2010.

[101] Concept of five positive actions/verbalizations for every one negative

477

Chapter 14
[102] Ron Blue and Jeremy White, *Surviving Financial Meltdown*, Carol Stream, Ill.: Tyndale House Publishers, 2009.
[103] Pilar Gerasimo, "Resolution Workshop," *Experience Life*, January/February 2003.
[104] G. T. Doran, "There's a S.M.A.R.T. way to write management's goals and objectives," *Management Review*, vol. 70, no. 11 (AMA FORUM), 1981, 35–36.
[105] Bahram Akradi, "Opportunity Costs," *Experience Life*, July/August 2011.
[106] IBIS World, Toon VAnBeeck, Ten Key Industries that will decline, available at, http://www.ibisworld.com/Common/MediaCenter/Dying%20Industries.pdf, accessed May 12, 2012

Chapter 15
[107] Bureau of Labor Statistics. http://www.bls.gov/news.release/ecopro.toc.htm, Accessed May 8, 2012
[108] Emily Listfield, "Generation Wired," *Parade*, October 9, 2011.
[109] David Kinnaman and Aly Hawkins, "The Generation of Contrast," *Relevant*, September/October 2011.
[110] Brett McCracken, "In Defense of Slow," *Relevant*, September/October 2011.
[111] Maria Halkias, "Holiday Shoppers Hold the Reigns," *Dallas Morning News*, November 13, 2011; Robin Lewis and Michael Dart, "The New Rules of Retail", Palgrave and Macmillan, New York, NY, 2010.
[112] Taylor Clark, *Nerve: Poise under Pressure*, New York, NY, Little, Brown and Company, 2011.
[113] Inspired by Daniel H Wilson, "The Terrifying Truth about New Technology," *Wall Street Journal*, June 12, 2011.
[114] Jeremiah 32:17; 1 Peter 5:7

Chapter 16
[115] Inspired by a wake-up event watching Rod Parsley on the topic of faith, Mark 9:23–24, April 2012
[116] Sarah Young, *Jesus Calling*, Nashville, TN: Thomas Nelson, 2004.
[117] Inspired by Mike Bickle, *After God's Own Heart*, Lake Mary, Fla.: Charisma House, 2009.
[118] Sarah Young, *Jesus Calling*, Nashville, TN: Thomas Nelson, 2004.
[119] "Money and Happiness," *Money*, October 2003.
[120] Thanks to Steve Roemerman, Andy Postema, Kaylee Featherly, Cheri Wilke, Alisa Minner, Sharon Frampton, Odet Kent, Deb Jager, Georgia Emry, and Mary Stouten for their Facebook posts of March 26–29, 2011.
[121] Ecclesiastes 2:11, 17

Chapter 17
[122] "Study: For Men, Family Comes First, Life's Work," *Generational Attitudes Toward Work and Life Integration*, Radcliffe Public Policy Center, *Harvard University Gazette*, May 04, 2000.
[123] Study: American 'Millennials' Value Family Most, May 11, 2010, www.christianpost.com/news/study-american-millennials-value-family-most-45113
[124] Beatrice Gottlieb, *The Family in the Western World*, New York: Oxford University Press, 1993.
[125] Ibid.
[126] Ibid.
[127] Kevin Swanson, "The Re-Integrated Family and the Return of Love," www.generationswithvision.com/Articles/11, December 4, 2006
[128] Patrick F. Fagan, Leonie Ten Have, and Wendy Chen, "Marriage, Family Structure and Children's Educational Attainment," September 19, 2011. Marriage and Religious Research Institute
[129] Available http://entertainment.blogs.foxnews.com/2011/05/05/cameron-diza-says-the-instutition-of-marriage-is-dying/?test=facesww.fox, May 5, 2011.
[130] Ken Ham and Britt Beemer, *Already Gone*, Green Forest, Ark.: Master Books, 2009. Available http://www.victoriansociety.org.uk/publications/redundant-churches-who-cares/
[131] Barna Research Online, "Teenagers Embrace Religion but Are not Excited About Christianity," January 10, 2000. (Available www.Barna.org.)

Chapter 18
[132] Carl W. Wilson, *Our Dance Has Turned to Death*, Living Books, 1981.
[133] Ed Vitagliano, "The Decay of Greatness," *AFA Journal*, June 2011.
[134] Ibid.
[135] Pitirim A. Sorokin, The American Sex Revolution, Porter Sargent, 1956
[136] David Barton, *America: To Pray or Not to Pray?* Aledo, Texas, Specialty Research Associates, 1988.
[137] NCHS Data Brief, No. 18, U.S. Department of Health and Human Services, Centers for Disease Control and Prevention, National Center for Health Statistics, May 2009
[138] Steve Smallwood, "New estimates of trends in births by birth order in England and Wales," Population and Demography Division, Office for National Statistics, United Kingdom, 2002.
[139] Fox News interview with Jon Stossel and Dr. Walter E. Williams, June 4, 2011. Jeff Poor, "Walter E. Williams on welfare: As government plays father, black males have become dispensable," *The Daily Caller*, June 4, 2011 (available www.dailycaller.com/2011/06/04).

[140] John Stossel, "Is Government Aid Helping or Hurting Blacks?" www.foxnews.com/opinion/2011/06/02, June 2, 2011.

[141] Vital Statistics of the US, 1947, Monthly Vital Statistics Report, Final Natality Statistics 1972, National Vital Statistics Report, Births: Final Data for 2008, www.cdc.gov/nchs/data/nvsr/nvsr51/nvsr51_12.pdf (2000 census)

[142] "Out of wedlock births surge for young moms," *Dallas Morning News,* February 18, 2012.

[143] "Breaking moral barriers one song at a time," *American Family Association Journal,* AlMenconi.com, January 2000.

[144] Nicholas Paphitis, "Furor in Greece over pedophilia as a disability," Associated Press, Jan. 9, 2012.

[145] Statistics courtesy of www.familysafemedia.com. Most statistics are from 2006, so they are much worse now.

Chapter 19

[146] Carl W. Wilson, *Our Dance Has Turned to Death,* Living Books, 1981.

[147] 1 Samuel 8

[148] George Washington's Speech to Delaware Indian Chiefs, May 12, 1779, in John C. Fitzpatrick, editor, *The Writings of George Washington,* Vol. XV (Washington: U.S. Government Printing Office, 1932), p. 55.

[149] Barack Obama, *The Audacity of Hope: Thoughts on Reclaiming the American Dream,* New York: Crown Publishers, 2006.

[150] Proverbs 22:6

[151] John C. Maxwell, *Failing Forward,* Nashville: Thomas Nelson Publishers, 2000.

Chapter 20

[152] Ed Vitagliano, *The Decay of Greatness,* www.onenewsnow.com.

[153] Ibid.

[154] Mark Holmen, *Faith Begins at Home,* Ventura, Calif.: Regal Books, 2005

[155] Search Institute, Effective Christian Education: a National Study of Protestant Congregations

[156] Dave Simmons, *Dad the Family Mentor,* Little Rock: Victor Books, 1992.

[157] James 5:16

[158] Robert Lewis, *Raising a Modern Day Knight,* Wheaton, IL, Tyndale House, 1997.

[159] Matthew 7:24–27

[160] James 1:22

Chapter 21

[161] Stu Weber, *Along the Road to Manhood,* Sisters, Ore.: Multnomah Books, 1995.

[162] Dennis and Barbara Rainey, *Growing a Spiritually Strong Family,* Sisters, Ore.: Multnomah Publishers, 2002.

[163] *The State of Our Nation's Youth,* Horatio Alger Association, 2008–2009, 2005–2006, www.horatioalger.com/pdfs

[164] Edith Schaeffer, *What is a Family?* Grand Rapids: Baker Book House, 1975.

Chapter 22

[165] Nancy Gibbs, "The Magic of the Family Meal," *Time,* June 4, 2006.

[166] Judy Scharfenberg, *Secure Families in a Shaky World,* Enumclaw, Wash.: Pleasant Word, 2010.

[167] *The State of Our Nation's Youth,* Horatio Alger Association, 2005–2006, www.horatioalger.com

Chapter 23

[168] Inspired by Leo Rivera as he shared his wisdom with our small men's group.

Chapter 24

[169] Jan Cullinane and Cathy Fitzgerald, *The New Retirement,* Emmaus, Pa.: Rodale, 2004. Stephanie Brown, "5-year study of older married adults," *Psychological Science,* July 2003.

[170] Courtesy of Brad Northcutt, 2011.

Chapter 25

[171] Philippians 3:10

[172] Jeremiah 29:13

Chapter 26

[173] Inspired by Brad Northcut, Adult Bible Fellowship teaching, April 3, 2011.

[174] Ephesians 6:1–2

175 "Parents accept responsibility for their child's spiritual development, but struggle with effectiveness, Barna Research Online, www.barna.org/barna-update/article/5-barna-update/120-parents-accept-responsibility, May 6, 2003.
176 Inspired by Marshall Shelley, "Planting Trees," *Leadership*, Summer 2003.
177 "Did You Know?" *World Relief Magazine*, Winter 2000. Barna Research Group, 1999.
178 Inspired by Perry Stone, *Purging Your House, Pruning Your Family Tree*, Lake Mary, FL, Charisma House, 2011.
179 Isaiah 61:3
180 Dennis and Barbara Rainey, *Growing a Spiritually Strong Family*, Sisters, Ore.: Multnomah Publishers, 2002.

Chapter 27
181 Hebrews 12:5–6
182 Tedd Tripp, *Shepherding a Child's Heart*, Wapwallopen, Pa.: Shepherd Press, 1995.
183 Mark 10:16
184 Malachi 4:6
185 Ephesians 5:15–16, Colossians 4:5

Chapter 28
186 Inspired by Steve Wester as he shared a parenting truth in our small men's group.
187 James Dobson, *The Strong-willed Child*, Wheaton IL: Tyndale House Publishers, 1987, pp. 198–207.
188 James 1:19
189 Ibid.
190 1 Samuel 2:12–17, 22–25, 27–34; 3:11–14; 4:1–3, 10–22
191 Inspired by message by Dr. Charles Stanley, First Baptist Church, Atlanta, GA, January 23, 2011.
192 Cara Hedgepeth, "Talk to your kids about drinking," *USA Weekend*, June 3–5, 2011.
193 Michael P. Farris, *The Homeschooling Father*, Hamilton, Va.: Michael P. Farris, 2002. Christy Farris, "Character Qualities for My Future Husband," B&H Publishing Group, Nashville, TN
194 Ibid.
195 *Generation M2: Media in the Lives of 8 to 18 year olds*, A Kaiser Family Foundation Study, Victoria J. Rideout, Ulla G. Foehr, Donald F. Roberts, January, 2010.
196 Ibid.
197 Ibid.
198 Ibid.
199 Ibid.
200 Ibid.

Chapter 29
201 These men in my weekly accountability "Men's Challenge" group have had a major influence in my life and challenged me greatly. Thanks, Brad, Danny, Dave, David, and Leo.
202 Thank you, "Mr. Idea," David Narramore.
203 Jim McBride, *Rite of Passage,* Chicago: Moody Publishers, 2011.
204 Stormie Omartian, "Breaking Family Ties," *Charisma*, May 2011.

Chapter 30
205 Thanks for the insight, Jorge Diaz. Ephesians 5:32.
206 Ed Vitagliano, "I DO. I do. I do. I do," *AFA Journal*, November 2011.
207 Inspired by H. Norman Wright, *The Marriage Check-up Questionnaire*, Ventura, Calif., Gospel Light, 2002.
208 John Gottman, *Why Marriages Succeed or Fail*, New York: Simon and Schuster, 1994.
209 National Center for Health Statistics, Vital *Statistics Report, Final Divorce Statistics,* Vital Statistics of the United States, 1947, p. LI, the divorce-marriage ratio.
210 EurLIFE Divorce rate, www.eurofound.europa.eu/areas/qualityoflife/eurlife, 1999 data column.
211 William Doherty, University of Minnesota, 2009–10.
212 "Ponder This," *New Man Magazine*, March/April 2003.
213 Phil McGraw, *Family First*, New York: Free Press, 2004.

Chapter 31
214 Willard F. Harley Jr., *His Needs Her Needs for Parents*, Grand Rapids: Fleming H. Revell, 2003.
215 www.loveandrespect.com
216 Matthew 16:24–25
217 Matthew 20:28
218 Inspired by Adult Bible Fellowship teaching, Danny Locklear, 2011.
219 Daniel 6:10

Chapter 32

[220] Bill C. Dotson, *From Faith to Faith*, Bloomington, Ind.: Crossbooks, 2011.

[221] Steve Farrar, *Finishing Strong*, Sisters, Ore.: Multnomah Publishers, 1995.

[222] Dennis Rainey, *Building Strong Families*, Wheaton, Ill.: Crossway Books, 2002. Ideas based on Bob Lepine, *The Christian Husband, Servant*, Ann Arbor, Mich.: Regal Books, 2005.

[223] 2 Chronicles 26:5, 16

[224] Proverbs 16:18

[225] Steve Farrar, *Finishing Strong*.

[226] Stu Weber, *Along the Road to Manhood*, Colorado Springs, CO, Multnomah, 2006.

Chapter 33

[227] 1 Peter 2:5–6, Collin County Cornerstone Christian Academy's naming

Chapter 34

[228] Exodus 17

[229] Ezekiel 22

[230] Nehemiah 2–4

[231] Matthew 16, Mark 8

[232] 1 Peter 1:7, Zechariah 13:9

Chapter 35

[233] Galatians 1:10

[234] 2 Timothy 2:3–4

[235] 2 Timothy 2:3

Chapter 36

[236] *A Profile of the American High School Senior in 2004: A First Look*, National Center for Education Statistics, U.S. Department of Education, Steven J. Ingels, Michael Planty, Robert Bozick, Washington DC, October 2005.

[237] National Center for Education Statistics, *120 Years of American Education: A Statistical Portrait*, US Department of Education, Thomas D. Snyder, Editor, January, 1993

[238] Donald R. Howard, *Crisis in Education*, Green Forest, Ark.: New Leaf Press, 1990.

[239] National Center for Education Statistics, *120 Years of American Education: A Statistical Portrait*, US Department of Education

[240] Ibid

[241] David Barton, *Four Centuries of American Education*, Fort Worth, Tex.: Wallbuilder Press, 2004.

[242] Marlin Maddoux, *Public Education Against America, New Kensington, PA*, Whitaker House, 2006.

[243] John William Turner Jr., *Character-Driven College Preparation*, Magnolia Media Group, GPA Ministries, 2001.

Chapter 37

[244] Voddie Baucham Jr., *Family Driven Faith*: Wheaton, Ill.: Crossway, 2007. George Barna, *Parents Describe How They Raise Their Children*, www.Barna.org, George Barna Research online, February 28, 2005.

[245] Baucham, *Family Driven Faith*.

[246] Josh McDowell, *The Last Christian Generation*, Holiday, Fla.: Green Key Books, 2006.

[247] Ibid.

[248] Probe Ministries, Worldviews and Philosophy, http://www.probe.org/site/c.fdKEIMNsEoG/b.4475191/k.7213/Worldview_and_Philosophy.htm

[249] Aline Sullivan, "Private Education, Framing Children's Future," *Robb Report Worth* magazine, May 2004.

[250] Glen Schultz, *Kingdom Education*, Nashville: Lifeway Press, 1998.

[251] Marlin Maddoux, *Public Education Against America*, New Kensington, PA: Whitaker House, 2006.

Chapter 38

[252] Dave Veerman, *Letting Them Go*, Nashville: Integrity Publishers, 2006.

[253] *Education Longitudinal Study of 2002*, Institute of Education Sciences, U.S. Department of Education, Second Follow-up 2006

[254] Gary Lyle Railsback, "An Exploratory Study of the Religiosity and Related Outcomes Among College Students", 1994. Doctoral dissertation, Ronald Nash and J.F. Baldwin, *Summit Ministries Guide to Choosing a College*, Manitou Springs, Colo.: Summit Ministries, 1995.

[255] Ibid.

Chapter 39

256 Ibid.

257 Lori Greene, "Writing Your College Application Essay," Loyola University Chicago, 2011 Health & Medicine Edition, www.careersandcolleges.com, accessed 5/22/12

Chapter 40

258 Mike and Danae Yankoski, "Beyond Fourth Grade," *Relevant*, September/October 2011.

259 Ibid.

260 *Help Wanted: Projections of Jobs and Education Requirements through 2018*, Georgetown University, Center on Education and the Workforce, June 2010.

261 College Board, *Trends in College Pricing 2010*. www.collegeboard.org, accessed 5/25/11

262 Ibid.

263 Tamar Lewin, "Student Debt Mounts, Shifting Graduates' Options," *Dallas Morning News* and *New York Times*, April 13, 2011.

264 "Finance 101: A Freshman Parents' Guide," *Money*, September 2003.

265 Jane Bennett Clark, "Smart Ways to Save for College," *Kiplinger's Personal Finance*, October 2011.

266 Kimberly Lankford, "Caught in the Middle," *Kiplinger's Personal Finance*, November 2011.

Chapter 41

267 Inspired by Greg Vaughn, *Letters from Dad*, Nashville: Integrity Publishers, 2005.

268 Ibid.

269 Edith Schaeffer, *What is a Family?* Grand Rapids. Baker Book House, 1975.

Chapter 42

270 Deuteronomy 6:9; 11:20

271 "Drinking by Example?" WebMD the Magazine, October 2011.

272 Michael P. Farris, *The Homeschooling Father*, Hamilton, Va.: Michael P. Farris, 1992.

273 Tim Stafford, *Never Mind the Joneses*, Downers Grove, Ill.: InterVarsity Press, 2004.

274 Perry Stone, *Purging Your House, Pruning Your Family Tree*, Lake Mary, FL:Charisma House, 2011.

275 www.livingwaters.com

276 "Measuring the Culture, One Hope Survey of 5108 teens between ages 13 and 18," Charismamag.com, April 2011.

277 Thanks, Aaron Corcoran, for the inspiration.

Chapter 43

278 Historical Background and Development of Social Security, www.ssa.gov/history/briefhistory3.html

279 Historical Background and Development of Social Security, www.ssa.gov/history/briefhistory3.html

280 *National Vital Statistics Reports*, vol. 54, no. 19, June 28, 2006. National Center for Health Statistics, available at www.cdc.gov/nchs.

281 Social Security Administration (SSA) 2011 Annual Report

282 Congressional Budget Office Summary, July 2010

283 John David, "Misleading America: How Social Security Trust Fund Really Works," Heritage Foundation, Executive memo #940, available at www.heritage.org

284 David Wiedemer, *Aftershock*, Hoboken, N.J.: John Wiley & Sons, 2011. Joseph P. Quinlan, *The Last Economic Superpower*, Columbus, OH: McGraw Hill, 2011.

285 Ibid.

286 Inspired by Larry Burkett and Ron Blue, *Your Money After the Big 5-0*, Nashville: B&H Publishing Group, 2007.

287 Glenn Beck, *Broke*, New York: Threshold Editions, 2010.

288 Ibid.

289 Ian Bremmer, "Careful what you wish for," *Washington Post* and *Dallas Morning News*, July 31, 2011, available at www.foreign-policy.com.

290 Ibid.

291 Ibid.

292 Joseph P. Quinlan, *The Last Economic Superpower*, Columbus, OH: McGraw Hill, 2011.

293 "The 50 most innovative companies," Bloomberg/*Business Week*, April 15, 2010.

Chapter 44

294 "Population comparison, GDP, External Debt," available at www.cia.gov/library/publications/the-world-factbook, accessed 8/10/11.

295 Addison Wiggins, "The next financial crisis will be hellish," Yahoo News, Forbes.com, November 16, 2011.

296 U.S. Department of Commerce, Bureau of Economic Analysis.

Chapter 45
[297] Scott Burns, "Writer explores what's next in debt nightmare," *Dallas Morning News*, September 25, 2011.

Chapter 46
[298] David Wiedemer, *Aftershock*, Hoboken, N.J.: John Wiley & Sons, 2011.
[299] Carmen M. Reinhart and Kenneth S. Rogoff, "This Time is Different," Princeton: Princeton University Press, 2009.
[300] Michael Lewis, *Boomerang*, New York: W.W. Norton and Company, 2011.
[301] David Wiedemer, *Aftershock*, Hoboken, N.J.: John Wiley & Sons, 2011.
[302] www.ronpaul.com/congress/legislation/audit-the-federal-reserve-fed-hr-459-s202/ HR1207, HR 459
[303] Walker Todd, "The Long Goodbye: The Declining Purchasing Power of the Dollar," American Institute for Economic Research, August 5, 2009, available at www.aier.org/reserach/briefs/1826-the-long-goodbye-the-declining-purchasing-power
[304] "Overview of the Federal Reserve System," available at www.federalreserve.org, accessed 9/20/11.
[305] Michael Lewis, *Boomerang*, New York: W.W. Norton and Company, 2011.
[306] Ibid.
[307] Dennis Cauchon, "Federal benefits, pensions explode," *USA Today*, September 29, 2011.
[308] Ibid.
[309] Carl F. H. Henry, *Twilight of a Great Civilization*, Westchester, Ill.: Crossway Books, 1988.
[310] Isaiah 5:20

Chapter 47
[311] Thomas J. Stanley and William D. Danko, *The Millionaire Next Door*, New York: Simon and Schuster, 1996.
[312] 1 Timothy 6:17
[313] "A Century of Family Budgets," *Monthly Labor Review*, May 2001, p. 32.

Chapter 49
[314] Maria Halkias, "Holiday Shoppers Hold the Reigns," *Dallas Morning News*, November 13, 2011.

Chapter 50
[315] "Reinventing Aging," Center for Health Communication, Harvard School of Public Health, Boston, MA, 2004
[316] American Express Financial Advisors, *A Common Sense Guide to Personal Money Management*, Minneapolis, MN, 1996
[317] "The Global Shift," Charles Schwab on Investing, Investment Company Institute, Summer 2011.
[318] "The New Generation Gap," *Smart Money*, December 2011.
[319] Charles Schwab, *On Investing*, Spring 2011.
[320] Andrew Hallam, *Millionaire Teacher*, Hoboken, N.J.: John Wiley and Sons Pte Ltd, 2011. David F. Swensen, *Unconventional Success, a Fundamental Approach to Personal Investment*, New York: Free Pres, 2005, (p. 217).
[321] Andrew Hallam, *Millionaire Teacher*, Hoboken, N.J.: John Wiley and Sons Pte Ltd, 2011. Linda Grant, "Striking Out at Wall Street," *U.S. News and World Report*, June 20, 1994.
[322] Andrew Hallam, *Millionaire Teacher*, Hoboken, N.J.: John Wiley and Sons Pte Ltd, 2011. John C. Bogle, *The Little Book of Common Sense Investing*, 2007 (pp. 47–48).

Chapter 51
[323] 2011 Fidelity Investments Couples Retirement Study www.fidelity,com, May, 2011
[324] Jena McGregor, "Love and Money," *Smart Money*, November 2003.
[325] Andrew Hallam, *Millionaire Teacher*, Hoboken, N.J.: John Wiley and Sons Pte Ltd, 2011.
[326] 2011 Fidelity Investments Couples Retirement Study, www.fidelity,com, May, 2011
[327] "Expenditures on Children by Families," U.S. Department of Agriculture, 2010.
[328] www.guardian.co.uk/news/datablog/2010/feb/23/cost-raising-child#
[329] Carrie Schwab-Pomerantz, "Talking to Kids about Financial Worries," *Charles Schwab On Investing*, Fall 2011.

Chapter 52
[330] "Grandparent money gaffes," *Dallas Morning News*, November 6, 2011.

Chapter 53
[331] Emily Yoffe, "Just take the gold watch, already!" *Dallas Morning News*, May 1, 2011.
[332] Ibid.
[333] Gail Sheehy, "To American women in midlife, the sky is indeed falling," *USA Today*, July 11, 2011.
[334] Scott Burns, "Have dessert, but indulge wisely," *Dallas Morning News*, April 30, 2011.

335 Larry Burket and Ron Blue, *Your Money After the Big 5-0*, Nashville: B&H Publishing Group, 2007.
336 M.P. Dunleavey, "Retirement: Get Pedaling Together," *Money*, April 2011.
337 *The Future of Retirement, The Power of Planning*, HSBC, US, UK, France, China and India reports, 2011.
338 Ibid.
339 Ibid.
340 *Reinventing Aging*, Center for Health Communication, Harvard School of Public Health
341 *The Future of Retirement, The Power of Planning*, HSBC, US, UK, France, China and India reports, 2011.
342 Ibid.
343 CNNMoney.com, March 2012.
344 Catey Hill, "6 Secrets of Early Retirees," *Smart Money*, October 26, 2011.

Chapter 54
345 Kathy Chu, "Design a countdown-to-retirement plan," *USA Today*, December 16, 2011.
346 Joel Kotkin and Wendell Cox, "Where the Boomers are," *Forbes*, September 12, 2011.
347 Missy Sullivan, "Empty nesters filling the void," *Smart Money*, October 2011.
348 Kimberly Lankford, "Caught in the Middle," *Kiplinger's Personal Finance*, November 2011.
349 Ibid.
350 Glenn Rufenach, "Planning not to retire is not a viable retirement strategy," *Smart Money*, October 2011.
351 Shelly K. Schwartz, "Holding on to a house note," thestreet.com, Survey: 2007, *Dallas Morning News*, October 9, 2011.
352 "2002 Consumer Expenditure Survey," U.S. Department of Labor, Bureau of Labor Statistics.
353 Harry Dent, *The Roaring 2000s*, Simon and Schuster, New York, NY, 1998, p. 37. Ty Bernicke, *Reality Retirement Planning: A New Paradigm for an Old Science*, Eau Claire, WI, 2005.
354 Ty Bernicke, *Reality Retirement Planning: A New Paradigm for an Old Science*, Eau Claire, WI, 2005

Chapter 55
355 Inspired by Ron Blue and Jeremy White, *Surviving Financial Meltdown*, Carol Stream, Ill.: Tyndale House Publishers, 2009.
356 Term from Alan Gotthardt, *New Man*, March/April 2004, p. 27.
357 Immaculate Conception Youth Ministry, Barna Research Group survey,2003, available at www.icmalden.com.
358 Ibid.
359 According to World Bank economist, Branko Milanovic
360 The State of World Evangelization, 2000 Global Mission Statistics, available at www.missionfrontiers.org/neslinks/statewe.htm, February 6, 2001
361 David A. Livermore, *Serving with Eyes Wide Open*, Grand Rapids: Baker Books, 2006. David Barrett and Todd Johnson, eds., *World Christian Trends: AD 30–AD 2000*, Pasadena, Calif.: William Carey Library, 2011, pp 3–9.
362 World Mission Statistics, Frontier Harvest Ministries, available at www.frontierharvestministries.net, accessed 8/11/11
363 The Joshua Project, Unreached Listings, Great Commission Statistics, available at www.joshuaproject.net, accessed 8/11/11.
364 Richard Wurmbrand, *Tortured for Christ*, Bartlesville, Okla.: Living Sacrifice Books, 1967; reprint, 1998.
365 Frontier Harvest Ministries, World Mission Statistics, www.frontierharvestministries.net, accessed 8/11/11.
366 Gospel For Asia, January 3, 2012, available at www.gfa.org.
367 Bill Craver, Dream Center International
368 David A. Livermore, *Serving with Eyes Wide Open*, Grand Rapids: Baker Books, 2006.
369 Carl F.H. Henry, *Twilight of a Great Civilization*, Westchester, Ill.: Crossway Books, 1988.
370 Inspired by Michelle Wallace, "In Everything You Do," *Living*, September 2011.
371 1 Corinthians 10:31, Colossians 3:23
372 Exodus 4:10

Chapter 56
373 David Platt, *Radical*, Colorado Springs, Colo.: Multnomah Books, 2010.

Chapter 57
374 Inspired by K.P. Yohanon, "Don't Ignore the Warning Signs," Gospel For Asia, May 2012.
375 2 Peter 3:8

Chapter 58
376 Kerby Anderson, *The Decline of a Nation*, Probe Ministries, available at www.eaderu.com/orgs/probe/docs/decline.html, July 14, 2002.
377 Ibid.
378 Bill O'Reilly, *America in Decline*, BillOReilly.com, The Hill Newspaper poll, October 25, 2011.

[379] Henry Chu, "Critics see moral decay in Britain," *Los Angeles Times* and *Dallas Morning News*, August 28, 2011.

[380] "Barna examines trends in 14 Religious Factors over 20 years (1991 to 2011)," State of the Church Series, 2011, Part 1, General Trends, July 26, 2011.

[381] Mary Faulds, "Husband, father, shepherd," *AFA Journal*, March 2011.

[382] *Reinventing Aging*, Center for Health Communication, Harvard School of Public Health, 2000 Roper Report Survey.

[383] Ibid.

[384] Troy Anderson, "At a Loss for the Word," *Charisma*, April 2011.

[385] *Abortion Surveillance Report, United States, 2007, Morbidity and Mortality Weekly Report*, Centers for Disease Control and Prevention, February 25, 2011, available at www.cdc.gov/mmwr.

[386] *Abortion Surveillance Report, United States, 2007, Morbidity and Mortality Weekly Report*, Centers for Disease Control and Prevention, available at www.cdc.gov/mmwr. (Annual reports, note: not all states reported for each year; does not include illegal abortions.)

[387] "American War and Military Operations Casualties: Lists and Statistics," Congressional Research Service, CRS Report For Congress, February 26, 2010, available at www.defense.gov/news/casualty.pdf.

[388] National Vital Statistics Reports, Volume 58, Number 19, May 20, 2010, U.S. Department of Health and Human Services.

[389] "Induced Abortion Facts in Brief," Guttmacher Institute, (2002) (13,000 out of 1.31 million abortions in 2000 were on account of rape or incest). Retrieved via InfoPlease 2007-01-07. Bankole et al., "Reasons Why Women Have Induced Abortions: Evidence from 27 Countries", International Family Planning Perspectives (1998). Also see Lawrence B. Finer, Lori F. Frohwirth, Lindsay A. Dauphinee, Susheela Singh, and Ann M. Moore, "Reasons U.S. Women Have Abortions: Quantitative and Qualitative Perspectives", Perspectives on Sexual and Reproductive Health, 37(3):110-118 (September 2005). www.wikipedia.org/wiki/Abortion_statistics_in_the_United_States, 4/11/11.

[390] National Vital Statistics Reports, Volume 57, Number 2, July 30, 2008, CDC, US Department of Health and Human Services.

[391] Brannon Howse, *Grave Influence: 21 Radicals and Their Worldviews that Rule America from the Grave*, Collierville, Tenn.: Worldview Weekend Publishing, 2009.

[392] "App Store pulls Manhattan Declaration," Christianity Today liveblog, November 29,2010.

[393] Don Wildmon, "The Truth Hurts," *AFA Journal*, February 2010

[394] "A Historic Event," Wallbuilders, August 9, 2011, available at www.wallbuilders.com.

[395] Ibid.

Chapter 59

[396] Buddy Smith, "Can prayer save America?", AFA Journal, November 2011.

[397] When Revival Ran Epidemic, Worcester, MA, Glimpses, Issue 41, Christian History Institute, 1992.

[398] The Fourth Great Awakening of 1857 Onwards,*Revival Library*, www.revival-library.org, accessed: 5/15/12.

[399] David Smithers, Why Did the Fire Fall in 1857? www.watchword.org, accessed: 5/15/12.

[400] Ibid.

[401] Cathy Lynn Grossman, ""Almost all denominations losing ground, survey finds, *USA Today*, March 9, 2009.

[402] James Denison, Texas Baptist Convention, "Texas Faith," *Dallas Morning News*, May 14, 2011

[403] "Trends among Christians in the U.S.," available at www.religoustolerance.org, accessed 6/28/11.

[404] "Largest denominational families in U.S., 2001, growth from 1990–2001," available at www.adherents.com, accessed 6/28/11.

[405] "Is American Christianity turning Charismatic?" The Barna Group, January 7, 2008, www.barna.org, Barna Research Institute

[406] "Top 10 Largest International Religious Bodies," available at www.adherents.com/adh_rb.html, accessed 6/28/11.

[407] "The Praises in the Persecution," www.Joshuaproject.com, Charisma, May 2011. Accessed: 5/21/12.

[408] Tom Hess, "The World's Largest Praying Church," Charisma, May 2011.

[409] "Church attendance in England, 1980–2005," *British Religion in Numbers*, available at www.brin.ac.uk/news, accessed May 15, 2011.

[410] George Barna, "What Americans Believe About Universalism and Pluralism," available at www.barna.org, April, 18, 2011.

[411] Ibid.

[412] Ibid.

[413] Jimmy Stewart, "Do All Paths Lead to God?" Charisma, October 2009.

[414] Kerby Anderson, *A Biblical Point of View on Islam*, Eugene, Ore.: Harvest House, 2008.

[415] Ibid.

[416] Frank Bartleman, Azusa Street, South Plainfield, NJ: Bridge Publishing, 1980. (Available at http://cupandcross.com/index.php/azusa-street-and-frank-bartleman/)

[417] "Is American Christianity Turning Charismatic?" The Barna Group, January 7, 2008.

Chapter 60

[418] Tim LaHaye and Jerry B. Jenkins, *Are We Living in the End Times?*, Carol Stream, Ill.: Tyndale House Publishers, 1999.

[419] Brannon Howse, *Grave Influence, 21 Radicals and Their Worldviews that Rule America from the Grave*, Collierville, Tenn.: Worldview Weekend Publishing, 2009.

[420] Misty Edwards, As in the Days of Noah, Always on His Mind, Forerunner Music, 2008.

Chapter 61

[421] 1 Corinthians 15:33

[422] Hebrews 9:27

[423] John 3:16

[424] Psalms 46:10

[425] John 3:16

[426] Voddie Baucham Jr., *Family Driven Faith*, Wheaton, Ill.: Crossway, 2007.

[427] Matthew 7:13–23

[428] Psalms 103:12

[429] 1 John 1:9

[430] Psalms 145:8

[431] Mark 12:30

[432] John 3:3

[433] Robert Andrescik, "Ponder This," *New Man*, March/April 2003.

Chapter 62

[434] Dr. Tony Evans, KCBI, The Alternative Radio Program, September 16, 2011.

[435] Inspired by Brian Haynes, *The Legacy Path*, Nashville: Randall House Publications, 2011.

[436] George Barna, "Maximum Faith," *Charisma*, May 2011.

[437] Philippians 3:10

Chapter 63

[438] Ed Vitagliano, "Can't Help Myself," *AFA Journal*, April 2011.

[439] Ed Murphy, *Handbook for Spiritual Warfare*, Thomas Nelson Publishers, Nashville, TN, 2003

[440] Ibid.

[441] Inspired by Gary Rosberg, *Guard Your Heart*, Sisters, Ore.: Multnomah Books, 1994.

[442] Stephen Arterburn, *Being God's Man in the Face of Temptation*, Colorado Springs, CO: Waterbrook Press, 2003.

Chapter 64

[443] Matt Friedeman, "Thank God my college football team is losing, *AFA Journal*, January 2011.

[444] James 5:16

[445] Stephen Arterburn, Kenny Luck, and Todd Wendorff, *Being God's Man in Leading a Family*, Colorado Springs, CO: Waterbrook Press, 2003.

[446] Erin Pognet, "Dads make a difference in child development," *AFA Journal*, November 2011.

[447] Genesis 3:6

Chapter 65

[448] http://www.worldchallenge.org/en/in-memory-of-david-wilkerson/

[449] Inspired by Don Carson quotation, available at www.bullartistry.com, June 13, 2009.

[450] David A. Livermore, *Serving with Eyes Wide Open*, Grand Rapids: Baker Books, 2006.

[451] Frank Bartleman, *Another Wave of Revival*, New York: Whitaker House, 1982.

Chapter 66

[452] The Westminster Confession of Faith and the Westminster Shorter Catechism, available at http://www.reformed.org/documents/WSC.html, accessed: 2/14/12

[453] Ibid.

[454] Acts 9:16

[455] 2 Timothy 2:9

[456] John MacArthur Jr., *How to Study the Bible*, Chicago, IL: Moody Publishers, 2009.

Chapter 67

[457] Og Mandino, *The Greatest Salesman in the World*: Bantam Books, 1968.

www.futurefoundationbuilders.com

- Get additional web resources

for your future, finances, family and faith

- Get additional copies of *A Lasting Legacy* at a <u>discount</u>

- Get copies of *Ease the Squeeze* at a <u>discount</u>

- Seminars / Speaking engagements

Future Foundation Builders

P.O. Box 3764

McKinney, TX 75069

www.futurefoundationbuilders.com

Secure Future. Strong Family.

Real Faith. A Lasting Legacy.

CPSIA information can be obtained at www.ICGtesting.com
Printed in the USA
LVOW112053211012

303746LV00001BD/7/P

9 781622 305933